All Things
Shakespeare

All Things Shakespeare

An Encyclopedia of Shakespeare's World

J–Z

Kirstin Olsen

Greenwood Press
Westport, Connecticut • London

Library of Congress Cataloging-in-Publication Data

Olsen, Kirstin.
  All things Shakespeare : an encyclopedia of Shakespeare's world / Kirstin Olsen.
    p.   cm.
  Includes bibliographical references and index.
    ISBN 0–313–31503–5 (set : alk. paper)—ISBN 0–313–32419–0 (A–I. : alk. paper)—
  ISBN 0–313–32420–4 (J–Z : alk. paper)
    1. Shakespeare, William, 1564–1616—Encyclopedias.   I. Title.
  PR2892.O56   2002
  822.3′3—dc21   2002069732

British Library Cataloguing in Publication Data is available.

Library of Congress Catalog Card Number: 2002069732
ISBN: 0–313–31503–5 (Set Code)
        0–313–32419–0 (A–I)
        0–313–32420–4 (J–Z)

First published in 2002

Greenwood Press, 88 Post Road West, Westport, CT 06881
An imprint of Greenwood Publishing Group, Inc.
www. greenwood.com

Printed in the United States of America

The paper used in this book complies with the
Permanent Paper Standard issued by the National
Information Standards Organization (Z39.48–1984).

All line illustrations, except where otherwise noted, credited to Kirstin Olsen.

10 9 8 7 6 5 4

For my mother, Nancy Olsen, who taught me how to read,
For Nancy Goodyear Rice, who taught me how to write,
For Geraldine Warren, who taught me why both matter,
And for all other good teachers everywhere.

Contents

Acknowledgments

The study of Shakespeare's works has such a long and fruitful history that I have had the benefit, and the curse, of a wealth of excellent scholarship in compiling this volume. It has been a benefit in that almost every word of every text has been perused with such diligence that someone, somewhere, has explained virtually everything. It has been a curse because no one could possibly digest all the material available in ten years, let alone the two in which I needed to complete this book. I have therefore the constant, nagging suspicion that I have undoubtedly missed the one academic article or the one perfect illustration that would have made all the difference. Nevertheless, to all the scholars who have dedicated their careers to elucidating a set of centuries-old texts, thank you. The format of this book prevents the inclusion of footnotes or endnotes, but there is a bibliography that I hope will enable readers to pursue subjects of interest to them, and when quoting primary sources I have attempted to mention the name of the author so that readers can locate the original work.

I am indebted to the staffs of several fine institutions. In particular, I would like to thank Kate Harris of Longleat House, Mary Lineberger of the Cleveland Museum of Art, Michael Bates and Sharon Suchma of the American Numismatic Society, and the staffs of the Rare Book Collection, Map Collection, and Photoduplication Service at the Library of Congress, especially Daniel DeSimone, curator of the Rosenwald Collection, for their assistance. They have been extremely patient and helpful. Thank you also to my editor, Lynn Malloy, and to everyone at Greenwood.

On a personal note, I would like to thank my husband, Eric Voelkel, for not saying "I told you so" and for being, astoundingly, the most decent man I know, the funniest man I know, *and* my best friend. My children,

Acknowledgments

Emily and Devon, as always, have been extremely patient with my disappearances into my office to write, and I am immensely grateful. I am also aware that they have been sneaking extra TV time while I've been writing. Guess what, guys? You're busted. I am grateful every day of my life to have had parents who encouraged me to read, teachers who taught me to look at books with a critical eye, and anyone who uses the English language with grace, precision, and enthusiasm. Thank you to Dave Mackie for the ball, box, and stick remark quoted in the Games entry, and to Erica Olsen for researching the saints. Thanks also to Mindy Klasky for providing housing on a research trip and to Bill for starting it all.

Introduction

For those interested in the physical surroundings of Shakespeare's world, this book is an invaluable reference. More than 200 entries illuminate such subjects as the coins, clothing, food, drink, animals, occupations, architectural methods, symbolism, agriculture, and rites of passage of the Renaissance. From the most common gifts at a baptism to the elements of a funeral procession, information about the objects and customs of Shakespeare's world are gathered in one resource in an unprecedented combination of scope and detail. A wealth of charts and tables explains the symbolism of animals and birds, the properties attributed to the constellations of the zodiac, the meanings and derivations of Shakespearean insults, and the names and uses of the heraldic devices found on coats of arms. The appendix contains an extensive chronology that details the historical events mentioned in the plays and places them in their proper sequence so that readers can understand Shakespeare's manipulation and compression of the historical record. More than 200 illustrations depict Renaissance coins indicating their actual sizes in diameter, unusual animals, farming methods, items of clothing and jewelry, weapons, armor, household tools and furnishings, craftsmen's workshops, and many other items. Illustrations include copies of rare photographs and many original renderings that allow readers to appreciate detailed aspects of the items. Maps pinpoint many of Shakespeare's settings and geographical allusions.

While there are shelves and shelves of useful books and journal articles about Shakespeare's works, none has addressed his physical world in quite this way. I have attempted to compile a reference that is both comprehensive and easy to use, for not every reader has access to a university library or the time to wade through those aisles of books and journals. Most public libraries, due to limited space and acquisitions budgets, do not have all the resources that readers require if they are to discover the details of shillings, ships, witches, warfare, cucking stools, and butter churns. Summaries of the Shakespearean world have been published before, notably the monumental two-volume *Shakespeare's England* (1916), which is still a useful resource. However, much has been learned about Renaissance England since 1916, and *Shakespeare's England* omits many topics that are addressed in the present work. Many recent books describing the same historical period tend to be overviews, excellent at sketching the broad outlines of a topic but weak on detail. The really interesting material— how beer was brewed, pewter was made, weapons were fired, and furniture was built—tends to be found in primary sources or in specialized texts or articles that can be challenging to locate.

This book, *All Things Shakespeare*, attempts to summarize much of the interesting but sometimes less accessible material available about Shakespeare's world. Throughout, the primary concern has been the convenience of teachers, actors, directors, audiences, and readers of Shakespeare's works. This text can be used by students writing essays on either Shakespeare or Renaissance England, by book clubs trying to understand a particular play, by instructors explaining *Macbeth* or *King Lear* to their students, by audiences who want to be well-informed before heading out to their local Shakespeare festival, and by theater companies seeking to stage a play with a better understanding of how the original audiences would have reacted to certain lines.

This book is not primarily a work of literary criticism or biography. Shakespeare's dramatic techniques, the traditions from which they arose, his use of poetry and figurative language, the known details of his life, speculation about the aspects of his life that remain a mystery, and the evolution of his skills as a playwright are sources of ongoing and interesting debate, but they are not the subject matter of this volume. This book purports to explain what the *things* in Shakespeare's works are, leaving it to the reader and the critics to determine what the things mean. If you want to know about clothing as metaphor in the plays, this is not the book for you. If you want to know the difference between a doublet and a jerkin, however, or what a bodkin was, or what a clock looked like, or who could legitimately be called "Your Grace," then you have come to the right place.

There are multiple ways to read and use this book. Those interested in a broad content area, such as warfare or government, can consult the bibliography and topic list. This list includes not only suggestions for further reading in the subject area but also a complete list of relevant entries within this book. For a more specific topic, such as breeds of dogs or types of chairs and stools, readers may prefer to consult the index to find applicable entries. The organization and grouping of these entries proved to be one of the most challenging aspects of writing this book. For example, under the heading "Clothing," Shakespeare uses more than 120 different terms, including pomander, doublet, farthingale, smock, caddis, inkle, and round hose. If each of these terms were defined separately, this book would resemble a dictionary more than an encyclopedia, and valuable information about the way the pieces were worn together would be lost or needlessly repeated in each entry. If all terms were included in the entry, it would resemble a chapter more than an entry, and readers might become bogged down in the details of ruff-making when they only wanted to know how hose were different from breeches. Accordingly, most of the terms in this category are discussed under the heading "Clothing," with supplementary entries wherever necessary. For the same reasons, most of the fauna mentioned in Shakespeare's works appear in the Animals and Birds entries, while animals mentioned hundreds of times and requiring much fuller descriptions, such as deer, dogs, and horses, merit their own entries.

At the end of many entries, cross-references to supplementary entries appear. For example, at the end of the Clothing entry, the reader is referred to additional entries on doublet, fabric, gloves, hair, hat, inkle, jewelry, pomander, ruff, and tawdry lace. The best procedure for readers interested in a topic likely to include a multiplicity of terms is to find the most general heading, such as clothing, food, weapons, animals, or entertainment, and proceed through cross-references to related or more specific entries, such as ruff, dishes, sword, dog, or games.

Readers looking for a particular Shakespearean word, such as "tester" or "targe," should head directly to the index. Here they will find the words for which they are most likely to need definitions. Those interested in researching particular plays should also refer to the index for discussions of major themes in particular plays, such as debt, Jews, marriage, or witchcraft.

This book is intended as a companion to any Shakespeare text. Therefore, it tends not to repeat the material likely to be found in almost any well-edited edition of a work by Shakespeare. Most such editions begin with interpretation, character analysis, the date the work is assumed to have been composed and a justification of that assumption, the reliability and provenance of the text itself, a brief biography of Shakespeare, and, inevitably, a description of London theaters in his lifetime—their construction, stages, audiences, actors, and use of props and costumes. In the case of history plays, a discussion of the resemblance of Shakespeare's text to the historical record is also customary. I have touched lightly or not at all upon these subjects. I have instead focused on the sort of material not typically found in introductions to individual plays, such as the difference between a carpenter and a joiner, the text and translation of the inscriptions on contemporary coins, the composition of different grades of bread, and the manufacture of ink, movable type, and paper.

As for the citations found within the entries of this encyclopedia, my concern was to offer a variety of points of reference without attempting a concordance, and without permitting the citations to be more intrusive than necessary. I have therefore tried to include citations that are relevant to the words near which they appear, to include only the most representative or interesting references to a particular concept, and to keep the citations themselves as brief as humanly possible. Most contain only two or three letters, numbers, or symbols, followed by act, scene, and line numbers, so that (*Cor* I.i.26–28) stands for *Coriolanus* Act 1, Scene 1, lines 26 through 28. A complete list of abbreviations can be found on page xxiii. I have, on occasion, omitted the title from the citation when the title of the work concerned is clear from the context. Citations in series should be presumed to refer to the same work unless a new title is introduced, and to the same act and scene unless a new act and scene are listed; thus (*2GV* IV.iv.21, 23, V.i.1; *Oth* I.iii.330–31) refers to *The Two Gentlemen of Verona*, Act 4, Scene 4, lines 21 and 23; *The Two Gentlemen of Verona*, Act 5, Scene 1, line 1; and *Othello*, Act 1, Scene 3, lines 330 and 331. That a scene is set in a particular location is indicated by the word "set" in the citation, as in (*Oth* I.iii.set). Stage directions are abbreviated as "s.d.," and references to characters in a particular scene are abbreviated as "ch." For example, a discussion of meat processing or occupations might include a reference such as (*2H6* IV.ii.ch.), meaning that a butcher appears as a character in *2 Henry VI*, Act 4, Scene 2.

Line numbers, and even scene divisions, can be a problem when quoting from Shakespeare, since the innumerable editions of his works often differ in both respects. I have chosen to use *The Complete Signet Classic Shakespeare*, largely because its copious notes are of great help to readers. Readers using one of the other fine editions of Shakespeare's works should, if they cannot find a relevant word in the line(s) cited, search back or forward a few lines to find the appropriate passage. When Shakespeare's wording differs significantly enough from the language used in my text that I am concerned about readers searching for the wrong word, I have tried to list the key word or phrase in parentheses along with the citation. I apologize in advance to anyone who has difficulty in finding a specific quotation; this is a problem common to all Shakespeare concordances and references.

Where other primary sources are concerned, I have tried to strike a balance between sixteenth-century and twenty-first-century typographies. The former can be obtrusive, even incomprehensible, to modern readers unfamiliar with its quirks, such as writing the number *four* as *iiij* and the word *that* as *y*; the latter saps some of the life out of the texts it corrects and, I think, brings the reader closer to the ideas of the text while distancing her from the atmosphere in which Renaissance readers and writers operated. I have therefore retained irregularities of spelling and capitalization but have modernized the use of *i* and *j*, *u* and *v*, and the "long s." The word "upon," which often appears in Renaissance texts as "vppon," will therefore be written in this volume as "uppon," "rea*f*on" as "reason," and so on. Readers who remain confused by the spellings should try saying words that mystify them aloud; often this enables an immediate identification of the word, for Renaissance writers were often attempting to write more or less phonetically.

Measurements are given first in U.S. units and then in metric equivalents. However, it should be remembered that Renaissance measurements were seldom consistent from one place, or even one person, to another, and that there is, therefore, a certain amount of inaccuracy built into the system. Since I am an American, I have used the terms first, second, and third story when referring to building levels, rather than the British terms ground, first, and second story.

In choosing illustrations, I had great latitude, for Shakespeare's works are set in times that span two millennia. However, it is not clear how much he really knew of the artifacts of ancient Greece, Egypt, Rome, or Britain, or even of medieval Europe, especially since his plays are littered with anachronisms and since we know that his actors were dressed in more or less contemporary costume. I have therefore tried to select illustrations from the late sixteenth and early seventeenth centuries, and have concentrated only on artifacts from that period unless there is good reason to expand the discussion. I have rarely continued the discussion of objects or ideas past the year of Shakespeare's death.

Many debates about Shakespeare focus on intriguing but ultimately unresolvable questions about what he believed. Usually, these controversies arise when a modern-day reader who fully appreciates Shakespeare's dramatic and poetic gifts runs smack into a very sixteenth-century attitude about Moors, Jews, or women. For example, a female reader may feel uneasy about the conflict between her admiration for Shakespeare's language and her disgust at the racist, sexist, or ignorant statements that come out of his characters' mouths. There are several ways for her to resolve this conflict. She can conclude that Shakespeare fully believed the worst views expressed in his plays, and then determine whether or not this attitude spoils the plays for her. She can decide that Shakespeare's tendency to give even his most stereotypical characters comprehensible motives and emotions makes him ahead of his time, perhaps even a sympathizer with more progressive views, but also a realistic businessman who knew that audiences preferred and expected a barbaric Moor, a greedy Jew, and a shrewish woman. This eternal question—how much is art, how much is personal belief?—has been the meat of countless books, theses, and doctoral dissertations, and ultimately remains largely a matter of speculation.

It is possible that Shakespeare believed every word of his writing, that he believed none of it and simply wrote what brought people to the theater, that he believed only the views of the sympathetic characters, or that he thought he was saying one thing and actually ended up conveying another. What an author intends to say, what he believes, what he thinks will sell, and what he actually gets on paper are often very different things. In most cases, however, the bulk of the evidence implies that Shakespeare shared, or at least was willing to echo, some of the least appealing beliefs of his society. This assessment will doubtless meet with disagreement in some quarters. But in the case of Shakespeare, we are dealing with a distance of 400 years from the present day, and though human emotions have changed little in that time, society has changed substantially. It should not surprise us that Shakespeare's values, and those of his contemporaries, are different from our own. What is surprising is the length to which lovers of Shakespeare will go to ignore or explain away those differences.

I adore Shakespeare and have done so since my first encounters with him in the eighth grade. Yet all my affection for his obvious genius cannot blind me to his appalling views regarding the second-class citizens of his society, including women and Jews. As a woman, a Jew, and an admirer of Shakespeare, I have had to find a way to appreciate the man's work without sharing or accepting all of his opinions. All his genius cannot disguise or erase the fact that he had (or at least perpetuated) many strong prejudices, and I attempt in this volume to explain the prejudices without minimizing them, apologizing for them, or pretending that they do not matter. I have attempted to outline the prevalent views of the time and to assess, briefly, how the works reflect or differ from those views. I have not attempted to enter into a lengthy discussion of all the arguments about whether and how much prejudice is evident in the works, for that has been done much better and more thoroughly elsewhere, and in any case is beyond the scope of the present work. I feel that it is ultimately the reader's decision whether the plays are racist and sexist, whether Shakespeare himself was a racist or a sexist, and whether the answers interfere with one's enjoyment of the works.

As to the authentication of certain plays, or scenes within plays, I am not inclined to disagree with majority opinion. *Henry VIII* and *The Two Noble Kinsmen* are generally acknowledged to be collaborations, and *Pericles* is thought to be an adaptation of another text, partially revised by Shakespeare and then rendered in a corrupt quarto by a person (or people) who recorded it from memory. Some editors have recently adopted another play, *Edward III*, into the Shakespeare canon. The present volume is not concerned with these controversies, but with making the objects of

Shakespeare's time and works accessible to people today. Therefore, I have chosen to include references to all parts of *Pericles, Henry VIII*, and *Two Noble Kinsmen*, on the grounds that readers and audiences of these plays would like to understand everything in the texts, regardless of whether Shakespeare was the author of any given line. Likewise, I have not included any material from *Edward III*, since only a minority of readers are yet likely to come into contact with it, and much of its historical context is already addressed in the entries that follow. When making decisions of this sort, my criterion has been the convenience of the majority of readers, rather than the requirements of Shakespeare scholars.

Alphabetical List of Entries

Alphabetical List of Entries

Abbreviations for Shakespeare's Works

A&C	*Antony and Cleopatra*
AW	*All's Well That Ends Well*
AYLI	*As You Like It*
CE	*The Comedy of Errors*
Cor	*Coriolanus*
Cym	*Cymbeline*
2GV	*The Two Gentlemen of Verona*
1H4	*Henry IV, Part 1*
2H4	*Henry IV, Part 2*
H5	*Henry V*
1H6	*Henry VI, Part 1*
2H6	*Henry VI, Part 2*
3H6	*Henry VI, Part 3*
H8	*Henry VIII* (also known as *All Is True*)
Ham	*Hamlet*
JC	*Julius Caesar*
John	*King John*
LC	*A Lover's Complaint*
Lear	*King Lear*
LLL	*Love's Labor's Lost*
MAAN	*Much Ado About Nothing*
Mac	*Macbeth*

MM	*Measure for Measure*
MND	*A Midsummer Night's Dream*
MV	*Merchant of Venice*
MWW	*The Merry Wives of Windsor*
Oth	*Othello*
Per	*Pericles*
PP	*The Passionate Pilgrim*
P&T	*The Phoenix and the Turtle*
R2	*Richard II*
R3	*Richard III*
R&J	*Romeo and Juliet*
RL	*The Rape of Lucrece*
S	Sonnet (followed by sonnet number, as S 22)
TA	*Titus Andronicus*
T&C	*Troilus and Cressida*
Temp	*The Tempest*
Tim	*Timon of Athens*
TN	*Twelfth Night*
TNK	*The Two Noble Kinsmen*
TS	*The Taming of the Shrew*
V&A	*Venus and Adonis*
WT	*The Winter's Tale*

Jewelry

Jewels (*R2* III.iii.146; *R3* I.ii.201, 203) were of the utmost importance in the Renaissance, not only for their beauty or their intrinsic value, but also for what they said about their wearers. Jewels, especially if one could afford to make a statement, announced one's rank, marital status, family connections, religious affiliation, political alliances, medical concerns, beliefs, and, sometimes almost as an afterthought, aesthetic taste. The number of jewels worn depended both on gender and on personal wealth.

Women's Jewelry

Jewels were worn on more parts of the body than they are today, at least by members of the upper class. Women adorned their dresses with brooches (*Ham* IV.vii.93), which were jewels attached to the clothing by pins. By the 1580s brooches were somewhat out of favor with the fashionable (*AW* I.i.157–60), though they remained popular among the middle and lower classes, if we are to judge by the cheap versions marketed by traveling peddlers (*WT* IV.iv.601). Throughout the period that concerns us, however, women who could afford them wore fancy buttons, often with floral motifs, made of gold, jewels, enamel, or semiprecious stones carved into cameos. They also wore gems called flowers or ouches (*2H4* II.iv.49), similar to brooches in shape and style, that were sewn rather than pinned onto garments, or hung from rings or chains. Perhaps the "rubies" in the "gold coats" of the cowslips in *A Midsummer Night's Dream* (II.i.10–12) are supposed to be buttons or ouches. Men and women alike wore aglets (*TS* I.ii.78)—matched pairs of tiny metal tags that adorned hats, buttons, or the meeting points of slashes in sleeves, doublets, and bodices. The hard tips at the ends of shoelaces today are still called aglets and are about as long as the Renaissance variety.

Around her waist a woman might wear a girdle (*LLL* IV.i.51; *MND* II.i.175–76)—a simple belt if she were middle or lower class, with perhaps a silver buckle as the sole ornament; a magnificent chain or series of jewels set in gold if she was wealthy. From the girdle she could hang any number of decorative or useful objects, common choices being a jeweled and clasped prayer book called a girdle-book, a scented pomander to ward off infectious air, a pendant, a watch, a tablet (what we would call a locket today, a pendant that opened to reveal something inside, usually a picture of a loved one), keys, a perfume bottle, a mirror, a whistle to summon servants or dogs, or a toothpick or earpick. Obviously, lower-class women owned few of these trifles, and no woman wore all these things at once, or her waist would have resembled an extremely expensive Swiss Army knife. Usually, she chose one or two, hanging one from the girdle and perhaps another from a chain around her neck.

This simplified composite drawing of an upper-class woman from c. 1592 shows, from top to bottom, a biliment, several bodkins, a pear-shaped pearl earring, a pearl necklace with a jeweled pendant, a rope of pearls, a jeweled girdle, rings on both hands, and a pendant suspended from the girdle by a ribbon.

Neck ornaments came in many varieties. There were long ropes of pearls like the impressive waist-length strands worn by the wealthy widow Bess of Hardwick in a 1592 portrait. Thick gold chains were also popular—one knight's widow, who died in 1574, left a chain worth £65 5s—as were strings of beads and gold links set with gems. Bead necklaces with crosses at the ends were worn until about 1600, when they fell out of fashion. In addition to the chains (*2H4* II.iv.48; *CE* IV.iii.134–35; *AYLI* III.ii.182), there were collars, which often hung quite low, and carcanets or necklaces that were more like chokers in length. The typical carcanet (*CE* III.i.4) was made of gold studded with a few large "captain jewels" (S 52) separated by pairs of pearls. Some carcanets were composed of separate pieces that could be detached and worn as bracelets or a biliment (a jeweled headband). Carcanets, like brooches, were considered unfashionable by the end of the sixteenth century. Necklaces (*WT* IV.iv.223) were, however, popular with lower- and middle-class women, who might buy cheap beads (*MND* III.ii.330) from a peddler and string them together. A child might make a pendant out of a small pierced silver coin. Pendants (*2H6* III.ii.106–9) were hung from chains, collars, and carcanets, or even from sleeves, ruffs, and bodices, as well as from the girdle.

The arms and hands, too, were adorned. Armlets, worn tightly around the upper arm, were uncommon, but bracelets (*WT* IV.iv.223, 602) were increasingly popular. Usually formed of chains or links in Elizabeth I's reign, they were more likely to be formed of pearls or large gems with a clasp in James I's, when the jewels themselves became more important than fancy gold settings. Bracelets were often given as tokens of romantic attachment. Posthumus gives Imogen just such a "shackle of love" (*Cym* I.i.121–22) when he leaves Britain, and she in return gives him the most common love token of all, a ring.

The ring was the most common item of Renaissance jewelry (*R&J* III.ii.142, V.iii.31–32; *Per* V.ii.38; *Cym* I.iv; *2GV* IV.iv.71, 85, 97, 132–37). Worn by men and women alike, it was exchanged at betrothals and weddings (*TN* V.i.155–60; *TS* II.i.316). Therefore, participants in mock marriages gave rings made of rushes as a form of flirtation (*AW* II.ii.23; *TNK* IV.i.88–89). Expensive rings might be set with jewels or contain hidden compartments, but even fairly humble people owned a ring or two, even if it was just a simple band of gold (*TS* IV.iii.55) or silver.

Rings, especially wedding rings, often contained an inscription inside the band (*AYLI* III.ii.271–73). This "posy" (*Ham* III.ii.155; *TNK* IV.i.88–91; *LC* 45) might be a statement of love or the date of a wedding, and was increasingly in Roman rather than Gothic lettering and in English rather than Latin. In the case of the ring that Nerissa gives to Gratiano, the posy is "Love me, and leave me not" (*MV* V.i.150). Posies also figure in *As You Like It*, when Orlando is told,

> You are full of pretty answers. Have you not
> been acquainted with goldsmiths' wives, and conned
> [learned] them out of rings? (III.ii.271–73)

Sometimes the ring was a "gimmal" or "joint-ring" (*Oth* IV.iii.76–77) that looked like one ring when worn on the finger but, when removed, could be separated into two linked rings, sometimes with a hidden message or picture between the bands.

The head might house several different pieces of jewelry. Earrings (*R&J* I.v.48) became popular after about 1575, when changing hairstyles began to reveal the ears. Jewels such as diamonds were certainly used in earrings, but by far the most popular type were pierced earrings made of pear-shaped pearls (*MND* II.i.14–15). Atop the head there might be a biliment, replaced in James's reign by wire frames threaded with jewels or seed pearls. Throughout Shakespeare's career, women wore bodkins (*LLL* V.ii.609)—clusters of gems or pearls fixed into the hair with long pins. Elizabeth I owned sixty-six bodkins, and James's Queen Anne owned more of them than of any other kind of jewelry. Philip Stubbes, in his *Anatomie of Abuses* (1583), complained of the overornamentation of women's hair, which he claimed was littered with "ouches, rings, gold, silver, glasses, & other such gewgawes and trinckets besides."

Women and men of very high rank might also wear a crown or crownlike ornament. Various sorts of crowns, coronets, and circlets, for example, are worn in the coronation procession of *Henry VIII* (IV.i.36 s.d.), and cor-

A portrait of James I shows him with a large hat badge, called the "Mirror of Great Britain"; a collar studded with large stones and pearls; a diamond pendant; jeweled buttons and ouches; a cape studded with ouches of gold and jewels or pearl clusters; an elegant girdle and sword hanger; trunk hose worked with seed pearls; the Garter; and beaded shoes with a large pearl in the center of each decorative flower. Most men did not wear this much jewelry, but as king, James had a responsibility to display his wealth and power.

onets (*1H6* III.iii.89, V.iv.134) and diadems (*2H6* I.i.244, I.ii.7, 40; *Ham* III.iv.101) are mentioned elsewhere.

Men's Jewelry

Men's jewels were similar to women's, though men tended to wear fewer. Men wore watches, belts, and girdle-books on occasion, and they also wore the occasional jeweled badge or pin. Furthermore, they carried items that women did not, such as swords, scabbards, and pistols, all of which could be highly decorated with gilding, engraving, and ivory inlays. The sword and dagger, girdle-book, and perhaps a showy bunch of keys hung from a belt or girdle (*2H4* I.ii.37–39; *1H4* III.iii.159; *Tim* III.iv.90). Men, like women, wore earrings (*MAAN* V.i.307–8), though this practice was discouraged in James I's reign.

Men had no equivalent to the bodkin, but they did wear jeweled badges in their hats, alone or as a pin for ostrich plumes. James I himself had a magnificent specimen, called "The Feather," that contained twenty-size sizable diamonds and stood several inches high. Sometimes such a hat badge could be a symbol of one's profession; Shakespeare refers to such a brooch "worn in the cap of a toothdrawer" (*LLL* V.ii.617).

By far the two most common pieces of jewelry worn by men were the chain (*MWW* IV.v.30–35; *MAAN* II.i.183–84) and the ring (*TA* II.iii.226–27; *AW* II.ii.58; *1H4* II.iv.334). Chains were worn even by boys, if their families could afford them, and any man with a pretense to gentility had to have at least four of varying quality. Long chains were preferred, for these could be worn wide across the shoulders or twisted into short loops nearer the neck. Chains went out of fashion for men around 1617, but this was after Shakespeare's writing career was finished.

Rings for men were decorative, but often also served a practical purpose. Sir Thomas Ramsey, Lord Mayor of London who died in 1590, owned eight rings, and one of them was a signet ring (*Ham* V.ii.49–52), used to impress his coat of arms into the warm wax with which he sealed letters. Most men of middle class or above probably owned signet rings, engraved either with a coat of arms or a business trademark. A ring known to belong to a certain man (or woman) served as proof of the authenticity of letters, documents, and messengers (*R2* II.ii.91–92; *Lear* III.i.47).

Materials, Manufacture, and Sale

The simple jewelry worn by the middle and lower classes was of silver or gold in small quantities, or of cheap substitutes for gems, such as glass, topaz, zircon, and rock crystal (*LC* 37; *S* 46). The jewelry of the rich, however, might be made of almost any precious or semiprecious material. Jewels were typically set into gold foil (*R3* V.iii.251; *Ham* V.ii.257–59; *R2* I.iii.265–66), often shaped to resemble acanthus leaves, at least until the reign of James I and the decline of the goldsmith. The gold (*2GV* II.iv.171) for gilding (*1H4* V.iv.156; *R2* I.i.179), chains, rings, and gem settings, as well as the silver for rings and buckles, came either from Europe or from South America. The gold came in several degrees of fineness and a wide range of prices; one goldsmith, Nicholas Herrick, who died in 1592, carried eleven different grades.

Beads for necklaces and bracelets might be made of polished jet (*2H6* II.i.111–13; *MV* III.i.38; *TA* V.ii.50; *LC* 37), a hard black coal. Other common materials for beads were mother-of-pearl, crystal, lapis lazuli, jasper, agate, amber (*LLL* IV.iii.84; *TS* IV.iii.58; *WT* IV.iv.223; *LC* 37), marble detailed in gold, and opals (*TN* II.iv.74–75; *LC* 215) from Hungary. Beads were usually round or hourglass-shaped.

Jewels for pendants, rings, carcanets, ouches, brooches, and so forth came from around the world. Diamonds were shipped from India to Lisbon merchants, then to Antwerp cutters, and finally to jewelers throughout Europe; a few diamonds also came from Borneo. The diamond (*MV* III.i.80–81; *LLL* V.ii.3–4; *MWW* III.iii.54; *Lear* IV.iii.24; *Tim* III.vi.121; *Per* II.iii.37, III.ii.102–3) was, then as now, an expensive and popular gem, used in rings, carcanets, bracelets, earrings, girdles, brooches, ouches, and bodkins. Small diamonds called "sparks" were sprinkled liberally over expensive accessories. Gems employed in similar ways included rubies (*MND* II.i.12; *MM* II.iv.100; *Cym* II.ii.17) from Burma, emeralds (*LC* 213) from South America, and sapphires (*LC* 215) from Sri Lanka. Topazes came from South America, turquoise from the Sinai and Persia, garnets (the "carbuncle" of *Cym* V.v.189; *A&C* IV.viii.28; and *Cor* I.iv.55–56) from Bohemia and Sri Lanka, and pearls (*MND* V.i.55; *2GV* II.iv.170, III.i.225,

V.ii.11–13; *LLL* IV.ii.90, V.ii.53–56, 459; *TA* II.i.19, V.i.42; *TS* II.i.346; *Oth* V.ii.346–47; *Lear* IV.iii.24; *A&C* I.v.41; *R3* I.iv.26, IV.iv.322)—round, pear-shaped, huge, or tiny, incorporated in almost every kind of jewelry—from the Persian Gulf, the Indian Ocean near Sri Lanka, the coast of Venezuela, and even the rivers of Scotland. Inlays and carvings of coral (*TS* I.i.174; *V&A* 542) or ivory (*MV* III.i.38; *TS* II.i.343; *V&A* 363) could be found in jewelry as well as in the other decorative arts. Hard stones such as agate (*MAAN* III.i.65; *2H4* I.ii.16–17; *R&J* I.iv.55–56), onyx, and sardonyx for signets, cameos, and rings came from within Europe. Cameos were sometimes decorated with gold and were, in this case, known as *commessi*.

Various types of tradesmen and artisans handled these gems, stones, and metals. London had at least dozens, perhaps hundreds, of workers in the jewelry trade—goldsmiths (*CE* IV.iii.ch.; *AYLI* III.ii.271–73), miniaturists, button makers, jewelers (*Tim* I.i.ch.), and lapidaries (stonecutters)—many of them Protestant refugees from other parts of Europe. There were some provincial goldsmiths, but most English jewelry was manufactured in London, and much of what was owned by the fashionable was either made abroad or influenced by foreign designs. Jewelers traveled widely, and came to England to display their wares to the wealthy and fashionable:

Methought all his senses were locked in his eye,
As jewels in crystal for some prince to buy;
Who, tend'ring their worth from where they were glassed,
Did point you to buy them, along as you passed. (*LLL* II.i.242–45)

Buyers looked both to the "water"—the clarity or luster of the gem—and its "form" (*Tim* I.i.17–18).

Forms were, however, somewhat limited. There were only a few shapes into which gems were cut, and these contained relatively few facets. Simplest of all was the cabochon, a rounded form. The table cut had a large, flat surface, and the point had four facets rising to a point, like a pyramid. Other available cuts, such as the lozenge and the triangle, were similarly basic. The first rose-cut gem in England was one made for Queen Anne in 1605. The development of better cutting and more facets helped to shift the emphasis away from the gold settings and toward the gems themselves.

Jewelry Motifs

How much jewelry one wore, and the value of the gold and gems in each piece, spoke volumes about one's wealth. The style of jewelry—the pictures, designs, and mottoes incorporated into it—said a great deal about the wearer's taste and preoccupations. Scenes from classical mythology or history advertised one's education, to be sure, but they also said something about the way the wearer wished to be perceived, or was perceived by the giver of the gem. For example, Elizabeth I was given jewels that portrayed the virgin goddess Diana, thus emphasizing her unmarried life and reputation for virtue. (It probably also didn't hurt to flatter the queen by likening her to a goddess.) A courtier-soldier might choose to wear a badge with a picture of Mars, the Roman god of war, or a model citizen from Roman history. Cameos often had such classical subjects.

Another common motif for jewelry was a picture, motto, or set of letters that identified the giver or the wearer. A family motto might be engraved on a ring or around the border of a pendant, or an animal or other symbol from the family crest—a griffin, pomegranate, dragon, greyhound, rose, bear, phoenix, or such—created out of a carved gem, an assemblage of stones, metalwork, or colored enamel. Coats of arms and heraldic devices were especially common on signet rings but might also be added to badges or even earrings. Sometimes the name or initials of the giver or wearer appeared on a piece of jewelry; if the piece was a gift from a lover or spouse, it might feature the couple's intials interwined, or a saying such as I LIKE MY CHOICE. Anne of Cleves, Henry VIII's fourth wife, had GOD SEND ME WEL TO KEPE engraved on her wedding band, and thought so little of the marital luck it brought her that she asked to have it destroyed after she died.

Love gifts might also have the shapes of hearts (*2H6* III.ii.106–9) or clasped hands worked into their designs. Celtic-style knotwork and letters twined to look like rope knots or woven twigs were also popular. There were several different styles of knots, some of them specific to individual families, and there was also a type called the true-lover's knot that appeared on many pieces of jewelry given as gifts.

Much jewelry bore purely decorative designs of animals, birds, fish, or flowers, but sometimes even a simple picture of an animal was drenched in symbolism. The pelican, for example, was believed to feed its young with its own blood, and was thus a symbol of parental love and sacrifice. Other animals had heraldic or mythological significance.

Jewelry might also announce one's religious devotion. Crosses of various shapes were worn, as were Gothic-letter IHS pendants. Biblical scenes were portrayed on pendants, badges, brooches, and girdle-books. Catholic religious jewelry was outlawed in 1571, including the rosary (sometimes called a "pair of beads"), reliquaries to hold saints' relics or true-cross fragments, and the Agnus Dei, a bit of Easter candle wax stamped with a picture of a lamb and blessed by the pope. However, some Catholics continued to wear the rosary in a surreptitious form, the rosary ring, which had ten small bumps on the hoop. Catholics and Protestants alike tried to remind themselves of the unimportance of the temporal world and the promise of heaven with jewelry decorated with skulls or skeletons. The most common example of this "memento mori" was the death's-head ring, a ring with a skull on the bezel (*1H4* III.iii.32–33; *LLL* V.ii.610).

Loyalty to God was followed closely (and sometimes superseded) by loyalty to monarch and country. Jewelry announced one's obedience in a very public way. Thus there were many pieces of jewelry adorned with a portrait of the king or queen. Royal servants and officials often bore a portrait of the ruler or a royal symbol, such as a rose, in their signet rings. St. George (*LLL* V.ii.615), patron saint of England, was another popular motif. The few who belonged to the Order of the Garter had a full set of paraphernalia to wear, including a collar of Tudor roses encircled by blue garters alternating with tasselled knots, garter, and emblems called "Georges"—the "Lesser George," for example was for everyday wear. They were not, however, the only ones who liked to flaunt their patriotism, and many who were not knights wore St. George's image.

The Purposes of Jewelry

The most common raison d'être for jewelry—at least in Shakespeare's works—was to be given. Again and again, characters present their lovers with jewels (*LLL* V.ii.455–59; *TN* II.iv.123; *2GV* III.i.90–91). The portrait miniature (*TN* III.iv.213), perhaps set in a tablet, was an intimate gift. Olivia gives Sebastian a pearl (*TN* IV.iii.2), and rings are given to Romeo by Juliet (*R&J* III.iii.163), to Bassanio by Portia (*MV* III.ii.171–74, 183–85), to Gratiano by Nerissa (*MV* IV.ii.13–16, V.i.147–58), to Proteus by Julia (*2GV* II.ii.5 s.d.), to Posthumus by Imogen (*Cym* I.i.112), and to the disguised Viola by Olivia (*TN* I.v.299–300). Jewels were also exchanged between hosts and guests. When Queen Elizabeth made her progresses through the country, stopping for rest and entertainment at the country homes of her nobles, she was usually presented with a magnificent jewel by her host at arrival and again at departure. Courtiers also gave her jewels at New Year's; on January 1, 1587, alone she received eighty different pieces of jewelry. Duncan reverses the process, giving his hostess, Lady Macbeth, a diamond (*Mac* II.i.15–16). As this example shows, the giving of jewelry was not always a one-way transaction to curry favor. Monarchs gave jewels in return as a mark of favor or to reward some particular service to the crown. Ordinary people also gave gifts of jewelry out of friendship, or to mark an occasion like St. Valentine's Day, when giving gifts was to some extent customary. Jewels were also exchanged between rulers as part of the diplomatic process, marking ambassadorial visits, marriages, courtship, treaties, and negotiations.

In Shakespeare's plays it would appear that a ring was a significant gift when given to a man by a woman, but not as binding as the gift of a ring to a woman by a man, which might be construed as a kind of common-law marriage. Indeed, a rare instance in Shakespeare of such a gift from a man to a woman takes place in *All's Well That Ends Well*. The king gives Helena a ring, but it is clear that no promise of marriage is intended, since Helena is already married to Bertram. Bertram gives Diana a ring (IV.ii.39–72) as a promise to marry her when Helena is dead. And Helena, posing as Diana during the night, gives Bertram the king's ring, which in the end, along with her possession of the ring given to Diana, proves her claim that Bertram has consummated their marriage (V.iii.76–127, 311–14); in other words, the exchange of rings, however convoluted, makes her a wife.

Another occasion for giving a ring was death. Bequests of jewelry were common, especially bequests of rings. Printer Johanne Woolfe, who died in 1574, left her "ringe of golde with a harte Rubie in yt" to a cousin. Rings of this latter sort might very well not fit the recipient and were worn, often suspended from strings, on the ruff, neck, ear, sleeve, or hat. Particularly in the Jacobean era, rings were tied to a black string that ran through the hoop of the ring and back up into a loop around the wrist.

Jewels were also a way of storing one's wealth in a time before savings accounts and the stock market. Gems were small, easily transported, and worth a great deal. People who had to flee suddenly, as Shakespeare's characters sometimes do, could not take their houses or their furniture, but they could take their jewels (*MV* II.viii.20–21; *AYLI* I.iii.133).

People usually wore jewels for sentimental reasons or to make a fine display of their riches (*TN* II.v.58–59), but sometimes jewelry was worn for magical protection. John Monson, for example, was born in 1597 with the caul—the amniotic sac—around his head. This was considered a lucky sign, so the caul was saved for him, dried, and mounted in a pendant that he could wear. Certain stones were held to have magical properties, and these were frequently set without backing so that their virtues could be transmitted directly to the wearer's skin. Amethyst was thought to protect the wearer against melan-

The method of wearing rings in the early seventeenth century, from a portrait c. 1618. The black strings set off the whiteness of the wearer's skin.

choly; carbuncle and coral, to suppress fear and nightmares. Toadstone (*AYLI* II.i.13–14), not a product of the toad but actually a fossilized fish tooth, was thought to protect the kidneys and all newborns. Slices of narwhal tusk, known commonly as unicorn's horn, were worn as proof against poison. Pregnant women and those with nervous disorders such as epilepsy or palsy wore "cramp rings" blessed by the king or queen on Good Friday, which were supposed to ameliorate tremors and labor pains. *See also* Clothing; Crown.

Jews

Much controversy surrounds Shakespeare's attitudes toward Jews, particularly as those attitudes are revealed in the character of Shylock in *The*

Merchant of Venice. Some accuse him of virulent anti–Semitism; others defend him on the grounds of Shylock's famous "If you prick us" speech (III.i.52–70); others acquit him on the grounds that he was trying to make a living and had to appeal to the lowest common denominator, while arguing that no one can say definitively what his private views may have been; still others find him guilty of prejudice but a prejudice in part excused by the mores of the time. Many are the literary critics who employ their considerable intellects in proving that their idol was not a bigot. What is less frequently mentioned is the demographic and legal oddity that made Shakespeare's, or any Englishman's, opinions about Jews inherently strange. England had no Jews—at least not officially—and it was rare for anyone in England to meet a Jew who had converted to Chrisitianity, let alone a Jew who practiced Judaism openly. Though there were said to be a few of the latter, especially in East Anglia and Houndsditch, their numbers are almost impossible to gauge reliably. In name at least, all of England's Jews had been banished in 1290 and not permitted to return, even 300 years later. Therefore, those who were still practicing Jews had good reason to hide or to feign Christian conversion, as did those who returned to teach Hebrew or to serve as physicians to the nobility and royalty.

It is likely, then, that Shakespeare never met a Jew who would actually admit to being one. It is likely that the same could be said of everyone he knew, of his parents, his grandparents, and his great-great-great-grandparents. This makes it all the stranger that Shakespeare would profess to know anything about them, yet he presumes to know more about their character and customs than he does about the Muscovites, the Persians, or even the Danes. Where did he get his ideas?

English attitudes about the Jews had their root in Catholic stories of miracles. A common plot for such a story began with a Jew, always a cruel, stubborn, selfish person, who for some reason committed or attempted to commit some unspeakable atrocity. Typical offenses included killing Christian children for use in Passover rites or even killing the Jews' own children for minor faults. At this point, sometimes before and sometimes after the commission of the crime, the Virgin Mary interceded, sent a vision, or caused a miraculous salvation to occur, and the wicked Jew was either horribly punished or converted to Christianity.

One such tale, a fifteenth-century English translation of a story by Etienne de Besançon, recurred in various forms over the centuries, most notably in *Merchant of Venice*. In the fifteenth-century version, the Roman emperor Constantine's mother, Helena, travels in search of the True Cross, accompanied by a goldsmith. The goldsmith is in debt to a Jew who claims either the repayment of the money or an equal weight of the goldsmith's flesh. Helena's messengers judge the dispute and rule that the flesh may be taken, but none of the goldsmith's blood, and they sentence the Jew to lose his property and his tongue.

At the heart of all such tales were two assumptions. The first was that the Jew was inherently greedy, brutal, freakish (there was a popular belief that Jewish men, as well as women, menstruated), in league with the devil, and murderous. Any punishment of such a person, no matter how severe, was well deserved. Christopher Marlowe's play *The Jew of Malta* (c. 1589) fits neatly into the pattern; the Jew Barabbas is a sorcerer, poisoner, traitor, miser, and usurer who successfully plots the deaths of Christians and is boiled to death at the end of the play, no doubt to the crowd's satisfaction. The second assumption was that only stubbornness prevented the Jews from converting, for once they were exposed to the glories of the Virgin Mary or Jesus by means of miraculous visions or experiences, they were sure to see the light. The perverse refusal of the Jews to convert en masse, therefore, could be attributed only to stubbornness, to the stiff-neckedness spoken of so often in the Old Testament.

The Bible was what kept the Jews foremost in the English imagination. In the New Testament, they were portrayed as the ungrateful villains who arranged the killing of Christ. In the Old Testament, they were often faulty, and when they were truly laudable, the Christian view was that their virtues could be rationalized by chronology: If the heroes of the Old Testament had known of Jesus, it was argued, *they* would have converted. After the Reformation, this sort of thinking continued, and it was reinforced by the continued popularity of works—such as *The Canterbury Tales, Confessio Amantis, Piers Plowman*, and many a scurrilous ballad—that reviled the Jews. Ministers, while eschewing the old miracle tales, still used the Jews in their sermons as examples of "a most wicked and ungodly people."

On occasion, the Jews were praised, but usually it was a rhetorical device to further shame Christians into good behavior. Look at the Jews, authors would write. Look at how they help others in their communities (*MV* I.iii.54–55). Look how well they keep the Sabbath (*MV* IV.i.36). If even they, with all their faults, can be so good, surely we, as Christians, can do much better. Authors sometimes qualified even this lukewarm praise of Judaism by pointing out that the Jews went too far in their Sabbath observance and had too many dietary restrictions and silly laws (*MV* I.iii.31–35, III.v.23–26). More rarely, authors denounced the supposed faults of Jews and, at the same time, demonstrate the equally bad or even worse failings of the Christians around them, implying that the Christians had no just cause to claim superiority.

Shakespeare's views are a combination of his society's prejudices and his instincts as a dramatist. His best villains are the ones who have reasons for their behavior, and Shylock's denunciation of the character of Christians (*MV* I.iii.103–26, 157–59) is typical of Shakespeare's attempts to make his antagonists three-dimensional. Yet this should not necessarily be taken as an endorsement of Shylock's viewpoint. It is tempting to view Shakespeare retroactively as a tentative voice for tolerance, but the fact is that English audiences would have found Shylock's arguments inherently flawed. In their eyes, it was natural and right that a Christian should spit on and insult a Jew, should address him as "Jew" rather than by his proper name (*MV* IV.i.34), should use the word "Jew" as an insult (*1H4* II.iv.180; *2GV* II.v.48), should convince the Jew to convert if possible and force him to convert if the opportunity presented itself (*MV* IV.i.385–99).

In most respects, Shakespeare's attitudes fall squarely into the English Renaissance mainstream. The Jew is "faithless" (*MV* II.iv.37), diabolical (*MV* II.ii.23; III.i.18–20, 75; IV.i.216, 286), "stubborn" (*R2* II.i.55), stingy (MV II.ii.104–7), sneaky (MV I.iii.68–87), "blaspheming" (*Mac* IV.i.26), and hard-hearted (*2GV* II.iii.11; *MAAN* II.iii.255–57; *MV* IV.i.3–5, 78–80). Shakespeare makes much of the apparent opposition of both "gentle" and "gentile" to "Jew" (*MV* I.iii.174–75; II.iv.33–37; II.vi.51). The Jew who converts willingly, like Jessica, is to be admired and lauded for her good sense; all other Jews are worthless and malevolent.

Jobs
See Occupations.

Jousting
In retrospect, the tournament of arms, with its colorful heraldry, glittering armor, thundering horses' hooves, silk pavilions, eager spectators, and valiant knights, seems to embody what most people today think of as knighthood. However, when it first developed, in the twelfth century, the tournament was felt by kings and the church alike to be a dangerous sport—not merely for the participants' bodies but also for their souls, and for the kings' peace of mind. The church found the sport far too violent and worried that Christians might accidentally kill other Christians when they should be out killing Turks on crusades (*R2* II.i.54, IV.i.92–100). Accordingly, it excommunicated early participants and refused them burial in consecrated ground. Kings were not concerned about accidental death or injury, but they were anxious about a band of armed and mounted men, meeting for purpose of sport, noticing their collective strength, and enforcing their will on the crown or each other.

In England, the sport was banned under Henry II. Richard I licensed tournaments for the first time in 1194, naming controllers, licensers, and knights and clerks to keep the peace; conveniently for the crown, he made the holding of tournaments subject to a tax. The bureaucracy involved was considered necessary to preserve order. In *The Two Noble Kinsmen*, Theseus is angered, just as a king of England would have been, that two men are fighting in his domain "Without my leave, and officers of arms"

(III.vi.136). Perhaps there was not enough order to please some monarchs, for tournaments were discouraged again under Henry III, but Edward I enjoyed jousting, and prohibitions were less common after his reign. Events were usually banned only when the monarch was abroad or leading his troops in wartime. Jousts were still regarded with caution until the mid-fourteenth century, when the decreasing importance of cavalry in warfare made gatherings of horsemen less threatening to the king.

Procedures

The first step in the holding of a tournament was a proclamation. This announcement might be quite detailed, listing the dates, times, rules, and prizes for specific events. An example from 1570, issued at Hampton Court, proclaimed a tilt for a gold chain on the first day, a tourney for a diamond on the second, and a combat at barriers with short pike and sword for a ruby on the third. Participation in such events was, in theory, limited to those of good character and demonstrable noble lineage, but no one was likely to inquire too closely into either if a combatant was adequately skilled and equipped.

The tournament traditionally began several days before the actual fighting. Dances were held each preparatory day, with a display of the knights' coats of arms, helms, and crests taking place on the day of arrival. At the end of the days of preliminary socializing, the ladies chose a "knight of honor" to begin the fighting on the following day. At this time, the knights also swore an oath to keep the peace. Two or three days of events followed, with another dance each night, and then the various entourages dispersed. A knight was expected to have a group of followers; according to the *Statuta Armorum* of Edward I (1267), they had to be dressed in his livery, and none could be armored except cadets, standard-bearers, squires, heralds (*R2* I.iii.chs.), and the knight himself. Only the last three could bear swords.

Events

The first of the tournament combats invented, and often the first to be conducted in multiday spectacles was the *mêlée*, a mock battle fought by two teams of variable size. The knights rode up to cords stretched across the lists (*Per* I.i.62; *V&A* 595–96), an enclosure about 200 by 160 feet (70 × 49 m) surrounded by an inner wall 6 feet (1.8 m) high, a narrow open area, and a 12-foot (3.7 m) outer wall. A grandstand outside the outer wall held ladies and distinguished onlookers. The space between the walls was a safe zone to which knights with wounds, fatigue, or damaged equipment could retreat. There they were attended to by their followers, if they could reach one of the openings in the inner wall. A squire who saw that his master was in danger or trying to reach safety was expected to wade into the fray to effect a rescue. If he failed, his master could be captured, and a captured knight forfeited his horse and armor as a ransom. The *mêlée* began at a signal, with the cords lowered for the battle to begin, and it ended at a specific time, often sundown. On occasion flambeaux were lit, and the brawl continued into the night. Fighting after the retreat had been sounded meant immediate disqualification from the rest of the tournament.

From the mid-thirteenth century, a new event was added. This was the joust (*R2* V.ii.52, V.iii.16–19), a single combat with lances in which the

Leonhard Beck, German, c. 1480–1542. *The Art of Jousting and Tilting*, 1513–1518. Woodcut, 21.7 × 19.6 cm. © The Cleveland Museum of Art, 2001, Dudley P. Allen Fund, 1960.29.

two knights charged at one another on horseback, each attempting to unhorse his opponent or to break his own lance on the opponent's helmet or shield. After several unintentional collisions between the horses, the tilt (*2H6* I.iii.53; *MM* IV.iii.16; *LLL* V.ii.484), a barrier abut 3 feet (1 m) high was erected along the length of the field, with each horse charging along one side at a canter to the sound of trumpets and drums. Additional safety equipment included, as the centuries passed, reinforced shoulder armor on the left side that eventually replaced the shield, a brace on the right side of the armor against which to balance the lance butt, and helmets with only minimal eye slits and no ventilation holes on the left side. The last of these precautions reduced the chance of taking a piece of splintered lance in the eye or face, as did the knights' habit of raising their helmets at the last instant, which impaired their ability to see but lifted the eye slit away from most fragments. The price of the armor's safety was weight; by the sixteenth century, a suit of tournament armor could weigh 100 pounds (37 kg), with the helmet alone weighing as much as 23 pounds (8.6 kg). The groin, which could not be covered with plate mail, was protected by a tall, wide saddle pommel. Another precaution, introduced in the fourteenth century and optional but customary unless the joust was a personal duel, was the substitution of blunted swords and lightweight lances tipped with coronals—crown-shaped tips with three blunt projections—(*armes courtoises*) for the sharpened weapons used in real battles (*armes à outrance*).

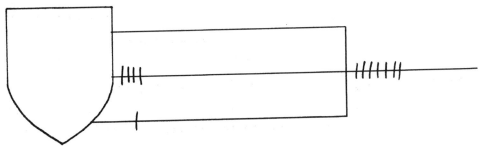

A joust's scoring diagram or "cheque." The contestant's coat of arms was drawn on the shield at left. The top bar was for hatch marks that indicated the number of "attaints"—hits to the body or head. The middle line within the box was for lances well broken; the lower line, for lances ill broken. The portion of the middle line that extended beyond the box was for the number of courses run.

Scoring was based on how often and how well the knights hit their targets. Unhorsing the opponent (*R2* I.ii.49–52) was worth the most points, followed by a tip-to-tip (coronal-to-coronal) lance strike, followed by three blows in a row to the opponent's helm, followed by any broken lance (*Per* II.iii.35–36) that hit the opponent's shield, helm, or pauldron (protective shoulder plate). It was common for none of these things to happen, and for neither of the knights to hit the other at all. Worse still was a clumsy hit such as a "staff . . . / broke cross" (*MAAN* V.i.138–39) by flopping sideways into the opposing knight's path. Knights lost points for breaking a lance within one foot of the tip or hitting the tilt or an opponent's saddle; they were disqualified for hitting a rival's horse (*AYLI* III.iv.41–42).

Sometimes the joust was structured so that when one combatant was knocked off his horse, or after three passes without either being unhorsed, the battle continued on foot with swords. By the end of the fifteenth century, swordplay, either mounted or on foot, with a wooden barrier or without, was a common element of the tournament. It became increasingly important as the years passed. In the sixteenth century, combat with halberds was introduced as well.

Shakespeare's Jousts

Though knighthood as an institution essential to the conduct of war was all but dead by Shakespeare's day, the joust, with its pageantry and its opportunities to celebrate the monarchy, was alive and well. Champions doing battle for the greater glory of their ladies, the tiltyard, and the weapons of the tournament appear in *2 Henry VI* (I.iii.59–61), and a pavilion of the kind set up by each combatant for the duration of the multiday festivities is mentioned in *Love's Labor's Lost* (V.ii.652). The most complete description of a tournament, with its courtly love, clever symbols and mottoes, and the dancing afterward, is that in *Pericles*, occupying much of act II. The entire spectacle, except for its geographical setting, could have come from one of Elizabeth I's Accession Day tilts, so closely does it resemble descriptions of those pageants and their elaborate allegorical compliments to the Virgin Queen. One of the few aspects of all this fuss not described by Shakespeare is the immense expense. The followers, their livery, the weapons, the armor, the tent, the festival clothes, and the ransoms in money or horses could—and did—bankrupt some participants. *See also* Armor; Army; Duel; Knight; Weapons.

Key

Locks (*V&A* 575–76; *Cym* II.ii.41; *MND* I.ii.34–35) and keys (*1H6* II.iii.2; *MAAN* V.i.307–8; *LLL* III.i.5; *R3* I.iv.95; *Cym* I.i.73) were common pieces of hardware in middle- and upper-class homes. The poor had little worth stealing and few chambers or chests to lock up, but in finer homes there were locks on chests, coffers, caskets (*MV* II.vii.59; *MWW* II.ii.268), garden gates (*MM* IV.i.28–33), and private rooms such as bedchambers and closets (*R2* V.iii.35; *2GV* III.i.35–36; *MWW* III.iii.156–58; *Oth* IV.ii.22; *Cym* III.v.43). In fact, the more keys a person carried, the more goods he had to protect, and thus a large bunch of jangling keys on a ring or chain became a symbol of status (*2H4* I.ii.39; *MV* II.v.12; *WT* IV.iv.614–15). Keys could also be a mark of trust; they were kept by such important servants as stewards and bailiffs as a mark of authority and responsibility. Conversely, when a servant or official lost his job, he was stripped of the keys belonging to his post (*MM* V.i.463–64), in the same way that a suspended or fired police officer today is deprived of his badge and gun.

The key itself was a simple tool, with a round or oval ring at the top, a long, thin shaft, and a flat square or rectangular tab at the bottom, notched on one or more of its edges. The notches fit along grooves inside the lock, allowing the key to bypass the grooves and lift the "ward" (*RL* 303) that kept the lock from opening. Some doors had no locks, merely latches that could be lifted (*RL* 339, 358–59) or large wooden bolts that fit into metal cradles and could be lifted or slid out of the way.

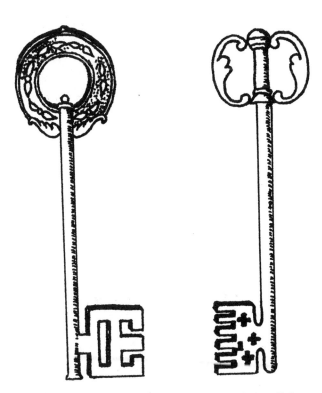

Two Renaissance keys, adapted from Claude Paradin's book of emblems, *Heroicall Devises*.

Superstition surrounded the closing and opening of locks. Many people in the Renaissance believed in sympathetic magic, the idea that an action could have an anologous consequence in a similar but unrelated situation. Therefore, all locks in the house were opened when a woman was giving birth, because it was believed that things closed or tied shut would magically prevent the womb from opening. By the same token, locks were unfastened when a death was imminent, to allow the soul to be released to heaven.

Knight

Reaching the apogee of its dominance in the eleventh and twelfth centuries, when only the clergy rivaled its power, knighthood was an intergral part of national and regional defense in the Middle Ages. A knight in those days was a warrior born and bred, sent out at about seven years old to act as a page (*R&J* V.iii.280) in another knight's household. After a few years of education and laborious service, the boy became a squire (*Lear* I.iv.242, III.ii.87; *1H4* I.ii.24; *A&C* IV.iv.11), learning the art of warfare and assisting his master in battle, practice at arms, and the joust. At last, when it was felt that he was ready to lead troops in combat, the squire became a knight (*R&J* III.ii.142; *LLL* I.i.171; *2GV* I.ii.9–10); it was common to make such promotions on the eve of a battle, for knighthood conferred not only a military command but also better pay and a greater likelihood of being kept alive and ransomed if captured.

There were several ways that the ceremony of knighthood—often referred to as an accolade, a girding-on of the sword, or, later, a dubbing—could be completed (*3H6* II.ii.58–62; *TA* I.i.196; *2H6* V.i.76–78; *TN* III.iv.239–41). The simplest way was on the field of battle, either by being formally presented with arms (the girding-on of the sword) or by being gently struck with the patron's hand or sword (dubbing). Any knight could create another; the king's or baron's presence or approval was not strictly necessary. In peacetime a more complicated (and expensive) ritual was followed. The squire's hair and beard were neatly trimmed, and then he bathed and dressed himself in white, with a scarlet coat, black surcoat, and white belt on top. A nightlong vigil in church or chapel was followed by morning confession and Mass, the blessing of his sword, his vow before his patron (who was often the local lord or one of the squire's close relatives), and the arming of the squire with hauberk and spurs. He knelt, received the accolade or dubbing, and his sword was buckled (or girded) around his waist. Mass knightings sometimes occurred, but individual ceremonies were the norm.

Knighthood began its long decline in power in the thirteenth century. An increase in royal and municipal power and a decrease in the relative importance of agriculture compared to trade were factors, causing knights to lose some of their national influence, as well as direct and complete local control. Changes in wafare, particulary the introduction of crossbows and gunpowder, led gradually to the introduction of plate-mail armor, but even that solid protection at last became vulnerable to improved weapons.

Too many knights were poor; the knight-errant of romantic fiction, wandering the countryside in search of injustice to avenge and glory to win, was "errant" precisely because he was landless, usually because he was unfortunate enough to be a younger son with no prospects of title or fortune. Many knights, landed or not, had no armor and no horse and lacked enough money to pay for either in time of war (*Lear* III.ii.87). Despite these conditions, which would seem to imply a surplus of knights, there were actually too few of them to sustain an extended military campaign. At least, that was the fear of the kings who felt that their safety depended on the knighthood. In 1254, Henry III of England mandated that landowners worth £60 be knighted and equip themselves accordingly, but later in the century, there were only about 1,500 knights in England, of whom only about 500 could be called ready for war.

Yet the institution was far from dead. In fact, it was flowering in other ways, producing a code of honor and chivalric (from the French word for knight, *chevalier*—see *1H6* IV.iii.14; *T&C* I.ii.235) behavior that would be, in retrospect, one of its most colorful and endearing qualities. The knight was expected to worship fair ladies and to seek to win their favor by glorious deeds and spiritual and moral improvement. He was to be courteous, truthful, discreet in love affairs, brave, just, and virtuous. Knightly honor was supposed to be preferred above all worldly possessions, above family, king, country, and life itself, though few knights managed to value their honor quite so highly. Honor—which became an important issue in later centuries in the ritual of the duel—was the privilege of the gentry, nobility, and military only; commoners, women, children, and clergy were incapable of possessing it. This was one of knighthood's less endearing qualities. Chivalry and knightly honor, however, were not the only new aspects of the rank to develop. In England, knights were acquiring new peacetime duties as judges, jurors, and administrators. They were, for example, the original members of the House of Commons.

In the fourteenth century, knighthood became associated less with military service and more with male-line descent from the nobility. The actual ceremony of dubbing, which once could take place when any knight admired another's prowess on the battlefield, was now of less importance than high birth in determining who had a right to the title. Knighthood and nobility separated again, however, not because nonnoble knights were created in large numbers but because fewer and fewer of the nobles entitled to knighthood actually wanted it. Becoming a knight meant pledging military service, paying a variety of often steep fees, and investing in armor, weapons, and a well-trained horse. Typically, those who anted up were those who wanted careers as professional soldiers.

In 1348, England's most famous order of knighthood, the Order of the Garter (*1H6* IV.i.15), was created. It was one of a number of religious or patriotic military orders, such as the Knights Templar, the Knights Hospitallers, and France's Order of the Golden Fleece, established over the centuries. Various versions of the legend describing the founding of the Order of the Garter exist; they all, however, center on the loss of a lady's blue-and-gold garter, the chiding of the lady in question for the loss of such an intimate item, and the response, "Honi soit qui mal y pense" (Evil be to him that thinks evil of it). This reply, which became the Garter motto, can also be taken, along with the blue and gold colors of the order (the national colors of France at the time), to be a defense of England's claim to the French throne.

The Garter was an exclusive order, consisting of only twenty-six members, one of whom was the king. Its patron was St. George, and there was a grand procession of the knights on St. George's Day, and an annual feast at Windsor. As marks of his membership, a new knight was entitled to a banner, sword, helm, crest, mantle, red velvet surcoat or gown lined with white, blue-and-gold garter for his left leg (*R3* IV.iv.366, 370), a 30-Troy-ounce (.93 kg) shoulder-spanning special-occasion Garter collar of Tudor roses within blue garters alternating with tasseled knots, a picture of St. George (*2H6* IV.i.29) killing the dragon to be suspended from the collar and a "lesser George" for daily wear that hung from a chain or ribbon (*R3* IV.iv.366, 369). He also had a stall—the one that had been vacated by the death or treason of his predecessor—in the chapel at Windsor Castle set aside for his arms, crest, and mantle (*MWW* V.v.58–74). Much of this gear he had to supply himself, making membership in the Garter an expensive privilege. Inclusion in the Order of the Garter was a great honor, however, usually reserved for prominent military commanders, powerful statesmen, and foreign leaders whom the English wished to flatter or befriend. William Cecil, Lord Burghley, Elizabeth I's trusted adviser, was a knight of the Garter, as were Frederick, Duke of Württemberg, and James I's brother-in-law, Christian IV of Denmark. The order maintained twenty-six impoverished knights on the grounds of Windsor Castle; in 1592, Frederick's secretary wrote that there were only seventeen at the moment, and that each received housing, a gift of clothes from Elizabeth I, and an annual stipend of 100 crowns.

Elizabeth, in the last two decades of her rule, encouraged an interest in knighthood and the code of chivalry. It had little to do with the actual conduct of war; the last attempts in England to raise an army by feudal levy (*3H6* III.iii.251, IV.i.131, IV.viii.6) occurred in 1327 and 1385. But Elizabeth could not fail to love a system that praised fair ladies, and she was thoroughly entertained by jousts and courtly addresses. One of the highlights of her year was Accession Day, the anniversary of her inheritance of the crown, which was celebrated with magnificent pageants and tilting. These tournaments, and those staged on other special occasions, were often framed by a device or story line, such as knights repesenting Desire besieging the Castle of Beauty. Elizabeth was not alone in her interest;

there was a general enthusiasm for tales of chivalry, but this was all mock knighthood and nostalgia for the Middle Ages. In the seventeenth century, full plate-mail armor, even for ceremonial occasions, passed out of use, and knighthood was entirely a thing of the past.

It cannot be said that Shakespeare himself fell victim to the renewed cult of knighthood. Certainly he was capable of delineating a gallant speech, a chivalrous gesture, and many a masque whose pageantry and symbolism evoked that of the tournaments. But his actual knightly characters are, on the whole, not personifications of chivalry. Valentine and Sir Eglamour, in *The Two Gentlemen of Verona* (IV.iii., V.i., V.ii.) are notable exceptions, but Sir Andrew Aguecheek and Sir Toby Belch of *Twelfth Night* are vulgar, uneducated, greedy, lazy, and dissipated, and Sir John Falstaff, for all his endearing self-parody, is cowardly, impoverished, thieving, drunken, and an absolute boor in the art of love. Down to his perilous indiscretion about his amours in *The Merry Wives of Windsor*, he is the antithesis of the thirteenth-century ideal, a knight so bad that not even his friend, the newly crowned Henry V, will acknowledge him. *See also* Armor; Fealty; Flags; Jousting; Titles; Weapons.

Land

Land was farmed by four types of people. The first was the aristocratic landowner, who held so much land that he rarely took a direct interest in it at all. His own private lands were supervised by a steward, who brought only important matters to his lord's attention, and the rest of his lands were rented out to tenants. The second type of farmer was the freeholder or franklin (*1H4* II.i.57, *WT* V.ii.164; *Cym* III.ii.77), of whom the aristocratic landowner was merely an extreme example. The freeholder held his lands outright rather than leasing them, and might be very wealthy or barely scraping by. In legal terms, he had the "fee-farm" (*T&C* III.ii.48) or "fee-simple" (*MWW* IV.ii.204; *AW* IV.iii.283–86) of his land, the right to keep it forever unless he sold it to someone else. An estate with an entail—a restriction governing inheritance or sale—was not a fee-simple, though there was a legal procedure, called fine and recovery (*CE* II.ii.73–74; *MWW* IV.ii.205), that enabled an estate to be cleared of entail.

Leaseholders held the right to rent a particular piece of land for a given number of years (often ninety-nine years—see *2H6* IV.iii.7–8), or for the lifetime of the leaseholder and perhaps those of his next two heirs (*R2* II.i.60, 110, 113; *Lear* I.iv.136–37). Copyholders usually paid a smaller yearly rent than leaseholders but were charged a fee every time the land changed hands, at which time the transfer was recorded in the court roll of the manor and the tenant (*Lear* IV.i.13–14) was given a copy of the record—hence the origin of the term "copyholder." Copyholders as a whole farmed between a third and half of English soil. The rents of copyholders and leaseholders were paid in days of labor on the lord's manor, cash, produce, or a combination of these.

In many places, however, farmers did not own a particular field or block of acres. Instead, they farmed on commonly held land or "commons" (*2H6* I.iii.22, IV.ii.69–70; *JC* IV.i.21, 25–27) divided among the villagers into fields and strips. Each field had several strips, which were distributed according to formulas that varied from village to village. Each farm was allotted a certain number of animals to graze on the commonly held meadows. This system meant that an individual farmer's strips might be widely scattered and might adjoin those of a neighbor who was not as scrupulous a weeder. The commons also required a great deal of maintenance and intervention from local authorities, who had to decide when plowing, sowing, and harvesting should take place; when animals would be allowed to graze in pasture or stubble; when repairs to fields or fences needed to be made; which male animals should be allowed to breed with the common herd; and when someone was exceeding his rights.

A frequent complaint was that people with no right of tenancy were putting up ramshackle cottages on the waste areas of the manor, sometimes with the lord's permission but frequently without it. These people, desperate to survive and crammed into a smoky, one-room hovel of only 80 to 250 square feet (7.44 to 23.25 m²), represented a threat to the livelihood of the villagers and were often driven out, their hastily built cottages pulled down by a team of horses or oxen.

The difficulties of "champion" or open-field farming, with its scattered strips and common land, were eventually too much for some people. They exchanged strips with neighbors to consolidate their land, a strategy known as "farming in severalty," or even won the legal right to enclose their land with fences and hedges (*LLL* II.i.219–23). Enclosure (*2H6* I.iii.22), which was a source of increasing controversy in the next two centuries, enabled farmers to improve their own land and avoid conflicts with neighbors. It also enabled them to concentrate on sheep and take advantage of rising wool prices, which had the added advantage of concentrating the flock and improving the distribution of manure, which in turn increased crop yields. However, enclosure harmed the poor, at least in the short term, by removing their rights to glean and depriving them of pasturage for their few animals. *See also* Farming.

Law

There was not one law in England, but many. William Harrison mentions civil, canon, statute, common, and customary branches of the law and three different methods of conducting a trial. An additional type of law, Salic law (*H5* I.ii.11–100), was not valid in England but governed the inheritance of many Continental crowns and was thus of interest to the English kings, who claimed the right, with varying success and then ultimate failure, to the French crown. (At issue was whether the crown could descend through daughters as well as sons; Salic law forbade inheritance through the maternal line, but English law did not.) There were local, manorial, national, criminal, consistorial, and maritime courts, and matters were complicated still further by archaic court language and stenography, laborious and sometimes insufficient training of lawyers, and an extremely limited court calendar that was often interrupted by feast days.

The two main branches of law were the civil and common laws, and of these two, common law was the more widely practiced. This was the law governing most criminal and civil actions (*TS* III.ii.232–34) and the type of law that governed the courts of Common Pleas, King's (or Queen's) Bench, and Exchequer. The Court of Common Pleas dealt with lawsuits in which one private party, the plaintiff (*MAAN* V.i.304, *TN* V.i.354), sued another, the defendant (*S* 46). King's Bench was a criminal court, in which the crown attempted to prove that a defendant had committed some offense against the law. Exchequer began as a court to decide cases involving crown revenue but evolved into a quicker venue for the sorts of cases heard in Common Pleas. The Court of Chancery, under the supervision of the Lord Chancellor, was one of the nation's highest courts; it issued "original" common-law writs, that is, the writs that opened a case, and had a separate division in which the common law could be bypassed or sped up through appeal. One of its specialties was cases involving land held in "copyhold," a kind of long-term, transferrable lease. The Court of Requests, governed by the Lord Privy Seal and the Masters of Requests, had a similar function. It permitted petitioners to request justice, pardon (*2H6* IV.viii.9, 14, 22; *AW* V.iii.58), or some other action directly from the crown. It served as a cheap, quick legal avenue and was one means by which the Privy Council exerted its power, though the court's authority was much reduced in 1599 after the Court of Common Pleas exerted its right to adjudicate many of the cases (*Lear* III.ii.86) that had previously gone to Requests. Another type of national court was the Court of the Star Chamber (*MWW* I.i.2, 32), whose bench consisted of the Privy Council, the chief justice of King's Bench, and the chief justice of Common Pleas. It had few limits on its authority and was used primarily in cases of riot, violence, forgery (*3H6* III.iii.175), and slander (*MAAN* IV.i.210; *MM* II.i.178).

Civil law was less widely practiced than common law. It was used primarily in ecclesiastical and admiralty courts, and to a lesser extent in some of the same courts where common law was dominant. Customary law, and its close relative, prescription, dealt with purely local matters and amounted to little more than established customs. If, for example, a dispute between tenants broke out on a lord's lands, the matter was likely to be settled in the manorial leet (*TS* Ind.ii.87), a court in which the local lord or his representatives arbitrated such disputes, ordered improvements made to fields or ditches, and regulated the use of common land. Franklins, or freeholders, had the right to be judged by their peers in manorial courts, while villeins, or base tenants, were subject to the rulings of a jury and the lord's steward, who acted as judge. Prescription was an even narrower type of law, dealing with the customary or hereditary rights of specific individuals in specific situations, for example, variations in the payment of tithes, an easement to use part of a neighbor's land, or long-standing agreements about rights to pasture on the commons. To add to the complexity of the legal system, there were also "piepowder" courts, which had the authority to settle all disputes arising at fairs.

There were three kinds of trial mentioned by Harrison, but only one of them was used with any frequency. One could be tried by Parliament, a right typically invoked by peers, who were heard and judged by the House of Lords. Or one could choose to prove one's innocence through ritualized combat. Neither of these two methods allowed for any sort of appeal, so the most common type of trial was a jury trial. Much preparation and discussion took place before a case was resolved by the jury, however. First, a bewildering array of charges, countercharges, responses, and interviews, called the plaint, declaration, bar, answer, replication, rejoinder, rebut, sur-rebut, and so on, flew back and forth between the lawyers on both sides. These documents were written in court hand (*2H6* IV.ii.92–93), a type of cursive unintelligible to the untrained modern reader, and much of the writing, as well as much of the speech in court, was delivered in either Latin or "court French," the latter a legacy of the Norman Conquest. Shakespeare mostly ignores court French (though "oyes," the cries at the opening of a court session, make an appearance in *T&C* IV.v.142), but he alludes to a few of the legal terms that appeared in other languages, such as *in capite*, a Latin term for property leased directly from the monarch or "head" of state (*2H6* IV.vii.124); "Emmanuel," or "God is with us," a Hebrew word found at the beginning of some legal documents (*2H6* IV.ii.99); and *noverint universi per praesentes*, "be it known to all by these presents," another opening phrase found on documents (*2H6* IV.vii.30–31; *AYLI* I.ii.120–21).

Some of these trials (*2H6* III.iii.8) took place at the special courts mentioned above, but most were held locally. Minor matters were settled by the sheriff or justice of the peace; more serious crimes were dealt with, according to Harrison, "by the justices and gentlemen of the country" at quarter sessions, held, as their name implies, four times a year. Petty sessions, under the governance of bailiffs and high constables, heard cases pertaining to unfair weights and measures, cheating by merchants, and misbehavior by servants, employees, and common rogues. Some matters, particularly capital cases, were heard by circuit courts called assizes, roving courts consisting of a few judges and their staff traveling from county to county. Juries at the assizes were composed of twelve men (*MV* IV.i.397–99), four of whom had to be from the hundred (a term for a section of a county) "where the action lieth or the defendant inhabiteth." The jury (*R3* I.iv.185–91; *TN* III.ii.16–17, *Tim* IV.iii.341; *1H4* II.ii.93), or "quest" (*S* 46), Harrison wrote in *The Description of England*, deliberated, sometimes without eating or drinking, until they had rendered a verdict in writing, but lawyers, then as now, were often skilled in jury selection and would manage to include "some one or more into the jury that will in his behalf never yield unto the rest but of set purpose put them to this trouble." Many of Harrison's complaints sound like those still being made today about the legal system. He bemoans the fact that some jurors, in order to avoid being sued for a false verdict,

> bribe the bailiffs to be kept at home, whereupon poor men, not having in their purses wherewith to bear their costs, are impaneled upon juries, who very often have neither reason nor judgment to perform the charge they come for.

He complains, too, about the increasing litigiousness of his society and the overpopulation of the country with lawyers. Harrison was not alone in finding fault with the legal system. There was a popular, and well-founded, belief that the system favored the rich. One of the fishermen in *Pericles*, for example, says of a fish that it "hangs in the net like a poor man's right in the / law: 'twill hardly come out" (II.i.122–23), and Shakespeare's fellow playwright Thomas Heywood has his anti-hero, Chartley, plan to disavow a clandestine marriage because "there is none [to bear witness to it] but she and her father, and their evidence is not good in law. And if they put me in suit, the best is, they are poor, and cannot follow it." Other complaints included the length of time it took to resolve a lawsuit (*Ham* III.i.72; *Cor* II.i.72–75), the laziness or greediness of lawyers, and the ability of a good lawyer to make a bad cause seem just (*MV* III.ii.75–77).

The most famous trial scene in Shakespeare is undoubedly that in which Portia successfully opposes Shylock in *The Merchant of Venice*. This scene perhaps represents the way in which some lesser courtrooms operated, with the lord or justice, like the duke, asking questions, listening to various arguments, and then making a determination based on the facts of the individual case and his knowledge of the participants as much as on law or precedent. However, the best accounts of the English trial system are not attempts by Shakespeare to depict an actual courtoom. One of these accounts takes up much of *King Lear* III.vi and concerns the imagined arraignment, or trial, of Goneril and Regan (20–55). Here we see a facetious version of many courtoom elements: Edgar, Kent, and the Fool as robed justices of the king's commission; the questioning of witnesses (*Oth* III.iv.152–53; *MAAN* IV.ii.80; *MM* II.i.152—for the term "interrogatories," which was applied to these sorts of questions, see *MV* V.i.297–303); testimony from Lear under oath; and accusations of bribery, or "Corruption in the place" (*Lear* III.vi.54) that results in the mock-Regan's escape. Another good description of courtroom behavior occurs in *Henry VIII*, where a spectator recounts the Duke of Buckingham's treason trial:

> The great duke
> Came to the bar, where to his accusations
> He pleaded still not guilty, and allegèd
> Many sharp reasons to defeat the law.
> The king's attorney on the contrary
> Urged on the examinations, proofs, confessions
> Of divers witnesses; which the duke desired
> To him brought viva voce to his face. (II.i.11–18)

Officers of the Courts

The "bar" referred to in the account of Buckingham's trial was the railing surrounding the judge's seat, and it was to this bar that prisoners came to be arraigned, tried, and sentenced (*H8* II.i.31–32; *R3* V.iii.199–

200). The bar could also refer to an upper rank within the Inns of Court that served as training schools for common lawyers. (A third meaning of "bar" meant an obstacle, or a defense so irrefutable that it completely destroyed the plaintiff's case—see *TS* I.i.135). The bar was where the forces of law and the forces of disorder met, the place where one thing became another, where a prisoner emerged as a free man or one condemned, and a law student emerged as a lawyer. It was the point around which all legal officials' work revolved.

Chief among the officials were the justices, ranging in power from the justices of the peace (*2H6* IV.vii.42–44) in the smallest parishes to the chief justices of London's greatest courts. The least competent magistrates (*3H6* I.ii.22–27; *Temp* II.i.154) were the justices of the peace, who had only the power to hear cases; the more qualified justices of the peace and quorum, also known as justices of oyer and terminer, could hear cases and also pass judgment. Shallow and Slender's discussion in *The Merry Wives of Windsor* I.i turns, in part, on Shallow's exact rank; he is not only a justice, but a "Justice of / Peace, and Coram [Quorum]" and, furthermore, a "Custalorum"—a garbled version of *custos ratolorum*, or chief justice (3–7). Judges (*1H4* I.ii.63–65; *R2* I.iii.236; *MM* II.ii.176–77; *Cym* IV.ii.128; *TA* III.i.chs.) wore long robes (*MM* II.ii.60–61) that would be recognizable even today, though the wigs still worn by British judges had not yet come into fashion. Shakespeare's justices are fat, sententious fellows (*AYLI* II.vii.152–55), ambitious, and, if not corrupt, at least willing to do a friend a favor (*2H4* V.i.39–54).

Among the most numerous representatives of the legal profession were the lawyers, with attorneys (*CE* V.i.100; *R3* IV.iv.127–28) being those accorded less prestige, less glamour, and more day-to-day work. Attorneys were, for the most part, the individuals who drafted wills (*JC* III.ii.129–60, 235–51; *A&C* III.iv.4), deeds of gift or sale (*MV* IV.ii.2–4, V.i.292), and other documents, while the lawyers made courtroom presentations. This distinction was not, however, as strict or extreme as it would be in later centuries. Shakespeare, for example, uses "attorney" mostly as a metaphorical term for any go-between or agent (*AYLI* IV.i.91; *V&A* 335–36; *R3* IV.iv.413), but in the case of the Duke of Buckingham's trial, he uses it for the lawyer interrogating the duke (*H8* II.i.15). The list of land-related transactions and terms in *Hamlet* V.i represents, perhaps, the bread and butter of the attorney—purchases, statutes to gain control of the land of one's debtor, fines for the conversion of entailed land to a fee-simple, "double vouchers" or repeated warrants of title, recoveries of title through court decrees, indentures (agreements), and conveyances, or documents of transfer (103–10).

Shakespeare uses the term "lawyer" more frequently, and he paints a complex picture of the profession. His much-quoted plan to first "kill all the lawyers" (*2H6* IV.ii.77) comes, in fact, from the distasteful mouth of

Jack Cade, who also advocates the killing of worthy noblemen and clerks. Cade's advice thus cannot be taken at face value, though unquestionably there was much resentment directed at lawyers in Shakespeare's day, and the plays reflect this. Shakespeare's lawyers are collegial (*TS* I.ii.276–77) but adversarial (*1H6* II.v.45–46), learned and professional (*2H6* IV.iv.36, *WT* IV.iv.204–7) but little more than calculating talkers (*AYLI* IV.i.14; *Lear* I.iv.131–32), greedy (*R&J* I.iv.73; *AW* II.ii.21–22), and dissembling (*Tim* IV.iii.155). They are seemingly embodiments of Latin jargon (the "quiddities" of *Ham* V.i.99, from *quidditas*, "whatness") and quillets (petty verbal distinctions—see *Ham* V.i.100; *Tim* IV.iii.156). Harrison agreed with Shakespeare on the issue of lawyers' greed, as indeed did almost everyone writing at the time. Harrison complained that lawyers sometimes charged high fees and then never bothered to show up in court. He claimed that some would not even stir from their chambers for less than £10. Robert Greene, writing in *A Quip for an Upstart Courtier* (1592), agreed that

> if a poore man sue a gentleman, why he shootes up to the skie, and the arrowe fals on his own head, howsoever the cause goe, the weakest is thrust to the wall, lawiers are troubled with the heate of the liver, which makes the palms of their hands so hot that they cannot be coold unlesse they be rubd with the oile of angels.

In other words, lawyers would do nothing unless some angels—gold coins—were placed in their hands, and of course a poor man could not afford this sort of fee. In *The Anatomie of Abuses*, the Puritan Phillip Stubbes accused lawyers of ambition and ostentation; he granted that they would do their best for the client, but only as long as the client had any gold left, and he was impatient with the excuses they made if they lost a case.

The apprehension and interrogation of criminals were in the hands of a host of local officials who often carried metal-tipped staffs as signs of office and were thus called tipstaffs (*H8* II.i.53 s.d.). The highest-ranking peace officer in each county was the sheriff, "shire-reeve," "shrieve," or some other similar variation (*1H4* II.iii.68, II.iv.487–95; *2H4* IV.iv.99; *AW* IV.iii.191). The bailiff (*WT* IV.iii.96–99; *TN* III.iv.182) was a sheriff's deputy who served writs and warrants (*R3* I.iii.341, I.iv.112–13; *H8* I.i.216–17) and made arrests (*Ham* V.ii.338–39; *TN* III.iv.322–75, S 74). A similar function was performed by the paritor (*LLL* III.i.185), who served summonses for the ecclesiastical courts. The beadle was a lesser official with similar functions who might also serve as a town crier, a law-court official, and a whipper of minor offenders, such as prostitutes, bawds, and beggars (*2H4* V.iv.ch.; *LLL* III.i.174; *Lear* IV.vi.160–65; *Per* II.i.92–97). A constable (*2H4* V.iv.4; *MAAN* IV.ii.ch., V.i.ch.; *Temp* III.ii.27; *R&J* I.iv.40), either "high" and serving at the hundred level, or "petty" and serving the parish, was a peace officer. Shakespeare calls him a "nut-hook," from the staff he carried (*MWW* I.i.158–60), and provides three excellent portraits of him in *Measure for Measure*'s Elbow, *Love's Labor's Lost*'s Dull, and *Much Ado About Nothing*'s Dogberry. A third kind of constable, the thirdborough or thirdbarrow, appears to have served as a keeper of the peace in a town or on manorial lands (*LLL* I.i.183; *TS* Ind.i.12). Constables, like bailiffs, could make arrests, though they could pursue offenders only to the boundaries of their parish or other area of authority. At times, a "hue and cry" would be raised, with neighboring parishes notified of a fugitive's flight so that he could be hunted from one territory to the next. Still, as William Harrison pointed out, a victim of theft who asked the neighboring parish's constable to pursue the thief was likely to be told, "God restore your loss! I have other business at this time."

Any or all of the parish and county peacekeepers—bailiffs, constables, beadles, and so forth—could be known collectively as "officers" (*3H6*

Night watchman with dog and lantern, from the *Roxburghe Ballads*, which borrowed the illustration from *The Belman of London*. Reproduced from the Collections of the Library of Congress.

I.iv.43, V.vi.12; *2H4* II.i.chs., V.iv.chs.; *MAAN* IV.ii.81; *Oth* I.i.179; *TS* V.i.89–95). The humblest of all the officers were the night watchmen (*MAAN* III.iii.ch., IV.ii.ch., V.i.ch.; *JC* II.ii.16; *T&C* I.ii.271; *R&J* III.iii.148, V.iii.158; *A&C* IV.iii.17). The watch went about the streets of towns, hoping to discourage criminals by their mere presence. A contemporary woodcut shows one armed with a staff, a bell, a lantern, and a dog; he does not look particularly intimidating. In fact, in *Richard II*, far from being able to arrest a set of young thugs, the watch is actually beaten by them (V.iii.9–10). Some of the loftiest enforcers of the law were the pursuivants (*R3* III.ii.ch., III.iv.87), who were royal messengers empowered to serve warrants.

Courts employed various functionaries to make and keep their records. In most cases, these were simple clerks (*2GV* II.i.110; *MV* V.i.143) or secretaries. Constables might have an assistant to take notes during the interviews of suspects (*MAAN* III.v.46–65). In London, the officer entrusted with recording and recalling the decisions of various courts was known as the recorder (*R3* III.vii.30), and his evidence as to precedent was considered practically irrefutable.

The Court Calendar

The legal year was divided into four terms (*AYLI* III.ii.331–33; *2H4* V.i.82–83), each of which was interrupted by feast days and "returns." On the return day, the sheriffs of each county had to report to the court on the progress of all writs issued since the last return. The terms were named for the holidays after which they began. Hilary term thus began on January 23, unless January 23 was a Sunday, and then it began on January 24. It ended February 12 and had four return days, three holidays on which no business could be conducted, and several other feasts that were sometimes observed and sometimes omitted. Easter term began seventeen days after Easter, ended four days after Ascension Day, and had five returns. Trinity term began the Friday after Trinity Sunday and ended two weeks from the following Wednesday, with four returns. The last term, Michaelmas term, began October 9, unless that was a Sunday, and ended November 28, with eight returns. *See also* Crime; Duel; Execution; Farming; Inheritance; Inns of Court; Prison.

Lead

When Shakespeare mentions lead, it is often as a symbol of emotional or physical heaviness (*Cor* III.i.313; *A&C* III.xi.72). Elsewhere, he uses it in a variety of negative contexts: when "molten," it "scalds" (*Lear* IV.vii.48); when used to make spoons, it is one of the most worthless things imaginable (*Cor* I.v.5–7); when used to make or line a prosperous person's coffin, it is one of the many symbols of death (*JC* IV.iii.265). However, lead in Shakespeare's England was one of the most readily available and widely used metals.

It was plentiful in Britain, often appearing so close to the surface that small groups, or even individuals, could mine it. Those who found a source had to register a claim, extract the ore, and smelt it (*AW* III.vi.37–38; *Ham* IV.i.25–27). Usually this was done simply by digging a shallow pit with channels leading into molds. A fire was built in the pit, the ore added, and the whole pit covered with turf but left open to the wind on one side. As the metal melted, it drained into the molds, forming "pigs," which were left to cool. The miners then paid a percentage of their yield as a tithe to the lord of the field, often the monarch but sometimes a local landowner.

The lead, once smelted, was used not only in coffins but also in printers' type, pewter for dishes and utensils, and construction. It was sometimes employed for plumbing, downspouts, and gutters because it did not rust, and the same quality made it a good roofing material. Unlike most roofs, a lead roof did not leak and could therefore be flat. It would gradually oxidize and thin, but this could take a couple of centuries, and then the remaining lead could be melted, supplemented, and recast. Roof lead was melted and gently poured onto large sand-covered tables with rims and allowed to solidify into sheets. If the roof was to be patterned, a mold could be pressed into the sand before the melted lead was poured.

The disadvantage of lead was its cost. The metal itself was expensive, but most of all, it was heavy, and its weight required more and bigger supports, which also cost money. It was therefore employed chiefly in churches and the houses of the rich; ordinary houses seldom had roofs of lead. This did not mean that lead was absent from such houses, however. Lead was the material into which window panes were set, and glass windows were becoming increasingly common in middle-class homes. *See also* Architecture.

Leather

English leather (*AYLI* IV.iii.25) was made from a variety of animals, including sheep, lambs, cows, calves (*John* III.i.55–59, 125–27), and deer. It was used for clothing, including breeches, coats, and gloves. It was also the basis of parchment, fine book bindings, straps, laces, boots, saddles, and even gunpowder flasks. Neat's (cow's) leather was used for the soles of shoes (*Temp* II.i.70–71). The most desirable leather, because of its softness and pliability, was cheveril (*R&J* II.iv.86; *H8* II.iii.32), made from French kidskins, but all leather had a reputation for being durable and water-resistant.

The making of leather—in this example, for gloves—began with the delivery of hides (*Lear* III.iv.103) to the tanner (*2H6* IV.ii.24; *TNK*

II.ii.44; *Ham* V.i.167), who determined which side of the skins to dress. The side on which the hair grew, the grain side, produced a smooth finish when dressed; the flesh side produced suede. The tanner determined which was the better side depending on the quality of the hides and the purpose for which they were intended. Next, he soaked the skins to clean them of grease and dirt. The need for plenty of water in the tanning process demanded that his yard, like so many other businesses of the time, be located near a stream or river.

Lime was applied to remove the hair, and after sitting in lime pits for a few weeks, the hides were scraped of any remaining hair or flesh, washed again, and soaked in a mixture of warm water and manure, which softened them. They were again rinsed and then rotted in a tub of water and flour or bran until they were thick and pulpy. They were rinsed and scraped yet again, then tanned with oil, alum, or extracts from bark or berries. After drying, they were "staked"—rubbed back and forth on the flesh side over a tool called a staking knife, which softened them one last time.

The process differed somewhat when the leather was intended for other purposes. For example, hard objects, including powder flasks, helmets, and armor, were sometimes made of a material called *cuir bouilli. Cuir bouilli* was made by boiling the leather and pressing it into a mold, then cooling it. The process produced a very hard leather. *See also* Armor; Clothing; Gloves.

Letters

Letters feature prominently in Shakespeare's works, not only because they were one of the few forms of long-distance communication available in his day, but also because, as an indirect means of discourse, they offer all sorts of dramatic possibilities for misunderstanding, delay, and misdirection. There are love letters in great quantities, of course (*LLL* V.ii.775, 783; *2GV* I.iii.45–81, II.i.89–141, 150–67; *LC* 47–49), but there are also letters on other matters exchanged between wives and husbands (*JC* IV.iii.180), between nobles and kings (*1H6* IV.i), and between travelers and those at home, assuring each other of their mutual good health (*2GV* II.iv.50–51, III.i.57).

The typical letter was written with a quill pen on a single sheet of paper, either flat or folded once to make four "pages." A space was reserved on the back of the leaf for the address (*LLL* V.ii.8). There were no envelopes; once completed, the letter was simply folded so that the address showed on one side, and sealed with wax (*LLL* IV.i.61; *TN* II.v.90–92; *Lear* IV.vi.260; *Cym* III.ii.35–36; *MAAN* IV.i.165; *JC* II.i.37; *John* IV.ii.215). It was a procedure so familiar that Lady Macbeth can perform it in her sleep:

> I have seen her rise from her bed, throw her nightgown upon her, unlock her closet, take forth paper, fold it, write upon't, read it, afterwards seal it, and again return to bed. (*Mac* V.i.5–8)

There was no requirement that the sealing wax be decorated in any way, but many people chose to imprint it, while still warm, with a "signet," often engraved into a ring. The signet or stamp (*MM* IV.ii.198; *Tim* II.ii.208; *TA* IV.ii.69; *Ham* V.ii.49–52) guaranteed that the letter had not been broken open and read in transit, and also served as a sort of return address for those familiar with its design.

Letters were delivered in one of two ways. They could be sent with one of the postboys (*MWW* V.v.190), usually not boys at all but grown men, who traveled from one station to another, carrying government dispatches. At each station, they handed their letters over to a new postboy and horse. The post (*2H6* I.iv.77; *3H6* II.i.109, IV.iv.ch.) had right-of-way on the roads and first right to fresh horses at post stations; he blew a horn (*3H6* III.iii.162–67) to announce his approach. Since the post was initially reserved for government communications, private letters had to be sent by a carrier or hauler, who took a much slower path back and forth between London and various towns.

The second way of sending a letter was to send it with a friend who was traveling to or near the recipient's home, or with a servant or apprentice. Friends would perform such a service for free, but servants expected to be tipped for this extra duty, and they kept track of who gave how much: Costard is given only three farthings by Armado to carry a love letter, but a whole shilling by Berowne for the same service (*LLL* III.i.6, 50, 129, 167–68). Letters sent in this way needed little in the way of a written address; the messenger knew to whom the letter was sent and where he or she was likely to be found. Lucrece simply addresses her letter to her husband "At Arden to my lord with more than haste" (*RL* 1332).

One type of letter was not really a piece of correspondence. This was the letter patent (*H8* III.ii.251), a legal document and a matter of public record. It was used to convey a royal command or grant, such as an order for the founding of a charitable institution or the granting of a monopoly. *See also* Literacy; Writing.

Lighting

For many people in the Renaissance, light was almost entirely derived from natural sources. One rose with the sun and went to bed soon after it set; nighttime was lit only by the moon, the stars, the glow of the dying hearth, and the bonfires of occasional festivals. Many other people made do with the cheapest forms of artificial light: torches (*MAAN* V.iii.24; *JC* V.v.2; *V&A* 163; *R&J* I.v.46; *A&C* IV.ii.41), rushlights (peeled rushes dipped in fat or pitch and set on fire), or candles made of the rendered animal fat called tallow. Many tallow candles were made by housewives at home from kitchen drippings caught in a "candle-mine" or "tallow-catch" (*2H4* II.iv.306; *1H4* II.iv.229); these were dark and cloudy, and gave evidence of their humble origins. They also smelled bad (*Cym* I.vi.109–10). They were molded rather than dipped, and had wicks of hemp, tallow, or rushes. Better-quality white tallow candles with cotton wicks and the even more expensive wax variety (*2H6* II.iv.17 s.d.; *MWW* IV.iv.50) could be bought at chandlers' shops (*1H4* III.iii.47–48) or from traveling candlemakers who could be hired to work on-site for 4d per day. Butchers, like house-holders, saved animal fat for this purpose, cutting it off and rolling it into lumps called keeches (*H8* I.i.55).

In many cases, the exact composition of the candles mentioned by Shakespeare is unclear. They are simply called candles or tapers, with no indication of whether they are tallow or wax (*1H4* II.i.46; *MAAN* V.i.18; *LLL* IV.iii.266, V.ii.268; *JC* II.i.7–8, 35, IV.iii.161, 272; *Oth* I.i.137–38; *Per* I.Cho.15–16). Usually, context hints at whether the character speaking would be likely to afford wax or not. Imogen is so rich, as a princess, that she can afford to leave the candle burning even after she falls asleep, just in case she needs something during the night (*Cym* II.ii.3–7); surely she, for example, has wax candles.

Candles could be lit easily at the kitchen or chamber fire, but if it was the middle of the night, the fire might well have gone out. In this case it was necessary to use a tinderbox and flint to generate sparks that could be transferred to the candle wick (*RL* 176–79). Candles could be placed in a candlestick or in a lantern, often spelled "lanthorn" because its translu-cent sides were made of thin slices of cow's horn (*2H6* II.iii.25; *1H4* II.i.36–37, III.iii.26–27; *MAAN* III.iii.23–24; *MWW* V.v.80). Light could also be rented in the form of torch bearers or linkboys, who could be hired or drafted from among one's servants to assist on the walk home from a party or tavern (*1H4* III.iii.44–46).

Oil lamps had an advantage over candles and torches because they were less susceptible to the drafts that could make torches smoke (*RL* 310–12) and candles go out. Their disadvantage was cost, for they were usually imported and thus expensive. The oil that they burned could also be costly, and bitumen—mineral pitch, or asphalt—was sometimes used as a cheaper substitute. Shakespeare has a preference for oil lamps in classical settings (*T&C* III.ii.158; *A&C* I.iv.4–5, IV.xv.88; *V&A* 755–56), but they appear in some of his plays set in other times and places as well (*1H6* II.v.8; *R2* I.iii.220–22; *AW* I.ii.58–60). *See also* Fire; Household Objects.

Literacy

No one knows for certain how many people in Shakespeare's day could read and write, though many scholars have attempted to estimate the num-ber. Unfortunately, there were many levels of literacy in late Tudor and early Stuart England, and the more widespread varieties are the hardest to spot from surviving documents.

The easiest way to quantify literacy is to look at a set of documents—parish records, for example, that register marriages—and see how many of the parties involved could sign their names and how many made an X instead (*2H6* IV.ii.102–3). According to this type of study, about 70 percent of adult men and 90 percent of adult women were illiterate, in the sense that they could not (or chose not to) sign their names. There were wide regional differences; only 22 percent of London men were illiterate in this sense, whereas at least 75 percent of Nottinghamshire men were. There were also gender differences, as noted above, and class differences. The gentry and professionals were universally literate by 1600, but farm laborers and servants were far less so. In this context, it makes perfect sense that Capulet's servant cannot read the guest list (*R&J* I.ii.38–44), that Jaquenetta needs to have Armado's letter read to her (*LLL* IV.ii.91–145), that the noble lovers and conspirators scattered throughout the plays seem to have no difficulty reading books and each other's letters, and that George Seacole is made a constable simply because he can read and write (*MAAN* III.iii.9–16). A more ominous example of the literacy gap is the murder of the clerk Emmanuel by a mob simply because he can write (*2H6* IV.ii.85–109).

However, writing is not the only measure of literacy, simply the easiest to track. It was also one of the last and highest levels of literacy available to sixteenth and seventeenth-century people, who started their education, if they were educated at all, at a "petty school." These petty schools focused almost exclusively on reading. Reading furthered religious study, a prime consideration in Reformation England; writing did nothing to enhance one's knowledge of the Bible. Reading was easier to teach in the short time available; most children could be spared from the tasks of home and farm for only a few months to two years, and writing required small-muscle control, extensive practice, the making of quill pens, a knack for dipping into the ink just so, and other skills that took time and practice to master. Finally, reading was cheaper to teach than writing, needing only a bench or a stool to perch upon and a paddle-shaped horn book or primer. Writing, on the other hand, required paper, ink, quills, penknives, and desks. Those who wished to make notes and had not mastered the art of writing had to make do with their memories, or with notches made on a stick.

The question of literacy is further complicated by the types of reading that could be undertaken. Roman type, the sort usually used for books today, was coming into fashion, but black-letter or "Gothic" type was used for many reading materials, particularly those directed at the common people. It was possible to be black-letter literate, therefore, and unable to read Roman type. It was also possible to be able to read both black-letter and Roman fonts and be unable to read handwriting, for there were multiple styles of handwriting, each with its own abbreviations and letter formations. The commonly used "secretary hand" had at least nine ways of making the letter "r," for example.

Shakespeare must naturally have encountered both literate and illiterate people, but to judge from the plays he must have thought the inability to read a truly lower-class trait. The characters who have not attained this basic level of literacy are always bumpkins or servants. Even his servants can sometimes read; Launce, for example, reads his own list of a milkmaid's qualities (*2GV* III.i.273–375), as does Speed. *See also* Books; Education; Letters; Writing.

Magic

The lines between science and magic were extremely blurry in the Renaissance. Medicine was half sorcery, consisting often of such "cures" as smearing a salve on a weapon in the hope that this would heal the person wounded by it. There was great faith in analogy and symbolism in all aspects of life; if thing A resembled thing B, surely there was some mystical link between the two, not always demonstrable but present nonetheless. The crucial question was the origin of special knowledge and power. If it came from God as a privilege of holiness or royalty, it was of course perfectly harmless. If it came from nature and could be discovered by lawful study and research, it was likewise appropriate for humans to know and use. If it came from demonic interference, it was to be shunned and even, after 1541, prosecuted as a felony.

The trick was knowing the derivation of practices and, if one was the practitioner, avoiding a negative interpretation. For example, a local wise woman prescribing the herb savin as an abortifacient was actually operating, whether she knew it or not, on its scientifically demonstrable (albeit dangerous) efficacy at ending pregnancies. This use would be perceived as white magic by the women who used her services and as black magic by others in the community, with the balance, and the wise woman's fate, resting on her local popularity. The moment she became obnoxious to her neighbors, she could be accused as a witch. The delicate balance is represented in Shakespeare by the presence in *As You Like It* of "a magician, / most profound in his art and yet not damnable" (V.ii.60–61)—a man who uses magic for good, yet recognizes that its practice daily puts him in danger of execution (70–71).

Magical practices consisted mostly of trying to avoid a malevolent influence, cause a beneficial event, cause harm, determine the true nature of something in the present, or foresee the future. Often, Shakespeare mentions magic without specifying which of these goals is intended, settling instead for vague references to "art and baleful sorcery" (*1H6* II.i.15), "spells and medicines bought of mountebanks" (*Oth* I.iii.61), or "devilish charms" (*2H6* III.i.46). Sometimes, he is more specific, though charms (*Mac* I.iii.37; *R3* I.iii.214) or practices to avoid evil crop up only occasionally. It was believed to be unlucky to untangle "elflocks" (*R&J* I.iv.90–91), or clumps of matted hair brought by the fairies, so these were probably cut out instead. A reference to horse hair alludes to the practice of putting a horse hair into water to avert snakes (*A&C* I.ii.194).

On the subject of magic worked to bring a benefit, Shakespeare is almost entirely silent, except for the use of love charms (*Oth* I.ii.64, III.iv.55–58, 69), which, along with spells to locate lost property or fairy treasure, were among the most commonly used "white" magics. Benign magic was also used in cases of illness or physical travail. Cramp rings, blessed by the king or queen, were believed to relieve seizures and labor pains, and the monarch was also believed to have the power to cure scrofula by touching the afflicted. Catholic women used church relics to ease them through labor, while women of all denominations were convinced that opening locks and untying knots would sympathetically open the birth canal and speed the baby's emergence. Less common, though much sought, were charms that enabled the sorcerer (*CE* I.ii.99; *1H6* I.i.24–26) to become invisible. Owen Glendower, who appears in *1 Henry IV*, was noted as a wizard (*1H4* III.i.44–48, 52, 55–56, 152–55) and was rumored to possess a stone of invisibility that had been expelled by the pet raven of the Earl of Arundel. There were also claims that ferns, whose reproduction by spores was not yet understood, produced an invisible seed that could transmit its powers to the eater (*1H4* II.i.89). Some magic was benign only to the user; Jennet Device of Lancashire testified that she and her brother had learned a charm, "Crucifixus hoc signum vitam Eternam," to bring other people's beer to her own vessels.

Not everyone believed that such uses of magic were actually beneficial. Some held white witches or wizards (*2H6* I.iv.16; *R3* I.i.36) to be just as blameworthy as those who trafficked with evil spirits, or even more guilty because they encouraged the belief that magic was effective and safe. On the subject of dark magic, however, nearly everyone was in agreement. Raising spirits to do one's bidding, consorting with familiars, and cursing people or animals with illness were all dangerous, foul practices that came from the devil. It is surprising that Prospero, since he routinely raises spirits, is portrayed as heroic, but perhaps he is exempted from the rules because he uses the spirits only for good, or to torment the evil Caliban (*Temp* II.ii.4–14). He is alone among Shakespeare's magicians, however, who are otherwise consistent with the popular condemnation of conjuring and other dark magic. The only people who disagreed with this verdict were those few who disbelieved in magic altogether.

Most people, however, believed in the power to see more than was visible to the naked eye. This was true even of scientists, who perceived that there was much knowledge of the world waiting to be discovered and left themselves open as to the form it might take or the source from which it might come. There were therefore many clever and even skeptical people who held that mind readers (*Oth* III.iv.55–58) could perceive people's thoughts, or that astrologers and numerologists (*MWW* V.i.3–4) could perceive connections between the individual and the universe. Reginald Scot, who rejected the notions of witchcraft and possession, nevertheless believed in the curative power of unicorn horns, the existence of stones with magical powers and special connections to specific planets, and the popular superstition that a corpse could identify its murderer by bleeding in the murderer's presence or at his touch.

When it came to knowledge of the future, people were always credulous. In *The Description of England*, William Harrison wrote of farmers' attempts to predict next year's grain prices by observing

> the first flock of cranes that flee southward in winter, the age of the moon in the beginning of January, and such other apish toys, as by laying twelve corns upon the hot hearth for the twelve months, etc., whereby they show themselves to be scant good Christians.

Many educated people read the works of Paracelsus, a physician and alchemist who identified several branches of secret knowledge. He divided "Hermetic Astronomy" into seven branches: astrology, magic, divination, nigromancy, signatures, uncertain arts, and physics. Astrology was the reading of future events and influences in the stars; it was widely practiced, and even the skeptics on this subject were not inclined to debunk all magic. George Carleton, who wrote a tract attacking astrology, in 1624, claimed that it was clearly a false science, "Because particular events . . . cannot bee foretold but by the help of a spirit."

Magic, according to Paracelsus's definition, "brings down and compels heaven from above to stones, herbs, words, etc. It teaches also the change of one thing into another, as well as the knowledge of the supernatural stars, comets, etc." It enabled the practitioner to interpret celestial phenomena such as comets, cure diseases and wounds by instilling heavenly properties into images, effect cures and become invisible by using carved stones, cast spells with spoken or written words, change people into animals, control the will of others, and deal with spectral illusions. Divination enabled the future to be foretold in dreams, animal behavior, ideas that appeared suddenly in the mind, rational consideration and guesswork, and sheer luck. Nigromancy allowed the magician to view things that were secret or yet to happen, but this discipline used tools such as mirrors (*MM* II.ii.95–96) and crystals. It also gave the user control over astral spirits (like Ariel in *The Tempest*) and inanimate objects brought to life. Signature concerned the perception of destiny through physical characteristics, including the lines on the hands and body, features of the face, height, and gait. The uncertain arts used the four elements—earth, air, fire, and water—to make predictions—for example, by reading images in a fire. The branch dealing with water, hydromancy, could reveal "secret and hidden things, closed and sealed letters, and persons who are travelling in distant countries, whether they are living or dead." Physics, or the material arts, contained virtually all of Paracelsus's areas of study that are still considered valid branches of learning: mathematics, geometry, geography, and the manufacture of scientific instruments.

Almost all Shakespeare's references to specific magical practices fall into one or more of Paracelsus's categories. The plays, particularly those set in the ancient world, are thick with soothsayers (*JC* I.ii.19; *A&C* I.ii.3,

II.iii.ch.; *Cym* IV.ii.ch., V.v.ch.), fortune-tellers (*TNK* III.iv.14–16), and augurers, who told the future by examining the internal organs of sacrificial animals (*JC* II.i.200, II.ii.37–40; *A&C* IV.xii.4–6, V.ii.33). There are even more examples of omens, and while there were some phenomena that in Shakespeare's day were accounted as omens of good fortune, the ones in the plays are overwhelmingly negative. Bad omens usually involved some disruption of the natural order—monstrous births, animals behaving contrary to their nature, comets or other celestial anomalies, earthquakes, storms, the appearance of ghosts, or unusual tides (*2H4* IV.iv.122–28; *JC* II.ii.17–31; *John* IV.ii.182–86; *3H6* V.vi.44–54; *TS* III.ii.93–95; *Mac* II.iii.56, 59–61, II.iv.14–18).

Sometimes it was not necessary for animals to behave unusually for their appearance to bode ill. Some animals, such as ravens (*Oth* IV.i.20–22), crows, and kites (*JC* V.i.79–87), were unlucky in themselves, and the appearance of such a creature always betokened imminent death; since such animals were scavengers, their association with death was not accidental. Other omens had nothing to do with the nature of the animal or with any especially unsual behavior, but simply with the timing of an event, as when a man or his horse stumbled or faltered at a moment that seemed significant in some way (*R3* III.iii.83–85). The mistake would be interpreted as part of a larger pattern of bad luck, just as someone today might have several setbacks in the morning and take it as a sign that the entire day would turn out badly.

The question of whether Shakespeare personally believed in such prophecies is a tricky one. He includes several speeches that seem to debunk prophecy. Cicero, responding to Casca's reports of unnatural happenings (*JC* I.iii.15–32), does not dispute the fantastic reports, but declares that "men may construe things after their fashion, / Clean from the purpose of the things themselves" (34–35)—in other words, people see what they fear or desire, not the truth. Cicero does not, however, deny the possibility of prophecy altogether, but simply warns against misinterpretation, and as events fall out, he is dead wrong. Cassius, too, scoffs at Casca's fears, but only to put his own spin on the auguries of nature (57–78). Even Caesar, who at first dismisses superstition, yields to it (*JC* II.i.195–201), and then falls victim to the events it foretells. The strongest denunciations of prophecy by omens occur in *King John* (III.iii.151–59)* and *1 Henry IV* (III.i.12–42), and even they incline rather to warnings against misinterpretation rather than outright accusations of inefficacy. It is, of course, possible that Shakespeare had no belief in magic but found it too useful a dramatic device to exclude from his works, but in light of the prevalence of belief in the supernatural, and in the absence of any over-

---

*The *Complete Signet Classic Shakespeare* combines two scenes in *King John*, so that the text regarding prophecy by omens appears in many other editions of the play in III.iv.

whelming proof of disbelief, it would seem that he had some faith in what we would call magic. *See also* Alchemy; Astrology; Demon; Fairy; Witch.

Maps

The sixteenth century was a turning point in the cartographer's art, in England as elsewhere in Europe. By 1570 the Italian superiority in map-making had yielded to the Low Countries, where the Flemish cartographer Abraham Ortelius published his *Theatrum Orbis Terrarum*, the first collection of maps on a uniform scale of the whole world to be based entirely on postclassical data. It was extremely popular, passing through forty-two folio editions from 1570 to 1612 and thirty-seven smaller editions from 1576 to 1697. Many of these editions were translated into other languages or updated; the first to be printed in English appeared in 1606. Ortelius's countryman and friend Gerard Mercator (1512–94), whose maps exemplify the shift away from the pictorial style, published excellent maps of Europe in 1554 (revised 1572), Great Britain in 1564, and the world in 1569. His masterwork, a three-volume atlas, was published from 1585 to 1595 and was the first to use the term "atlas" for a collection of maps. After his death, Mercator's plates were bought by Jocodus Hondius, who continued to issue them with additions of his own.

Englishmen, too, published maps (*2H6* III.i.203; *R2* V.i.12; *S* 68). Christopher Saxton's detailed maps of individual English counties, first drawn between 1574 and 1579 under royal patronage, were revised but barely improved upon for the next century. He issued a complete twenty-one-sheet map of England and Wales, *Britannia Insularum in Oceano Maxima*, in 1579. Drawn on a scale of eight miles to the inch, it was reused and adapted by other printers for 200 years. Maps showing the progress of the Spanish Armada were popular after its defeat in 1588. In the 1590s, John Norden published maps of some counties, and Emery Molineux constructed a globe (*2H4* II.iv.291). English explorers compiled maps and charts during their expeditions, and though they did not always publish them, professional cartographers sometimes took advantage of their data. Hondius, for example, used information from Sir Walter Raleigh's voyages for a map he published in 1599 and based a map of c. 1590 on the travels of Sir Francis Drake.

Edward Wright, an expert on navigation, published an excellent map to accompany Richard Hakluyt's *Voyages* (1600); it is perhaps this that is "the new map with the augmenta / tion of the Indies" (*TN* III.ii.76–78). There were also a few maritime atlases published during Shakespeare's lifetime, but not until 1627 did John Speed publish the first world atlas by an Englishman. Many maps remained the hand-drawn kind, meant for a particular purpose at a particular moment, to give directions (*Cym* IV.i.2) or to plan military strategy (*1H4* III.i.5).

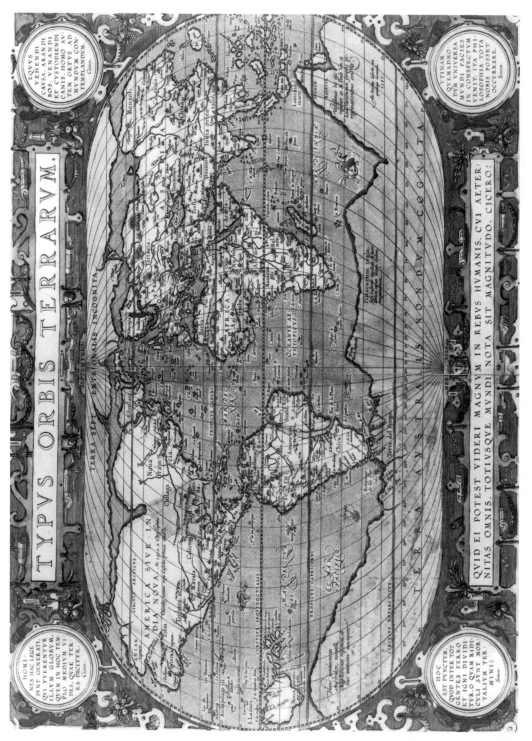

Map of the world, from the first English translation of Abraham Ortelius's *Theatrum Orbis Terrarum* (1606). Reproduced from the Collections of the Library of Congress.

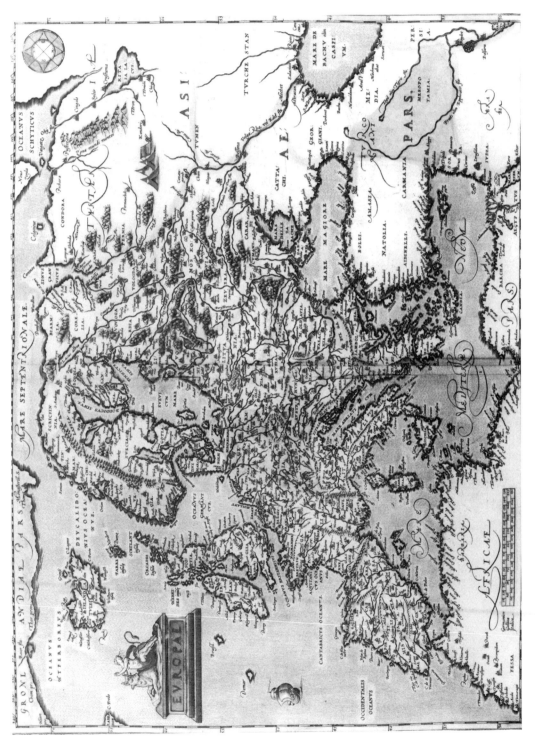

Map of Europe, from *Theatrum Orbis Terrarum*. Reproduced from the Collections of the Library of Congress.

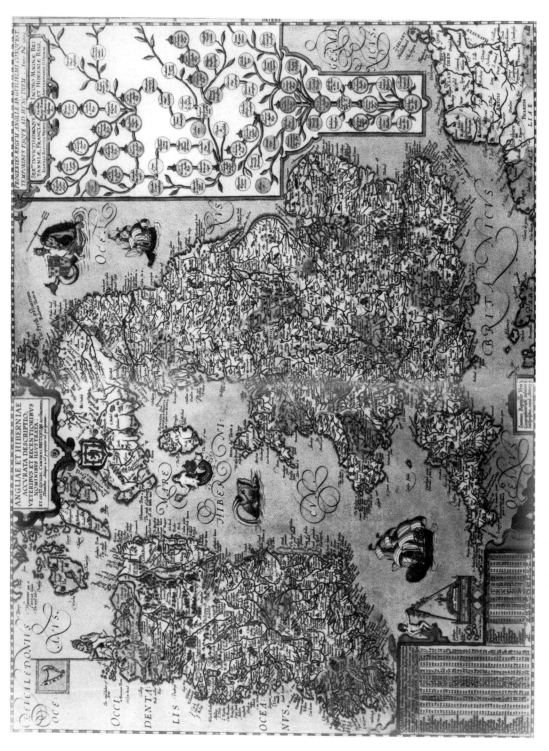

Map of England and Ireland, from *Theatrum Orbis Terrarum*. Reproduced from the Collections of the Library of Congress.

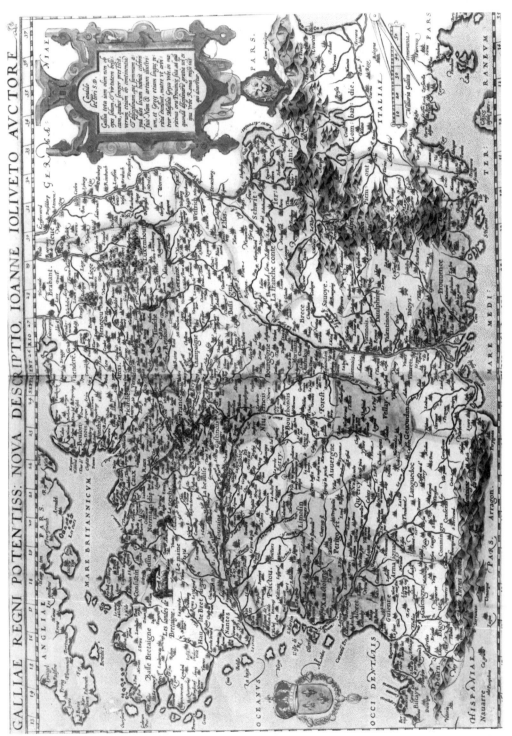

Map of France, from *Theatrum Orbis Terrarum.* Reproduced from the Collections of the Library of Congress.

Mark

The mark (*CE* I.i.21; *2H6* V.i.79; *MM* IV.iii.4–8) appears frequently in Shakespeare's works as a unit of money, even though it was not actually issued as a coin in Renaissance England. For example, Falstaff owes Mistress Quickly 100 marks (*2H4* II.i.31), Petruchio bets 100 marks on Kate's newly minted submissiveness (*TS* V.ii.35), and 30,000 marks, plus five provinces, constitutes Blanche of Castile's dowry (*John* II.i.530). The mark was also a unit of weight equal to 8 ounces of either gold or silver. In *The Description of England*, William Harrison indicates that one mark was worth 13s 4d. *See also* Money.

Markets and Fairs

English commerce took place in shops between merchants and their customers, in private homes between itinerant artisans or peddlers and housewives, and most of all at markets (*CE* III.i.12, III.ii.151; *1H6* III.ii.4–5, 10, 16; *LLL* III.i.109; *TS* V.i.10; *Mac* IV.ii.39–41) and fairs. The two institutions are often confused, but they were actually quite different. The market was found in virtually every sizable town; one estimate puts the number of market towns at 809 between 1500 and 1650. In *The Description of England* (1587), William Harrison drew up a partial list of counties and numbered the parishes and market towns within them; he said that Middlesex had three market towns; Surrey, six; Sussex, eighteen; Kent, seventeen; Buckinghamshire, eleven; Oxfordshire, ten; and so on. It was held at least once a week at a prominent location within the town itself, often at a crossroads marked by a cross, a pole, a gazebo-like open-walled structure, or a gloriously appointed and impressive market house. Goods brought to market were regulated by the town corporation, members of which ensured that weights and measures were fair and that produce was up to standard; they paid particular attention to the quality of bread and beer.

The market was where the daily staples of life were bought, in quantities appropriate to single households. Farmers and their wives (*AYLI* III.ii.96–97; *A&C* III.vi.50–51; *AW* IV.i.41–44) sold chickens, cheese, butter, pigs, cows, beer, and vegetables; the local butcher set up slabs of meat and, one suspects, spent much of his time keeping them free of flies; the bakers brought out their loaves of bread, which had to conform to certain requirements regarding their content and weight. Each merchant had his particular stall (*Cor* II.i.213). London was so large that it could not be content with just one market. It had several, each specializing in a particular commodity. The one at Smithfield, for example, was for livestock, and was held several days a week.

Because almost everyone came to the marketplace on a regular basis, this was where the public events in a town often occurred (*MAAN* IV.i.305–6; *JC* I.iii.26–28, III.i.228–30; *A&C* II.ii.217, III.vi.3–5; *Cor* II.i.236). Proclamations were made here (*1H4* V.i.73; *Cor* I.v.26), notices were posted, and criminals were punished (*2H6* II.i.157, IV.ii.59). In Shakespeare's works, it is "in the marketplace, / The middle center of this cursèd town," that Salisbury's body is displayed (*1H6* II.ii.5–6); it is in the market that Marina's would-be pimp searches for customers (*Per* IV.ii.3–5). The marketplace is, in short, the heart of the town (*John* II.i.41–42). It was so vital to the life of the community that it often evoked complaint. There were charges, repeated with increasing intensity in the centuries to come, that middlemen—"purveyors" and "corn-badgers"— were buying up goods, especially grain, before it could even reach the marketplace, with the result that poor husbandmen could find none to buy. Merchants and artisans from out of town complained that they were unable to break local monopolies or near-monopolies on certain goods, for the town's tradesmen controlled the right to sell and could always find fault, somehow, with the goods brought in from elsewhere.

By contrast, the fair (*WT* IV.iii.103) was open to virtually everyone. It was held outside of the town, to avoid just these sorts of restrictions. It came once a year, sometimes more, but certainly not once or twice a week; the most common time of the year for fairs was at the end of summer or the beginning of fall, after the harvest was in. A fair might last for weeks rather than a single day, three to fourteen days being a usual length, and it was attended with entertainment, revelry, trade disputes, and inevitably the sort of disorder that the temporary "pie-powder" courts on the fair-grounds were authorized to investigate and punish. (The term "pie pow-der" came from the French *pied poudre*, "dusty foot," alluding to the distances walked by participants.) Whereas the market was local, the fair was a national and even international event, and goods and livestock were sold in huge quantities. At the Yarmouth herring fair in September, mer-chants from France, Holland, and Scandinavia brought silk, china, and timber to trade for the fish that were being salted and sold along the seashore. The scale of the event was enormous by the standards of the time; in 1614 Yarmouth had approximately 1,000 fishermen working from 200 boats, and the Dutch often brought in their catches as well.

There were fairs for almost every conceivable commodity—horses, sheep, cattle, cloth, wool, trinkets, grain, silk, cheese, geese, hides, herring, and even servants, who were hired at "statute fairs." Goods were brought to the fair, and the sellers paid a toll for the right to market their goods or livestock within the grounds. For days before the fair opened, the roads were choked with wagons or, in the case of livestock fairs, the herds of drovers. Once they arrived, buyers and sellers alike found a place to sleep, either at an inn or in the fields. Pens were set up for the animals, and fiddlers, peddlers, and pickpockets descended on the area. Local house-holders opened temporary alehouses by hanging a bush over their doors. The fair opened with speeches and sometimes with a church service or the tolling of a bell.

Then the chaos began. Peddlers sold books, describing the contents from atop their stools. Men bet on their horses or dogs, diced, drank, and socialized. People paid to see performing animals and humans who had physical defects. Thieves, prostitutes, and professional gamblers prospered. To guard against thieves, guards were appointed to watch the paddocks at horse fairs, and toll collectors were required to note each animal's distinguishing marks in case there should be disputes about ownership.

The country's two largest fairs were the Stourbridge and Bartholomew fairs; Shakespeare mentions the roast pork that was a traditional delicacy at the latter (*2H4* II.iv.234–35). He also mentions Stamford Fair (*2H4* III.ii.40) and Hinckley Fair (*2H4* V.i.19–20), which was held near Stratford in late August. To Stourbridge, as to most of England's other hundreds of fairs, he makes no specific reference. *See also* Business.

Marriage

When the wedding bells had finished ringing, when the feasting was over and the guests had been sent home, a husband and wife had to get down to the practical business of being married. This meant that each of them had rights and responsibilities, though most of the rights belonged to the man. Each, however, was an important partner in the happiness and prosperity of the household and the continuation of the family, and each was valued by society if he or she played the appropriate role.

For the husband, this meant providing his family with its basic needs and with any luxuries within his means. If his wife was shabbily dressed or his daughters undowried, this was his fault and no one else's. He was also ultimately culpable for any lapses of discipline in his household, since he was supposed to be the master within the marriage (*CE* II.i.10–31; *TS* V.ii.110–81; *LLL* IV.i.36–40); if his wife scolded him in public or his children appeared disobedient, he would be blamed by his community for failing to control them. Some husbands handled this aspect of their responsibilities with restraint and kindness, but others abused their legal power. They could not legally kill their wives, but they could do almost anything else, including beatings with fists, feet, or sticks (*CE* IV.i.16–18, V.i.183; *Oth* IV.i.); rape; and confiscation of all the wife's possessions (*H5* II.iii.48; *TS* III.i.128–36, II.i.379–90). Actually, this last is a misnomer, for the wife, under the law, owned no possessions. Nothing she used, wore, or earned was hers; all belonged to her husband to dispose of as he liked. She could not sue, be sued, make a will, enter into a contract, or incur a debt, for all her actions were subsumed in her husband's legal identity.

Society at large did not take kindly to a woman's usurpation of her husband's prerogatives. If she upbraided him, shouted shrilly at other men, or seemed too confident of her own power, she could be termed a scold or a shrew and threatened with public humiliation to teach her her place. Of course, carrying out such a punishment was an implied humiliation of her husband as well, for it pointed out his inability to keep her quiet and subservient. The woman's role was, ideally, to have children, care for the children, keep the house in as thrifty and efficient a manner as possible, supervise the servants, and keep her husband happy (*TN* II.iv.27–39). That not all women succeeded, or even wanted to, is reflected in the proverbs of the day: "Wedlock is a padlock," "A ship and a woman are ever repairing," "Husbands are in heaven whose wives chide not," and "Swine, women, and bees cannot be turned." Shakespeare, too, recognized that controlling women was easy to prescribe and hard to do:

LEONTES   . . . lozel [worthless fellow], thou art worthy to be hanged,
                That wilt not stay her [your wife's] tongue.

ANTIGONUS   Hang all the husbands
                That cannot do that feat, you'll leave yourself
                Hardly one subject. (*WT* II.iii.107–11)

Some wives even went so far as to beat their husbands (*WT* II.iii.90–91).

There was much dispute over whether the advantages of marriage outweighed its inconveniences, and both sides tended to exaggerate their claims. Certainly it was a disadvantage that divorce (*H5* V.ii.366; *AW* V.iii.317–18; *Oth* I.ii.13) in the modern sense, especially after 1620, was impossible, and that separation and annulment were difficult. Husbands and wives blamed one another for being capricious, fickle, and illogical (*AYLI* IV.i.143–52). However, there was much happiness to be found in marriage (*MWW* I.i.235–41; *TS* IV.ii.37–41), as contemporary letters, diaries, and testimonials demonstrate. Husbands wrote fond and tearful encomiums on wives who had died in childbirth; wives wrote wistful reminiscences about husbands who had been faithful to them in their darkest hours. Spouses gave one another nicknames, used terms of endearment, teased one another (*1H4* II.iii, III.i), and expected to know all one another's secrets (*JC* II.i.280–87). Their wishes were not always gratified, but they hoped to find and preserve love (*1H6* IV.v.13; *2H6* I.i.21–36). Not all the popular literature, moreover, made fun of marriage and of the foibles of wives. Some material praised the simple pleasures of married life. The song "Jacke and Jone," for example, describes a happy rural couple enjoying themselves at fairs, drinking "nappy Ale," telling one another stories in wintertime, and demonstrating their individual, gender-appropriate skills; Joan, for example, knows the names of all her dairy cows and can make a wedding cake trimmed with plums. And despite the legal status of wives, they had more freedom than the women of many other

European countries and were trusted with important tasks—and, often, control of the household funds (*CE* IV.i.36–38, 103–6). Few women, given the choice, preferred to remain single, even when the alternative was the second-class citizenship of wifehood. As wives, they ran households, set many of their own rules, and became mothers; as single women, they were ridiculed as old maids (*MAAN* II.i.38–39; *TS* II.i.34).

Adultery, from the *Roxburghe Ballads*. The Devil tempts a housewife to betray her husband, while horns appear numerous times as symbols of cuckoldry: on the beam extending from the house, on the deceived husband watching from the window, on the Devil's head, and in the hand of the man who calls, "Looke out." Reproduced from the Collections of the Library of Congress.

The most feared disadvantage of marriage was the possibility of a spouse's sexual infidelity (*Lear* IV.vi.111–13; *TA* IV.ii; *MV* V.i.223–35, 258–65, 281–85; *MWW* II.ii.295–99). For men (*CE* III.ii.5–15, V.i.56–89), adultery was considered more forgivable and natural than for women, though religious prohibitions for both sexes carried a great deal of weight (*TNK* IV.iii.50–55). The fear of being betrayed, of having another man's offspring passed off as his own, of being made to appear stupid and ridiculous, was so powerful that men needed to make jokes about it to stave off misfortune. The apprehensions and jealousies of husbands form the basis for at least three of Shakespeare's plays: *Othello*, *The Merry Wives of*

Windsor, and *The Winter's Tale*, and it plays a lesser role in many more. The symbol of the cuckold (*AW* I.iii.46)—the betrayed husband—was a pair of horns (*LLL* IV.i.113–14, V.i.67, V.ii.253–54, 896–99, 904–7; *TA* II.iii.67–71, IV.iii.72–76; *MAAN* I.i.234–36, V.iv.43–51, 123–24; *MND* V.i.238–39; *John* II.i.290–93; *2H4* I.ii.46–47; *AYLI* IV.i.49–60; *2GV* I.i.80), an image whose origins are obscure but may be connected, according to the *Oxford English Dictionary*, to an old practice of grafting the severed spurs of a castrated rooster to its head. Horns are almost always the symbol of adultery in Shakespeare's works, though he does make a reference to "Vulcan's badge" (*TA* II.i.89) as another symbol of this illict act; a well-known Roman myth related how Vulcan's wife, Venus, was caught in the act of adultery with the war god Mars. *See also* Courtship; Wedding.

Mask

The mask, "visor," or "vizard" (*LLL* II.i.123, V.ii.127–35, 157, 228, 243, 246–47, 272, 296–98, 386–88; *MAAN* II.i.91; *3H6* I.iv.116) had not yet assumed the cultural importance that it would in the masquerades of the eighteenth century, but it was not unknown. Masks could serve several purposes. As ladies' accessories, they served as sunscreens, keeping the skin white and creamy while walking or riding (*Oth* IV.ii.9; *WT* IV.iv.222; *2GV* IV.iv.153–56). Men or women might wear them as part of a full-blown masque or pageant at a banquet. Stage productions of masques, like all theatrical productions, might portray women taking part in such a masque, but the actors playing the women were all male. A mask might also be worn for the sake of anonymity, particularly if one was engaged in a disreputable activity, like robbing travelers (*1H4* II.ii.52) or attending a party without a proper invitation (*R&J* I.iv.1 s.d., 29–32). *See also* Clothing.

Masque

A popular form of theatrical presentation, the masque (*MV* II.iv.21, II.v.23, 28–37; *MND* V.i.32; *JC* V.i.62; *TN* I.iii.109–10) was employed at all sorts of festive occasions, from coronations and royal holiday revels to aristocratic weddings and private parties. The masque usually began with a procession, led by a presenter who explained aloud what the theme of the masque was to be; Romeo and Benvolio dispense with the role of the presenter in their masque at Capulet's feast (*R&J* I.iv.1–10). The presenter, usually a boy, was followed by torchbearers and by performers, called mummers (*Cor* II.i.78) or masquers (*3H6* IV.i.94), dressed in outlandish clothes and often disguised with full-face velvet masks. Since most masques took place at night, inside great halls or specially constructed buildings, their costumes were often made of cloth-of-gold, sequin-studded fabric, or other materials that would reflect the flickering candle-light. These mummers were meant to represent gods, goddesses, historical figures, or foreigners (Moors and Amazons being especially popular). A contemporary illustration of a masque in progress shows a presenter, a performer disguised as the goddess Diana (recognizable from her moon-shaped headdress), and several ladies in masks. Usually, the theme of the masque was designed as a compliment to the host or the guest of honor, praising his or her chastity, military prowess, generosity, honor, family history, or some other characteristic by choosing appropriate characters to portray.

The theme of the masque could be an elaborate construction, requiring the audience to interpret multiple layers of symbolism, or it could be nearly nonexistent, providing little more than an opportunity for viewing or wearing unusual costumes. The appearance of the courtiers of Navarre in Muscovite attire is in keeping with the simpler sort of masque, though it is less formal than a masque with hired performers. Another simple masque, with noble revelers dressed as shepherds, is incorporated into *Henry VIII* (I.iv.64 s.d.) The more elaborate type of performance, which might end with carefully rehearsed music and dances, appears in *Timon of Athens* (I.ii.130 s.d.). The whole purpose of the masque was to delight one's guests with the cleverness of the symbolic devices employed, the thoroughness of the diguises, and the expense lavished on the costumes and props. The most elaborate masques were those staged at court, often for the delight of foreign dignitaries. They were orchestrated by the Master of the Revels, who employed court officials, local merchants, wardrobe and jewel house keepers, architects, carpenters, painters, embroiderers, tailors, and other craftsmen and functionaries in the preparations.

Similar to the masque was the pageant (*2H6* I.ii.67; *R3* IV.iv.85; *T&C* III.ii.74; *A&C* IV.xiv.8), in which amateur or professional actors carried a masquing theme to the next level of complexity. They performed a scene or short play illustrating an episode from the Bible, a classical myth, or a newly invented interaction between characters of symbolic significance. Pageants performed by the London Drapers' Company on Midsummer 1521 included "The Castle of War," "The Story of Jesse," "St. John the Evangelist," "St. George," and "Pluto." Mummers dressed as devils, halberdiers, and the king of the Moors were also present. Ben Jonson wrote a pageant in 1604 for James I's procession through London that contained a dialogue between actors personifying the Thames and the Genius of the City. *See also* Dance; Entertainment; Theater.

(Medical Practitioners

Today, when we think of "going to the doctor," we usually mean traveling to the office of a physician with an M.D. and a medical license, or to a sterile hospital full of equipment, proven medications, and a staff that includes surgeons, general practitioners, nurses, aides, and specialist technicians. In Shakespeare's day "going to the doctor" was almost as different from our experience as it could be.

Physicians

The vast majority of people never consulted a physician. Physicians were few and expensive, largely because of the extensive education their occupation required. It might take seven years to acquire the M.A. degree, followed by another seven for the M.D. Medical students read texts in Latin, English, and occasionally other languages as well; these texts were a new feature of medical education, since only a century or so before, in the days before movable type, there were few books available, and knowledge had been acquired by taking dictation. Students rarely had any hospital experience, for hospitals (*LLL* V.ii.848–62, or "spital," as in *H5* II.i.76–79) existed mostly to offer the poor a clean bed, good food, and sleep rather than diagnosis, surgery, and extensive medication. They also seldom saw a human dissection; such anatomical displays were still confined primarily to the annual dissection of a small and legally specified number of hanged felons by the Royal College of Physicians and the Company of Barbers and Surgeons. Instead, would-be physicians studied the

A physician examines a patient's urine. From *Panoplia*, illustrated by Jost Amman. Reproduced from the Collections of the Library of Congress.

centuries-old theories of their Greek predecessors, Asclepiades (*MWW* II.iii.27; *Per* III.ii.112), Hippocrates (*MWW* III.i.62–63), and Galen (*AW* II.iii.11; *MWW* II.iii.27; *2H4* I.ii.118). If they were very adventurous, they might explore the iconoclastic theories of the sixteenth-century alchemist Paracelsus (*AW* II.iii.11), whose ideas about the cause and treatment of disease were strongly resisted by the Royal College. Galen and Paracelsus were both wrong, but in completely different ways: Galen divided everything into four prime qualities (hot, cold, wet, dry) and four elements (earth, air, fire, and water), whereas Paracelsus divided everything into salt, sulfur, and mercury.

Medical students learned about the nature of matter and of the bodily humors, disease and treatment, case studies, the use of plants and other ingredients in medicines. Many, if not most, of the remedies learned were the same ones prescribed for the past dozen centuries. Unless they wanted to go abroad for their degrees (and some did go to universities on the Continent, particularly in Italy or the Netherlands), medical students had to attend one of England's two universities, Oxford and Cambridge. These institutions provided not only degrees but licenses to practice medicine or surgery throughout the country.

London physicians, of whom there were about fifty at any one time between 1580 and 1600, could opt to jump through another set of hoops to join the Royal College of Physicians, established in 1518. The College, like medical education itself, offered little in the way of innovation or practical experience but did supply status and the right to charge higher fees. Membership in the College was limited to thirty from 1590, including royal physicians, and offered the chance to associate with other physicians and to attend an annual anatomical lecture.

However, no physician, even the most lofty member of the Royal College, operated out of an office to which patients came at his convenience. Physicians attended their patients, making house calls on the affluent and the noble. The cost of such a house call often kept patients from calling until it was too late to help, and in any case, medicine could do little in an age before rigorous scientific method, antibiotics, X-rays, or even an accurate knowledge of the circulatory system. The physician, therefore, was stigmatized as an expensive parasite, and he frequently appears in this context in Shakespeare's works (*Tim* III.iii.11–12, IV.iii.432–34; *RL* 904). Even so, the physician's opinion carried weight. When Hotspur's father is "grievous sick" and "keep[s] his bed" for four days, it is considered extremely significant that he is "much feared by his physicians" (*1H4* IV.i.16, 21, 24), that is, that they have given up hope of a cure. It was, after all, the physician's job to *do* something—even though physicians recognized that often nature needed to work unhindered by medical intervention—and when physicians failed even to pretend to have a cure, it was a serious matter. The king, for example, in *All's Well That Ends Well* is resigned to death on the advice of his doctors:

We . . .
. . . may not be so credulous of cure,
When our most learned doctors leave us, and
The congregated College have concluded
That laboring art can never ransom nature

From her inaidable estate.
I say we must not
So stain our judgment or corrupt our hope,
To prostitute our past-cure malady
To empirics [unlicensed physicians, mountebanks]. (II.i.117–25)

(The "doctors" in this case are clearly physicians, as shown by the mention of a college and by the medical context, but Shakespearean doctors are not always physicians. A doctor was, and remains, anyone holding a doctoral degree, and might be a scholar or a theologian. In some cases, he might be both, since many clergymen in Shakespeare's day also studied medicine.) In the king's case, the overwhelming authority of the College of Physicians is not subverted by any implication on Helena's part that their diagnosis is flawed; such a claim, especially from a woman, would be unthinkable. Instead, she overrides their despair with a superior prescription from a superior physician, in this case her deceased father. Medical opinion remains authoritative.

Physicians appear frequently in Shakespeare's plays. References to them, their treatments (*TS* Ind.ii.121–23, 130–35), and their diagnoses are common, and they also appear as characters, for example, in *Macbeth* IV.iii. and V.i., *Lear* IV.vii., and *Two Noble Kinsmen* IV.iii. Shakespeare knew a useful symbol when he saw one; despite the fact that few people consulted physicians and the fact that many thought their fees exorbitant and their services dubious, most recognized their knowledge and believed that they had a superior degree of skill. After all, lesser practitioners could offer nothing better in the way of diagnosis and cure, only lower prices. Therefore, when the voice of medicine speaks in Shakespeare, it is likely to come from the mouth of a licensed physician.

Surgeons

Below the physician on the social scale stood the surgeon. Physicians prescribed and diagnosed, but they shed no blood. Phlebotomy, stitching up dueling wounds, removing "stones" from internal organs, boring into the skull to relieve pressure caused by head wounds (trepanning), amputations, and such procedures were the exclusive domain of the surgeon or barber-surgeon. In the last two decades of the sixteenth century, there were about 100 surgeons in London's United Company of Barbers and Surgeons, which was the largest of the London livery companies. In theory, the surgeons and apothecaries alike were controlled by the College of Physicians, but in practice they governed themselves.

Surgeons, even those licensed by the universities, tended to be less educated than physicians, but not necessarily less practiced or skilled. They served an apprenticeship under an experienced surgeon, learned Latin, and were eventually examined (in London, at least) by members of the Company. They were more numerous than physicians, which implies but does not singlehandedly prove that they were in more demand. Certainly they were in great demand in the military, which always had more than its fair share of open wounds to be sutured.

There was a wide range of prestige. At the pinnacle were those who studied the latest advances in anatomy, attended the dissections of the Company's four alloted corpses of felons per year, availed themselves of the Company's library and instrument collection, and performed complicated procedures on the wealthy. At the bottom were the part-timers like the Chelmsford surgeon who was really a shoemaker by trade (and who makes an interesting companion to the cobbler of *Julius Caesar* I.i.24–26) and the barber-surgeons, who had shops where they cut hair, shaved, bled, pulled teeth, and dressed simple wounds. Shakespeare mentions some of these functions of surgeons. Drawn teeth are "the forfeits in a barber's shop" (*MM* V.i.322). Battles and duels frequently require a surgeon to attend to their aftermath (*H5* IV.i.138–39; *Oth* V.i.30; *Mac* I.ii.44; *TNK* I.iv.30–31; *R&J* III.i.95). There is also a possible reference to trepanning when Lear cries, "Let me have surgeons; / I am cut to th' brains" (IV.vi.192–93).

Apothecaries

Surgeons and physicians appear so often in Shakespeare's plays because his subjects are exactly the sorts of people who consulted them: lords, kings, queens, soldiers, and brawlers. For the minor tradesman or artisan, the two authorized medical practitioners who would be most familiar were the apothecary and the midwife. Apothecaries are mentioned only occasionally by Shakespeare; it is not very dramatic to see someone shopping for a cold remedy or asking about that pain in his right thigh, and the only intense encounter with an apothecary is the one in which Romeo buys his poison—an example of an apothecary acting *counter* to his typical duties.

Apothecary. From *Panoplia*, illustrated by Jost Amman. Reproduced from the Collections of the Library of Congress.

There were approximately as many apothecaries (*2H6* III.iii.17; *Per* III.ii.9) in London as there were surgeons, and there was just as wide a range of income and reputation. Members of the Grocers' Company, apothecaries offered walk-in diagnoses for much less than a physician would charge, filled prescriptions written by physicians, and prescribed on their own. They also apparently sold perfumes, if we are to judge from *Lear* (IV.vi.130–31). In London, they often set up shop in Bucklersbury, near Cheapside. Sometimes, particularly toward the end of the sixteenth century, they worked with hospitals. The best Shakespearean description of an apothecary is unquestionably that in *Romeo and Juliet* (V.i.37–84). His shop, a poor, bare example of its kind, is nevertheless stocked with animal specimens, skins, boxes, pots, bladders, seeds, "simples" (medicines made from one ingredient rather than many), perfume components, thread, and poisons.

Midwives

The midwife (*Per* III.i.10–12; *WT* II.iii.159; *2H6* IV.ii.45; *R2* II.ii.62–66) was present at virtually every birth. From palaces to hovels, she sat by the birthing mother, examined the birth canal, lubricated the way with oil or grease, cleaned the newborn and tied off the cord, gave it medicine if necessary, delivered the placenta, stitched up any vaginal tears, and helped with the start of breast-feeding. If serious complications developed, she called in the local surgeon, and if she could tell that even a surgeon would not be able to save the baby's life, her church-issued license (if she had bothered to apply for one) authorized her to perform an emergency baptism. The midwife was a respected local figure, often enlisted to examine suspected witches, rape victims, unwed mothers, and female prisoners. Midwives were sometimes criticized by physicians and surgeons, but this criticism usually consisted of a call for better education and practice among midwives, rather than their replacement by male practitioners.

In the long hours preceding the birth, the midwife might fortify herself with spirits, provided by the laboring woman's family (*TN* II.v.191–92). Assuming all went well during the birth, she was often accorded the honor of carrying the baby to church for its christening and given a gift for doing so. If something went wrong—for example, if the baby was born deformed or so unlike the woman's husband as to be scandalous—the midwife might be the first to spread rumors of the monstrous birth (*WT* IV.iv.269–71; *TA* IV.ii.140–45, 167–69).

Midwifery, incidentally, was not the only medical career open to women. In the late sixteenth century, there were about sixty women practicing medicine in London alone. Lady Grace Mildmay was a noted upper-class herbalist and practitioner, and a Mrs. Cook served as surgeon-apothecary to Christ's Hospital.

Unlicensed Practitioners

Though formal medical education was becoming increasingly important to practice, there were still at least as many unlicensed "empirics" as authorized practitioners. There were perhaps 250 of these at any one time in London between 1580 and 1600, as many as the physicians, surgeons, and apothecaries combined. In addition to the women mentioned above, there were about 200 unlicensed male practitioners. In the countryside, the unlicensed caregivers dominated the trade to an even greater degree. Cost, accessibility, and a vast and general medical ignorance that made astrology or magic as likely to produce a cure as an expensive medicine contributed to the influence of the outsiders.

People without vast resources seeking a cure might consult a wide variety of more or less casual practitioners. Care began at home, with the women of the family, who nursed, washed, ventilated, fed, and distributed home remedies. They may have been helped in this task, if they were literate, by some of the new English-language medical texts for the general public, but perhaps these texts were primarily read by the empirics so feared by the established medical profession. Certainly someone was reading these books; Thomas Moulton's *Mirror or Glass of Health* alone went through at least seventeen editions between 1530 and 1580. Such texts included recipes for herbal medicines, the symptoms of the plague, symptoms by which death or recovery could be predicted, and treatments for the most common "diseases," such as jaundice, dropsy, fever, toothache, and cough. Though such books were not available to everyone, almanacs, which contained some medical advice, especially on propitious times to be bled, were extremely widespread. Bathhouse keepers, who sometimes encroached on the hair-cutting privileges of barbers, sometimes also encroached on their medical territory as well, offering leeching or cupping services to their customers. Finally, virtually every village or parish had access to a "wise woman" (*TN* III.iv.104–6), a village herbalist who could offer comfort, advice, and a handful of flowers, leaves, or seeds to ease the pain. The title character of Thomas Heywood's 1633 play, *The Wise-Woman of Hogsdon*, is such a practitioner; he portrays her as a complete fraud whose patients are sometimes ashamed to consult her, but no doubt wise women provided comfort, physical or psychological, to people who could afford no other care. *See also* Alchemy; Anatomy and Physiology; Astrology; Bleeding; Disease and Injury; Insanity; Pregnancy and Childbirth.

Mermaid

Mermaids (*3H6* III.ii.186; *A&C* II.ii.209; *Ham* IV.vii.176) had existed in mythology for centuries before Shakespeare's birth, though sixteenth- and seventeenth-century explorations of North and South American waters gave rise to new reports of sightings. On June 13, 1608, two of Henry Hudson's men claimed to have seen one, human "From the Navill upward," white-skinned, long-haired, with a "tayle which was like the tayle of a Porpoise, and speckled like a Macrell." Whether such sightings were actually sightings of seals or manatees, illusions, or fabrications is not clear.

The mermaid of mythology was not always a lovely creature with a single fishy tail. She was a descendant of the Greek Sirens, and as such, associated with death, known for her song, and sometimes winged (*CE* III.ii.45, 165; *MND* II.i.149–54). Medieval mermaids, sometimes pictured with two tails, were treated as a symbol of temptation by the Catholic Church. Supposedly they lured or seized sailors off ships, either from love or from a desire to devour or drown them. Paracelsus thought they had no souls but could gain souls by marrying humans. The mermaid was often portrayed holding a mirror and a comb, symbols of vanity and femininity; such a mermaid can be seen near the Isle of Man in the entry on Maps, in the map of Europe).

Mirror

The mirror was an expensive luxury item, if it was a true "glass" (*2H6* V.i.142; *2H4* II.iii.21, 31; *H5* V.ii.151; *LLL* IV.i.18; *Lear* V.iii.263–65; *WT* IV.iv.600–603; *Mac* IV.i.111 s.d.; *R2* IV.i.263–90). Cheaper versions, with greater distortion, could be made out of polished steel, but the really desirable object was made of a sheet of glass backed with a thin foil of tin that was stuck to the glass with a mercury amalgam. These mirrors, until well into the seventeenth century, were exclusively imported, usually from Venice's glassmaking center at Murano. Small mirrors, mounted in gold and gems, could be carried or kept on a dressing table. Large wall mirrors, set in carved or gilt frames, could cost more than a fine painting. Mirrors, because of their cost and the absorption with self that they induced, were associated with vanity (*Lear* III.ii.35–36; *WT* I.ii.116–17).

Money

The coinage of the Middle Ages and Renaissance differed a great deal from that of the present day. Perhaps the most striking difference was that it was a genuine, not a token, currency. A gold coin was worth exactly its face value in gold; today, the value of the metal in a given coin is almost always much less than the face value. The ramifications of this policy were significant for monarchs, who liked to use their coinage to disseminate their images and agendas.

In the first place, a king—for example, an English king claiming to be the legitimate ruler of France, or any king whose grip on the throne was uncertain—wanted to have as many coins in circulation as possible. This served both to keep people happy with a bountiful supply of gold and silver and to have plenty of tiny instruments of propaganda proclaiming one's God-given right to rule. It helped to have an imposing portrait of oneself, armed, armored, or bearing the symbols of kingship. To have room for such images, it was necessary that the coins be large, and for coins to be large, they had to be inherently valuable, which meant the monarch had to find and maintain a steady supply of gold and silver bullion. Despite Shakespeare's references to money as brass (*H5* IV.iv.19–21) or copper (*LLL* IV.iii.383), English coinage during the period that concerns us was always of gold or silver.

There were several ways to enhance the propaganda value of money. One was to mint more of it by debasing the quality of the metal. This was never a popular stratagem, and a whole series of coins might be rejected by the public if diminished value was suspected. Kings used the technique only in truly desperate times; Henry VIII resorted to it for much of the later part of his reign, and his son Edward VI was quick to restore the coinage to its true value.

Another means of increasing one's presence in the public mind was to melt down rival currencies. Newly elevated kings and queens quickly replaced their predecessors' coinage with their own, sometimes destroying and reminting old coins to do so. Foreign currency, too, was melted as it entered the country and reissued as English coinage. Several governments dealt with the problem of foreign coins by minting their own versions of similar weight and design. For example, the Dutch kroon, French écu, and English crown were virtually interchangeable. This stimulated international trade by making exchanges easy; it also spread English monarchs' reputations to foreign lands.

The correspondence of coins between nations was assisted by an eighth-century method of accounting that was still in use in many countries. This Carolingian system, based on the units of coinage of the Roman Empire, divided each pound of silver into twenty solidi and each solidus into twelve denarii. The pound (libra in Latin, livre in French) was abbreviated as "£," the solidus (which became the English shilling, rendered as "solidares" in *Tim* III.i.44) as "s," and the denarius (the English penny, the French denier) as "d." This £ s d system was abandoned in other countries in the early modern period, but in England it would survived into the twentieth century.

Accounting under this system was a little awkward, but it could be made significantly more so by fluctuations in the prices of gold or silver. An increase in the value of gold could make a coin worth more without any change in size or face value, and monarchs periodically had to adjust their coinage or its nominal value to reflect the price of precious metals. Thus a coin designed to fit into the Carolingian system—worth, say, 5 shillings

Roman solidus, 273 C.E. Actual size is 20 mm in diameter. © 2002 The American
Numismatic Society. All rights reserved.

(a quarter of a pound)—might be worth a truly confusing and inconvenient amount if the price of gold rose by 10 percent.

Another disadvantage of the use of real, largely unalloyed gold and silver
was the great inducement to fraud it created. There was strong motivation
to "clip" coins—that is, to shave bits off the edges—or to counterfeit them
(*John* III.i.25; *H8* III.i.171; *H5* IV.i.225–29; *MM* II.iv.44–45).

Coin Manufacture

English coins were produced at several mints (*T&C* I.iii.193; *LLL*
I.i.177; *TN* III.ii.22) from which they emerged "fire-new." At various
times, there were mints in London, Canterbury, York, Durham, Bristol,
and elsewhere. Each mint had its own mint mark that was stamped on its
coins, and the mark of each mint changed periodically. It was always a tiny
symbol, sometimes chosen for its associations with the ruler, as in the case
of the thistle (during James I's reign, a reference to his kingship of Scotland), the fleur-de-lis (symbol of France and of the English monarchs'
continuing claims to its throne), the crown, and the rose (symbol of the
Tudor dynasty). Other mint marks might reflect the name or heraldic arms
of the mint's supervisor.

Coins began as ingots (*MM* III.i.26) of gold or silver, divided into pieces
of the correct size and placed on an engraved hard metal die embedded
into a block or anvil. This engraving would stamp (*WT* IV.iv.728; *Cym*
II.v.5; *Cor* V.ii.22; *H8* III.ii.325–26) the coin's obverse—the side with
the monarch's image, symbol, or claims to rulership. The mint worker then
placed another tool atop the blank, this one a metal cylinder with a flat-
tened area on one end and an engraving of the coin's reverse on the other.

A coin-maker striking coins, from *Panoplia*, illustrated by Jost Amman. Reproduced from the Collections of the Library of Congress.

The engraved end was placed on the blank coin and struck with a hammer, impressing both sides of the coin simultaneously. The coin was then filed if necessary to bring it down to the proper weight, and there were periodic trials or weighings of chests of coins to ensure that they were of the desired size. Coins produced in this way were said to be "hammered."

Some coins were produced with the help of machines, usually in the form of a water mill that generated the striking force. Coins so minted were said to be "milled." Both milled and hammered coins were produced in the reign of Elizabeth I, though by the time Shakespeare came to London, all new coins were hammered.

The Appearance of Coins

Each coin had two sides, and obverse and reverse, as described above. Most coins had, on both obverse and reverse, a central section devoted to some sort of picture and a circular band around the outside for a "legend"—a Latin motto of some kind. This legend was often heavily abbreviated, even more so on the smaller coins, so that one frequently had to be familiar with it in the first place to be able to ascribe any meaning to it at all. A typical obverse legend might be EDWARDVS D G AGL FR ET HIB REX, indicating that Edwardus (the Latin form of Edward) was king (rex) by the grace of God (Dei Gratia) of England (Anglia), France (Francia), and Ireland (et Hibernia). Sometimes, there was no room to spell out the ET and it was represented instead by the letter Z.

Coins tended to take their names either from their value or from the pictures on either side. Hence there were pennies, threepences, shillings, and pounds, whose names respresented values. There were also crowns (which bore a picture of a crown), sovereigns (which bore the image of the ruler), and angels (which showed the Archangel Michael slaying a dragon). Units of value seldom appeared. One had to tell the difference between a penny, a twopence, a threepence, a groat, a shilling, and a sixpence—all silver coins—by the size, the motto or abbreviation thereof, or a slight difference in style, such as the addition of a rose behind Queen Elizabeth's head. Under James I this situation was ameliorated somewhat by the addition of Roman numerals to the smaller coins, such as XII for the shilling, which equaled twelve pennies.

Dates of minting appeared on only some coins. During Shakespeare's lifetime, all gold coins were undated, as were the silver shilling, twopence, penny, and halfpenny. All other silver coins bore the date in Arabic numerals.

Certain motifs appeared again and again, with only minor changes, for decades. The portrait of the Archangel Michael was one such example. Others were symbols of royalty—a Tudor rose, crowned or uncrowned; the royal coat of arms, crowned or uncrowned; the French fleur-de-lis; the English lions; the Scottish thistle; and the royal portrait. An element on the reverse of many coins was the "long cross," a cross whose thin arms reached into the border of the coin, where they branched into two or more leaflike protrusions. Shakespeare uses the word "crosses" synechdochally for such coins (*LLL* I.ii.33; *2H4* I.ii.229).

Shakespeare's Coins

In general, Shakespeare sticks to units of English coinage when referring to money in his plays. This may be because he was uncertain of the value of foreign coins, particularly ancient coins; his usage of the talent in *Timon of Athens* (II.ii.200) is notoriously incorrect, vastly undervaluing this unit of weight. Perhaps he simply felt his audience would be unfamiliar with archaic units of money. He makes occasional reference to drachmas, "sicles" (shekels, *MM* II.ii.150), or, more vaguely, "an old Roman coin" (*LLL* V.ii.611). However, it is far more common for him to insert anachronistic English units of currency into a play set in ancient Greece or Rome than it is for him to use the correct ones.

Units of English Coinage

Coin Name	Value	Composition	Notes
Three-farthings	¾d	silver	
Penny	1d	silver	
Three-halfpence	1½d	silver	
Twopence	2d	silver	
Threepence	3d	silver	
Fourpence	4d	silver	Also called a groat, this coin was discontinued after 1582.
Sixpence	6d	silver	
Shilling	12d	silver	

Coin Name	Value	Composition	Notes
Quarter-angel	2s 6d	gold	
Half-crown	2s 6d	gold or silver	The value of this coin increased in 1611; see Crown. The silver half-crown was introduced in 1601.
Half-angel	5s	gold	The half-angel, like the crown, was worth 5 shillings. The crown, however, was made of 22-carat "crown" gold, while the half-angel was made of purer "fine" gold.
Crown	5s	gold or silver	The value of the gold version coin increased due to a rise in gold prices in 1611; see Crown.
Noble	6s 8d	gold	The noble was introduced in 1344 and discontinued in 1465 after a brief revaluation of the coin at 8s 4d; see Noble.
Angel	10s	gold	The value of the angel was set at 10 shillings during Shakespeare's life, but it was worth different amounts in the preceding centuries.
Half-pound	10s	gold	Like the angel, the half-pound was worth 10 shillings (or 120 pence). The difference between the two coins lay in their designs and in the quality of the gold used; from 1583 to 1603, for example, the angel used a purer form of gold (23 carats, 3.5 grains, compared to the half-pound's 22-carat gold).
Ryal (royal)	15s	gold	The 15-shilling value is for the last coinage of Elizabeth I, issued between 1583 and 1603. James I, her successor, did not issue ryals until 1606, when a very limited issue of rose-ryals worth 30s and spur-ryals worth 15s was produced. An increase in the value of gold resulted in a revaluation of the coins in 1611; the rose-ryal was acknowledged to be worth 33s and the spur-ryal worth 16s 6d. Similar adjustments were made to other gold coins at this time.

Coin Name	Value	Composition	Notes
Pound	20s	gold	
Sovereign	30s	gold	From 1583 to 1603, the sovereign was a 30-shilling fine-gold coin. Under James I, however, it was synonymous with the 20-shilling pound, and the half-pound of 10 shillings became known as the half-sovereign.

The Storage of Money

There was no national bank in Shakespeare's day, though wealthy merchants, especially goldsmiths, might serve as bankers. Generally speaking, money was kept close to one's person or home, in bags (*Lear* II.iii.49; *WT* IV.iv.262–63; *MV* II.v.18; *Per* III.ii.41), small chests called coffers (*TN* III.iv.350), or purses (*TS* I.ii.56; *1H4* I.ii.128; *2H4* II.i.115; *H5* IV.iii.36–37; *AYLI* II.iv.12–13; *2GV* IV.iv.176). The printer Richard Jugge, who died in 1577, left his son-in-law "all my oulde goulde and silver of forraine coine and of any other coine whatsoever being in a box in my comptinge howse."

Purses were generally simple leather bags drawn closed with strings (*Oth* I.i.2–3) and hung from the waist. Women wore theirs between the farthingale and skirt, reaching the purse through a slit in the skirt; men's were more exposed and thus more vulnerable to the "cutpurse," who haunted crowds and "picked and cut most of their festival purses" (*WT* IV.iv.617–18).

The rich could afford some variations on the theme of a simple leather pouch containing a few coins. In some cases, the purse might be held by a page or other servant (*2H4* I.ii.237–40). The wealthy also had embroidered "sweet bags" to hold sachets, as well as decorative purses for money. Shakespeare seldom describes his characters' purses in any detail, but he does make reference to such a decorated bag when he includes the "tassel of a prodigal's purse" (*T&C* V.i.36) in a list of effeminate objects. Finally, merchants and the gentry might have other objects to keep handy in a purse; Hamlet, for example, keeps his father's signet ring there (*Ham* V.ii.49 52). *See also* Angel; Crown; Crusadoes; Doit; Dollar; Drachma; Ducat; Farthing; Groat; Halfpenny; Mark; Noble; Penny; Pound; Quart d'Écu; Sequin; Shilling; Sixpence; Threepence.

Music

Music (*MV* V.i.51–88, 97–101), as one of the chief forms of entertainment, was widely studied, especially, but not exclusively, among those with leisure. Those who could not play an instrument were expected at least to be able to carry a tune, and some trades had their own songs that served as mnemonic devices and pleasant ways to pass the time while working. Music played an essential role in court life, warfare, festivals, weddings (*AYLI* V.iv.141–46; *R&J* IV.iv.22–23; *TNK* I.i.1 s.d.), royal processions, and theatrical presentations (*Cym* IV.ii.186 s.d., V.iv.29 s.d.; *Mac* IV.i.132 s.d.; *Temp* III.iii.17 s.d., 82 s.d.); almost no public occasion or lavish private party could be considered complete without it. Those with money hired musicians (*AYLI* IV.i.11–12; *2H4* II.iv.380) to play at their feasts, but being able to pay for a band did not exempt one from knowing how to play. A thorough knowledge of musical theory and practice was an indispensable part of a genteel education (*TS* I.i.93, I.ii.130–33, 170–74, IV.ii.10–17; *Oth* IV.i.188). The opening of composer Thomas Morley's *Plaine and Easie Introduction to Practicall Musicke* (1597) describes the embarrassment of a fictional gentleman when his supper companions discover his inability to sing from written music:

> . . . after manie excuses, I protested unfainedly that I could not, [and] everie one began to wonder. Yea, some whispered to others, demaunding how I was brought up.

Even servants to the great were expected to play well, so that they might entertain their employers (*TS* Ind.i.50–51, Ind.ii.35–36; *TN* I.ii.57–59; *2H4* IV.v.3–4; *H8* IV.ii.78–80 s.d., 94–95).

Music was usually associated with a festive mood, but not always. Sometimes it was contemplative or even mournful. It was also closely linked to love (*A&C* II.v.1–2; *TN* I.i.1, II.iv.1–22, 42–68), and wooers might sing to a woman or hire musicians (*Cym* II.iii.chs.; *R&J* IV.v.chs.) to serenade her (*2GV* III.ii.82–85, 91, IV.ii.39–72). Music could also be used as a gesture of friendship or deference, as when the wealthy sent their small private orchestras to play at the houses of friends (a service for which the musicians expected to be tipped by the lucky recipient). It is by means of such a compliment that the disgraced Cassio seeks to ingratiate himself with Othello (III.i.1–13). Sometimes, musicians who were not part of a nobleman's household attempted the same maneuver to acquire tips, and they apparently made a nuisance of themselves, particularly at taverns, so that they were subjected to much criticism. The reputation of musicians, like that of actors, was not high, and they were often accounted vagabonds and rogues. Phillip Stubbes, who admittedly had a high opinion of almost no one, called them "bawdye parasits as range the Cuntreyes, ryming and singing of uncleane, corrupt, and filthie songs [at] Tavernes, Ale-houses, Innes, and other publique assemblies." Those who were fortunate enough to be part of a nobleman's household had to wear badges identifying their employer.

Musical Terminology

Those instructed in music would have understood the various technical terms used by Shakespeare. They would, for example, have known that a clef was a marking on a musical staff that indicated pitch, and they would have understood that the remark about Cressida, "any man may sing her, if he can take / her cliff; she's noted" (*T&C* V.ii.11–12), was both a reference to the term clef and a sexual slur. The important term here is "noted," alluding both to musical notes and to the idea that Cressida is well known as a whore. The use of the clef may be an allusion to the shape of certain musical symbols; the bass clef and the symbol for B flat, then also called a clef, bear a rough resemblance to breasts. Similarly, they would have known such terms as "key" (*MAAN* I.i.181–82), which also referred to the tone or pitch of a particular piece of music.

Notes were drawn somewhat differently, but on a staff of lines that would be familiar to modern musicians. New tunes could be learned either by ear or by reading this "pricksong" (*R&J* II.iv.22), the writing out of vocal music. There were, at the beginning of the Tudor period, notes organized in octaves, corresponding to the letters G, A, B, C, D, E, F, and G again. The notes were also divided into groups of six, or "hexachords," bearing the familiar names *re, mi, fa, sol,* and *la* (*TS* I.ii.17; *Lear* I.ii.140), and the less familiar *ut* (*LLL* IV.ii.101), which, like, the others, was the Latin syllable sung on the relevant note in a medieval hymn to St. John the Baptist; in a later era, the Italian *do* was substituted for *ut* and the syllables *la* and *ti* added to the scale. The scale itself, from *ut* around again to G or gamma, was called the gamut (*TS* III.i.66–78). Then as now, notes were determined not only by pitch but also by duration. What is today a whole note was then called a semibreve; today's half note was the minim (*R&J* II.iv.23), and the quarter-note was a crotchet (*R&J* IV.v.118).

These notes, arranged in some sequence, formed a melody, sometimes called the "division" (*R&J* III.v.29) when each long note was divided into several shorter ones. A simple melody was called "plain-song" (*H5* III.ii.5, 7) and usually consisted of a low melody punctuated by a higher-pitched melody called the descant (*2GV* I.ii.94). Melodies that altered in pitch at some point were said to have a "change" (*2GV* IV.ii.68–69) or modulation. Combinations of notes were deemed to be harmonious and pleasant (and thus in "concord") or not, resulting in "jar" (*AYLI* II.vii.5; *TS* V.ii.1) or "discord" (*AYLI* II.vii.6; *R&J* III.i.49). Oddly enough to modern readers, "broken" (*H5* V.ii.245; *T&C* III.i.50) music did not necessarily have anything wrong with it. Like the term "division," "broken" merely implied that the music was divided into parts in some way, in this case into differently pitched parts rather than groups of notes. Each instrument or voice took a different part, such as bass (*Temp* III.iii.99) or "mean" (alto or tenor—see *LLL* V.ii.328–29), resulting in a pleasing harmony (*2H6* II.i.55–56; *T&C* III.i.54). Shakespeare often uses discord and harmony as metaphors; in *Henry V* he likens the latter to the different but related functions of different branches of government.

> For government, though high, and low, and lower,
> Put into parts, doth keep in one consent,
> Congreeing in a full and natural close,
> Like music. (I.ii.180–83)

In the case of vocal harmonies, or part song (*WT* IV.iv.289–313), one or more singers might sing the "burden" (*MAAN* III.iv.44; *TS* I.i.67; *Temp* I.ii.383 s.d.), a chorus or repeated phrase sung more or less continuously under the main lyrics. An example in *The Two Noble Kinsmen* has the burden "Down-a down-a" (*TNK* IV.ii.10–11), and "Willow, willow" was a burden common to many songs. Some burdens, like "down-a down-a," were pure nonsense; popular examples included "with a fading" and "dildo," the latter used either as a nonsense syllable or for its meaning as an artificial phallus (*WT* IV.iv.194).

The last of Shakespeare's commonly used technical terms is "time" (*R2* V.v.41–45), which refers not to the duration of the music but to its tempo. This element of a piece of music is the subject of an punning exchange between Touchstone and two pages who take exception to his criticism of their singing. They respond that they have kept the rhythm perfectly:

FIRST PAGE   You are deceived, sir. We kept time, we lost not our time.

TOUCHSTONE   By my troth, yes; I count it but time lost to hear such a foolish song. (*AYLI* V.iii.36–39)

By the time this passage was written, it was already to some extent old-fashioned. The vocal or predominantly vocal songs so popular in the six-teenth century, and so accessible to the public, were in James's reign being eclipsed by pieces in which the instrumental music was dominant. The wealthy, who could afford to buy and play instruments, thus began to separate their musical tastes from those of working people, who could still sing at their labors but could not stop to play chamber music. In the years after Shakespeare's career, a further change took place, with the polyphonic part songs being replaced by homophonic songs with a single melody.

Instruments

Almost every contemporary instrument makes an appearance in Shake-speare's works, from the bone clappers (*TNK* III.v.86–87), hammered tongs (*MND* V.i.28–30), and bagpipes (*1H4* I.ii.76–77; *WT* IV.iv.183; *MV* I.i.53, IV.i.49) of the common man to the virginal (*WT* I.ii.123–27; *TNK* III.iii.34), an instrument like an upright piano played by genteel women. The stringed instruments he mentions include the cittern (*LLL* V.ii.608), harp (*R2* I.iii.159–65; *LLL* V.ii.406; *Temp* II.i.88–89), viol (*R2* I.iii.159–65), lute (*1H6* I.iv.96; *MAAN* II.i.90; *H5* III.ii.43; *LLL* IV.iii.339–40; *Tim* I.ii.130 s.d.), psaltery (*Cor* V.iv.50), rebec, and violin, the last of which had a bow or "fiddlestick" (*R&J* III.i.49) strung with horsehair and strings of calfgut (*Cym* II.iii.31) or catgut (the catlings of *T&C* III.iii.304; *R&J* IV.v.130). Some of these require additional description. The virginals were, like a piano, a stringed instrument, though the striking of keys, which on a piano causes a hammerlike peg to hit a string, in a virginal caused a similar piece called a jack (*S* 128) to pluck the corresponding string. The cittern was a guitarlike instrument with eight strings, two each tuned to the notes G, B, D, and E. The lute was also somewhat guitarlike, but without a waistlike indentation and with a sharply angled tuning head. It had eight frets formed by glued cord and eleven or twelve strings, all but one (if there were eleven) being grouped in identically tuned pairs. The viol was the viola da gamba (*TN* I.iii.24–26; *Per* I.i.82), a six-stringed, fretted, bass viol thought unfeminine under Elizabeth I but an acceptable instrument for ladies by the time of James I. The psaltery, of all these instruments the one least likely to be seen today, was similar to a harp, in that it had a wooden frame and strings, but also was like a dulcimer in having the soundboard behind and parallel to, rather than arranged around, the strings. It could be either strummed or plucked with a pick. The rebec was a three-stringed violin used as the surname of one of the musicians in *Romeo and Juliet* (IV.v.133); his colleague, James Soundpost (136), is named for an internal support that was part of a violin.

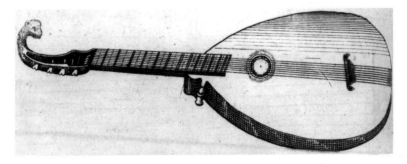

A cittern, from Robert Fludd's *Utriusque Cosmi Historia*. Reproduced from the Collections of the Library of Congress.

String instruments, including lutes and citterns, were often kept in barber shops for the use of the customers while they waited to be shaved or bled. Like the woodwinds, stringed instruments were often made in different sizes. The larger instruments had lower tones, and the smaller ones a higher pitch, so that together they created a similar but harmonious

A harpist and lutenist, with a third musician, from *Panoplia*, illustrated by Jost Amman. A second lute lies face down on the ground and serves as the harpist' foot rest. Reproduced from the Collections of the Library of Congress.

sound. Many of these instruments were heard only in aristocratic homes, but the fiddler (*T&C* III.iii.303), tipped fourpence or sixpence for his work, was a common figure at fairs, wakes, markets, and weddings.

A similar variety of wind instruments appears in Shakespeare's works. The pipe is a simple tube of wood or reed (*R&J* IV.v.96; *Ham* III.ii.70–71; *Oth* III.i.19; *MAAN* V.iv.128–29; *2H4* Ind.15) associated with rustic materials and the pastoral life (*LLL* V.ii.900; *MND* II.i.67). A much grander kind of instrument with pipes, the organ (*Temp* III.iii.98; *TN* I.iv.32–33; *John* V.vii.23), was so huge and expensive that its use was restricted to churches. The other wind instruments mentioned by name are the recorder (*Ham* III.ii.348 s.d.–380; *MND* V.i.122–24; *TNK* V.i.136 s.d.), fife (*MV* II.v.30—this one has, perhaps, an angled mouthpiece), flute (*A&C* II.ii.197, II.vii.132), cornet (*AW* I.ii.1 s.d.; *Cor* I.x.1 s.d., II.i.207 s.d.), horn, trumpet (*H5* IV.vii.55; *MV* V.i.75; *John* II.i.198, 200 s.d., 205), sackbut (*Cor* V.iv.50), and hautboy (oboe—*Mac* IV.i.106 s.d.; *A&C* IV.iii.11 s.d.; *2H6* I.i.1 s.d.). The "treble hautboy" of *2 Henry IV* (III.ii.331) is, because high-pitched, one of the smaller versions of the instrument. The flute looked very little like the instrument of today, having its mouthpiece at the end like a recorder, not on its side. It had six holes in a row, with two others for the little finger and thumb elsewhere, and measured more than two feet in length. The sackbut was a bass trumpet with a trombone-like slide.

Wind instruments were often associated with the military or with announcements of one kind or another. The cornet, for example, appears in Shakespeare in the context of battle, duels, and outdoor sports (*TNK* I.iv.1 s.d., II.iv.1 s.d., III.i.1 s.d., V.iii.55 s.d.). Horns—the exact type often unspecified, but sometimes clearly the hunting horn made, literally, of a hollowed animal horn—appear paired with a drum, in hunting calls, and as the instrument played by couriers and heralds to sound an approach (*1H6* II.iii.61 s.d.; *MAAN* I.i.234–36, *MND* IV.i.139 s.d.; *John* I.i.219; *MV* V.i.39–46). The fife, along with the drum and trumpet, was associated with military marches and signals (*Oth* III.iii.349), but the trumpet was clearly the chief musical instrument of the army, crucial for sending several types of messages across long distances (*TS* I.ii.205; *2H4* IV.i.52; *R&J* III.ii.67; *1H4* V.ii.100 s.d.; *T&C* I.iii.256–57, IV.v.6–11, V.iii.14). The trumpet gives the signal to parley, or negotiate with the enemy (*Tim* V.iv.2 s.d.; *H5* III.ii.90, 138 s.d.–39; *1H4* IV.iii.29 s.d.); to retreat (*T&C* I.ii.179 s.d., *H5* III.ii.90; *1H4* V.iv.156 s.d.–157); to mount horses; and to charge into battle (*TNK* V.iii.55 s.d.). The call to mount horses and march was the tucket (*T&C* I.iii.212 s.d.; *H5* IV.ii.35–36; *AW* III.v.1 s.d.; *Lear* II.iv.178 s.d.).

Even when it is not actually shown in the context of warfare, the trumpet is an extremely official instrument. It conveys the signals at jousts (*R2* I.iii.4, 6 s.d., 25 s.d., 117, 121) and announces the approach of kings and other important people (*1H4* V.v.1 s.d.; *2H4* V.v.2–3; *H5* II.ii.11 s.d.; *LLL* V.ii.156 s.d.). This latter call, also played at an important person's departure, is called a sennet (*2H6* III.i.1 s.d.; *JC* I.ii.24 s.d.; *Lear* I.i.33 s.d.; *A&C* II.vii.17 s.d.; *Mac* III.i.10 s.d.). The more important nobles in the plays have their own personal trumpet calls, allowing their followers to make ready for their arrival in camp or at home. Great public occasions, such as the betrothal of Henry V and Katherine, or Caesar's refusal of a crown, are marked with

Aut in diuersis fistulis unico instrumenta inseruientibus cuiusmodi sint Regalia seu Organa et huiusmodi alia.

Vel intensiorj aut remissiorj flatus mensura, sine mutatione digitorum de aliquo foramine ad aliud diuersæ voces eduntur quemadmodum in Tubæ clangore, cornuq; sonitu euidenter explicatur.

Various musical instruments from *Utriusque Cosmi Historia*, including horns and bagpipes. Reproduced from the Collections of the Library of Congress.

trumpet fanfare—the "flourish" so common in stage directions (*H5* V.ii.358 s.d.; *JC* I.ii.78 s.d.; *Lear* I.i.187 s.d.). Here, art imitated life, for real monarchs were often heralded by trumpets. Paul Hentzner, a traveler who saw Elizabeth I in 1598, noted that she came to dinner accompanied by twelve trumpets and two kettledrums.

The second most important martial instrument was the drum, often paired with the trumpet in Shakespeare as a symbol of war (*1H6* I.iv.80; *1H4* IV.ii.18; *R2* I.iii.134–35, III.iii.50; *LLL* I.ii.177; *John* II.i.76, III.i.229, V.ii.164–79). If the trumpet was the chief means of signaling, the drum set the rhythm of the army, pacing the marching of the soldiers (either accompanied by other instruments or alone—see *1H6* III.iii. s.d.; *JC* V.i.20 s.d.; *Lear* V.iii.328 s.d) or investing the approach of a party with *gravitas* (*H5* III.vi.87 s.d.; *Mac* I.iii.30–31; *Cor* I.iii.29). Nonetheless, not every drum was put to martial use. Kettledrums, like those at Elizabeth's dinner above, were used for the music in grand households (*Ham* III.ii.89 s.d., V.ii.277), and drums set the pace at masques (*MV* II.v.29) and dances as well as in the rank and file. The tabor, a small vellum-headed drum, was a popular instrument for dancing and was often used to accompany the morris (*WT* IV.iv.181–183; *Temp* IV.i.175–77; *TNK* III.v.31; *LLL* V.i.150). Shakespeare even contrasts the martial and civilian varieties of instruments when he has one character complain of another, "I have known when there was / no music with him but the drum and the fife; and / now had he rather hear the tabor and the pipe" (*MAAN* II.iii.12–14). The other percussion instruments mentioned by Shakespeare are the "tabourine" (a kind of drum beaten with one drumstick while the other hand held a flute—*A&C* IV.viii.37) and the cymbals (*Cor* V.iv.51).

Songs

Since music was used for many purposes, there were many different kinds of songs. They were sad, spiritual, joyous, and bawdy, as the occasion demanded, and because they could often be sung unaccompanied, they were the most popularly accessible form of music. Almost anyone could afford to buy a printed ballad, and anyone who could carry a tune could learn one by ear. The ballad (*MAAN* I.i.245; *LLL* IV.i.66–68; *MND* IV.i.214–19; *AW* I.iii.61) was the musical lowest common denominator of Renaissance society. It was the national newspaper, informing the public about attacks on the monarch, foreign affairs, or whatever topic the "ballet" maker found of interest or was paid to advertise (*2H4* IV.iii.46–54). The ballad was the scandal sheet as well, offering tales of monstrous births (*WT* IV.iv.259–65), bizarre omens (*WT* IV.iv.275–78), miraculous events, or grisly crimes—there was no worse fate, in the opinion of some, than to be the subject of such a composition (*1H4* II.ii.44–46; *A&C* V.ii.215–16). The ballad was the radio station, offering entertainment while one worked or played. It was, like television and film, a medium that fed off itself with reckless fervor, as each ballad writer copied, answered, or parodied his rivals.

The ballad was all the mass media in one, and it was so popular not only because it offered information and entertainment but also because it was easy to perform, having only one melody to learn, little or no musical accompaniment, and as many stanzas or verses (*AYLI* II.v.17–18) as were necessary to tell the story. Different songs could be set to the same tune, or different tunes to the same verses, because the meters were often interchangeable; an example of this is Jaques's humorous rewriting of Amiens's "melancholy" song (*AYLI* II.v). The form was held in contempt by some, partly for its unchallenging simplicity, partly because the stories told could be so absurd, partly because they resented the pushy salesmanship of the ballad sellers who haunted the streets and fairs singing bits of their merchandise (*Cor* IV.v.232; *1H4* III.i.124–31; *WT* IV.iv.181–99, 259–313; *LLL* I.ii.107–12). Critics were, however, in the minority, and the public bought ballads almost as fast as they could be turned out.

Not every song was a ballad. Shakespeare includes a dirge or funeral song, though he calls it a "solemn hymn" (*MAAN* V.iii.11–21); a related type of music was the anthem, in which prose, such as a biblical passage, was set to solemn music (*V&A* 839; *2H4* I.ii.191). Hymns (*John* V.vii.22; *MV* V.i.66) and carols also had religious themes, though hymns tended to be serious and carols joyful (*MND* II.i.102). Flemish immigrant weavers spread the popularity of singing psalms in the latter part of the sixteenth century, and this tendency is remarked upon by Falstaff, among others (*1H4* II.iv.133–35; *TN* II.iii.57–59).

Secular music included canzonets (*LLL* IV.ii.122), short solos; hays (*LLL* V.i.150), a type of lively music meant to accompany dancing; dumps, which were slow dance tunes (*R&J* IV.v.105, 107); and catches (*TN* II.iii.18, 60–79, 94, 102–14; *Temp* III.ii.120), what we would today call "rounds," in which one voice begins the song, and each new voice begins the melody anew after the previous singer has completed one line of the song. The one sung in *Twelfth Night* begins "Hold thy peace, knave," and must have been a comic catch (there were serious and plaintive ones as well). Catches were usually arranged for three voices, but madrigals (*MWW* III.i.17), while they could sometimes be sung by three, were part songs usually intended for five or six singers. They were among the most complex pieces of vocal music at the time, sung a cappella in different and harmonious melodies, the lyrics of each usually different from but echoing the others. They could be extraordinarily beautiful, but they were never as popular as ballads.

Those who were already sad usually chose to sustain the mood rather than drive it away, selecting mournful or solemn songs rather than those that were cheerful or facetious. These might be of a religious character or reflections of one kind or another on death. "Oh Death! Rock Me Asleep," possibly written by Anne Boleyn's brother, was one example; "Fortune My Foe," traditionally played at hangings, was another. The *Hamlet* gravedigger's song, "I Loathe That I Did Love," is a typically gruesome example, full of the trappings of mortality:

A pickax and a spade, a spade,
  For and a shrouding sheet;
O, a pit of clay for to be made
  For such a guest is meet. (V.i.94–97)

A similar song, though sung with greater earnestness than the gravedigger's, is that sung over Fidele's grave in *Cymbeline*, with its refrain emphasizing that all people must at last "come to dust" (IV.ii.258–75). Less macabre was "Loth to Depart," which was often sung as a farewell. Those who were frustrated in love often preferred songs about people in similar situations (*MM* IV.i.1–6). Many of these included the word "willow" (*TNK* IV.i.80), because the willow was associated with unrequited love. So common was it for the lovelorn to resort to heartwrenching ballads that a tendency to song was one of the signs by which others recognized their melancholy (*AW* III.ii.6–9).

Those who were in love but had greater reason to hope for a positive outcome favored songs of consummated love or enthusiasm for the beloved's charms (*T&C* III.i.115–24; *2GV* II.i.21–22; *TN* II.iii.35–53). Composing such songs, like composing love poetry, was a popular gesture of affection. A man in love with a woman might bring her tangible gifts as well as "musics of all sorts, and songs composed / To her unworthiness" (*AW* III.vii.40–41). It was common for such songs to praise the various aspects of the beloved's appearance, using complimentary comparisons of natural objects to her skin, eyes, lips, teeth, hair, and so on. Jaques considers amateur composition an indispensable aspect of the infatuations of youth; his seven ages of man progress from infant to schoolboy to "the lover, / Sighing like furnace, with a woeful ballad / Made to his mistress' eyebrow" (*AYLI* II.vii.146–48). One of the most popular, and thus most imitated and adapted, love songs of the day was "Greensleeves" (*MWW* II.i.61, V.v.19–20), a plaintive song from a rejected lover to his lady. One of the many versions begins thus:

Alas! my love, you do me wrong,
  To cast me off so discourteously,
And I have loved you so long,
  Delighting in your company.
    Greensleeves was all my joy,
    Greensleeves was my delight,
    Greensleeves was my heart of gold,
    And who but my Lady Greensleeves.

Some songs were neither serious nor amorous but bawdy (*1H4* III.iii.14–15; *Temp* II.ii.46–55), riotous, humorous, pastoral, or simply silly. Silence sings bits of several in *2 Henry IV* V.iii that chiefly concern women, wives, and drinking. A single line (106) is from a ballad about Robin Hood; heroes and their adventures were popular subjects for songs. Several such tunes, about the archer Adam Bell (*MAAN* I.i.250–52), King Arthur (*2H4* II.iv.33), and Childe Roland (Charlemagne's nephew, in a possible ballad reference from *Lear* III.iv.180), turn up in other plays. Iago sings a drinking song (*Oth* II.iii.90–97), for music was almost as closely associated with inebriation as it was with romantic love.

Shakespeare mentions many other songs, sometimes including whole stanzas, at other times merely alluding to a popular song with a few words or a couple of lines. Among those that have been identified are "Peg-a-Ramsey" or "Peggie Ramsey" (*TN* II.iii), a dance tune whose lyrics could be sung to at least two different melodies in Shakespeare's time, and "Three Merry Men Be We," mentioned in the same scene, whose lyrics include the following:

> Three merry men and three merry men,
> And three merry men be we a,
> I in the wood, and thou on the ground,
> And Jack sleeps in the tree.

The ballad "The Friar of Orders Gray" shows up twice, once with the title line and another (*TS* IV.i.134–35), and once, less obviously, in a line from the song "Through the / sharp hawthorn blows the cold wind" (*Lear* III.iv.45–46). "Light o' Love," another popular song, is mentioned in both *The Two Noble Kinsmen* (V.ii.53) and *The Two Gentlemen of Verona* (I.ii.83). A complete catalog of the songs that appear in the plays would be prohibitively long, but would include "Heart's Ease" (*R&J* IV.v.100–103); "Jog On, Jog On" (*WT* IV.iii.126–29), whose tune was also used for a ballad about the Spanish Armada; "Bonny Sweet Robin" (*TNK* IV.i.108); and "All the Flowers of the Broom" (*TNK* IV.i.107), a song about a shrub, not a household implement. The line "My heart is full" (*R&J* IV.v.105) comes from a love song beginning with a maid's lament that her absent lover has forgotten her, whose burden was "my heart is full of woe." In general, characters who sing lines or stanzas are repeating parts of songs that would have been familiar to Shakespeare's audiences.

In most cases, the characters use these songs in the appropriate contexts. Silence's songs about drinking and the woes of married life, and Enobarbus's song to "Plumpy Bacchus" (*A&C* II.vii.114–19), are exactly the sorts of songs that groups of men would have sung to entertain each other. The Clown's song at the end of *Twelfth Night* is the sort of merry, nonsensical song that was often used to express lightheartedness (V.i.390–409). The singing of girls as they do needlework (*MND* III.ii.203–8; *Cor*

I.iii.1) and of servants to their masters (*LLL* I.ii.120–22; *MAAN* II.iii.36–87) are similiarly consistent with what we know of the role of music in Renaissance life. The places where music seems the strangest are in the scenes of insanity, specifically the insanity of Ophelia (*Ham* IV.v.22 s.d.–67), the jailer's daughter (*TNK* III.iv.19–24, III.v.60–72, IV.iii.56), and, to a lesser extent, Edgar (*Lear* III.vi.41–44). Edgar's madness is feigned, which perhaps makes him less musical, but the emphasis on song of the two women may be due to the fact that both go mad for love, and music was the "food of love" (*TN* I.i.1). In Renaissance eyes, they have taken love, and its natural penchant for song, to an unnatural extreme. In Ophelia's case, the inappropriate nature of the continual singing is magnified by her choice of songs; she is a virgin, yet one of her songs concerns the bedding and betrayal of a maid. The fact that this theme probably reflects her feelings at being mysteriously jilted by Hamlet would in no way have excused her immodesty to a Renaissance audience. The same contrast between maidenhood and bawdiness is used for humorous effect in *The Winter's Tale*, when a country bumpkin defends the propriety of an obviously indecent song:

> He has the prettiest love songs for maids, so without bawdry, which is strange; with such delicate burdens of dildos and fadings: "Jump her, and thump her"; and where some stretch-mouthed rascal would, as it were, mean mischief, and break a foul gap into the matter, he makes the maid to answer, "Whoop, do me no harm, good man"; puts him off, slights him, with "Whoop, do me no harm, good man." (IV.iv.192–99)

The rustic either is trying to titillate his audience while pretending to be guiltless or truly believes that the song is harmless merely because it includes a scornful refrain. Since Shakespeare's rustics are usually profoundly dimwitted, the latter interpretation is likely. In this scene, as in hundreds of other places in the plays, music can shed light on a character's mood, intelligence, personality, and circumstances. *See also* Army; Dance.

Mythology

Knowledge of Latin was essential for a well-educated man during the Renaissance. It crops up frequently in Shakespeare's works, often as quotations from the Bible or liturgy spoken by parsons or priests, as legal jargon in proclamations and documents or from the mouths of lawyers and justices, and in the stage directions of the plays: *exit* (he leaves), *exeunt* (they leave), *manet* (he stays), *manent* (they stay), and so on. Quotations found in the standard children's Latin text of the day, known popularly as *Lily's Latin Grammar*, crop up here and there. Professionals and noblemen are expected to know Latin well, and if they are chided on the subject of this ancient language, it is because they use it too often or too pedantically.

Even some of the less noble characters use an occasional *quondam* (former) or *ergo* (therefore), and the only characters who truly butcher the language are those, like Costard, who are meant to look like fools. *Love's Labor's Lost* IV.ii and *The Merry Wives of Windsor* IV.i. demonstrate Shakespeare's attitude—and that of all educated people—toward those who did and did not know Latin well. That Shakespeare expected a significant percentage of his audience (or at least the percentage of it most likely to pay for the good seats) to understand some Latin is reflected in the fact that he rarely translates the Latin passages of his plays.

It is therefore quite natural that the subject matter of the Latin classics, principally history and mythology, should be well known also. Shakespeare mentions about 150 characters from Greek and Roman mythology, usually in their Roman incarnations, since the study of Latin was far more widespread than the study of Greek. In fact, one of the very few references to Greek in the plays is as a language so foreign as to seem like gibberish, the famous "it was Greek to me" (*JC* I.ii.282). When we hear of Greek being studied, it is in addition to, not instead of, Latin (*TS* II.i.81, 100). Nonetheless, some of the plays are set in ancient Greece, often with gods or heroes as characters, so clearly the mythology was fairly well known, even if the language was not. Since Shakespeare tends to use the gods' Latin names, this entry does so as well, including the Greek name, when it differs, in parentheses.

Major Gods and Goddesses

The king of the Roman pantheon was Jupiter or Jove. Never in Shakespeare's works is he called by his Greek name, Zeus. Because of the comic possibilities of metaphors involving bulls and cuckolds' horns, his wooing of the mortal Europa (*MAAN* V.iv.446–48; *MWW* V.v.3–4), daughter of King Agenor of Phoenicia (*TS* I.i.168–70), is often alluded to. His other loves, including Leda, whom he ravished while disguised as a swan (*MWW* V.v.6–8), and his cupbearer Ganymede (*AYLI* I.iii.123; *TNK* IV.ii.15–18) are occasionally mentioned as well. He is often enlisted as a symbol of kingship or power (*Per* I.i.105, II.iii.28) and, because he was powerful, is often enlisted as an enforcer of oaths (*H5* IV.iii.24; *LLL* V.ii.495; *AYLI* II.iv.1; *R&J* II.ii.92–93). His sacred grove of oak trees (*Temp* V.i.45) was in Dodona, though he had temples elsewhere, even in Roman Britain (*Cym* V.v.481–83). Other than the oak, his principal symbols were his shield, the Aegis; the eagle, considered by Renaissance people to be the noblest of birds (*Cym* IV.ii.348); and the lightning bolt and its accompanying thunder, which he was said to wield as a weapon (*LLL* IV.ii.115; *Lear* II.iv.224–25; *Cor* III.i.256; *T&C* IV.v.135; *Cym* V.iv.62 s.d.).

Jupiter's wife was Juno (Hera) (*LLL* IV.iii.115; *Lear* II.iii.21). She spends much of her time in the myths attempting and failing to enforce Jupiter's fidelity, for which reason she "is queen of marriage" (*Per*

493

Mythological figures were common devices in pageantry, art, and literature. This detail from the title page of the 1633 edition of John Gerard's *Herball*, for example, incorporates Ceres and Pomona, the Roman goddesses of grain and fruit, respectively. Reproduced from the Collections of the Library of Congress.

II.iii.30). Shakespeare treats her well, praising her fine mantle (*TNK* I.i.63) and the beauty of her eyelids (*WT* IV.iv.121). He mentions her role as patroness of childbirth as Lucina, a Roman name she shared with Diana (*Cym* V.iv.37–38; *Per* I.i.9, III.i.10–12), but oddly, he gives her swans (*AYLI* I.iii.74), when swans were more commonly associated with Venus. Juno's traditional bird was the peacock, whose tail she decorated with the hundred eyes of her slain servant Argus (*T&C* I.ii.29; *LLL* III.ii.198; *MV* V.i.230).

Neptune (Poseidon) (*Ham* III.ii.159; *Mac* II.ii.59; *MND* III.ii.392; *John* V.ii.34) was Jupiter's brother and the god of the ocean (*TNK* V.i.50; *A&C* IV.xiv.58). He was associated with storms, earthquakes, bulls, horses, and his three-pointed spear, the trident (*Cor* III.i.255; *Temp* I.iii.204–6). Jupiter's other brother, Pluto (*JC* IV.iii.101, *T&C* III.iii.197), known in Greek as Hades and in Latin as either Pluto or Dis (*TNK* III.v.114; *Temp* IV.i.89), ruled the underworld, Hades (*2H4* II.iv.159–62). He was also sometimes thought of as the god of wealth, perhaps because minerals were found underground, or perhaps because his name was similar to that of Plutus, the god of wealth (*Tim* I.i.285).

Pluto's kingdom was the subject of many myths. It was divided into several realms. Erebus (*JC* II.i.84; *MV* V.i.87) was the entry point for the recently departed; Elysium (*2H6* III.ii.399; *3H6* I.ii.30; *H5* IV.i.274; *TN* I.ii.4; *TNK* V.iv.94; *V&A* 600; *2GV* II.vii.38) was for the virtuous and for warriors who had died honorably in battle; Tartarus (*CE* IV.ii.32) was a place of punishment for the wicked. One of the residents of Tartarus was Tantalus (*V&A* 599), who had invited the gods to dinner and then served them a dish made of his own son, Pelops. The gods brought Pelops back to life, though one of his shoulder bones was missing and had to be replaced by a piece of carved ivory (*TNK* IV.ii.21). Tantalus they sent to Tartarus, where he was tormented by perpetual hunger and thirst, with a river and branches full of fruit forever just out of his reach. Around the regions of Hades ran five rivers: Acheron, the river of woe (*Mac* III.v.15); Lethe, the river of oblivion (*2H4* V.ii.72; *A&C* II.i.27, II.vii.109; *TN* IV.i.63); Phlegethon, the river of fire; Styx (*T&C* V.iv.19), the sacred river by which oaths were sworn; and Cocytus, the river of weeping. Depending upon the myth, it was the Styx, the Acheron, or the Cocytus across which the ghostly ferryman Charon carried the souls of the dead. Charon would take no one across without payment, however, so the dead were buried with a coin on their tongues for the fare (*T&C* III.ii.7–12; *TNK* IV.iii.19–20). In the midst of all this sat Pluto on his throne, with his massive three-headed dog, Cerberus, as a guard (*2H4* II.iv.171; *LLL* V.ii.585; *T&C* II.i.33). Jupiter also had two sisters, Vesta (Hestia in Greek), goddess of the hearth, never mentioned by Shakespeare; and Ceres (Demeter in Greek), goddess of grain and the harvest (*2H6* I.ii.2; *TNK* V.i.53; *Temp* IV.i.ch.).

Jupiter's children were also included in the pantheon. His daughter Minerva (Athena) (*TS* I.i.84)), goddess of wisdom, weaving, and warfare, had the olive as her special tree and the owl as her bird. Apollo (Phoebus) and Diana (Artemis) were twins, born of Jupiter and Latona (Leto), the daughter of Titans. Apollo was god of the sun, medicine (*TNK* I.iv.46), truth, and music (*TS* Ind.ii.35; *LLL* V.ii.925). His special instrument was the lyre, fashioned for him by the god Mercury, but Shakespeare gives him a lute instead (*LLL* IV.iii.339–40). As the sun god, Apollo was supposed to ride across the heavens daily in a flaming chariot (*MND* I.ii.36; *MV* II.i.5; *R&J* III.ii.1–2; *Ham* III.ii.158; *A&C* IV.viii.29); in this incarnation he was often called Phoebus, a word that meant "bright" or "shining" (*MAAN* V.iii.26; *H5* IV.i.273; *T&C* I.iii.230; *Cym* V.v.190; *WT* IV.iv.123–24). On only one occasion did another person drive his chariot, Phaethon (*2GV* III.i.153–55), the nominal son of the African king Merops and his wife Clymene. Phaethon's real Father, however, was the sun-god Helios (in some versions changed to Apollo), who permitted him to drive the sun-chariot for a day. Phaethon, however, drove so wildly and dangerously that the gods were forced to kill him (*3H6* I.iv.33, II.vi.10–12; *R2* III.iii.177; *R&J* III.ii.2–4). Apollo's oracle was at Delphi (*WT* II.i.184) and his sacred plant was the laurel, because a nymph he once pursued, Daphne, changed into a laurel tree rather than be ravished by him (*MND* II.i.230–31; *TS* I.ii.49–60; *T&C* I.i.101).

Diana (Artemis) was goddess of the moon (*1H4* I.ii.25–39; *LLL* IV.ii.39; *MV* V.i.66; *R&J* II.ii.4–9), of hunting, and of chastity (*3H6* IV.viii.21; *MAAN* IV.i.56–57; *MV* V.i.66). She had many names—Cynthia (*Per* II.v.11), for her birthplace on Mt. Cynthus; Phoebe when she was in the heavens; Diana on earth; Hecate in the underworld, or in the dark of the moon (*1H6* III.ii.64; *Lear* I.i.110; *MND* V.i.383; *Mac* II.i.51–52, III.ii.40–43). She appears as a character in *Pericles* (V.i) as Diana and in *Macbeth* (III.v) as Hecate.

Venus (Aphrodite) was born from the sea foam near Cythera, for which reason she is somethimes called Cytherea (*TS* I.ii.49–60; *WT* IV.iv.122; *Cym* II.ii.14). The goddess of love and beauty, she rode in a chariot pulled by doves (*R&J* II.v.7; *V&A* 153, 1190–93; *RL* 58; *MND* I.i.171; *MV* II.vi.5). She was married somewhat unwillingly to the lame god of the forge, Vulcan (Hephaestus) (*MAAN* I.i.181; *T&C* I.iii.168; *Ham* III.ii.84; *TN* V.i.52). She was not, however, a faithful wife (*MAAN* IV.i.58–59; *A&C* I.v.18). *Venus and Adonis* details her seduction of the doomed but beautiful mortal Adonis (*1H6* I.vi.6; *S* 53), and it was well known that she had committed adultery with Mars (Ares) (*1H6* I.ii.1–4; *1H4* III.ii.112, IV.i.115–16; *LLL* V.ii.642; *Cym* IV.ii.310; *TNK* I.i.62, I.iv.17; *R2* II.iii.100), the god of war and the son of Jupiter and Juno.

Of this illicit union of Mars and Venus came Cupid (Eros), god of love, who made people fall in love with one another by shooting them with magical arrows. Shakespeare frequently shows him as an archer (*MAAN* I.i.38, 180, II.i.371–72, III.i.22; *LLL* I.ii.171; *R&J* I.i.212; *MND* I.i.169–70; *Temp* IV.i.92–94), sometimes as a blind archer (*AYLI* IV.i.211–12; *R&J* I.iv.4–5, II.iv.17). Cupid was a winged (*T&C* III.ii.13; *R&J* I.iv.17–20, II.v.8) boy or youth whose age and temperament varied according to the individual myth.

Mercury (*TN* I.v.97; *LLL* V.ii.924; *T&C* II.ii.45; *Ham* III.iv.59), known in Greek as Hermes (*H5* III.vii.18), is one of the few gods called by both his Greek and Roman names in the plays. Mercury was a trickster and rogue who at various times stole Apollo's cattle, invented the lyre, and talked hundred-eyed Argus to death. He was the patron of thieves and merchants. His feet and traveler's hat were winged (*H5* II.Cho.7; *1H4* IV.i.105; *Cym* IV.ii.310–11), and this gave him the speed to be the messenger of the gods (*MWW* II.ii.77). His symbol was the caduceus, a short staff with wings and two entwined serpents (*T&C* II.iii.11–12), which was later adopted as a symbol of the medical profession.

Bacchus (*LLL* IV.iii.336; *A&C* II.vii.114–19), known in Greek as Dionysus, was the son of Jupiter and Semele, a mortal woman. The god of wine, he was often represented wearing a crown of grape leaves and a garment made from a leopard's skin. The secret rites of his female worshippers, the Bacchantes, were said to be extraordinarily wild, even murderously violent.

Lesser Deities

There were gods even older than Jupiter. In the beginning, the stories went, Uranus (the heavens) and Tellus (Gaea, the earth; *Ham* III.ii.159) gave birth to several races: three hundred-armed, fifty-headed monsters, the Centimani (Hecatonchires), named Briareus (*T&C* I.ii.28–29), Cottus, and Gyges; a group of giants with one eye each, the Cyclops; and the Titans. The male titans were Saturn (Cronus), Oceanus, Hyperion, Iapetus, and Ophion. Their sisters were Ops (Rhea), Themis, Tethys, Mnemosyne, and Eurynome.*

The titans began to pair off and have children of their own. Helios (*T&C* V.x.25), the sun god, was the child of Hyperion (*H5* IV.i.275; *Tim* IV.iii.185; *Ham* III.iv.57); Shakespeare sometimes refers to one or both of them, vaguely, by calling the sun "Titan" (*Cym* III.iv.164; *V&A* 177). Hyperion's other children were the dawn, Aurora (Eos) (*R&J* I.i.139; *MND* III.ii.380, 389), and the moon, Selene. Both fell in love with mortals. Aurora tried and failed to woo Cephalus, fell in love with Orion, and took Tithonus as her husband, securing for him the gift of immortality. She did not, however, remember to make him eternally young, and he withered away until he turned into a grasshopper. Selene fell in love with the shepherd Endymion (*MV* V.i.109) and learned from her sister's error. Endymion was kept eternally young, and forever asleep on the hillside where she first saw him, so that every night she could admire his beauty as she passed.

Iapetus's sons were Prometheus (*LLL* IV.iii.301, 348), who stole fire to give to humans; Epimetheus, sometimes credited with the creation of humans; and Atlas (*3H6* V.i.36; *A&C* I.v.23), who was punished for a rebellion against the gods by having to bear the sky on his back for eternity. Ophion and Eurynome took control of Mt. Olympus, where the gods had their home, only to be ousted by Saturn and Ops.

Saturn, in turn, was overthrown by Jupiter, who took Olympus for himself. It was at this point that the other Titans and their descendants, except Prometheus, rose up in revolt against Jupiter and his siblings. The effort failed, however, and Jupiter buried most of his rivals in Tartarus. The blood of Saturn, seeping into the earth, gave rise to the goddesses who punished sin, the Furies (*2H4* V.iii.109; *A&C* II.v.40). They had hair made of snakes and eyes that wept blood instead of tears. Another rebellion was staged by a pack of giants. They stacked Mt. Pelion on top of Mt. Ossa (*MWW* II.i.77–78) in an attempt to reach Olympus, but were defeated when Jupiter knocked Pelion off with a thunderbolt, burying the rebellious giants beneath it.

Jupiter became king of the gods, ruling over heaven and earth, but the

*These are the Titans listed by Thomas Bulfinch, who relied on many of the same Roman mythologists who informed Shakespeare and his contemporaries. Bulfinch's sources recounted a myth in which Ophion and Eurynome were the original rulers of Olympus before Cronus and Rhea seized control. Other sources, however, differ regarding the identities of the original Titans. One list gives Cronus, Iapetus, Oceanus, Hyperion, Crius, and Coeus as the male Titans and Rhea, Themis, Tethys, Theia, Mnemosyne, and Phoebe as their respective spouses. In this view, Eurynome is not one of the original Titans but an Oceanid, a daughter of Oceanus and Tethys. In still another version of the creation, Eurynome was one of the first beings, existing before all the Titans. She gave birth to a serpent, Ophion, whom she then took as a mate.

waters were controlled by other gods. Neptune was the chief of these, ruling the Mediterranean and the Black seas, but there were others, including the nymphs (*TNK* I.i.1 s.d.; *2GV* V.iv.12), or naiads (*Temp* IV.i.128), of individual rivers and the gods in the genealogical chart below.

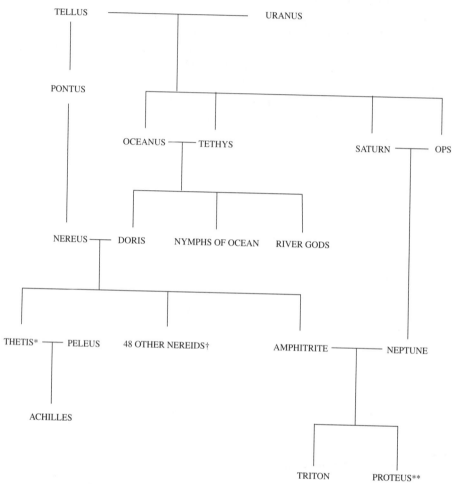

*(*Per* IV.iv.39; *T&C* I.iii.39)
†(*A&C* II.ii.208)
**Some myths identify Proteus as the offspring of Oceanus and Tethys.

Proteus (*3H6* III.ii.192) was best known for his ability to change shape, and Triton (*Cor* III.i.89) was known for his horn made of a massive seashell.

There were numerous minor goddesses in both Greek and Roman mythology. Ate (*MAAN* II.i.247; *JC* III.i.271; *John* II.i.63; and as "Ates" in *LLL* V.ii.686) was the goddess of revenge and mischief. Echo (*R&J* II.ii.162–64) was a nymph punished by Juno with the inability to speak any words but those she had just heard; she faded away at last to only a lingering voice because of her unrequited love for the beautiful boy Narcissus (*TNK* IV.ii.32; *V&A* 161–62; *RL* 265–66), who fell in love with his reflection in a pool of water and drowned trying to kiss the lovely stranger.

Three of Jupiter's daughters, Aglaia, Euphrosyne, and Thalia, were collectively known as the Graces (*T&C* I.ii.242) for their joy and beauty. Iris was the goddess of the rainbow (*2H6* III.ii.407; *AW* I.iii.153; *Temp* IV.i.76–82). Nemesis (*1H6* IV.vii.78) was the personification of righteous anger and lived not on Olympus but among mortals. Jupiter had nine other daughters with the Titaness Mnemosyne. These nine were called the Muses (*H5* I.Pro.1; *S* 38; *S* 78; *S* 79) and were the patrons of the arts.

Muse	Domain
Calliope	Epic poetry
Clio	History
Erato	Love poetry
Euterpe	Lyric poetry
Melpomene	Tragedy
Polyhymnia	Hymns
Terpsichore	Dance
Thalia	Comedy
Urania	Astronomy

Astraea was the daughter of Jupiter and his aunt Themis. The goddess of justice and purity, she was set into the sky as the constellation Virgo (*TA* IV.iii.4).

Proserpina (Persephone) was the daughter of Ceres. While picking flowers with her maidens, she was kidnapped by Pluto and taken to the underworld to be his queen (*T&C* II.i.33; *WT* IV.iv.116–18; *TNK* IV.iii.24); there she lamented her fate and refused to eat anything but six pomegranate seeds. Her mother's longing for her resulted in a compromise: since Proserpina had eaten only six seeds, she would have to live in the underworld for six months of the year, but could return to her mother for the other six. Her mother's alternation of grief and joy was said to be the cause of winter and summer.

The Fates (*MV* II.ii.60–61; *H5* V.i.20; in Latin, Parcae) were minor in the sense that they were not active in the world at large, but they were not minor goddesses at all in terms of power. They controlled the lives of all humans, and not even Jupiter could overrule their decisions. These three sisters (*MND* V.i.335) were Clotho, who spun the thread of each human life; Lachesis, who determined destiny; and Atropos (*2H4* II.iv.202; *Per* I.ii.108; *John* IV.ii.91), who cut the thread and thus determined how long each person would live.

Lesser gods included Hymen, god of marriage feasts (*MAAN* V.iii.32; *Per* III.Cho.9–11; *Tim* IV.iii.383; *Temp* IV.i.23; *AYLI* V.iv.ch; *TNK* I.i.ch.). Aeolus (*2H6* III.ii.92) was keeper of the winds, among them Boreas (*T&C* I.iii.38), the fierce north wind. Typhon (*T&C* I.iii.160), one of the giants who rebelled against Jupiter, was the father of several monsters, including the Sphinx (*LLL* IV.iii.339), who had the body of a lion and the head of a woman, and the Chimera, who was part serpent, part lion, and part goat.

Magical beasts such as the Sphinx and Chimera were common in mythology. Some were beautiful, like the winged horse Pegasus (*H5* III.vii.14–17; *1H4* IV.i.108). Some were horrifying, like the Harpies (*Per* IV.iii.46–48; *Temp* III.iii.52 s.d.), half woman, half bird, filthy and screeching and violent. Some could be benign and frightening by turns, such as the often warlike Centaurs (*Lear* IV.vi.124), who were horses with men's torsos and heads, or the lustful Satyrs (*MWW* V.v.38 s.d.), who were men from the waist up and goats from the waist down.

Some gods were peculiar to the Romans and had no Greek equivalents. Those mentioned by Shakespeare are Bellona (*Mac* I.ii.54; *TNK* I.i.75, I.iii.13), a war goddess who is sometimes described as Mars's sister, sometimes as his wife; Flora (*WT* IV.iv.2), goddess of flowers and spring, and lover of Zephyrus, the west wind; Janus (*Oth* I.ii.32; *MV* I.i.50), the two-faced god who presided over beginnings and endings and thus gave his name to the month January; and Priapus (*Per* IV.vi.4), a fertility god.

Heroes and Mortals

Stories of Love

Stories of mortals were often told to illustrate a particular virtue—love, fidelity, strength, cleverness—or the consequences of faults like greed and pride. Stories of enduring and often tragic love are frequently alluded to by Shakespeare. He makes an indirect allusion to the story of Ceyx and Halcyone; Ceyx was drowned and Halcyone, after a vision in which she saw him dead, went to the sea, where she saw his body riding on the waves. She jumped in after it but was changed into a bird before her body touched the water, and Ceyx was changed into a bird as well so that they could always be together. Legend had it that this "halcyon" (*1H6* I.ii.131) bird nested on the water in calm weather.

Another love story was that of Pyramus and Thisbe, which forms the subject matter of the tradesmen's play in *A Midsummer Night's Dream* (I.ii., III.i., V.i.). Forbidden to see one another, they agreed to meet at night. A lion chased Thisbe (*R&J* II.iv.43; *MV* V.i.7–9) away from the rendezvous, smearing blood on her scarf but not killing her; Pyramus, finding the scarf and believing Thisbe dead, slew himself; Thisbe, returning, found his dead body and did likewise. The story of Hero and Leander

(*AYLI* IV.i.97–102; *2GV* III.i.119–20; *R&J* II.iv.43) also had a tragic ending. Leander used to swim the Hellespont every night to visit Hero, but one night the light Leander used to guide himself to shore went out, and he drowned; Hero, finding his body, killed herself. Another story with a violent conclusion was that of Cephalus and Procris. Cephalus refused the advances of Aurora and returned to his beautiful wife, Procris, but jealousy poisoned their marriage forever afterward, and one day during a hunt Cephalus accidentally killed his wife with a javelin. The inept players of *A Midsummer Night's Dream* know these myths, but only vaguely, calling Hero and Leander "Helen" and "Limander" and Cephalus and Procris "Shafalus" and "Procrus" (V.i.196–99).

The story of Philomela (*TNK* V.iii.123–28; *Cym* II.ii.44–46; *RL* 1079, 1128–34) and Procne was just as sad. Tereus, married to Procne, raped her sister Philomela, told Procne that Philomela was dead, and then cut out Philomela's tongue to keep his secret. Philomela wove a picture of her story and had it delivered to Procne, who in revenge stabbed to death the son she had borne to Tereus. The sisters cooked the boy's body in a stew and fed it to Tereus, then showed him the severed head and told him what he had eaten. Tereus chased the sisters and nearly caught and killed them, but at the last moment all three were changed into birds—Procne into a nightingale, Philomela into a swallow, and Tereus into a hoopoe.

Not every love story ended in sorrow. Baucis and Philemon (*MAAN* II.i.91) were a poor but happily married couple who were hospitable to a disguised Jupiter and in return were granted their wish: that they might die at the same time, so that neither would have the misery of outliving the other. After death, they were turned into trees that grew around each other, branches entwined. The sculptor Pygmalion (*MM* III.ii.46) created such a beautiful statue of a woman that he fell in love with his creation; his prayers were answered when she came to life.

Stories of the Gods' Vengeance

Some tales warned of hubris (excessive pride), or of attempting to take advantage of the gods. Niobe (*T&C* V.x.19) was the wife of Amphion (*Temp* II.i.88–89), a wonderful musician and the son of Jupiter, whose playing was so powerful that it raised the rock walls of Thebes. Niobe bragged that her seven daughters and seven sons outnumbered the mere two children of Leto. She claimed divinity for herself and demanded that Leto's temple be made her own. Unfortunately, Leto's children were Apollo and Diana, and they slew all her children with their arrows. Niobe was turned into a stone that was perpetually wet with her tears.

Icarus (*1H6* IV.vi.55, IV.vii.16), son of the great architect Daedalus (*TNK* III.v.114), also strove for godlike power and was struck down. He and his father flew from Crete on wings made of feathers and wax, but

Icarus, captivated by his new power, flew too high. The sun melted the wax in his wings, and he plunged into the sea and drowned.

Actaeon was more unlucky than proud. He chanced, while hunting, to see the nude Diana bathing with her attendants. The idea of having a mortal see her thus was too much to bear, and she turned him into a stag and allowed him to be killed by his own dogs. Shakespeare uses Actaeon as an emblem of cuckoldry, since the hunter was literally given a pair of horns (*MWW* II.i.116, III.ii.39).

Greed was the downfall of King Midas (*MV* III.ii.102). He wished for riches and was granted the ability to turn anything into gold simply by touching it. He regretted his gift after turning his own daughter to gold by mistake.

Sometimes, fatal consequences extended beyond the sinner. The unwitting incest of Oedipus and his mother, Jocasta, for example, tainted their four children as well. Their two sons, Eteocles and Polynices, fought one another for the Theban crown, and both were slain. The new king, their uncle Creon, forbade a proper burial for Polynices (*TNK* I.i.42), but a third Oedipal child, Antigone, disobeyed and buried her brother anyway. She was buried alive as punishment, and her lover Haemon, Creon's son, killed himself.

On one occasion, all of humanity offended the gods, and Jupiter decided to destroy the world and create a new race of people. He created a great flood that drowned everyone except one virtuous man, Deucalion (*WT* IV.iv.434; *Cor* II.i.95), and his wife, Pyrrha, who was descended from Titans. They rode on the flood in a chest and washed up on Mount Parnassus, where they created a new race of humans out of stones.

Stories of Adventure

Sometimes stories were simply good stories, meant to extol the deeds of great heroes and to inspire new adventures. Atalanta (*AYLI* III.ii.147, 277), for example, was a great huntress and athlete who participated, with other heroes, in a hunt for a great boar (*A&C* IV.xiii2) sent to ravage the lands of King Calydon (*2H6* I.i.232–33). She was the first to strike the boar and, after a dispute, was granted the skin by Meleager (*TNK* III.v.18), a young man who had fallen in love with her. There was a fight about this afterward, and Meleager killed his two uncles, brothers of his mother Althaea (*2H4* II.ii.85–89; *2H6* I.i.232–33). Bitterly angry, Althaea burned a log that the Fates had told her would last as long as her son's life. He died as it turned to ash, and she hanged herself out of remorse.

A hero from the time of Atalanta, Jason sailed with a host of companions in search of the Golden Fleece (*MV* I.i.170–72, III.ii.241). Since their ship was named the *Argo*, they became known as the Argonauts. They sailed to the land of Colchis, where a princess named Medea (*2H6* V.ii.58–59) helped them and murdered her own brother in order to escape, throwing the pieces of his body from their departing ship to detain their pursuers. Back in Jason's home, she restored his father, Aeson, to youth by using her magical arts (*MV* V.i.12–14) but was repudiated by Jason and killed the sons she had borne Jason and Jason's new bride, Creusa.

A whole host of heroes from the Trojan War and its aftermath appear in Shakespeare's works. *Troilus and Cressida* is set in and around Troy, and a host of characters from both sides appear or are mentioned. The Trojan characters include King Priam (*3H6* II.v.120; *AW* I.iii.74; *2H4* I.i.71–74), Queen Hecuba (*Cym* IV.ii.313; *Cor* I.iii.40–43), the wise elder Antenor, the prophetess Cassandra, and the princes Hector (*1H6* II.iii.20; *3H6* IV.viii.25; *2H4* II.iv.222; *LLL* V.ii.532, 630–88; *Cor* I.iii.40–43), Deiphobus, Helenus, and Paris, sometimes called Alexander (*1H6* V.v.104; *TS* I.ii.242–45). It was Paris who ostensibly began the conflict by judging a beauty contest involving Venus, Juno, and Minerva in Venus's favor. Each goddess offered him a bribe, but he liked Venus's best— the love of Helen, wife of King Menelaus of Sparta, one of four children of Jupiter and Leda (*TS* I.ii.242–45) and renowned as the most beautiful woman in the world. He visited Sparta and took Helen home with him, after which she was known as Helen of Troy (*3H6* II.ii.146–49; *AYLI* III.ii.145; *R&J* II.iv.43; *S* 53). Other Trojan characters in *Troilus and Cressida* include Andromache, wife of Hector; the foolish warrior Pandarus (*MWW* I.iii.74), whose breaking of a truce after single combat between Paris and Menelaus ruined a chance for peace; and the warrior Aeneas, son of Venus and a mortal father, whose adventures after the war form the basis of Virgil's *Aeneid*. Not included in *Troilus and Cressida*, but mentioned elsewhere, is Penthesilea (*TN* II.iii.176), queen of the Amazons (*1H6* I.ii.104; *3H6* I.iv.114; *Tim* I.ii.130 s.d.; *John* V.ii.154–58), a race of warrior women. She fought on the Trojan side and was slain by Achilles, who then paid tribute to her beauty and bravery.

The Greeks include Agamemnon, leader of the Greek forces (*3H6* II.ii.146–49; *2H4* II.iv.223; *H5* III.vi.6–7); Menelaus (*3H6* II.ii.146–49); the soothsayer Calchas; Achilles (*2H6* V.i.100; *LLL* V.ii.630), the war's greatest warrior and leader of troops called Myrmidons (*T&C* V.v.33); Patroclus, Achilles' best friend; Thersites (*Cym* IV.ii.252–53), who was slain by an angry Achilles; Diomedes; and Nestor, oldest and wisest of the Greeks (*1H6* II.v.6; *3H6* III.ii.188–90; *MV* I.i.56). Ajax (*LLL* IV.iii.6–7, V.ii.574; *Cym* IV.ii.252–53; *A&C* IV.xiv.38), son of the Argonaut Telamon (*2H6* V.i.26–27; *A&C* IV.xiii.2) and retriever of the bodies of Achilles and Patroclus, has a prominent role. Ajax committed suicide after the death of Achilles, not out of grief but out of anger at the presentation of Achilles' armor to Ulysses (Odysseus), rather than himself. Ulysses (*3H6* III.ii.188–90), who invented the stratagem of the Trojan Horse to breach the city's walls (*Per* I.iv.92), plays a large part in *Troilus and Cressida*. However, there is little mention in any of Shakespeare's works of Ulysses' postwar adventures, related in Homer's *Odyssey*. There are a few references to the witch Circe (*CE* V.i.271; *1H6* V.iii.35), who entertained him for a year during his voyage home, and one to his wife Penelope, who waited patiently, dutifully weaving, for his return (*Cor* I.iii.83–85). Sinon, a Greek who came weeping to the Trojans with a story of escaping an intended human sacrifice, convinced the Trojans to bring the massive horse filled with Greek soldiers into the city. He is not mentioned in *Troilus and Cressida* but is referred to elsewhere in Shakespeare's works (*3H6* III.ii.188–90; *Cym* III.iv.61; *TA* V.iii.85). The sight of the entire Greek army massed before Troy, with many of the same characters as *Troilus and Cressida*, is described in *The Rape of Lucrece* (1367–1568).

Shakespeare prefers the travels of Aeneas (*Cym* III.iv.60; *Temp* II.i.81; *A&C* IV.xiv.53) to those of Ulysses, probably because they were written in Latin and were therefore more accessible. After the war, Aeneas, carrying his old father Anchises on his back (*2H6* V.ii.62–64; *JC* I.ii.112–14), escaped from Troy. He and his band sailed past many dangerous obstacles, fleeing the Harpies and avoiding the narrow strait that contained the monster Scylla and the whirlpool Charybdis (*MV* III.v.16–17). Juno diverted him to the African city of Carthage, where its widowed queen, Dido (*TNK* IV.iii.14–15; *TS* I.i.154; *MV* V.i.9–12; *Temp* II.i.80; *R&J* II.iv.42; *A&C* IV.xiv.53), fell in love with him. He lingered, but when Mercury delivered a message from Jupiter to leave, he did so, and Dido killed herself in despair, her funeral pyre visible from the departing Trojan ship (*MND* I.i.173–74). Next Aeneas descended to Hades with the Sibyl (prophetess) of Cumae as his guide (*TS* I.ii.69). He eventually made his way to Italy, where his son Ascanius (*2H6* III.ii.116–18) founded the city of Alba Longa, in which the founders of Rome, Romulus and Remus, were born.

One of the greatest heroes, and certainly the strongest, was Hercules (Heracles), son of Jupiter and Alcmena. Jupiter had disguised himself not as an animal but as Alcmena's husband, Amphitryon, son of Alcaeus. It was Hercules' ostensible descent from Alcaeus that gave him the alternate name Alcides (*1H6* IV.vii.60; *TS* I.ii.255–56). A jealous Juno tried to destroy the baby Hercules, sending two snakes to kill him in his cradle, but he strangled them (*LLL* V.i.126–37). Hercules was brave and strong (*MAAN* IV.i.320), but subject to cycles of madness, violence, and penitence. After one such episode, he was sentenced to perform twelve labors under the supervision of his cowardly cousin Eurystheus (*MAAN* II.i.351–52; *Cor* IV.i.17–18). One of these labors was to kill the Nemean lion, which could not be harmed by any weapon. Hercules strangled the lion with his bare hands and wore its skin afterward as a cloak (*LLL* IV.i.90; *John* II.i.139–46; *TNK* I.i.66–68). Another of the labors was to kill the Hydra, a monster with nine heads, each of which sprouted two new heads if severed from the body (*2H4* IV.ii.38; *H5* I.i.35; *1H4* V.iv.23; *Oth*

II.iii.302; *Cor* III.i.93). Another task was to steal the golden apples of the Hesperides (*Per* I.i.28–30; *LLL* IV.iii.337–38), which required that Hercules slay a dragon and enlist the aid of Atlas.

After his labors were complete, Hercules went mad again. This time he was condemned to serve three years as a slave in the house of Queen Omphale of Lydia, with whom he fell in love. He performed feminine tasks like spinning while she ordered him about and wore his lion's skin (*MAAN* II.i.244; *LLL* I.ii.66–67). Freed from this confinement, he married again, but his new wife grew jealous and painted his robe with a substance she thought was a love potion. Actually, it was a powerful poison given to her by a dying enemy of Hercules, the centaur Nessus. When Hercules put on the robe that his page Lichas (*MV* II.i.32–35; *A&C* IV.xii.43–47) brought, he was consumed with pain He slew Lichas but could not die himself until he lay down on his own funeral pyre and, dying, ascended to Olympus as an immortal.

Theseus also had many adventures. A cousin of Hercules, he killed the notorious bandit Procrustes and ended the influence of the witch Medea over his father, Aegeus. Next he traveled to Crete, which had long demanded occasional sacrifices of Athenian youths and maidens to a beast called the minotaur, which had the body of a man and the head of a bull. Theseus entered King Minos's labyrinth (*1H6* V.iii.188–89; *T&C* II.iii.2), the maze in which the beast lived, killed it, and escaped with the help of Minos's daughter Ariadne (*2GV* IV.iv.167–68). He abandoned Ariadne on the island of Naxos and sailed home, where an incorrect signal from the ship caused Aegeus to think his son was dead. Aegeus flung himself into the sea now known as the Aegean, and drowned. Theseus, now king of Athens, traveled to the land of the Amazons and brought back their queen, Hippolyta, to be his wife. His marriage to her is part of two Shakespeare plays, *The Two Noble Kinsmen* and *A Midsummer Night's Dream*.

Other heroes mentioned in Shakespeare's works include Perseus, who slew the Gorgon (*Mac* II.iii.72) Medusa and rescued the princess Andromeda from a sea monster (*H5* III.vii.21; *T&C* I.iii.41–42, IV.v.185); Castor (*TNK* III.vi.137), Helen of Troy's brother, whose divine twin Pollux gave up half his own immortality to share it with his brother; Arion, a poet whose beautiful music caused a dolphin to rescue him from drowning (*TN* I.ii.15); and Cadmus (*MND* IV.i.113), brother of Europa, slayer of a dragon and founder of Thebes. Orpheus (*2GV* III.ii.77–80, *MV* V.i.80), a musician so gifted he could make trees and rocks move, is mentioned in connection with his doomed attempt to retrieve his beloved wife, Eurydice, from the land of the dead. His music won Pluto's consent, but there was one condition: he must not look back at her until they reached the surface. Unable to believe she was really behind him, he glanced back and lost her forever (*RL* 553).

Other Mythologies

Almost all mythological references in Shakespeare's works are to Greek and Roman tales, but there are exceptions. He does mention some legendary British kings, among them Gorboduc (*TN* IV.ii.15), a son of King Lear, and Uther Pendragon (*1H6* III.ii.95), father of King Arthur. The Kings Lear and Cymbeline, of course, had whole plays devoted to them. The Egyptian goddess Isis is, appropriately enough, Cleopatra's special guardian (*A&C* I.ii.65, III.iii.46), and Caliban's Algerian mother is said to have worshiped a god named Setebos (*Temp* I.ii.375, V.i.261), perhaps some form of the evil Egyptian god Set. *See also* Basilisk; Griffin; Mermaid; Phoenix; Religion; Salamander; Unicorn.

Navy

The navy (*A&C* IV.v.20) was, to a large extent, the nation's merchant fleet, extended somewhat by government resources. At Elizabeth I's death in 1603, there were only twenty-nine Royal Navy warships of 100 tons or more, and at James I's death in 1625, the number had been increased by only one ship. When war was declared or threatened, the navy simply hired merchant vessels, impressed merchant crews (*A&C* III.vii.34–36), and added a few more guns. Because the strength of the navy depended on the number and size of England's merchant ships, a reward of 5s per ton was paid to those who constructed merchant vessels.

Warships were rigged no differently than merchantmen, were sailed no differently, and differed chiefly in their crews and in the purpose to which the ships were put. The pinnace, for example, was in the navy a scout or advice vessel (a swift boat carrying orders or dispatches), though it could be used in combat if necessary. The regular officers and men present on a merchantman were supplemented, on a ship of war, by a master gunner (*Temp* II.ii.47), a captain, and a lieutenant who served as the captain's second in command. In some cases, an admiral might be aboard, and then his presence was indicated by a lantern hung in the stern of the ship (*1H4* III.iii.26–27). Naval discipline was generally stricter than on board a merchant ship. Liars were punished by being made subordinate to the lowest deckhands, the swabbers; more serious offenders were keelhauled (fastened to a line running from a yardarm, under the hull of the ship, and back to the opposite yardarm, and twice dragged along this path), ducked, whipped, or, in cases of mutiny or similarly severe crimes, hanged.

Naval tactics fell into two general categories, based either on gunnery or on boarding. Gunnery used cannon fire to cripple an enemy from a distance, but not many crews had the skill to fire very precisely, and the cannon of the day were not very accurate even when properly handled. Seizing the enemy ship with huge grappling hooks, drawing the two ships close together, and then engaging in hand-to-hand combat was the more popular approach (*TN* V.i.53–62). It was also preferred by Shakespeare, who found in the images of grappling, boarding, and invading the opponent's hatches (small entrances to the lower decks) a metaphor for sexual conquest (*MWW* II.i.88–91; *TS* I.ii.94; *TNK* II.ii.32; *LLL* II.i.218). He rarely uses any other metaphors lifted from naval battle tactics, though he makes reference to boarding a "lawful prize" (*Oth* I.ii.49–50), a legitimate enemy in whose sale price and cargo the triumphant captain and crew shared; another to "fights" (*MWW* II.ii.131), the colored cloth screens used to hide the crew from enemy fire; and another to "fetches" (*Lear* II.iii.87), which can mean either tricks and stratagems or instances of tacking (sailing at an angle in one direction, then another, in order to head into a contrary wind). A sea fight and the taking of a prize is depicted in *2 Henry VI* (IV.i). *See also* Army; Transportation.

Needlework

Sewing was a principal task of women in Shakespeare's time, which probably surprises no one. Without much difficulty, one can conjure an image of the Renaissance housewife, sewing or embroidering with her maidservants (*TNK* II.i.184–87) near the fire on stools that are perhaps covered with cushions of their own making. This picture is not inaccurate, but neither is it complete. Not all Renaissance needlework was done by women, and not all of it was done at home.

Many pieces came from abroad. Great houses might have silk damask from China with a pattern already woven in or stitched on, or an Indian cotton quilt already stitched in multiple colors on a plain white background. Some silk embroidery was imported from Italy, like the "Valance of Venice gold in needlework" of *The Taming of the Shrew* (II.i.347), and other types of work came from Flanders and France. Sometimes only the materials came from overseas; those who could afford it, for example, preferred Spanish silk thread, because it was considered more colorfast than that dyed in London. Even when items with decorative stitching did not come from Asia or from other parts of Europe, they might be manufactured in various parts of England. Norwich had at least some makers of "Turkeywork"—Turkish-style carpets—and London had professional "silkwomen" and male embroiderers whose wares were sold in other parts of the country.

Professional male needleworkers might belong to the staff of a great household; Bess of Hardwick, Countess of Shrewsbury, described certain items in her

A professional embroiderer at work, using a rectangular frame. From *Panoplia*, illustrated by Jost Amman. Reproduced from the Collections of the Library of Congress.

house as having been made by "grooms, women, and some boys I kept." A professional embroiderer might also travel between great houses, selling his services. He did fine work himself or simply drew patterns for the women of the house to fill in after his departure. If no itinerant embroiderer was available, the women might enlist any nearby craftsmen whose skills included drawing, and get him to set out their patterns for them. Failing this, they could sketch pictures from books, buy ready-made patterns printed either on paper or on canvas, or prick holes in a picture and "trace" it onto the cloth by rubbing charcoal through the holes.

Types and Techniques

There was plenty of ordinary sewing to be done, in which pieces of fabric were attached to one another to create garments or household items, but there were also several types of decorative sewing. One of these was embroidery, which did not simply mean any kind of pictorial sewing. Embroidery referred specifically to expensive thread such as silk, gold, or silver, applied to an equally expensive background of silk, velvet, or other fine material, and often incorporating appliqués of other expensive fabrics such as cloth-of-gold. It took a very long time, was done by professionals, and cost much more than adding braid or fringe to an object. Metal thread could cost £3 6s per pound, more than most servants made in a year; its cost, bulk, and stiffness meant that it was usually not passed through all the layers of fabric but simply pinned down ("couched" or "laid") at regular intervals with less expensive thread.

Some types of embroidery incorporated even more precious materials. Metal strips, spangles, and purl (a twisted, springlike metal thread) might be added to the design. Beads and seed pearls (*TS* II.i.346), too, were used. This type of embroidery was far too expensive for use in all but the homes of the rich, where it was employed on bed hangings, other furnishings, and clothing (*TNK* II.i.184–87).

"Wrought" work was stitched with linen on a linen ground and was created by seamstresses. Work in silk or metal on linen, on the other hand, was the province of silkwomen, who made silk and metal thread, decorated linen, and made braid and fringe. These types of sewing were done by amateurs as well.

When linen canvas was covered entirely by stitches, in either silk or worsted ("crewel") thread, it was known as "needlework." The most common stitches used in this technique were the cross, tent (half, petepoint, *petit point*), and Gobelin stitches. Other stitches used at the time included stem, whipped stem, chain, speckling, knotted, double-running, coral, overcast, blanket, back, plait or braid, brick, and satin. This technique was practiced by both sexes and by both amateurs and professionals. The resulting products were used to decorate chairs, stools, cupboards, tables, book covers, pincushions, purses, bed hangings, and especially cushions.

Often needlework was used to fill in "slips," preprinted or drawn patterns of flowers, birds, animals, or leaves (*Per* V.Cho.5–8), which were completed by the women of the house and then attached as appliqués to a more expensive fabric by a professional male embroiderer.

Another technique used many of the available stitches to place a picture or design on an exposed linen ground. This was often done to clothing such as smocks (*WT* IV.iv.208–11) and handkerchiefs (*Oth* III.iv.178; *LC* 15–17), or to bed and table linens too large to be completely covered with stitching. Sometimes white stitches were used on white fabric to create an effect of texture rather than color.

Motifs included stories from the classics or from the Bible, initials, heraldic devices and shields, frets (lattices), antics (grotesques such as masks, gargoyles, or distorted animals), realistic flowers (*TNK* II.i.184; *MND* III.ii.203–5), and arabesques.

Equipment

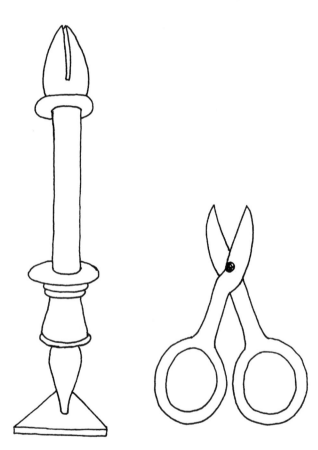

Broach and embroidery scissors.

Whether done by the women of the home or by professionals, sewing was a specialized skill. In his descriptions of it, Shakespeare demonstrates that he has been an observer of the process, but not a participant. He knows, for example, that women sit and sew; he places Volumnia and Virgilia on stools (*Cor* I.iii.1 s.d.) and Helena and Hermia on cushions (*MND* III.ii.205) for this purpose. He knows that sometimes they talk or sing to pass the time while working (*MND* III.ii.203–8). He places their basic tools in their hands—thimbles (*John* V.ii.156; *T&C* II.i.81), needles (*TS* II.i.25; *Cym* I.i.168; *John* V.iv.11; *Oth* IV.i.187–88), pins (*2H4* IV.iii.53; *1H4* IV.ii.22; *MM* II.i.94, II.ii.45; *MWW* I.i.109), and thread. He knows that thread wound into a ball is called a clew (*AW* I.iii.183) and that thread can be twisted (*Cor* V.vi.95) or "sleided," that is, smooth (*Per* IV.Cho.21). One of his finest renderings of women's sewing habits is Lucrece's placement of her needle not in a pincushion, but in a nearby glove (*RL* 317). One can imagine him watching his own wife finishing her sewing and storing her needle in just such a way.

However, he misses some of the details that a woman, or a professional needleworker, would no doubt have included. For him, all decorative sewing is embroidery (*3H6* II.v.44; *MWW* V.v.73), done with silk thread on the fine linen known as cambric (*Cor* I.iii.85–87). He skips entirely over other types of thread, other techniques, and the rest of the requisite tools, such as shears, broaches (used for winding metal thread), and beams or tents (rectangular wooden frames on which the fabric was stretched and held in place during stitching). *See also* Household Objects; Housework.

News

There were no daily newspapers and no magazines in Shakespeare's day. News, therefore, traveled in a haphazard fashion, spread by word of mouth, brought by messengers (*1H6* I.i.), carried in letters, and sung in ballads. It could be conveyed more slowly through printed pamphlets or broadsides (posters), and still more slowly through books. Government notices could be announced by heralds or criers (*Ham* III.ii.3–4), but a more common practice was to print up bills (*MAAN* I.i.37; *AYLI* I.ii.120) or proclamations (*3H6* V.v.9; *R3* IV.iv.517; *TA* I.i.190; *H8* I.iii.17–18), and nail them to posts (*WT* III.ii.99–100) so that the literate could read them aloud and the illiterate could listen. Sometimes the crown, when an important or controversial matter was being decided, issued its own pamphlet to counter arguments being made against its position. At other times, since there was no free press, it simply suppressed offending pamphlets and arrested the publishers or writers. In one case, an author who had written against a proposed French marriage for Elizabeth I was sentenced to have his right hand lopped off.

Christopher Barker, who held the patent to print royal proclamations, was fortunately safe from these sorts of punishments, but he had other problems. He complained to Lord Burghley in 1582 that new proclamations came in without warning and had to be printed quickly, requiring him to undo all his set type for other projects and then laboriously reset it when the proclamations were completed. He judged that he lost money six times for every one time that he made a profit from this royal patronage.

Nine Worthies

Masques, in which a group of players dressed up as historical personages, literary characters, or embodied virtues or vices, were a common element in plays and festivals during the Renaissance. One popular subject was the

Nine Worthies, who embodied masculine and warlike virtues. Traditionally, they included three classical, three biblical, and three medieval heroes.

The classical heroes were usually Hector, Alexander the Great, and Julius Caesar. Alexander seems a natural choice, because he conquered most of the world known to him. Caesar seems equally promising, since he, too, was a great military leader and headed the conquest of Britain. However, Hector may seem to have been an odd choice, since he was a great warrior, but the greatest of the Trojans—the defeated side in the Trojan War. It might seem more natural to pick Achilles, the greatest of the Greeks, who killed Hector in battle. The reason Hector was selected was probably the English belief that Rome had been founded by Trojan refugees and that Rome had passed along her sovereignty to England. Thus Hector was, in a convoluted way, the ancestor of Britain.

The biblical heroes were Joshua, who conquered Israel after Moses' death and destroyed the walls of Jericho; David, a mighty king and the slayer of Goliath; and Judas Maccabeus, who led a revolt against Rome and allowed the Temple in Jerusalem to be cleansed. The medieval heroes were King Arthur, a legendary British king; Charlemagne, founder of the Holy Roman Empire; and Godfrey of Bouillon (or Boulogne), of all the worthies the most obscure today. Godfrey participated in the First Crusade and was idealized afterward as the model Christian knight. He is the hero of Thomas Heywood's play *The Four Prentices of London*, which was probably written in the early 1590s.

Shakespeare mentions the Nine Worthies briefly in *2 Henry IV* (II.iv.224), but he makes them the subject of hundreds of lines in Act V of *Love's Labor's Lost* (V.i.114–40, V.ii.487–720). Here, perhaps because he found Hector and Caesar difficult subjects for comedy, he replaces them with Hercules and Pompey the Great (whose name sounds enough like "pompion"—pumpkin—to be funny all by itself). He was not alone in changing the cast; a 1578 pageant, for example, substituted Guy of Warwick for Godfrey. *See also* Masque.

Noble

A coin introduced by Edward III with a value of 80d (or 6s 8d), the noble's obverse showed the king, armored, aboard a ship, holding a sword and a shield decorated with the quartered arms of England and France. The legend read EDWAR D GRA REX ANGL Z FRANC DNS HYB, an abbreviated way of writing "Edward, by the grace of God (Dei Gratia) King (REX) of England (ANGL) and (Z—a shortened Latin "et") France, Lord (Dominus) of Ireland (HYB—for Hibernia). On the reverse a shape like a fat eight-petaled flower surrounded a cross with fleur-de-lis endings and a lion and crown between each two arms of the cross. The legend around the rim read IHC TRANSIENS PER MEDIVM ILLORVM IBAT (Jesus, passing

Henry VI noble. Actual size is 33 mm in diameter. © 2002 The American Numismatic Society. All rights reserved.

through the midst of them, went his way). The coin was abandoned in the reign of Edward IV and replaced by the ryal (or royal) and the angel, but Shakespeare uses it appropriately in his histories (*1H6* V.iv.23; *1H4* II.iv.290–94; *2H4* II.i.154; *H5* II.i.108–16; *R2* I.i.88), for it was the standard gold coin during the relevant reigns. *See also* Angel; Money.

Nursing

Breast-feeding was often performed by a child's own mother, particularly among the poor and the lower middle class. Among those of greater means, however, it was common to hire a wet nurse. This was a servant who had weaned a child of her own and, instead of allowing her milk to dry up, nursed another's child for pay. If the household could not afford to hire a full-time nurse, the newborn might be sent to a nearby village to stay in the nurse's home. The astrologer John Dee paid a nurse 6s per month to nurse his daughter, born in 1581.

The reasons for hiring a wet nurse included convenience, the inability of the mother to produce sufficient or satisfactory milk, the death of the mother in childbirth (*Per* III.i.79–80), and a fear that breast-feeding would be damaging to the mother's health or appearance. There was also a general medical prohibition against sexual intercourse during lactation, so it is possible that a desire for resumed sexual relations, on the part of the wife, the husband, or both, motivated the hiring of a wet nurse. The term "wet nurse" actually came into common use later, to distinguish it from the separate job of tending to the sick; Shakespeare always uses the term "nurse" without qualification (*2H6* IV.ii.141).

It was important to find the right sort of woman to be the nurse, for not only nutrition but character was believed to be carried in the breast milk (*AYLI* IV.i.170–72; *WT* II.i.56–58). Ideally, a nurse was supposed to be clean, ruddy-skinned, well-spoken, plump, and pleasant. It was believed, though this superstition was sometimes attacked by physicians, that it was best if the nurse's last child had been the same sex as her client's. This is the case with Juliet's nurse, who lost a daughter of her own at about the time of Juliet's birth (*R&J* I.iii.18–20). Those who argued against the hiring of nurses raised suspicions about allowing one's child to be formed and morally or intellectually contaminated by a woman of low education and dubious virtue. They pointed out that a nurse could never love the baby as much, or attend to it as scrupulously, as the birth mother (*Cor* II.i.209–11). Nevertheless, Shakespeare's nurses are often sympathetic characters. The one in *Romeo and Juliet*, if not very wise or consistent, loves Juliet very much, and Marina is heartbroken at the death of hers (*Per* IV.i.11). Sonnet 22 speaks of "thy heart, which I will keep so chary / As tender nurse her babe from faring ill." Shakespeare thus appears to have had no prejudice against nurses.

Shakespeare's works include many references to breast-feeding by both mothers (*1H6* V.iv.27–29) and nurses. There are a few unpleasant images, such as that of "the infant, / Mewling and puking in the nurse's arms" (*AYLI* II.vii.142–43), and a few tragic or brutal ones, such as Lady Macbeth's vision of slaying a nursing baby (*Mac* I.vii.54–59), or that of an infant dying as it nurses (*2H6* III.ii.392–93). However, for the most part the scenes of nursing are tender, domestic, and convincing. Most of them, except for the occasional presence of the nurse herself, could equally apply to breast-feeding mothers today. The nurse nods off as the baby sucks (*A&C* V.ii.309–10), sings a lullaby (*TA* II.iii.28–29), or tells it a story to stop its crying (*RL* 813–14). The mother feels a rush of love for the baby as it smiles up at her (*Mac* I.vii.54–56) or suffers if the baby is taken away (*WT* III.ii.96–98). The baby delays nursing (*Ham* V.vii.190–91) or, in a "testy" mood, "scratch[es] the nurse" (*2GV* I.ii.58). *See also* Pregnancy and Childbirth; Servants.

Oaths

Oaths were of two kinds: serious vows, usually of loyalty to a comrade, king, or lover; and frivolous oaths uttered for emphasis. The former were shocking only if broken (and if made out of sexual passion, not shocking even then). The latter were used expressly to shock or at least to call attention to something, and were often perverse uses of the same sorts of religious oaths used in the former case.

Serious oaths (*2H6* III.ii.153–58, V.i.179–90; *3H6* I.i.201; *JC* II.i.126–40; *R2* I.iii.14, 16–25, 178–92) like marriage vows (*Ham* III.iv.43–46; *R&J* III.v.207–10) and vows of fealty depended for their force on the religious faith of the person making them. It was usually necessary to call on some religious force—God, a saint, the Bible (*Temp* II.ii.130; *LLL* IV.iii.247), a Roman god or goddess—to punish the votary if he broke his vow (*3H6* II.iii.29, 34), and this of course was meaningless if the oath taker had no fear of real punishment. Nevertheless, there was a second kind of penalty that awaited the perjurer (*3H6* V.v.34, 40), the penalty of public disapproval. This made context all-important. One who broke a sacred vow was loathsome; one who merely accented his speech with oaths, even religiously based oaths, was perhaps distasteful, perhaps fashionable, but not forsworn (*2H4* IV.v.124–26; *H5* III.vi.76; *1H4* III.iii.15; *Lear* III.iv.87–88; *Ham* III.iii.91; *Cym* II.i.1–4). The subtleties of making and breaking oaths comprise much of the plot of *Love's Labor's Lost*; those interested in this topic should pay special attention to acts and scenes I.i, II.i, and IV.iii.

Most frivolous oaths, too, had a Christian basis, though this was not always readily apparent. The connection was easy to make in the case of explicit swearing by saints (*TS* I.i.249, III.ii.81; *R3* I.i.138, I.ii.36, I.iii.45, III.iii.75), the Holy Family (*2H6* II.i.51; *MWW* IV.ii.187), or the emblems of the church: the Mass (*2H4* V.iii.13; *MAAN* IV.ii.52; *MWW* IV.ii.196; *Ham* V.i.55), the rood or cross of the Crucifixion (*2H4* III.ii.3; *Ham* III.iv.15), the communion Host (*R&J* III.v.177; *TNK* III.v.48), a relic or some other sacred object ("halidom," *2GV* IV.ii.135), and the soul (*MAAN* V.i.274). Even plays set in pre–Christian times have explicit or implicit references to Christianity in their oaths, for in this as in so many other things, Shakespeare was not wedded to historical accuracy.

The relationship to religion was more distant in the case of oaths that had been distorted so as to make them gentler and less blasphemous. Thus "by the Virgin Mary" became "By'r Lakin" (*Temp* III.iii.1; *MND* III.i.12) or the mild "Marry," so inoffensive as hardly to be an oath at all but a simple interjection (*CE* II.ii.50; *2H6* I.iii.5). "God's light" became " 'Slight" (*TN* II.v.31), "God's foot" became " 's foot" or "Fut" (*Lear* I.ii.134), "God's mercy" became " 'Ods pittikins" (*Cym* IV.ii.293), and

"God's wounds" became "Od's nouns" (*MWW* IV.i.23), "by goggs woones" (*TS* III.ii.159), or "Zounds" (*Oth* I.i.83; *R&J* III.i.101, 150; *R3* I.iv.126, 147; *TA* IV.ii.71). In addition to "s" or "ods," "God's" was sometimes abbreviated to "cocks" or "cox" in references to the passion of Christ (*TS* IV.i.108; *AW* V.ii.40–41). "Perdie" (*CE* IV.iv.70) was a corruption of the French *par Dé*, "by God."

Even milder oaths, used by women or by Puritans, included "What the goodyear" (*MAAN* I.iii.1; *MWW* I.iv.116–17), "By cock and pie" (*2H4* V.i.1; *MWW* I.i.290), and "By yea and no" (*2H4* III.ii.9). "I' fecks" (*WT* I.ii.120) was an alteration of "in faith"; "Mehercle" of "by Hercules" (*LLL* IV.ii.78). "Beshrew" was a gentle condemnation followed by the object of opprobrium, often a part of the swearer's self, as in beshrew my heart, beshrew my hand, beshrew me, and so on (*MAAN* V.i.55; *R&J* III.v.223, *2GV* I.i.126). Similar to "beshrew" in usage, and resembling the "damn it" of today, were wishes for disease to befall the source of one's troubles, as in "Plague on't" (*TN* III.iv.288) or "Pox on't" (*TN* III.iv.285). That mild swearing was socially acceptable, at least in most circumstances and among friends, is revealed by the frequency of casual swearing in the plays and by the fact that Hotspur even teases his wife for her watered-down cursing (*1H4* III.i.244–53). That not everyone found swearing acceptable is revealed in some of the treatises of the day, such as Andrew Boorde's *Dyetary of Helth*, in which the author complains that "in all the worlde there is not such odyble swearyng as is used in Englande, specyally amonge youth & chyldren, which is a detestable thyng to here it, and no man doth go aboute to punysshe it." Yet even this denunciation of swearing reveals how common and how widespread the habit was.

Occupations

Though there were many types of jobs in Shakespearean England, training was almost always much the same. People learned by doing, whether they were farm children or craftsmen's apprentices. Generally speaking, workers fell into one of four classes: farmers and drovers, artisans, merchants, and service providers. (Many of the occupations included in these categories, such as tanner, mercer, glover, yeoman farmer, parson, lawyer, merchant, and midwife, are described elsewhere in this book. A fifth class (thieves), which preyed on the other four, is described elsewhere as well.) This entry is concerned with a few trades and with the manner in which trades were learned and regulated.

Farmers and Drovers

Farmers, who raised produce and livestock, and drovers (*MAAN* II.i.188–89), who moved the livestock from farm to market, were essential to the feeding of the nation. They do not, however, fare well in Shakespeare's works. His "clowns" (*AYLI* V.i.11) and "hinds" (*AYLI* I.i.18)—both terms for country bumpkins—are straightforward but often dim-witted, and a standard butt of his jokes. They are discussed in more depth in the Farming entry. Three other types of workers lived directly or indirectly off the land. One was the milkmaid (*MM* I.ii.176), who tended the dairy animals, milked them, and either carried the milk to market or made cheese and butter from it. The second was the poulter, who sold fowl (*1H4* II.iv.442), and the third was the gatherer of samphire, a pungent marine plant that was served pickled, whom Edgar pretends to see clinging to the cliffs of Dover (*Lear* IV.vi.14–15). All these trades were learned by watching and then doing, being taught and corrected by more experienced workers. However, the samphire pickers, the drovers, the dairymaids, and others like them had no guild or trade organization, and there were no restrictions on entering these occupations except the willingness to do the work.

Artisans

Opening a shop took greater resources. The shop building itself could be a sizable investment, though contemporary illustrations show most workshops as relatively small and bare. The most prominent, and usually the most costly, items were the tools and materials. There was a wide range of cost for tools. For a tailor or botcher (clothes mender—see *TN* I.v.47; *AW* IV.iii.189; *Cor* II.i.90–92), the tools—scissors, needles, pins, and a yardstick—were small, relatively cheap, and portable. Huge inventories were not carried, for a botcher's customer supplied the items to be mended, and a tailor's brought him the fabric to be made up into garments. Tinkers' tools, though slightly more cumbersome, were still portable enough to permit these pot menders to travel door-to-door fixing dents, holes, and broken handles. Some tinkers carried their tools in a pigskin "budget" or pouch (*WT* IV.iii.20); others traveled with a dog who carried a pack. Tinkers had a bad reputation as rogues, cheats, and thieves, and Shakespeare never intends it as a compliment when he compares some-one to this sort of itinerant scoundrel (*2H6* III.ii.277; *TS* Ind.ii.21, 73; *TN* II.iii.89; *WT* IV.iii.98).

There were plenty of more reputable craftsmen. Fullers felted wool cloth by washing it in fuller's earth (definined by the *Oxford English Dictionary* as "a hydrous silicate of alumina"). The process was sometimes assisted by mill-driven hammers, sometimes by "walkers" who walked across the cloth as it soaked. Glaziers made glass and set it into windowpanes, constructed stained-glass windows, or made dishes and glasses. Ceramic dishes were made by potters (*1H6* I.v.19); pewter ones, by pewterers (*2H4* III.ii.267), who prided themselves on their ability to make anything in pewter that could be made in silver. In the port towns, there might be shipwrights (*Ham* V.i.42), ropemakers, and sailmakers (*TS* V.i.75) as well. Craftsmen of all sorts wore simple, durable clothing and often protected their clothes with cloth or leather aprons (*Cor* IV.vi.97; *2H6* IV.ii.13–14). This singled them out as "mechanicals" (*2H6* I.iii.195; *JC* I.i.3–5), or manual laborers, and made it clear to all that they were not gentlemen. Nevertheless, some gentlemen had great respect for artisans. William Harrison praised them for producing objects that were "fine and curious to the eye" as well as "strong and substantial," and judged "that they were never so excellent in their trades as at this present."

Apprenticeship and Guilds

Of all occupations, crafts—in which some product was manufactured according to a time-honored and secret practice called a "mystery"—were the most likely to have organized trade guilds. These guilds, usually specific to a single town, were run by a board of master craftsmen and governed all aspects of the trade in that town. They regulated terms of apprenticeship, settled disputes between guild members, determined worthiness to enter the trade, limited the number of craftsmen to keep incomes high, and lobbied the government for regulations and relief that benefited their membership. (The heraldic shields of the London Livery Companies, the principal guilds of that city, can be seen in John Norden's map of London in the Places entry.)

They were often called upon to enforce the terms of apprenticeship. Under this system, a child, usually a boy but sometimes a girl, was signed over to a master craftsman for a specified period of time. This was usually, but not always, seven years, as outlined in the 1563 Statute of Artificers. The apprentice (*2H6* I.iii.ch., II.iii.ch.; *R2* I.iii.270) was required to be well-behaved, attentive, and industrious, doing and learning whatever was dictated by the master. In return, the master was to provide the apprentice with humble but serviceable clothing, room, board, and, if specified in the articles of indenture, an education. The control exercised over apprentices, and the discipline imposed on them, led some of them to run away, but those who stayed eventually became journeymen and then masters, with the right to enter the trade and open shops of their own.

Service Providers

Some workers provided services rather than goods. These included chimney sweeps (*Cym* IV.ii.263; *LLL* IV.iii.263), who went door-to-door with the thorn bushes they used to scrub flues; town criers (*MWW* V.v.43), who spread news; drawers (*2H4* II.ii.170–71), or tavern waiters; factors (*A&C* II.vi.10), or agents for other tradesmen or for gentlemen; and carmen (*2H4* III.ii.322), who carted goods from place to place and who were famous as skillful whistlers. One of Shakespeare's characters has held a variety of occupations, most of them service jobs:

he hath been since an ape-bearer; then a process-server, a bailiff: then he compassed a motion of the Prodigal Son, and married a tinker's wife within a mile where my land and living lies. (*WT* IV.iii.96–99)

In other words, the character in question has traveled with a performing monkey, served legal writs and summonses, been a bailiff or law officer, operated a puppet show, and finally married a tradesman's widow. All of the jobs mentioned were slightly disreputable or unsavory, required little training, and were unregulated by guilds. Incidentally, marrying a craftsman's widow was a common route to success, for it brought one a shop, tools, apprentices, and someone—the widow—who presumably knew the trade. *See also* Alehouse; Army; Education; Fabric; Farming; Gloves; Iron; Law; Leather; Medical Practitioners; Money; Needlework; Religion; Servants.

Penny

The silver penny was, for centuries, England's standard and often its only coin. It was based on an eighth-century French system that struck 240 denarii from each pound (*libra*) of silver. The libra gave its name to the French livre and the Italian lira and its abbreviations (£, lb.) to the English units of money and weight. The denarius became the French denier; as with the pound, the English kept the symbol but changed the name, borrowing *pfennig* from Germanic languages and turning it into "penny," but abbreviating it as "d."

By Shakespeare's day, however, the penny (*2H6* III.i.109, IV.ii.67; *AYLI* II.v.26; *AW* V.ii.37; *LLL* III.i.27, 101) was no longer the universal type of coin, but one of many pieces of small silver. A pennyworth was now a token amount (*2H6* I.i.220; *MAAN* II.iii.41; *R&J* IV.v.4)—enough to buy a bit of sugar (*1H4* II.iv.4–28), a piece of gingerbread (*LLL* V.i.68–69), nine sparrows (*T&C* II.i.71–73), or a gallows rope (*Cym* V.iv.136–37).

The 1583–1603 penny of Elizabeth I. Actual size is 13 mm in diameter. © 2002 The American Numismatic Society. All rights reserved.

Elizabeth I's pennies of 1583 to 1603 show her portrait bust on the obverse with E D G (for *Elizabeth Dei gratia*, Elizabeth by the grace of God) ROSA SINE SPINA (rose without a thorn). The reverse bore the royal arms and long cross, and the words CIVITAS LONDON. Elizabeth's successor, James I, altered the royal arms to include Ireland and his native Scotland, and left off the reverse motto entirely. On the obverse appeared his portrait and I (IACOBUS) D G ROSA SINE SPINA. From 1604 to 1618 the penny was simpler still, with the royal portrait and arms replaced by a

thistle on one side and a rose on the other, the thistle accompanied by
TVEATVR VNITA DEVS (May God protect united things, i.e., the kingdoms
of Scotland and England) and the rose by the ROSA legend. *See also* Groat;
Money; Shilling.

Phoenix

The phoenix, subject of Shakespeare's poem *The Phoenix and the Turtle*
and mentioned elsewhere in his writings (*AW* I.i.170; *A&C* III.ii.12; *S*
19), was a mythical bird. The Greek historian Herodotus reported hearing that it came from Arabia (*Cym* I.vi.17; *Temp* III.iii.21–24) and appeared once every 500 years in Egypt to bury its myrrh-covered dead
parent. However, he mentioned nothing about its death and rebirth in

fire, an integral part of the
bird's later mythology, and he
himself was disinclined to believe in its existence. Pliny the
Elder, too, treated the stories
with skepticism, but described
the phoenix as eaglelike, with
purple plumage, a gold neck, a
blue-and-rose-colored tail, tufts
at the throat, and a crest on the
head. He reported that it lived
540 years, was sacred to the sun
god, and died upon a nest it
had constructed of spices,
whereupon a new phoenix
emerged, not from fire or ashes,
but from a larva that emerged
from the dead bird (*H8* V.v.39–
42). Again, the story ran that it
took great care to bury its dead

Phoenix from *Mythologia Ethica*, 1579, by Arnold Freitag.

parent. Tacitus believed in the bird but not necessarily in the reports of
its habits, and he related the notion that the parent was consigned to
some sort of sacred flame after the new bird had been born. Not until
about 200 years after Tacitus did the myth take on the form by which it
was best known in the Renaissance, with an androgynous or female bird
living a thousand years, flying to Syria (because of the similarity of
"phoenix" and "Phoenicia") to make a spice nest, and bursting into
flames during or after death, with its offspring carrying its ashes and the
remnants of the spices to the temple of the sun.

The phoenix was a powerful symbol of renewal and eternity in Renaissance art, and Elizabeth I was particularly fond of it. No doubt her feelings were influenced both by the Christian symbolism of life after death and by the comforting idea of an unmated and childless creature being able to reproduce. The phoenix, even more attractively, was unique in all the world; an English translation of Claude Paradin's French book of emblems, used by those in search of symbolic representations of themselves or their families, showed a phoenix with the legend *Unica semper avis*: "But always one Phenix in the world at once." On an enameled pendant from c. 1570–80, it appears on the back of a gold bust of Elizabeth I, where it is depicted with a pheasant-like head and crest and eaglelike hooked beak.

Pitch

A byproduct of turpentine or tar production, pitch is a dark, sticky, flammable resin. The word "pitch" was also sometimes applied to evergreen saps or resins, even those which had not been through any manufacturing process. Shakespeare almost always uses the word in the sense of something black and defiling (*1H4* II.iv.418–19; *MAAN* III.iii.56; *LLL* III.i.196, IV.iii.3); occasionally, he speaks of it as something that catches fire or hastens combustion (*1H6* V.iv.57; *Temp* I.ii.3).

Places

The following maps are provided to assist readers in locating the places mentioned by Shakespeare. In using the maps, please be aware of the following:

1. The maps are drawn to different scales.
2. Numbers designate countries or regions. These countries or regions have had different borders at different times, and many of these borders changed during Shakespeare's life and were, in any case, not the same as those in Julius Caesar's day, or Henry VI's, or Mark Antony's. Therefore the borders are modern; and some borders, especially in eastern Europe, where Shakespeare tends to refer to regions rather than to nations, have been omitted altogether.
3. All locations are approximate.
4. Citations from Shakespeare's work follow the place name in each key.
5. The map of London and Westminster is greatly simplified.

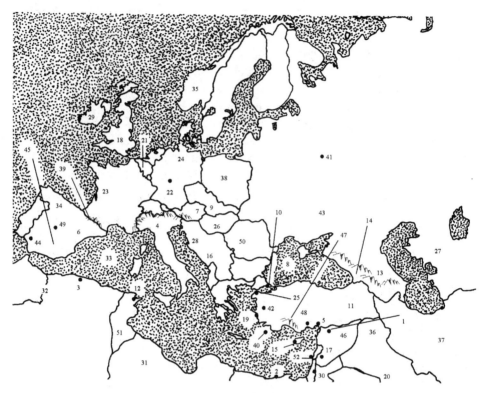

Europe, Asia, Africa.

1	Aleppo	*Oth* V.ii.351–55; *Mac* I.iii.7
2	Alexandria	Much of *Antony and Cleopatra* is set here. The city is on the western edge of the Nile (*A&C* I.ii.50, I.v.25, II.vii.18–24) delta.
3	Algiers	*Temp* I.ii.262
4	Alps	*John* I.i.202–3; *H5* III.v.51–52; *R2* I.i.64
5	Antioch	*Per* I.Cho.17–19, I.i.set
6	Aragon	One of the two powerful kingdoms united by the marriage of Ferdinand and Isabella in the fifteenth century to make up the basis of modern Spain (the other was Castile). Henry VII's first wife was Ferdinand and Isabella's daughter Katherine of Aragon, who appears as a character in *Henry VIII*. The characters Don Pedro and Don John in *Much Ado about Nothing* also hail from Aragon.
7	Austria	*AW* I.ii.5; *Measure for Measure* is set in Vienna, approximately where the number 7 appears on the map. Vienna is also the setting for the play-within-a-play in *Hamlet* (III.ii.242).
8	Black Sea	The "Pontic Sea" of *Oth* III.iii.450–53.
9	Bohemia	An archetypally wild place in *MWW* IV.v.18, the birthplace of Barnardine in *MM* IV.ii.133, and the home of King Polixenes and scene of much of the action in *The Winter's Tale*.
10	Byzantium	*Tim* III.v.62. An alternate name for Constantinople (*H5* V.ii.210), modern Istanbul, Turkey.
11	Cappadocia	*A&C* III.vi.70
12	Carthage	*Temp* II.i.84–87
13	Caucasus Mtns.	*R2* I.iii.294

14	Colchis	*MV* I.i.171
15	Cyprus	Most of *Othello* is set here. The dot locates the city of Paphos (*Temp* IV.i.93).
16	Dalmatia	*Cym* III.i.73
17	Damascus	*1H6* I.iii.39
18	England	*Mac* II.iii.139, IV.iii.set
19	Ephesus	*The Comedy of Errors* and some of *Pericles* are set here.
20	Euphrates River	*A&C* I.ii.102
21	Flanders	Now part of western Belgium and northern France. *H8* III.ii.318–20; *MWW* II.ii.295–99 ("Fleming"); *3H6* IV.v.21. The Flemings' neighbors in southern Belgium and northern France were the Walloons (*1H6* II.i.2).
22	Frankfurt	*MV* III.i.80–81
23	Gallia	*Cym* II.iv.18; Gallia was the Roman name for Gaul, or France.
24	Germany	*H5* I.ii.44–47; the rivers Elbe and Saale enclose a triangle of German land whose approximate center is indicated by this number.
25	Hellespont	*AYLI* IV.i.97–102. The strait leading into the Sea of Marmara and thence into the Black Sea; now called the Dardanelles. Troy (*1H6* V.v.106; *2H6* I.iv.18; *T&C* set) was located on the southern bank.
26	Hungary	*MM* I.ii.2; *MWW* I.ii.21. Pannonia, a Roman province, was located in present-day Hungary (*Cym* III.i.73).
27	Hyrcania	*3H6* I.iv.155; *MV* II.vii.41–43
28	Illyria	*Twelfth Night* is set here.
29	Ireland	*Mac* II.iii.140; *2H6* III.i.282–92; *R2* II.ii.42; *John* I.i.11
30	Jerusalem	*1H6* V.v.40; *2H6* I.i.47; *3H6* I.iv.122; *2H4* III.I.108; *John* II.i.378. The area around Jerusalem was part of the Roman province of Palestine (*John* II.i.4; *Oth* IV.iii.41–42). The numeral 30 marks what was once the ancient Roman province of Arabia (*Cor* IV.ii.24; *A&C* III.vi.72), which occupied much the same territory as does Jordan today.
31	Libya	*T&C* I.iii.328; *WT* V.i.157
32	Mauritania	*Oth* IV.ii.224. A Roman province incorporating parts of present-day Morocco and Algeria.
33	Mediterranean Sea	*Per* III.i.set; *Temp* I.ii.234; *LLL* V.i.56
34	Navarre	The setting of *Love's Labor's Lost*
35	Norway	*Mac* I.ii.31
36	Parthia	*JC* V.iii.37; *A&C* II.iii.31, III.i.1–5, IV.xiv.70; *TNK* II.i.107–8; *Cym* I.vi.20. In ancient Roman times, the Parthians were famous for their skill as archers.
37	Persia	*Lear* III.vi.80
38	Poland	*MM* I.iii.14
39	Pyrenees	*John* I.i.202–3
40	Rhodes	*Oth* I.i.26, I.iii.15
41	Russia	*MM* II.i.131–32, III.ii.89; *WT* III.ii.117. Moscow, marked by the dot, is mentioned in *LLL* V.ii.120–21 and *AW* IV.i.71.
42	Sardis	*JC* IV.ii, IV.ii.set. Sardis was the capital of the ancient kingdom of Lydia (*A&C* I.ii.103).
43	Scythia	*1H6* II.iii.6; *Lear* I.i.116. An ancient kingdom flourishing especially around 700–200 BCE. It covered much of the territory north of the Black and Caspian seas.
44	Seville	*MAAN* II.i.283
45	Spain	*JC* I.ii.119; *3H6* III.iii.81–82; Armado is from Spain (*LLL* ch.).
46	Syria	*A&C* I.ii.102, III.i.set.

47	Taurus Mtns.	*MND* III.ii.141
48	Tharsus	*Per* I.iv.set, III.iii.set, IV.i.set, IV.iii.set, IV.iv.set
49	Toledo	*H8* II.i.164
50	Transylvania	*Per* IV.ii.22
51	Tunisia	*Temp* II.i.72–73, 84–87
52	Tyre	*Per* I.i.1, I.ii.set, I.iii.set, II.iv.set

Not identified on this map: the Barbary Coast (*TNK* III.v.61), which stretched along northern Africa from Egypt to Morocco; some ancient kingdoms or provinces, including Media and Paphlagonia; and places in Italy, Greece, France, and England that appear on their own maps.

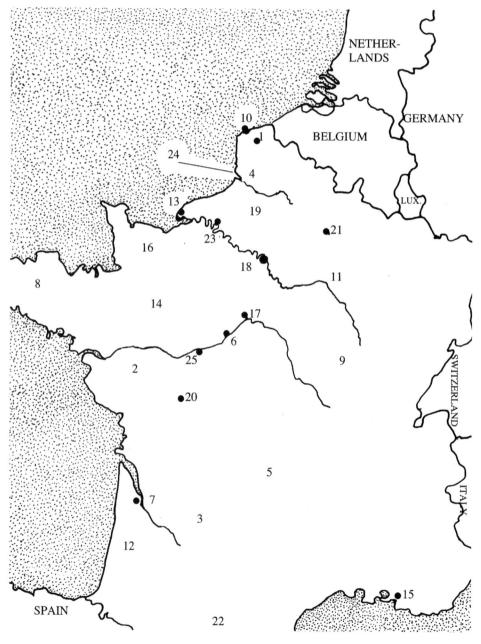

France.

1	Agincourt	*H5* III.vii.set, IV.set
2	Anjou	*1H6* V.iv.set; *2H6* IV.i.86; *John* I.i.11, II.i.527–28
3	Aquitaine	*LLL* I.i.136, II.i.8, 128–59, 248. A region that corresponds roughly to modern-day Guienne (*1H6* I.i.60).
4	Artois	*1H6* II.i.2
5	Auvergne	*1H6* II.iii.set. A region in south-central France.
6	Blois	*1H6* IV.iii.45. A town on the Loire River.
7	Bordeaux	*1H6* IV.ii.set, IV.v.set; *H8* I.i.95–96. A port near the mouth of the Garonne River.
8	Brittany	*3H6* IV.vi.97–101; *R2* II.i.277–78, *John* II.i.156. Sometimes simply called "Britain" by Shakespeare, this region was divided in a map by Abraham Ortelius into "Basse Bretaigne" and "Haulte Bretaigne."
9	Burgundy	*3H6* II.i.146–47, *Lear* I.i.258
10	Calais	*H5* V.Cho.6–10; *R2* I.i.126–27, IV.i.82; *John* III.ii.83. The last English stronghold in France, Calais was lost to the English during the reign of Mary I. The Field of the Cloth of Gold "Twixt Guynes and Arde" (*H8* I.i.7), at which Henry VIII met the French king, is located just south of Calais.
11	Champagne	*1H6* I.i.60
12	Gascony	*1H6* IV.iii.set, IV.iv.set. A region just north of the Pyrenees Mountains.
13	Harfleur	*H5* III.Cho.17, 127, III.i.set, III.ii.set, III.iii.set. A town near the mouth of the Seine River.
14	Maine	*1H6* IV.iii.45; *2H6* IV.i.86; *John* I.i.11
15	Marseilles	*AW* IV.iv.9, V.i.set
16	Normandy	*2H6* I.i.112, 213, IV.vii.66; *LLL* II.i.43
17	Orleans	*1H6* I.i.157, I.ii.set, I.iv.set, I.v.set, I.vi.set, II.i.set, II.ii.set
18	Paris	*1H6* III.iii.30, IV.i.set; *2H6* I.iii.174; *H5* II.iv.132; *AW* I.ii.set, II.i.set, II.iii.set, II.v.set
19	Picardy	*1H6* II.i.2; *2H6* IV.i.88
20	Poitiers	*1H6* IV.i.19, IV.iii.45; *John* I.i.11, II.i.527–28
21	Reims	*1H6* I.i.60, 92
22	Rousillon	Much of *All's Well That Ends Well* is set in this region adjacent to the Pyrenees and the Mediterranean.
23	Rouen	*1H6* I.i.65, III.ii.set, III.iii.set, III.iv.set, III.v.set
24	Somme River	*H5* III.v.1
25	Tours	*1H6* IV.iii.45; *2H6* I.iii.52. A town along the Loire located in the region of Touraine.

England, Scotland, and Wales.

1	Barnet	*3H6* V.i.110, V.ii.set, V.iii.set
2	Basingstoke	*2H4* II.i.169–71
3	Bristol	*2H6* III.i.328–29; *R2* III.i.set
4	Bury St. Edmunds	*2H6* III.ii.set, III.ii.240; *John* IV.iii.114–15, V.ii.set
5	Channel	*2H6* IV.i.115. The English Channel is also referred to as the Narrow Sea (*3H6* I.i.239, IV.viii.3).
6	Cirencester	*R2* V.vi.2–3
7	Cornwall	*H5* IV.i.50
8	Cotswold Hills	They appear as "Cotshill" in *R2* II.iii.9 and "Cotsall" in *MWW* I.i.84–85. This is also the approximate location of the county of Gloucestershire (*MWW* III.iv.44; *R2* II.iii.set).
9	Coventry	*3H6* IV.viii.32, V.i.set; *1H4* IV.ii.set near; *R2* I.i.199, I.iii.set
10	Daventry	*1H4* IV.ii.47
11	Doncaster	*1H4* V.i.142–45
12	Dover	*1H6* V.i.49; *2H6* III.ii.101; *John* II.i.23; *Lear* III.vi.90. Much of acts IV and V of *King Lear* takes place in or near Dover. The town was unusual for its proximity to the Continent, its white chalk cliffs, and its city walls (most towns in England were unfortified). It is located in the county of Kent (*2H6* IV.vii.55–65, IV.x.set; *3H6* I.ii.41–43, IV.viii.12).
13	Dunstable	*H8* IV.i.27
14	Forres	Much of *Macbeth* act III takes place here.
15	Greenwich	*H8* I.ii.189. There was a royal palace here.
16	Inverness	Scene of much of acts I and II of *Macbeth*. Cawdor (*Mac* I.ii.53) is located about midway between Inverness and Forres.
17	Ipswich	*H8* I.i.138, IV.ii.59
18	Isle of Man	*2H6* II.iii.13, II.iv.78, 94
19	Leicestershire	*3H6* IV.vii.15
20	Lincoln Washes	*John* V.vi.39–41. Tidal flats at the mouth of the Welland River.
21	King's Lynn	*3H6* IV.v.20
22	Monmouth	*H5* IV.vii.26–28
23	Norfolk	*3H6* IV.viii.12
24	Northamptonshire	*John* I.i.51
25	Oxford	*R2* V.iii.14; *H8* IV.ii.58–59
26	Pontefract	*2H6* II.ii.26; *R2* V.v.set; *John* IV.ii.147–52; *2H4* I.i.204–5. A castle called "Pomfret" by Shakespeare.
27	Reading	*MWW* IV.v.75
28	Rochester	*1H4* II.i.set
29	Saint Albans	*2H6* I.ii.57, 83, I.iv.72
30	Sarum Plain	*Lear* II.ii.85. The area around Salisbury.
31	Scone	*Mac* II.iv.31–35. Scottish kings were crowned here, over a revered stone that, after the thirteenth century, became part of the coronation chair in Westminster Abbey.
32	Scotland	*3H6* III.i.13; *H5* I.ii.144–73
33	Severn (River)	*Cym* III.v.17
34	Shrewsbury	*1H4* III.i.165–66, IV.i.set near, IV.iii.set near, V.i.set near, V.ii.set near
35	Southampton	*H5* II.ii.set
36	Stamford	*2H4* III.ii.40
37	Stratford-on-Avon	Shakespeare's birthplace.
38	Suffolk	*3H6* IV.viii.12

39	Tewksbury	*3H6* V.iv.set near, V.v.set near
40	Trent (River)	*TNK* Pro.12
41	Wales	*H5* IV.i.54, IV.vii.97–104; *1H4* III.i.set; *Cym* III.iv.set, III.vi.set, IV.i.set, IV.ii.set, IV.iv.set; *R2* II.iv.set, III.ii.set
42	Windsor	*2H4* IV.iv.14; *The Merry Wives of Windsor* is set in and near this town, and nearby towns and villages such as Frogmore (*MWW* II.iii.71), Maidenhead (*MWW* IV.v.75), and Eton (*MWW* IV.iv.74) are also mentioned. Windsor Castle, considered by some to be the most formidable royal palace, was located here.
43	Worcester	*John* V.vii.99–100
44	York	*3H6* II.ii.set, IV.vii.set

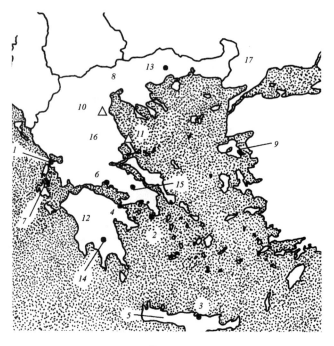

Greece.

1	Actium	*A&C* III.vii, III.viii, III.ix, III.x
2	Athens	*T&C* Pro. 3, 6; *Lear* III.iv.178; *A&C* III.iv.set, III.v.set. Much of *The Two Noble Kinsmen* and all of *Timon of Athens* and *A Midsummer Night's Dream* are set in or near Athens.
3	Candia	*TN* V.i.60. Cretan port now known as Iráklion.
4	Corinth	*Tim* II.ii.76
5	Crete	*MND* IV.i.114, 127
6	Delphi	*WT* II.i.184, II.i.1–11. Shakespeare confuses this, the site of Apollo's oracle, with the isle of Delos.
7	Ithaca	*T&C* I.iii.70; *Cor* I.iii.85
8	Macedon	*H5* IV.vii.22
9	Mytilene	*Per* IV.ii.set, IV.v.set, IV.vi.set, IV.vi.190, V.i.set
10	Olympus	*JC* III.i.74, IV.iii.91; *Cor* V.iii.30; *Ham* V.i.254
11	Pelion	*MWW* II.i.77–78
12	Peloponnesus	*A&C* III.x.30.
13	Philippi	*JC* V. set; *A&C* III.xi.35
14	Sparta	*T&C* II.ii.183; *MND* IV.i.115
15	Thebes	*Lear* III.iv.155; *TNK* I.i.42, I.ii.set, I.iv.set, I.v.set
16	Thessaly	*MND* IV.i.127
17	Thrace	*A&C* III.vi.71

Italy.

1	Adriatic Sea	*TS* I.ii.72–73
2	Mt. Aetna	*RL* 1042; the town of Hybla, famous for its honey, was located on the south slope of this volcanic mountain (*1H4* I.ii.42).
3	Antium	*Cor* III.i.11; many scenes in *Coriolanus* are set here.
4	Apennine Mountains	*John* I.i.202
5	Ardea	*RL* 1–4
6	Ferrara	*H8* III.ii.324
7	Florence	Much of *All's Well That Ends Well* is set in Florence; the character Claudio, in *Much Ado About Nothing*, is a Florentine (I.i.10–11).
8	Genoa	*MV* III.i.94, 103–4
9	Mantua	*TS* II.i.60; *2GV* IV.i.51, IV.iii.24, V.ii.47; *R&J* III.iii.169, III.v.89–90, IV.i.117, V.ii.3
10	Messina	*Much Ado About Nothing* and *Antony and Cleopatra* II.i are set here.
11	Misenum	*A&C* II.vi and II.vii are set near here.
12	Modena	*A&C* I.iv.57
13	Naples	*TS* I.i.205; *Oth* III.i.3–4; *Temp* I.ii.235; the king of Naples (*1H6* V.iii.52, 94, V.iv.78, V.v.40; *2H6* I.i.47) was the father of Margaret of Anjou, and several references are made to her Neapolitan origins (*2H6* V.i.117, 118; *3H6* II.ii.139).
14	Padua	*MV* III.iv.48–49, IV.i.108–9; *The Taming of the Shrew* is set here, and *Much Ado About Nothing*'s Benedick is from Padua. One reference to the city (*2GV* II.v.1) is a mistake for Milan.
15	Pisa	*TS* I.i.10, 21, 205, II.i.104
16	Po (River)	*TNK* Pro.12; *John* I.i.203
17	Rome	As the seat of the papacy, *1H6* III.i.51. Most of *Julius Caesar* is set in Rome, and there are mentions of several Roman landmarks, such as the Capitol (I.iii.20), the portico of Pompey's theater (I.iii.126, 152), and the Senate House (II.iv.1) in that play. Much of *Coriolanus* also takes place in and around Rome, and *Antony and Cleopatra* I.iv, II.ii, II.iii, II.iv, and III.ii are set there. See also *MM* III.ii.90; *RL* 1835.
18	Sardinia	*A&C* II.vi.35
19	Sicily	*2H6* I.i.6; *A&C* II.vi.35. Much of *The Winter's Tale* is set here, at the home of Leontes and Hermione. The two "Sicils" of *3H6* I.iv.122 are Sicily and Naples.
20	Siena	*AW* I.ii.1; *Cym* IV.ii.341
21	Syracuse	Egeon and his sons are from Syracuse in *The Comedy of Errors*.
22	Tiber (River)	*JC* I.i.46, 59, I.ii.101–15, III.ii.249; *A&C* I.i.33; *Cor* II.i.50
23	Tuscany	*AW* I.ii.14
24	Venice	*Oth* I.i.set, I.ii.set, I.iii.set. *The Merchant of Venice* is set here, and mention is made of the old shopping district near the Rialto Bridge (III.i.43–45).
25	Verona	*TS* I.ii.1, II.i.47; *2GV* IV.i.48, V.iv.130. Most of *Romeo and Juliet* is set here.

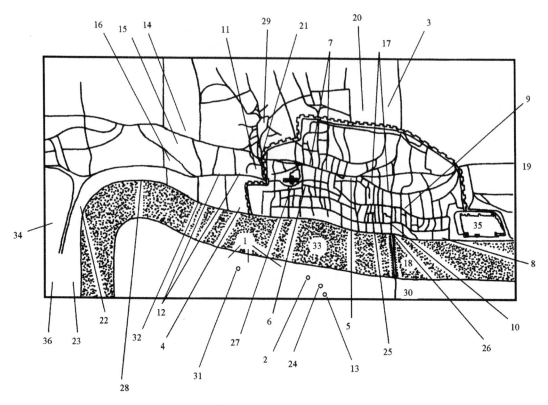

London and Westminster.

1	Bankside	A collection of brothels, alehouses, and other establishments clustered along Southwark's Thames bank. The westernmost area of Bankside was known as Paris Garden (*H8* V.iv.1–2).
2	Bearbaiting ring	
3	Bedlam	A lunatic asylum.
4	Bridewell	A prison for vagrants, prostitutes, and other minor offenders.
5	Bucklersbury	*MWW* III.iii.70–71. A street and district in which herbs were sold.
6	Cannon Street	*2H6* IV.vi.set. Another street, known as Candlewick in Shakespeare's day, was later dubbed Cannon Street.
7	Cheapside	*2H6* IV.ii.70, IV.vii.127. This street and the area around it, both known as Cheapside, were home to many shops.
8	Customhouse	
9	Eastcheap	*1H4* I.ii.130–31, II.iv.set; *2H4* II.i.69, II.iv.set, III.iii.set. A street and the neighboring district; Mistress Quickly's tavern is located here.
10	Fish Street	There was an Old Fish Street elsewhere in London, but since Jack Cade mentions the street (*2H6* IV.viii.1) almost in the same breath as "St. Magnus' Corner" (see below), it seems likely that he means this stretch of road just north of London Bridge, called either New Fish Street or Fish Street Hill. The Fishmongers' Company was located here.
11	Fleet Prison	*2H4* V.v.93
12	Fleet Street	As it continued westward, this road changed name and became the Strand (*H8* V.iv.51).

13	Globe Theater	
14–16	Inns of Court	*2H6* IV.vii.2; *2H4* III.ii.13–14, 23, 34; 14 shows the position of Gray's Inn, 15 that of Clement's Inn, and 16 that of Lincoln's Inn.
17	Lombard Street	*2H4* II.i.27–28
18	London Bridge	*1H6* III.i.23; *2H6* IV.iv.49, IV.v.3, IV.vi.14. In 1592, Frederick of Würtemberg's secretary called it "a beautiful long bridge, with quite splendid, handsome, and well-built houses, which are occupied by merchants of consequence."
19	Mile-End Green	The road indicated on the map continued eastward, and one mile beyond the city walls (hence the name) was Mile-End Green, where local militia troops drilled (*2H4* III.ii.283–90; *AW* IV.iii.275–76).
20	Moorfields	*H8* V.iv.32
21	Newgate	*1H4* III.iii.95. Newgate was one of the gates in the city walls; others were Aldersgate, Moorgate, Bishopsgate, and Ludgate. The Newgate area was home to one of London's most notorious prisons.
22	Palace	*1H6* V.set; *2H6* I.i.set; *3H6* III.ii.set; *H5* I.ii.set; *1H4* III.ii.set; *R2* I.iv.set. Too many scenes are set in "the Palace" in London to enumerate them all here. The palace in question is rarely specified, and England's kings and queens had several palaces in the London and Westminster areas alone. However, it may usually be assumed to refer to the palace of Whitehall, located along the bank of the Thames just south of the bend. The Elizabethan palace no longer stands and has been replaced by more recent government buildings. Whitehall began as York Place, the home of Thomas Wolsey, and was confiscated and renamed by Henry VIII (*H8* I.iv.set, IV.i.95–97).
23	Parliament	*1H6* III.i.set; *3H6* I.i.set; *R2* IV.i.set
24	Rose Theater	
25	St. Lawrence Poultney	*H8* I.ii.153–54. The church that anchored this parish in Tudor times burned down in the Great Fire of 1666.
26	St. Magnus' Corner	*2H6* IV.viii.1. The Church of St. Magnus stood at the northern end of London Bridge.
27	St. Paul's Cathedral	*H8* V.iv.15
28	The Savoy	*2H6* IV.vii.2
29	Smithfield	*2H6* II.iii.7, IV.v.10, IV.vi.12, IV.vii.set; *2H4* I.ii.50–51, II.iv.234–35
30	Southwark	*2H6* IV.iv.27
31	Swan Theater	
32	The Temple	*1H4* III.iii.207–8; *1H6* II.iv.set
33	Thames River	*2H6* IV.viii.2; *2H4* IV.iv.125–28; *H5* IV.i.115; *MWW* III.v.4–6
34	Tiltyard	*2H4* III.ii.327
35	Tower of London	*1H6* I.i.167, I.iii.46, II.v.set; *2H6* IV.v.set, V.i.41, 134; *3H6* III.ii.120, V.i.46, V.vi.set; *R2* IV.i.315–17; *H8* I.i.207, 212–13. The legend that Julius Caesar erected the Tower was a fabrication; it was actually built by William the Conqueror in the eleventh century. The Tower was used as an armory, a prison, a royal coronation eve residence, and a home for a small menagerie.
36	Westminster Abbey	*1H6* I.i.set; *2H6* I.ii.37, IV.iv.31; *2H4* IV.iv.set, IV.v.set

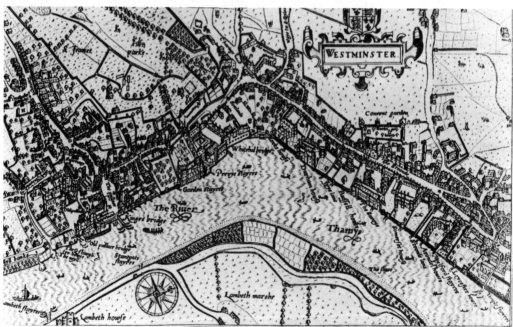

John Norden's maps of London and Westminster (*2H4* IV.iv.set; *H8* II.i.set, V.i.set), 1593. The simplified locator map of these areas is based partly on Norden's maps and partly on other maps of the area drawn between the mid-sixteenth and mid-seventeenth centuries. Reproduced from the Collections of the Library of Congress.

Plague

Although "plague" could mean any horrific misfortune, as in the biblical ten plagues sent against Egypt, by the late sixteenth century it usually meant bubonic plague specifically. Epidemics struck Europe periodically throughout Shakespeare's life, with particularly bad ones in England in the 1560s, the 1590s, and the 1600s.

The disease caused by the plague bacillus comes in two varieties, bubonic and pneumonic, and either or both may have been meant by the sixteenth-century term "plague." The bubonic form incubates in about six days and first emerges as nausea and limb and back pain, progressing to high fever and lymph node swellings called buboes in the groin or armpit, the "plague-sore" of *Lear* II.iv.221. About 60 percent of patients died. The pneumonic form arose when bacilli settled in the lungs and were expelled by coughing; this form was almost 100 percent fatal. The end must have been excruciating to watch, if we are to judge by a passage in *T&C* II.iii.177–78: "He is so plaguy proud that the death-tokens of it [symptoms indicating a fatal outcome] / Cry 'No recovery.' "

Watching the end were the patient's immediate family, if he or she had one. In some cases, plague victims were housed in established or impromptu hospitals, cared for by surgeons, nurses, and others. Having a nurse could be a blessing or a curse; some of the nurses, known as "night crows," were said to kill their patients and steal their belongings.

The plague was transmitted by a microscopic organism carried by fleas that bit both rats and humans. Both insect and rodent vermin were so common that no one thought to blame them for the spread of the disease. Instead, foreigners, a bad alignment of the planets, or putrid air was cited. Doctors came close when they recognized that animals might be to blame somehow, but they chose the wrong animals, and governments ordered the slaying of stray dogs and cats. The result was a rise in the rodent population and a continuation of the plague. Doctors also hit on part of the solution when they realized that the plague was a contagious illness, and houses in which plague had struck were quarantined. The victim's family was thus trapped in the house to nurse him or her, hope he or she recovered, and hope that they themselves would not be stricken.

Treatments and preventive measures were few. Theriac and mithridaticum, compounds of useless ingredients said to be effective against both poisoning and plague, were tried, but these were expensive. Those who could afford it fled afflicted areas, but plague epidemics could last several months. They usually broke out in late summer or early autumn and died away during the winter, since rodents and fleas thrived in warm weather. Ordinary people could seldom leave their homes and businesses for months at a time, and so they stayed and died. In London an outbreak killed 13 percent of the population in 1593; another, ten years later, killed 20 percent.

We know nothing of Shakespeare's personal reaction to the plague, but he must have been keenly aware of it. Aside from the natural physical fear that it must have engendered in everyone, for him it had significant monetary consequences, since in times of plague, the theaters were closed by the government. Nonetheless, most of the instances of "plague" in his writings are either general references that include plague as one of many misfortunes, as a shorthand for all misfortune, or as a general curse, such as "A plague upon" whatever unlucky subject the character despises.

There are a few specific references to the disease, other than the *Lear* and *Troilus and Cressida* examples above. A line in *Twelfth Night* asks how "quickly may one catch the plague?" (I.v.293); another in *The Tempest* refers to "The red plague" (I.ii.366), which may be either the bubonic plague, with its fever and sores, or to some other disease with a red manifestation, like smallpox or measles. Perhaps the best example is in *Timon of Athens*: "I . . . would send them back the plague, / Could I but catch it" (V.i.137–38). Shakespeare almost never refers to the plague's symptoms, but he hardly needed to. The word itself would have been sufficiently terrifying to his audiences, who were all too familiar, at least by reputation, with "the tokened pestilence, / Where death is sure" (*A&C* III.x.9–10). *See also* Disease and Injury; Disease and Injury.

Plants

Living lives closely connected to the earth and the seasons, Shakespeare and his contemporaries were familiar not only with the cultivated plants found in fields, orchards, and kitchen gardens but also with the wild ones that grew in woods, meadows, and fallow ground. Some of these plants— briars (*AW* IV.iv.32; *Temp* IV.i.179–81; *TA* II.iii.199), bushes, grasses, reeds, shrubs (*3H6* III.ii.156; *RL* 664–65), and thorns (*R&J* I.iv.26)— are so familiar today that they require no explanation here. Others had associations that are perhaps less obvious. Here we are concerned with plants that were considered weeds, that had medicinal or other uses, or that had some sort of symbolism that would have been recognized by Shakespeare's audiences.

Shakespeare offers two excellent lists of weeds, one in *Henry V*, the other in *King Lear*. In the first example, he describes "fallow leas" (unused arable land, usually plowed occasionally to keep weeds in check) overtaken by "darnel, hemlock, and rank fumitory" and meadows, normally used for grazing, choked with "docks, rough thistles, kecksies, burrs" (V.ii.43–55). Darnel was a kind of grass, *Lolium temulentum*, that grew in cornfields and was particularly susceptible to ergot; Shakespeare's contemporaries knew nothing of ergot, a fungus that could destroy and replace the seed of the grass, but they often saw ergotism, the hallucinatory, painful disease caused by consumption of the fungus. They did not know the name of the disease or even that it was caused by something the victims had eaten, blaming the symptoms on witchcraft or demonic possession. They did know, however, that darnel was not the barley or wheat they had sown, and so tried to remove it when they could. In his *Herball*, John Gerard, wrote that "among the hurtfull weeds Darnell is the first." Hemlock, related to carrots, had small white flowers and was highly poisonous, so it would be a most unfortunate plant to find among one's food supply. Fumitory (*Fumaria officinalis* or its close relatives) took its name from the Latin word for smoke, because it seemed to rise from the ground as swiftly and as abundantly as smoke from a fire. It had bitter leaves.

Of the meadow weeds, burrs (*AYLI* I.iii.13–17; *T&C* III.ii.110; *MM* IV.iii.180) need no explanation. The dock (usually *Rumex obtusifolius*) was a thick-rooted plant with small greenish flowers that was often used as a treatment for nettle stings. It is therefore appropriate that Shakespeare pairs it with nettles in an exchange from *The Tempest*:

ANTONIO   He sow'd it with nettle seed.

SEBASTIAN   Or docks, or mallows. (II.i.149–50)

The mallow was a hairy-stemmed, hairy-leafed plant with reddish-purple flowers that, like the dock, grew in meadows and near rivers. Thistles are fairly widely known, partly because of their distinctive bristly purple flower, partly because of the intimidating thorns that appear everywhere on the plant, and partly because it is a symbol of Scotland that, after the accession of Scotland's James VI as James I of England, appeared on the royal seal, on coins, and elsewhere. Kecksies were plants with hollow stems.

The passage from *King Lear* describes a madman

Crowned with rank femiter and furrow-weeds,
With hardocks, hemlock, nettles, cuckoo-flow'rs,
Darnel, and all the idle weeds that grow
In our sustaining corn. (IV.iv.3–6)

The "femiter" is fumitory again, and the "furrow-weeds" are generic, encompassing all the sorts of unwanted plants that might grow in the plowed furrows of a field. Hardocks are a species of dock; there were several such varieties, including red docks, white docks, fiddle docks, and burdocks. Hemlock has been discussed already, as has darnel. Nettles (*Urtica dioica*) grew on square stems up to four feet high and were covered with hairy leaves that, if touched, conveyed an intense burning, stinging sensation that lasted for some time after contact. This capacity to sting features often in Shakespeare's plays (*1H4* I.iii.238; *TNK* V.i.97; *R2* III.ii.18). Gerard states that the nettle (*Cor* II.i.194; *Ham* IV.vii.169; *Oth* I.iii.316) is edible and "stirreth up lust," especially when drunk with "cute" (boiled wine).

It grows, he writes, "in untilled places," and "groweth of it selfe neere hedges, bushes, brambles, and old walls almost everywhere."

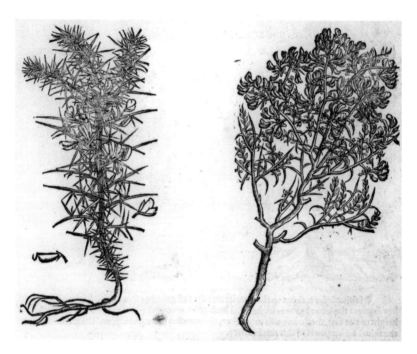

Furze or prickly broom, from John Gerard's *Herball.* The broom plant, in Latin *planta genista*, gave its name to England's ruling Plantagenet family. Reproduced from the Collections of the Library of Congress.

Other weeds mentioned in the plays include furze, gorse, heather, moss, sedges, speargrass, and toadstools. Furze and gorse were different varieties of prickly broom; both were thorny, hence "sharp furzes, pricking goss" (*Temp* IV.i.180). Heather, or "long heath" (*Temp* I.i.63–65) is paired with furze as a worthless plant found only on "barren ground." The Scottish term "heather" was not used in England until the eighteenth century, and in the south and midlands the shrubby plants of the genus *Erica* were called "heath." Mistletoe, now chiefly known as the plant hung in doorways at Christmas and associated with kissing of anyone who stands underneath it, is a parasitic plant with poisonous berries, hence "baleful mistletoe" (*TA* II.iii.95); it had some medicinal uses. Moss, like grassy weeds, was supposedly a sign of neglect (*CE* ii.ii.179; *Cym* IV.ii.228; *TA* II.iii.95). Edible fungi were called mushrooms (*Temp* V.i.39), and the poisonous varieties were known as toadstools (*T&C* II.i.20). Sedges and speargrass were both types of wild grass; speargrass or spearwort (*1H4* II.iv.312–13) had a leaf shaped like a spear point; when eaten or rubbed on the skin, it burned, and was used by beggars to raise sores to elicit pity.

Sedges were a common form of plant life in marshes and along the shores of lakes (*TS* Ind.ii.51, 53; *MAAN* II.i.196–97; *Temp* IV.i.129; *TNK* IV.i.32–34; *2GV* II.vii.29).

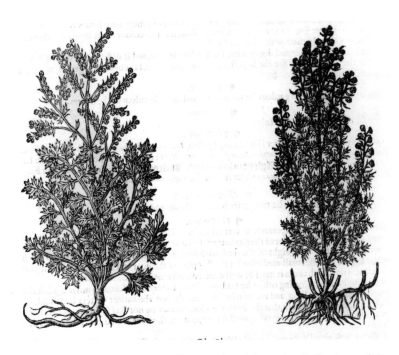

Wormwood, from Gerard's *Herball*. Reproduced from the Collections of the Library of Congress.

Some weeds had uses. *Carduus benedictus* (*MAAN* III.iv.73), or holy thistle, according to Conrad Heresbach (in *The Whole Art and Trade of Husbandry*), cured "dazing, or giddinesse of the head, [and] maketh a good memorie, and restoreth the hearing." The herb was also useful for those suffering from headaches or poisoning. John Fitzherbert (in *Booke of Husbandrie*) recommended it for quartan fevers if taken before the recurring fever set in. He added that it was good for worms, stomach problems, and complaints of the womb; taken with honey, it was good for the bowels and kidneys; taken with white wine, bread, and honey, it restored failing sight. Speargrass was a cure for sciatica or gout. Wormwood (*LLL* V.ii.845), a plant with feathery, grayish-green poisonous leaves, was used as an ingredient in cordials and as a purgative. Holly, fermented for about twelve days, could be used to make the sticky substance called birdlime; another kind of birdlime was made from mistletoe berries. Rushes (*Cor* I.i.183) could be dipped in tallow and used as substitutes for candles, or gathered and strewn on floors (*2H4* V.v.1), mixed with herbs, to make a sweet-smelling mat. They could also be made into temporary wreaths or

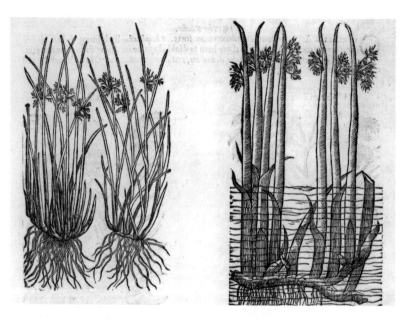

Two types of rushes, from Gerard's *Herball*: common rushes on the left, bulrushes (or great water rushes) on the right. Reproduced from the Collections of the Library of Congress.

rings (*TNK* IV.i.83–90; *AW* II.ii.23). Holly, because it was one of the few plants still green (*AYLI* II.vii.179) in the winter, was used to decorate houses and churches at Christmastime.

Mandrake was a plant with multiple associations. It was hallucinogenic and, in most circumstances, toxic. Those who ate any part of the plant might suffer vomiting, numbness, sleepiness, dilated pupils, slowed heart rate, coma, and death. Nonetheless, it was widely used in herbal medicine; Andrew Boorde recommended it as a sedative for men and a fertility drug for women. Its root split into two leglike projections, and it was therefore thought to resemble the human form (*2H4* I.ii.14–15). Legend had it that it would shriek when pulled from the ground, and that any who heard it would die soon (*2H6* III.ii.310; *R&J* IV.iii.47–48). Gerard had heard all the legends—that it grew under gallows, that it shrieked aloud, that one ought to have a dog pull it up so that the dog would die of its cry—and found them absurd: "There hath beene many ridiculous tales brought up of this plant, whether of old wives, or runnagate Surgeons or Physick-mongers I know not." All the stories were nonsense, he said, for he had uprooted it many times himself and was still very much alive.

Some plants were symbolic. Ivy (*WT* III.iii.64–67) and, more generally, vines (*TNK* II.i.100) were used as symbols of overly tight clinging or parasiticial behavior, because they twisted around and sapped the vigor from their hosts (*Temp* I.ii.85–87; *MND* V.i.44–45; *H8* V.v.49). Claude Paradin's *Heroicall Devises* shows a picture of ivy choking a tree and explains that it represents the twisting of the law by lawyers; however, Andrea Alciato, author of another popular book of emblems (*Emblemata*), lists ivy as a symbol of eternity because it is evergreen, so not all of the plant's connotations were negative. Knotgrass (*Polygonum aviculare*) was a creeping plant with many-jointed branches. Its low stature lent it the reputation for stunting growth if ingested, hence its appearance in a list of insults based on Hermia's shortness: "you dwarf; / You minimus, of hind'ring knotgrass made" (*MND* III.ii.328–29). *See also* Flowers; Food; Garden; Trees.

Mandrake or mandragora, from Gerard's *Herball*. The split root was thought to resemble the human form. Reproduced from the Collections of the Library of Congress.

Poetry

Poetry was employed for many purposes. A poem might be written to curry favor with a monarch or patron, or it might be sung to accompany music. Its themes might range from the uncertainty of mortal existence to the amorous doings of Roman gods to the rural pursuits of shepherds. It might be an ode, assessing someone or something, or an elegy, which was typically mournful or at least pensive in tone (*AYLI* III.ii.360–61). However, its most famous and satirized use was as a tool of seduction.

A man in love was expected to turn to verse, whether in person or merely in thoughts or letters, as a means of expressing his passion (*MAAN* V.ii.4–7, 25–41; *II5* III.vii 40–45, V.ii.135–38; when a woman engages in this form of wooing, as in *AYLI* IV.iii.40–63, it is considered overly aggressive). The sonnet was considered especially appropriate for this endeavor, though a "sonnet" at that time could mean any short poem (*AW* IV.iii.324; *2GV* III.ii.69–71, 77, 92; *LLL* I.ii.178–80, IV.iii; *TN* III.iv.22–23). The narrowly defined sonnet, consisting of fourteen lines of iambic pentameter, was then known as a quatorzain and came in three common rhyme patterns: *abba abba cddc ee*, the Italian, followed by Thomas Wyatt and Philip Sidney; *abab cdcd efef gg*, the "English" or "Shakespearean" pattern introduced to England by Henry Howard, Earl of Surrey; and the

Spenserian, rhyming *abab bcbc cdcd ee*, named for its chief practitioner, Edmund Spenser.

For those unfamiliar with rhyme designations, a line labeled *a* rhymes with another line labeled *a*, a *b* line rhymes with the other *b* lines, and so on. A collection of lines, separated from the others in a poem by a skipped line, is called a stanza. A collection of lines linked by their rhyme pattern is named according to the number of lines involved: two in a couplet (*TN* III.iv.381–82), four in a quatrain, six in a sestet, eight in an octave, and so on. The lines are further classified according to the number of their syllables and the pattern of stressed syllables. Each group within the line, composed of some number and order of stressed and unstressed syllables, is a "foot" (*AYLI* III.ii.165–66). For example, if we were to treat part of the preceding sentence as a line of poetry, marking emphasized syllables with a — and unstressed syllables with a u, we see that a pattern develops:

<pre>
u   — u —u —   u — u —
Each group within the line, composed of some
</pre>

The pattern here is unstressed, stressed, repeated five times—yielding five "feet." The pattern is one of many possible arrangements, usually of two or three syllables, and is called an "iamb." The line's rhythm is defined by the pattern—iambic—and the number of feet. Four feet, for example, would make tetrameter, five pentameter, six hexameter, and so on. The example above is iambic pentameter, Shakespeare's favorite. Iambic pentameter was the basis of sonnets. When unrhymed, it was the "blank verse" (*AYLI* IV.i.29–30; *MAAN* V.ii.34) introduced to England by Surrey and constituting a large portion of Shakespeare's dialogue.

Poetic rhythm is known today as "meter." Shakespeare used somewhat different terminology. When he means meter, he usually says "numbers" (*TN* II.v.99–100; *LLL* IV.iii.319), a reference no doubt to all that counting of stresses and syllables. He makes reference to stanzas, also using the alternate terms "staff" and "verse" (*MWW* III.ii.63–64; *LLL* IV.ii.105). There were many types of verses, some of which were simple four-line ballad stanzas, considered little more difficult to write than nursery rhymes (*H5* V.ii.161). More ambitious poets (*Tim* V.i.ch.) challenged themselves with difficult forms. The poulter's measure was a couplet in which the first line had twelve syllables and the second fourteen syllables; a fourteener was a pair of rhymed fourteen-syllable lines. When these types of verse were broken into four-line stanzas, they were known as short measure and common measure, respectively. The rhyme royal was a seven-line stanza rhyming *ababbcc*; Shakespeare used it for *The Rape of Lucrece* and adapted it as a six-line form for *Venus and Adonis*. Spenser reached extraordinary heights of complexity in his stanza structure. For *The Faerie Queene* he used nine-line stanzas: eight lines of iambic pentameter followed by a twelve-syllable "Alexandrine" that rhymed with the eighth line. For his *Epithalamion* he used eighteen-line stanzas composed of a sestet followed by couplets in various patterns. Each line had ten syllables except for line 18, which had twelve, and lines 6, 11, and 16, which had six.

Poison

Several poisons were known in the Middle Ages and Renaissance, though it is often unknown which poisons were used in which circumstances. Shakespeare seldom specifies which substance he means, referring to poison in general (*2H6* III.ii.45, 321; *AYLI* I.i.146, V.i.57). He does often speak of "ratsbane," for the extermination of rats was the most common household use of poison (*Lear* III.iv.53–54; *Cym* V.v.247–48; *1H6* V.iv.29). This is almost certainly arsenic, a metal that causes stomach pain, vomiting, loose and bloody stools, cold skin, dizziness, convulsions, and coma. It does not necessarily kill immediately, especially in smaller doses. Prolonged exposure can cause a jaundiced appearance, a flaking rash, headaches, dizziness, constipation, short-term paralysis, numbness, burning sensations, hair loss, liver failure, weight loss, and vision problems. The fact that it can be administered slowly and progressively, causing a general decline in health, makes it a likely candidate for the poison intended for King Cymbeline:

> a mortal mineral, which, being took,
> Should by the minute feed on life and, ling'ring,
> By inches waste you. (*Cym* V.v.49–52)

Though intentional arsenic poisoning was certainly frightening, in reality it was much more common to be poisoned by arsenic or mercury through environmental exposure in the workplace.

Another poison mentioned by name is aconitum, also known as wolfbane or monkshood (*2H4* IV.iv.48). The entire plant was poisonous, but especially the leaves and roots. Ingestion caused burning, tingling, numbness of the face and throat, vomiting, vision problems, respiratory paralysis, sweating, convulsions, and circulatory slowing. General numbness, cold, facial paralysis, and heart failure ensued in minutes or hours.

The poison sold to Romeo by the Mantuan apothecary (*R&J* V.i.50–86, V.iii.119–20) is unidentified. Certainly, it begins to work very quickly, a characteristic of many poisons, including prussic acid and some compounds of mercury. Unlike those poisons, however, it completes its work in mere seconds. There are poisons that work as quickly as that which Romeo uses to commit suicide, but they are usually not native to Europe or require injection rather than ingestion to be fatal immediately. Romeo's poison is likely a concoction of Shakespeare's imagination and dramatic necessity, made more believable to the audience by the reputation of Italians at the time as master poisoners.

Poisons known in Shakespeare's time included various plants or plant distillates such as henbane, belladonna, prussic acid, foxglove, and hemlock (*Mac* IV.i.25). Many poisons were actually ingested in small quantities on purpose (*2H4* I.i.137). Belladonna, for example, dilated the pupils and was used in some areas by women who wanted their eyes to appear larger and darker; its name literally means "beautiful lady." Some animals were also known or suspected to be poisonous, including adders and other vipers, spiders (*WT* II.i.39–45), and toads (*R3* I.ii.147, I.iii.245). Some toads are in fact capable of producing poisons, but since they can neither bite nor sting, the fact is usually of little consequence. However, poisoners were sometimes said to use and enhance this fact by feeding toads arsenic and then, when the animals were dead, distilling their juices to make a venomous concoction called *venin de crapaud*.

Fear of poison was widespread, especially among tyrannical husbands, who were at their wives' mercy when it came to the composition of their food (*AW* III.v.83–84), and among monarchs. Spurious remedies and preventives for poison were therefore popular. One was theriac, a concoction with as many as seventy-three ingredients, including vipers' flesh. Another was the bezoar stone, thought to be the cyrstallized tear of a snakebitten deer, but actually a gallstone-like concretion found mainly in the digestive systems of certain goats. It was thought to cure poison if swallowed, despite a failed test performed on a condemned criminal by the surgeon Ambroise Paré.

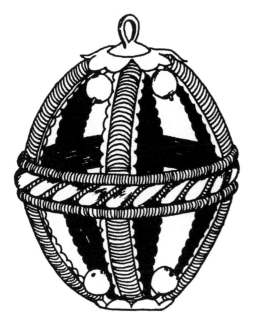

Gold and pearl pomander case.

Pomander

In a time when bad-smelling or infected air was believed to cause disease, hygiene was iffy at best, and streets were fouled with animal and human waste, the pomander (*WT* IV.iv.600–603) was more than a pretty accessory. It was considered an asset to health and well-being. The pomander was a metal cage or net filled with a mixture of sweet-smelling ingredients, such as cloves, cinnamon, musk, and civet. The physician Andrew Boorde recommended a healthful mixture of "lapdanum," ambergris, "wodde of Aloes," nutmeg, rosewater, and "storax calamite." Though many pomanders were held in jeweled balls and hung from the waist on ribbons or chains, they might also be incorporated into pendants, links of bracelets or necklaces, and even buttons. When a pleasant scent was required due to the foulness of the air, the wearer simply held the pomander, if it were worn on the hand or a chain, to her nose. *See also* Clothing; Cosmetics.

Pound

The standard that set one silver pound (*libra*) equal to 240 pennies dated back to at least the eighth century, but it was some time before gold pound coins were introduced in England. Elizabeth I issued a gold half-pound coin of 10s in 1558 and added a pound coin of 20s in 1561, both of which remained in circulation for the rest of her reign. Both the pound (*2H6* III.i.115, III.iii.13) and half-pound had a profile portrait bust of the queen on the obverse surrounded by the abbreviated Latin legend ELIZABETH D G ANG FRAN ET HIB REGINA—Elizabeth Queen of England, France, and Ireland by the grace of God (D G, Dei gratia)—further shortened as necessary. The reverse showed a crowned shield with the royal arms, flanked by the letters E R for "Elizabeth Regina," and surrounded by the legend SCVTVM FIDEI PROTEGET EAM (The shield of faith will protect her).

Under James I, the pound became known as the sovereign or unite, and the half-pound as the half-sovereign or half-unite. The term "sovereign" for a large gold coin had been used before, for a 20s coin in the reign of Henry VII and for a 30s coin later in the Tudor dynasty. The 10-shilling unit also predated both the half-pound and the half-sovereign; previously it was known as the royal or ryal, and it earns a couple of mentions in Shakespeare, most notably when Falstaff tries to cajole Hal into a robbery by saying, "thou cam'st not of the blood royal if thou darest not stand for ten shillings" (*1H4* I.ii.140–41).

The 1603–4 sovereign's obverse showed a crowned James with the legend IACOBVS D G ANG SCO FRAN ET HIB REX—short for James (Iacobus), by the grace of God (D G, Dei gratia) king (rex) of England, Scotland, France, and Ireland (Hibernie). The reverse bore the crowned royal arms as on Elizabeth's coin, but with two changes; the SCVTVM legend was replaced by EXVRGAT DEVS DISSIPENTVR INIMICI (Let God arise and let his enemies be scattered), and the E and R to the sides of the shield were replaced by I R instead, for Iacobus Rex (King James).

The 1604–18 coinage was similar. The sovereign showed a half-length portrait of James, crowned, holding an orb and scepter; the smaller half-sovereign (also known as a double crown) showed only a crowned bust. Both bore the IACOBVS D G and so on. Each had the crowned coat of arms and I R on the reverse. On the sovereign, the legend around this device was FACIAM EOS IN GENTEM VNAM (I will make them one nation), and on the half-sovereign it was HENRICVS ROSAS REGNA IACOBVS (Henry

Pound, or sovereign, 1558–1603. Actual size is 44 mm in diameter. © 2002 The American Numismatic Society. All rights reserved.

the roses, James the kingdoms), a reference to Henry VII's union of the houses of York and Lancaster (whose symbols were the white and the red rose, respectively) and James's union of Scotland and England.

Shakespeare usually mentions the pound when discussing large sums. These range from the ten-pound price of a "score of good ewes" (*2H4* III.ii.51–53) to the thousand pounds necessary to forestall an invasion (*R2* II.ii.91), satisfy Falstaff's debt to Shallow (*2H4* V.v.13–14, 72–73), or cure Claudio of "the Benedick" (*MAAN* I.i.82–86). It is also used when describing yearly income (*MM* II.i.120–21; *John* I.i.69).

The half-pound is specifically mentioned in Shakespeare only once, and then indirectly. In *2 Henry IV* (III.ii.226–27), an army conscript bribes Bardolph with £1 composed of "four Harry ten shillings in French crowns"—in other words, four crowns (of 5s each), which equal in value four of the debased ten-shilling pieces of Henry VIII's late reign. Such a coin would have been almost an antique by Shakespeare's time, yet it is obviously of later date than Henry IV's reign. *See also* Money.

Pox

When Shakespeare was born, "pox," or syphilis, was still quite a young disease in Europe. It first appeared in the 1490s in Naples, during an invasion by France, and was, on that account, promptly dubbed *morbus gallicus*, "the French disease." First illustrated in 1496, the French disease had spread to England and Scotland by 1497, where it wrought the same psychological and physical havoc that it had on the Continent. There is speculation, but no consensus, that it originally came from the Americas.

A chronic disease today, syphilis was acute and horribly disfiguring in its early years. It was marked by pustules or "pox," bone degradation, muscle and cardiovascular impairment, baldness, and, worst of all, the rotting away of the flesh of the joints, mouth, nose, and genitals. While it killed few people compared to tuberculosis, plague, and typhus, it was a visible link between sexual intercourse and death, and no disease was to have quite the same emotional impact until the emergence of the AIDS virus.

Sufferers would do almost anything to avoid the worst symptoms of the French disease. (Despite a 1530 poem blaming the origin of the disease on a shepherd named Syphilus, which gave the disease its eventual name, it was still "the French disease" or "the great pox" to Shakespeare's contemporaries.) Some tried verbena, an herb said to be under the influence of Venus. Others opted to be bled or to consume guaiacum bark from Hispaniola. A popular cure was mercury salve, a highly toxic substance that caused damage to the mouth lining, intense salivation, loose teeth, and sometimes the disintegration of the jawbone and the ulceration of the surrounding flesh. Without question, pox and plague were the era's most feared diseases.

It is fitting, then, that pox is mentioned frequently in Shakespeare, often in the same context as plague—that is, in curses, as in "a pox of that jest" (*LLL* V.ii.46) or "A pox damn you" (*2H4* II.iv.39). Its association with brothels is taken for granted (*MM* I.ii.46–47; *Per* IV.vi.15–16, 26–27, 102–3; *Tim* IV.iii.84–88; *T&C* V.x.50–55), as are its French-Neapolitan origins. When it is not called "pox," it is "malady of France" (*H5* V.i.83) or "the Neapolitan bone-ache" *T&C* II.iii.18), and the ensuing bald head is commonly called a "French crown" (*MM* I.ii.53; *MND* I.ii.95–96; *AW* II.ii.22–23), chiefly, one suspects, because there was a coin of the same name and thus a ripe opportunity for punning. Of its symptoms, pain and degradation of the bones and extremities are most often mentioned. It is the "bone-ache" as above, the possible cause of pain in a "great toe" (*2H4* I.ii.248), the "marrow-eating sickness" (*V&A* 739–43) that makes "bones . . . hollow" (*MM* I.ii.57–58). Its ability to cause the flesh to rot is recognized by the gravedigger in *Hamlet*, who observes that "we / have many pocky corses nowadays that will scarce / hold the laying in" (V.i.164–66). Of the many available treatments, the one mentioned most frequently by Shakespeare is the "tub-fast" (*Tim* IV.iii.84–88), in which the unlucky sufferer attempted to sweat out his sickness while sitting in a large tub. *See also* Disease and Injury; Prostitution.

Pregnancy and Childbirth

The bearing of children, especially among the aristocracy, was considered to be a woman's principal purpose for existing. Barrenness, particularly when there was a family fortune or title to be passed to the next generation, was the worst curse that could be laid upon a woman (*Lear* I.iv.277–91). She would, in her desperation, try charms, prayers, and all sorts of dubious medical advice to amend her condition. But if pregnancy was a near-necessity, it was also, in every class, one of the most exhausting and potentially dangerous experiences in a woman's life. There was a small but not inconsequential chance of dying (*Per* III.i.20–21; *H8* V.i.18–20; *JC* V.iii.70–71), either from complications during the birth or from infection afterward. As compensation, pregnant women were given special attention and indulgences that they received at no other time.

Conception and Discovery

There was a great deal of speculation, much of it thoroughly misguided, about the manner in which women became pregnant. Since most medical knowledge came from the ancient world, the prevailing theories were Aristotle's, that only men created seed and women were merely its incubators, and that of Hippocrates and Galen, who believed that each parent contributed something substantial. Galen argued that both male and female produced sperm, with the female's being less perfect and serving mainly as nourishment for the male's. Some authorities believed that a woman could not conceive unless she experienced orgasm. Many theories were also advanced regarding the means by which the fetus's sex was determined. Galen's opinion was that the right testicle and ovary, being in his opinion naturally warmer, produced the seed that developed into boys, while the cooler left testicle and ovary engendered girls.

Women discovered that they were "with child" (*AW* IV.iii.191; *TNK* IV.iii.42) in one of a number of ways. Hard nipples, swollen veins, cloudy urine, internal quivering, vomiting, loss of appetite, and food cravings were early signs, followed by the cessation of menses and the gradual swelling of the belly. The blood that had been expelled in menstruation was now believed to be reserved to feed the growing child (*3H6* I.i.222). There was no conclusive medical test for pregnancy; Mary I, Elizabeth I's half sister, went all the way to her supposed delivery date before her doctors determined that she was not pregnant, but suffering from a condition that was probably a combination of dropsy and wishful thinking. The best sign that all was well was the "quickening" of the child, when it began to move perceptibly in the womb and to kick (*AW* V.iii.301–3; *LLL* V.ii.70–79). Quickening literally meant coming to life, and it was believed that at 45 days, the fetus was fully formed and was given its soul.

Care During Pregnancy

Husbands were advised to take especially good care of their pregnant wives. Any food craving (*MM* II.i.87–89; *WT* IV.iv.264–65), no matter how fantastic, was to be granted, lest harm come to the fetus. Pregnant women could not be legally executed, so many women pleaded their bellies, truly or falsely, to avoid the noose, ax, or stake (*1H6* V.iv.62–85). In order to prevent miscarriages, women used herbs such as sage. They also tried to avoid cold, wind, frightening sights, loud noises like cannon fire or the sound of bells, dancing, immoderate sexual activity, overeating, and undue anger, fear, or other strong emotion, all of which were believed to bring on labor (*Per* III.Cho.44–52; *WT* II.ii.22–24). They also eschewed funerals and any motion of winding or grinding for fear of killing the child, or strangling it, by suggestion. Those seeking to induce an abortion, of course, applied these instructions in reverse. Instead of sage, they might ingest savin, ratsbane, and a host of other toxic substances, in the hope of miscarrying.

Lying-in and Delivery

As a woman approached the expected time of "eaning" (*Per* III.iv.5–7), or delivery, she began her lying-in (*Cor* I.iii.77–78). During this time, she kept to her home, or sometimes traveled to the home of a female relative. In middle-class homes, the husband was expected to take on many of the household responsibilities, and in most levels of society, the woman was surrounded by female friends and relatives, selected by her and entertained with food and drink during their visits. Many of these "gossips" (from "god-sibs"—see *TA* IV.ii.151; *2GV* III.i.269) would stay for the delivery, assisting the midwife by keeping the laboring woman cheerful. The best bed hangings that could be afforded were used to adorn the chamber, and a Bible, or a bit of bread or iron, was placed in the childbirth bed as a protection against the fairies. A woman might give birth in her own bed, but it was preferable to erect a special high bed topped with a straw mattress, along with plenty of clean white linen; the pallet was the origin of "in the straw," the common euphemism at the time for being in labor. The bed was placed away from the walls, so that the helpers could reach all sides of it, and near but not too near the fireplace. The woman might labor (*Oth* II.i.125–26) here, or standing, or leaning, or sitting in a birthing chair called a "groaning stool" or "midwife's stool." The husband, as soon as labor began, was banished from the chamber, along with all other men.

The room itself was dark, warm because of the fire, and closed at the doors and windows to prevent any cold air from striking the mother or the newborn. The laboring woman removed all her rings, as well as laces, buckles, and other fasteners. All knots nearby were untied, all locks unlocked. The reason for this precaution was a belief in sympathetic magic; closed and tied objects nearby would constrict the womb and make the delivery harder. The midwife, meanwhile, set up her tools: sponge, oils for the womb and her hands, the groaning stool, a knife with which to cut the umbilical cord, and herbal preparations to speed up the labor, ease the mother's pain, reduce bleeding, or increase lactation. The midwife checked

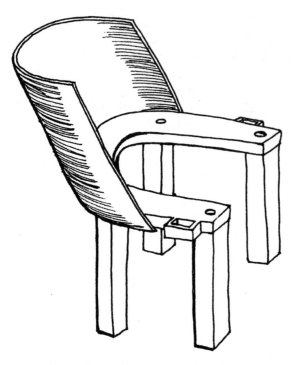

A groaning stool, late sixteenth century.

the presentation of the fetus, uttered encouraging words, and ordered broth, poultry, caudle (a thin porridge made with wine or ale—see *2H6* IV.vii.91), and other sustaining food for the laboring woman as necessary. If severe complications developed, she was to call a surgeon. There was not a great deal that even a surgeon could do for the mother, but if the mother died, he could cut open the womb in the hopes of saving the child (*Cym* V.iv.37–38; *Mac* V.viii.15–16). Cesarean section was never performed with any hope of saving the laboring woman. If the child seemed sure to die, the midwife could perform an emergency baptism on the doomed child, but most deliveries did not require extreme measures to save either the mother or the baby.

As the delivery progressed, the midwife lubricated the birth canal, checked contractions, and administered herbal medicines. Once the child emerged, she tied and cut the cord, and dressed it with an astringent to hinder bleeding. This part of her duties was invested with far more importance than today, for the shape of a child's navel after it healed was held to foretell all sorts of things about its future life, including its fertility and the size of its adult penis or vagina. The navel was held to be so important that some people carried the string used to tie it for the rest of their lives to ward off evil magic. The child's health and breathing were verified, and it was bathed and swaddled, or wrapped in cloth bands that bound its limbs firmly to its sides. The laboring mother was urged to push out the placenta, which was buried by the midwife.

Now the father, who had probably been waiting anxiously outside the delivery room, listening apprehensively to his wife's screams and groans (*H8* V.i.62–72), was given some role in the proceedings. The midwife carried the swaddled child to him (*TA* IV.ii.46–86, 140–51) with the traditional words, "Father, see there is your child, God give you much joy with it, or take it speedily to his bliss." Then the baby was taken back into the birth room, where it was laid beside the mother to send any diseases it carried into her, and out with the afterbirth, blood, and amniotic fluid. The room remained dark, warm, and quiet for a while, as the midwife massaged the baby to augment its future growth and administered any necessary salves or medicines to mother and child.

All these attentions were considered the mother's due, the basic courtesies merited by any woman undergoing such pain and effort. Not all women, however, received such treatment. Unwed mothers and prostitutes, without the support of their communities, might give birth far from home, or even outdoors (*Mac* IV.i.30–31), though the unwed and "groaning Juliet" is accorded "needful, but not lavish, means" (II.ii.15–16) in *Measure for Measure*. The wife of Pericles has not even what is "needful," for she gives birth aboard ship with "No light, no fire" (*Per* III.i.58). The unfortunate Hermione complains of the injustice of being forced to labor in prison with "The childbed privilege denied, which 'longs / To women of all fashion" (*WT* III.ii.101–2). It was highly unusual for women to forgo their lying-in; only some great event or necessity could draw them outdoors (*H8* IV.i.76–79).

Sometimes a child was born deformed (*WT* IV.iv.259–71). Elizabethans and Jacobeans took such incidents very seriously, often interpreting "monstrous" births as omens of tragic events on a national scale, or as proofs of divine punishment (*R2* II.ii.62–66). The moment of birth, even for a physically normal child, could be attended by any of a number of omens, positive and negative. The appearance of a bird of ill omen, such as a raven or a crow, was always feared; Shakespeare presents a good catalog of such omens when describing the birth of the future Richard III (*3H6* V.vi.44–54, 70–77; *R3* II.iv.28–29). It should be noted, however, that being born with teeth like Richard was not always considered an ill omen; an account of a Catholic life around Shakespeare's time listed the prenatal tooth as a miraculous event. Birth at an astrologically propitious moment, or with the "caul" (amniotic sac) still around the head, was held to be a positive sign. John Monson, born in 1597 with a caul, kept it in a pendant as a good-luck charm.

Upsitting and Churching

Conventional wisdom held that a woman should not go to sleep immediately after delivering a child. It was supposed to be more healthful to stay up for a few hours, making merry with the gossips. Sometimes the revelry became so loud, drunken, and bawdy that the authorities tried to put a stop to it, but this gossiping was another of the childbed privileges, and it was hard to suppress.

Another privilege—which does not sound very pleasant—was a period of time, between about fourteen and twenty-one days, during which the new mother lay on the same unchanged straw pallet and rested. At the end of this time, which ended when she felt ready to resume her household duties or when her husband had had enough of doing them himself, she was allowed to get up, to bathe, and to dispose of the soiled pallet. A feast generally followed this "upsitting" to celebrate the mother's safe recovery.

A more public festival, held about a month after the delivery, was "churching." The mother, who had been restricted from full participation in social, domestic, and religious life, was formally restored to her previous status. Some viewed the ceremony as a cleansing, but the principal purpose was to thank God for the mother's deliverance from danger. It was, of course, more joyous if the child had also survived and was safely baptized, and deeply poignant if the infant had already died, as many did during birth or shortly afterward. Shakespeare makes no direct references either to upsitting or to churching, though the aggrieved Hermione complains that, as the final insulting touch to her jailhouse delivery of Perdita, she has been "hurried / Here to this place, i' th' open air, before / I have got strength of limit" (*WT* III.ii.102–4), a clear violation of the woman's postpartum privileges. *See also* Baptism; Bastardy; Children; Marriage; Nursing.

Prison

Prisons (*2H4* V.v.35; *1H6* II.v.55–58; *2H6* IV.iii.16–17, IV.vii.44–45; *3H6* III.ii.70; *R2* I.iii.166–69; *2GV* III.i.236; *R3* I.i.121–28, 74–77; *AW* V.iii.281–82; *Oth* I.ii.84) were not intended as a final, or even long-term, destination for convicted wrongdoers. Instead, they were meant to be temporary holding areas for the accused awaiting trial. The exceptions to this rule were debtors (*CE* IV.i.107–9, IV.iv.108–20), who stayed in jail until they could repay their creditors; political prisoners (*3H6* I.iii.43); and those who, for one reason or another, had been forgotten and lost in the system. Barnardine's stay of nine years is, therefore, extremely unusual (*MM* IV.ii.134). Yet it was not legally inconceivable, for there was no right of habeas corpus until the late seventeenth century, and people could thus be kept in jail indefinitely, without cause or conviction, for as long as the ruler or Privy Council deemed appropriate. Often even the jailers forgot why certain prisoners had originally been incarcerated.

It was fortunate that long-term imprisonment was uncommon, for prison conditions were dreadful. Jails (*MAAN* III.v.59, 65; *TS* V.i.90–95, 129) were dirty, bare-floored or strewn with fetid rushes (*TNK* II.i.23), smelly (*TNK* III.i.86), and notorious as breeding grounds for disease (*MM* IV.iii.70–72). Shakespeare's jails (in the English spelling, gaols) are not precisely hellholes, and in this judgment we have more evidence than usual, for he sets a number of scenes (*MM* III.i, IV.ii, IV.iii; *WT* II.ii; *TNK* II.i, IV.i, IV.iii, V.ii) in jails and includes several jailers among his characters (*Cym* IV.iv; *WT* II.ii; *TNK* II.i, IV.i, IV.iii, V.ii, V.iv; *MV* III.iii; and the "provost" of *MM* II.i., II.iii, IV.ii). Yet we catch glimpses of what must have been a profoundly uncomfortable life. Jailers were notorious for extracting fees from their prisoners, since prisoners had few legal rights and did not even have to be fed a diet that could keep them alive and healthy. Jailers could, therefore, charge extra for decent food, beer, fresh rushes, lighter manacles and chains (also called irons, fetters, or gyves—see *Cym* V.iv.8–9, 14, 161; *1H4* IV.ii.41; *TNK* II.i.329–32, II.v.8; *MM* II.iv.92), the removal of all fetters, and better quarters. They were even paid a special fee upon each prisoner's release (*3H6* IV.vi.1–15; *WT* I.ii.52–54). In 1592 Robert Greene accused jailers of charging for "crossing and wiping out of the boke [in which prisoners' names were entered], turning the key, paieng the chamberlain, feeing for his jurie, & twenty such extortions."

The prisoners were grouped together without regard to sex, so that female prisoners were often raped or forced to engage in prostitution to secure enough money to pay their fees. The sad truth was that prisoners with little or no money, like debtors, were reduced to begging alms through the barred windows from passersby (*MM* IV.iii.19), while rich and influential prisoners lived comfortably with servants, visitors, and something nearly like normal life (*2H6* II.iv.110).

There were several different types of prisons. Bridewells, which were scattered across the country, housed vagrants, prostitutes, rioters, and other minor offenders who, it was thought, could be redeemed by forced labor. The first such bridewell, after which the others were named, was established in 1556, and by 1609 such institutions were mandated in every county. There were jails run by counties and towns, and even a few operated by bishoprics. London had several prisons that were famous throughout the nation, if only because they were subsidized by taxes paid by the counties. These included the Tower of London, which held mainly political prisoners; the Fleet (*2H4* V.v.93); King's Bench; Marshalsea (*H8* V.iv.85); and Newgate, which housed criminal defendants and served as a place of execution (*1H4* III.iii.95). Shakespeare does not mention the Clink, another famous London prison, but there were a few "counters," or compters—in Wood, Poultry, and Bread streets—that held mainly debtors (*MWW* III.iii.75–77).

The shortcomings of the system were apparent to many, but few alternatives were suggested or implemented during Shakespeare's lifetime. Long-term incarceration seems never to have been seriously considered. Transportation to a colony, which became a popular solution to English crime in the seventeenth and eighteenth centuries, was not suggested until 1611, and not implemented until 1615, when prisoners were first shipped to Virginia. A plan to man galleys with convict rowers was briefly implemented in 1601–2 but was unsuccessful. It would be many years before prisons would serve as the primary means of dealing with serious offenders. *See also* Execution; Law; Places.

Prostitution

During the sixteenth century, a fundamental shift occurred in attitudes toward prostitution. Under Catholicism, it had been a tolerated vice. The

Protestants were not so permissive, and across Europe they outlawed brothels (*MAAN* I.i.246–47; *1H4* III.iii.166–67; *Lear* I.iv.246; *Tim* IV.i.13; *Per* IV.ii.set), known as "stews" (*2H4* I.ii.54, II.iv.149; *1H4* III.iii.119; *MM* II.i.87–92; *R2* V.iii.16) because in the Middle Ages they were commonly public bathhouses (*MM* II.i.62–65). Prostitutes caught practicing their trade had their heads shaved. Then they were paraded through the streets, either riding in or tied behind a cart. Sometimes they were whipped at the rear of the cart in the public marketplace or even branded on the cheek. This crackdown gave rise to some interesting contradictions; for example, the Southwark brothels near the Globe Theater were under the administrative control of the Anglican Bishop of Winchester, for which reason some called the prostitutes there "Winchester geese" (*T&C* V.x.52; *R&J* II.iv.79).

Other terms for prostitutes included stale (from a term for decoy or snare—see *MAAN* II.ii.24, IV.i.64), drab (*T&C* V.ii.191–92; *WT* IV.iii.26), fitchew or polecat (because it was smelly, and so, presumably, were the prostitutes—see *Lear* IV.vi.122; *MWW* IV.i.26), hobbyhorse (*WT* I.ii.276; *Oth* IV.i.154), and punk (*MWW* II.ii.130; *MM* V.i.178, V.i.524–25). Some terms that are more familiar today, such as strumpet (*Oth* IV.i.97) and whore (*Oth* IV.ii.119–20; *Tim* IV.iii.84–88), were also in use. A courtesan (*Lear* III.ii.80; *Cym* III.iv.124; *2H6* I.i.221), from the Italian *cortegiana*, was an expensive, educated prostitute. At the opposite end of the spectrum was the doxy (*WT* IV.iii.2), a beggar's or thief's mistress; a young doxy was a "dell." The women or men who employed them were known variously as bawds (*1H4* I.ii.8; *H5* V.i.86; *MM* ch.; *Lear* III.ii.91; *R&J* II.iv.135) or panders (*H5* IV.v.16; *Per* IV.ii.ch.). Male accomplices were sometimes called "apple squires," and the women themselves might be called "bawdy-baskets" if they plied their trade door-to-door under the cover of selling cheap goods.

Attempts to suppress the trade did little good. In 1592, Robert Greene wrote of the gorgeously dressed streetwalkers, in rouged cheeks and enormous ruffs, who strolled along the roads or solicited in taverns and alehouses, and in the early seventeenth century, Thomas Heywood claimed that any schoolboy of fifteen or sixteen knew all about prostitutes and their ways. Shakespeare was well aware of the hypocrisies of his time; even as he uses whoredom as the ultimate insult to a woman, he recognizes that even the beadle whipping a prostitute in the marketplace "hotly lusts to use her in that kind / For which thou whip'st her" (*Lear* IV.vi.162–63).

Little is known about the conditions under which prostitutes worked in this period, or how much they charged, or how many men they entertained per night. What is known is that, even without the fear of arrest, it was a difficult job. Prostitutes, then as now, were especially vulnerable to disease (*T&C* V.x.54–55), beatings (*2H4* III.ii.321–22), and disrespect. Crucial to safety and reliable business was finding a place in which to work. Few alehouses actually functioned as brothels, but prostitutes were known to frequent alehouses looking for customers. At other times, drinkers at an alehouse might search for a prostitute and bring her back to the alehouse for a drink. Sometimes the alewife herself, or her daughter, was a part-time prostitute; in 1578 Margaret Fishe of Catton stated, "There cannot be any alewife thrive without she be a whore or have a whore in her house." Prostitutes commonly worked in the needle trades; there is a sly innuendo along these lines in *Henry V* (II.i.33–36).

Proverbs

Shakespeare's works are full of allusions to proverbs (*H5* III.vii.116–25; *Cor* I.i.207–10), songs, Latin literature, myths, and Scripture. A complete catalog of his proverbial references would consume an inordinate amount of space, but a few of the more common and, to modern minds, more obscure, deserve some explanation here. Expressions in quotations are taken verbatim from the plays; those not in quotations are referred to in the plays, sometimes with slight alterations, sometimes more indirectly. The initial letters of direct quotations have in some cases been capitalized for the sake of consistency.

Proverb	Citation(s)	Derivation or meaning
"Beggars mounted run their horse to death."	*3H6* I.iv.127	Those unaccustomed to good fortune ruin it through ignorance.
"Brag is a good dog, but Hold-Fast is a better."	*H5* II.iii.52	Actions speak louder than words.
(Our, my) Cake is dough	*TS* I.i.108–9 *TS* V.i.138	A reference to a baking mishap that must have been common enough among even experienced bakers, when ovens had no temperature gauges—the implication is that the cake is undercooked and doughy, and the meaning is that everything has gone wrong.
"The empty vessel makes the loudest sound."	*H5* IV.iv.70	The most foolish person is always the most talkative.
Fair face, foul heart.	*H8* III.i.145	The sixteenth-century version of "You can't judge a book by its cover."

Proverb	Citation(s)	Derivation or meaning
"Have is have, however men do catch."	*John* I.i.173	Similar to "all's fair in love and war" or "the ends justify the means"—any stratagem is authorized, as long as it succeeds. The proverb in the following line, "well won is still well shot," has the same meaning—"still," in this period, meant "always."
He that's born to be hanged need not fear drowning.	*Temp* I.i.29–30	Often said of perennial rogues, as a way of characterizing their absolute incorrigibility. The phrase "born to be hanged" survived as long as England's harsh felony sentences and crops up in the eighteenth-century novel *Tom Jones* in reference to the title character.
He who sups with the devil must have a long spoon.	*Temp* II.ii. 99–100	He who meddles with something dangerous had best be very careful.
"In at the window, or else o'er the hatch"	*John* I.i.171	If you can't get something one way, you may be able to get it another; the "hatch" is the lower half of a divided door.
Liquor will make a cat talk.	*Temp* II.ii.84	Liquor is a powerful substance; liquor makes everyone, even the most silent, garrulous.
"A little pot and soon hot."	*TS* IV.i.5	Just as a small pot will heat up more quickly than a large one, so a short person is something quick-tempered.
Nine days' wonder	*3H6* III.ii.113–14 *AYLI* III.ii. 175–76	Something only temporarily fascinating.
"Pitchers have ears."	*TS* IV.iv.52 *R3* II.iv.37	Anyone might be listening, so one should be discreet.
A poor dog that is not worth the whistling.	*Lear* IV.ii.30	Something utterly valueless.
The poor man always pays.	*H5* II.i.97	The person who can least afford to suffer always seems to be the one who does.
"A staff is quickly found to beat a dog."	*2H6* III.i.171	Dogs were poorly treated in the Renaissance and were often beaten. The implication is that one can always find

Proverb	Citation(s)	Derivation or meaning
		an instrument with which to oppress someone, particularly someone already routinely downtrodden.
The tailor makes the man.	*Lear* II.ii.56–57	Some people are all show (and are thus "made" by their clothes rather than their character). The phrase could also be adapted with a number—three, or four, or some other number of tailors making the man—and eventually became "nine tailors make the man," with the tailors being the nine tollings of the funeral bell that were traditionally rung at a man's funeral.
A tinker stops one hole and makes others.	*TNK* III.v.83–84	Tinkers, who traveled about mending pots and pans, were notoriously dishonest, sometimes stealing the pots and pans they mended or other goods belonging to the household. Here, the implication is that they pretend to find damage that they can then charge to repair; it is similar to the behavior of which auto mechanics are routinely suspected.
Wash a tile	*TNK* III.v.40–42	Various washing proverbs were current in Shakespeare's day. Most meant that the labor involved was done in vain. The most common versions involved washing an ass's ears or, in a racist version, a "blackmoor's" skin. Shakespeare's use of the tile may have to do with the fact that tile was common as a roofing material, especially in London, and would have been alternately dirtied by dust and smoke and rinsed clean by rain, both of which would make one's labor in washing them useless.
"Who dares not stir by day must walk by night."	*John* I.i.172	One should make the best of the realities of a situation; this is analogous to "making a virtue of necessity."

Pygmy

Pygmies (*Lear* IV.vi.167; *TNK* III.iv.14–16), a group of Africans whose adult height is unusually small, were mentioned by Herodotus and Homer, but they had disappeared from most travel accounts and histories until the sixteenth century. When they resurfaced in such books, they were at first thought to be mythical. Various accounts claimed the existence of pgymies in Africa, India, and an islet in the Hebrides. A 1625 book, *Purchas His Pilgrimes*, said they were native to Africa, as tall as twelve-year-old European boys, and skilled at hunting with bows and darts.

Quart d'Écu

This silver coin was worth one quarter of an écu, or French crown. It thus corresponded to roughly 15 pence. It appears twice in Shakespeare's works, both times in the same play (*AW* IV.iii.283, V.ii.32). It was introduced in the 1570s as part of a general reform of the French currency, in which the old system of £ s d was abandoned in favor of a system based on the écu as the standard unit.

Rape

Rape (*Per* IV.i.97–99), as a despised privilege of the nobility (*2H6* IV.viii.30–31, V.i.186; *R3* III.vii.7–8; *John* I.i.253–58), a wartime terror tactic (*H5* III.iii.19–21), a filthy and habitual vice (*AW* IV.iii.189–92, 254–57), or an act of power and vengeance, appears frequently in Shakespeare's works. His sympathies are usually with the victims, or at least with the male relatives of the victims (*Temp* I.ii.349–50), though he seems to view threats of rape, or jokes about it, as perfectly harmless as long as the act itself is not committed (*2GV* V.ii.57–59; *R&J* I.i.17–20, 24–28; *MND* II.i.214–20). Characters who utter such words are proven redeemable by the outcomes of the plays. The proper conduct of the victim, in Shakespeare's view (and in the dominant opinion of the time), was a visible sense of overwhelming shame, a desire for revenge for the sake of her family honor, and suicide (*RL*; *TA* II.i.110–35, II.iii.122–91, II.iv.1–43, IV.i.47–58, IV.ii.9, 40–43, V.i.63, V.iii.36–58). As for the reality, rather than the image on the stage, rape was probably at least as common then as it is today, and though some victims undoubtedly killed themselves, others survived and accused their attackers, or swallowed the shame, or bore bastards with or without the moral support of their families. In the eyes of society, even though they were not strictly to blame for their victimization, they were also not entirely guiltless, and they were forever afterward considered damaged goods. Rape within marriage was not a crime, and would not be so for centuries; rape outside of marriage was a felony with benefit of clergy (a lighter sentence if the condemned could prove his literacy) until 1575, when benefit of clergy was removed. *See also* Crime.

Religion

Christianity was obviously not the only religion in the world in Shakespeare's day. It was not even the only religion practiced in England. Nevertheless, to most people in England, it was the only one that mattered, and it mattered a great deal. For many people today, it is hard to conceive of dying for religion and even harder to conceive of dying for apparently slight differences in doctrine within the same religion, but it happened over and over again in sixteenth- and seventeenth-century Europe, and in numerous lesser ways, religion permeated almost every aspect of daily life. It had done so even in the early sixteenth century, when England was still Catholic, still ruled by a Catholic Henry VIII whose arguments against Lutheranism (*H8* III.ii.99–100) had won him the title of *Fidei Defensor* (Defender of the Faith) from the pope. It remained so during and after the religious turmoil that spread through England as Henry named himself, not the pope, head of the church in England; as he dissolved the monasteries and convents that had existed for centuries; as his Protestant son Edward VI authorized the further reform of the English church; as Protestant zealots raided the churches and destroyed altars, relics, and images; as Edward's half sister Mary I restored Catholicism for five years; and as their other half sister, Elizabeth I, came to the throne to return a compromising Protestantism to the nation. Ironically, Elizabeth, like her half siblings and all the English monarchs who followed her, retained the title *Fidei Defensor.*

Amid all the uncertainty, the extremism, the martyrdom of first one set of opposition clerics and then another, and the flight of many of the remaining opponents into exile, the common people of England strove to guess which way the wind would blow tomorrow and to search their own consciences for answers. The Protestants were, at the beginning of the sixteenth century, in a decided minority, and there was a great deal of anger about Henry's treatment of religious foundations, despite the undoubted indignation of some at abuses like the selling of indulgences (absolution from certain sins) and simony (the selling of church offices—see *H8* IV.ii.36). Even at midcentury, there was much celebration when Mary took the throne, a renewed outfitting of churches with Catholic paraphernalia, and a widespread (though not universal) enthusiasm for the return of the old faith. Mary might have succeeded in keeping England within the Catholic fold if she had done three things: refrained from her enthusiastic executions of Protestants, married a more popular figure than Philip II of Spain, and given birth to a child. However, she did none of the three, and Elizabeth's accession was greeted with a slow, tentative, and eventually overwhelming conversion of the population to conformity with the Protestant Anglican church. One element of her success was her reluctance to prosecute people for their inward beliefs. As long as they made an outward show of obedience and showed up at church on Sundays, they could do whatever they liked in their hearts. Like Mary, she resorted to executions, about 180 for various crimes of Catholicism between 1570 and 1603, and she approved of a 1584 law making the harboring of Catholic priests a felony and simply being a Jesuit priest on English soil an act of treason. However, unlike Mary, she was a public-relations genius who knew how to substitute her own cult of the Virgin Queen for the worship of saints. Moreover, she was long-lived; sheer persistence in breathing has always been a popular attribute for monarchs.

Like her predecessors, Elizabeth was plagued by extremism on both sides. On the one hand, there were plenty of Catholics, secret and professed, in England. Complaints were constantly being made by Protestants that the Catholics were smuggling in priests, holding Masses in their homes, and sending their children abroad to be educated in Catholic schools. On the other hand were the Puritans (a term coined in 1567), who longed for an even more complete Reformation and privately used the Bible and liturgy that came from Geneva. Elizabeth, who appears to have practiced a Protestantism that was very near Catholicism in many ways, was loath to give in to Puritan demands, but since the most conservative clergy had deserted on her accession, she was left with only reformers to guide her fledgling church.

Church Organization and Clergy

The Anglican Church ruled itself through a body called Convocation (*H5* I.i.76) and received orders from its supreme leader, Elizabeth, through her Court of High Commission. The next highest authorities within the church were the archbishops of Canterbury and York, who administered the archdioceses that bore the same names. The Archbishop of Canterbury, whose office was deemed the superior of the two, was head of most of England, plus all of Wales and Ireland; he crowned the king (or queen, if she ruled in her own right) and served as the monarch's personal chaplain. The Archbishop of York was responsible for the northern part of England, crowned the queen if she were a mere consort, and served as her chaplain. Each archdiocese was divided into dioceses, or bishoprics, administered by bishops and centered on the regional cathedrals (*1H6* II.ii.12–17; *2H6* I.ii.37). The bishoprics were further divided into archdeaconries, deaneries (*MWW* IV.vi.31–32), and parishes (*1H6* V.iv.11; *MM* II.i.270; *Cym* IV.ii.168; *H8* I.ii.153–54). Each parish had its own church (*MAAN* II.i.342–3, III.iii.88, III.iii.130–35; *Per* II.i.36; *AYLI* II.vii.52) and sometimes a "chapel of ease" for residents who could not travel all the way to the main parish church for services. In addition, there

From *Shakespear's England*. Preaching at St. Paul's Cross, 1621. St. Paul's was the great cathedral of London, dominating its skyline with its immense square spire.

were private chapels (*MAAN* V.iv.71; *WT* V.iii.set; *MV* I.ii.12–14; *Cym* II.ii.33) for noble families, staffed by a chaplain.

The typical staff of a parish church was headed by a priest (*Lear* III.ii.82), who read the liturgy, delivered sermons, and performed marriages, christenings, and funerals. He was responsible for administering penance to sinners (*2H6* II.iv.6–75; *MAAN* V.i.272; *2GV* V.ii.38; *LLL* I.i.115); making sure that the death bell was rung; instructing children and apprentices in the catechism (*MAAN* IV.i.77; *TN* I.v.62; *Oth* III.iv.16; *AYLI* III.ii.229), the Ten Commandments (*R3* I.iv.198–205; *2H6* I.iii.144; *TS* III.ii.229–31), the Lord's Prayer, and the Anglican Creed; and inspecting the community for particularly egregious breaches of the Sabbath (*R3* III.ii.110), such as gambling or the operation of alehouses during service hours. He was assisted by a clerk (*TS* IV.iv.94) who kept the parish records, served as a witness to rites, and called out antiphonal responses during services (*R2* IV.i.172–73). He might also have another type of assistant called a curate (*LLL* V.i.110, V.ii.533; *TN* IV.ii.1–12), whose duties were largely identical to the priest's, but who received less pay and had less seniority. The term "parson" (*LLL* IV.ii.83–84, IV.iii.191) was synonymous with parish priest, but the "vicar" (*AYLI* III.iii.ch.; *MWW* IV.vi.48; *TS* III.ii.167) was slightly different. The vicar was identical to the priest or parson except in the manner in which he was paid. Most parsons were paid by tithes (*R&J* I.iv.79–81; *MM* IV.i.76; *John* III.i.73–97)—a portion, ideally a tenth, but sometimes only a token amount, of all the produce generated in the parish. A 1601 record showed that, in one parish,

> tythe lambs is paid the third day of May, and the tenth night and the tenth morning we have tythe milk, and so every 10 night and 10 morning until Martinmas day in the morning, the tythe of a calfe if killed is in the shoulder, if it be sold the tenth penny, if it be weaned a halfpenny, the offering is a penny a piece at Easter; we have tythe eggs on Good Friday and at Easter every garden a penny; tythe wool when they sheare; . . . tythes pigges, tythes of bees; tythe fruit and apples and peares, etc.

In some parishes, however, tithes were collected but paid into the hands of a layman, often the local lord, who had acquired the rights to the tithes at some point. This layman, in turn, paid the salary of the parish priest, who, because he did not receive tithes directly, was termed a vicar. Clergymen, except in particularly rich parishes or higher church offices, were not especially well paid. Smaller "livings" (parish assignments) were worth only about £10 to £30 per year, and parsons were subject to a variety of taxes and tithes to their monarch and bishop. To supplement their incomes, they could teach school, collect fees for marriages and burials, and hold two livings at once, as long as these were within 30 miles (48.3 km) of each other.

Lay officials included the beadle (*John* II.i.188), who whipped sinners and vagrants; the overseer of the poor; the sexton (*MAAN* IV.ii.ch.; V.i.ch.; *Ham* V.i.ch.), who was the caretaker of the church building and grounds, and sometimes the chief ringer of bells (*Per* II.i.39–46; *TS* III.ii.172); surveyors of the highways; and churchwardens, who fined Sabbath breakers, helped to lead the annual procession along the parish boundaries (the "beating of the bounds"), and supervised public institutions such a hospitals, almshouses, and schools. The churchwardens, who also undertook the collection of poor rates and made sure that the church and parsonage were in good repair, tended to be substantial, well respected men. Most of the lay officials gave an account of their actions and expenses at Eastertime, when they were replaced by new officers chosen by the vestry.

The tumult of the sixteenth century had produced an intellectually impoverished clergy, and one of Elizabeth's priorities was to educate and recruit new priests. Clergymen, in theory, had to become fluent in Latin at a grammar school, then attend a university for several years, take holy orders (ideally as a deacon at age twenty-three, then as a priest at age twenty-four) after being recommended by professors or other clergymen and approved by a bishop, and then be lucky enough or influential enough to be preferred to the pulpit of some parish church. Overall, the London clergy tended to be good scholars and orators, but some of the provincial towns had priests, scornfully called "hedge-priests" (*LLL* V.ii.539), who were illiterate in Latin or otherwise poorly educated. Since the clergy was one of the few professions that allowed gentlemen's sons to retain their rank, there were a good many men who were in the pulpit simply because they had no other recourse. This is not to say that they were men of no religious conviction; it was as difficult to avoid religious conviction in sixteenth-century England as it is to avoid television today. Religion was everywhere, in everything from the horn book with which children learned the alphabet to the prayers included, as a matter of course, in texts on agriculture. It was as inconceivable to run a farm without God as it would be to run it without a plow.

The clergy had certain privileges under the law. Being literate (*1H6* III.i.100), they could plead benefit of clergy and accept a lesser punishment in the unlikely event that they were convicted of certain capital crimes. More useful on a daily basis was the prohibition against striking a minister (*MM* V.i.128–30), which was punished by an excommunication reversible only by royal decree. During the time of the excommunication, according to William Harrison, the affected party "can yield no testimony in any matter. . . . No bargain or sale that he maketh is available in law, neither any of his acts whatsoever pleadable," and of course he could not attend religious services, take Communion, or be buried in church ground. Historically, the rite of excommunication involved the use of a bell, book, and candle as symbols for the severance of the excommunicant's ties to the church (*John* III.i.99, III.ii.22).

The Anglican clergy could marry, unlike their Catholic predecessors. A word or two should be said about the latter, since many of Shakespeare's plays are set in Catholic eras or countries. The Catholic Church had priests (*1H6* I.vi.19; *3H6* I.iii.4; *R3* III.ii.ch.; *TS* III.ii.5, 157–64, IV.iv.88–89, 94, 102–3) who performed much the same function as Anglican parish priests. It also had friars (*1H6* I.vi.19; *MAAN* IV.i.ch, V.iv.ch.; *MM* I.iii.ch.; *2GV* IV.iii.46, V.ii.37; *R3* III.v.104; *R&J* ch.), who were mendicants and confessors, and monks (*H8* III.i.23), who lived in single-sex communities called monasteries (*MM* I.iii.set; *R3* I.ii.214; *MV* III.iv.26–32) governed by abbots (*John* III.ii.17–18; *R2* V.iii.136, V.vi.19). The "friar of orders gray" in *Taming of the Shrew* (IV.i.134–35) was a Franciscan, an order that wore gray robes and were thus known as "gray friars." Friar Lawrence, in *Romeo and Juliet*, is also a Franciscan (V.ii.1). The other principal orders of friars were the Augustinians, the Dominican (black friars), and the Carmelites (white friars). Monks and friars typically dressed in loose, sacklike robes with hoods and a rope to cinch the waist; their hair was shaved on the crown only, leaving a fringe around the sides, back and front; this centrally bald haircut was called a "tonsure." Monks, like friars, could belong to one of several orders, each with its own rules and guiding purpose. The "monk o' th' Chartreuse" of *Henry VIII* (I.i.221), for example, was a Carthusian; the name came from their monasteries, or "charterhouses," the chief of which was the Grand Chartreuse in Grenoble. It was an unusually strict order and had a notable house in London that became (and still is) a public school.

The female equivalent of the monks were nuns (*AYLI* III.iv.15–16; *TN* I.i.29; *MM* I.ii.180–81; *V&A* 752; *R3* IV.iv.202), who lived in communities called convents (*MM* I.iv.set; *R2* V.i.22–25; *MND* I.i.69–78). For some women, the opportunity to study and pray and the freedom from marriage and childbearing made the life of a nun attractive. Some also thrived on the discipline offered by strict orders like that of St. Clare (*MM* I.iv.5–19). If the convent was governed by an abbess (*CE* V.i), it was known as an abbey (*2H6* III.i.set; *2GV* V.i.set; *H8* IV.ii.6–30); a monastery governed by an abbot could bear the same title. Some convents, called priories (*CE* V.i.37, 94), were administered by a prioress, who, like her male counterpart, the prior, ranked just below an abbot or abbess. All of these men and women in holy orders were supposed to be poor, obedient, and chaste; their failure to be any or all of these in many cases had been part of the reason for Luther's Reformation (*AW* II.ii.26–27). The Catholic Church, like the Anglican one based upon it, had bishops (*1H6* V.i.60; *2H6* IV.iv.9; *H5* I.i.ch.; *R3* III.iii.ch.) and archbishops; higher up, it had cardinals (*1H6* V.i.28–33, 51–54; *2H6* I.iii.63; *R3* III.i.ch.; *John* V.i.ch.; *H8* II.ii.ch.), and at the top of the hierarchy, the pope (*1H6* V.i.51–54;

2H6 I.iii.64–65; *TA* V.i.76; *H8* II.ii.55; *John* III.i.73–97). The higher clergy, like abbots and bishops, were collectively known as prelates (*H5* I.i.40); this term achieved a certain notoriety in the 1580s and 1590s, when Puritan radicals published attacks on the Anglican Church under the pseudonym "Martin Marprelate."

Doctrine

Several aspects of church doctrine changed with the Reformation. Of the seven Catholic sacraments—baptism, confirmation, Communion, penance, ordination, marriage, and last rites—only baptism and Communion (*AW* IV.iii.139; *R3* V.v.18; *R2* V.ii.97) were retained as sacraments (rites prescribed by Scripture). Protestantism placed a lesser emphasis on both the Virgin Mary (*1H6* I.ii.74–86, 106; *2H6* II.i.51; *R3* III.vii.) and the saints, and many saints' days were removed from the religious calendar of feasts and fasts; William Harrison asserted that the ninety-five Catholic feast days had been reduced to a mere twenty-seven. Miracles, so important to the Catholic process of canonization (*John* III.i.103, III.iii.52), were declared false, for once Jesus had appeared on earth, there was no need for further miracles; everything that needed to be said and done for man's salvation had already been said and done. However, it was impossible to root the saints out of the spiritual mind altogether. Every trade, every town, every parish church had its own guardian saint, just as St. George was the patron saint of England (*3H6* II.i.204, IV.ii.29; *R3* V.iii.271, 302, 350), St. Patrick that of Ireland, and St. David that of Wales. Shakespeare mentions several saints who would have been well known to his audiences, including the omnipresent George; St. Martin of Tours, whose feast day, Martinmas, was November 11 (*1H6* I.ii.131); St. Denis, the patron saint of France (*1H6* I.vi.28, III.ii.18; *H5* V.ii.185); and St. Peter, who guarded the gates of heaven (*Oth* IV.ii.90–91).

If the saints could not be eliminated from the mind and heart, however, they could be eliminated from the map, and the reformers went about destroying statues of saints (*1H6* III.iii.14–15) and all purported relics and shrines (*R&J* I.v.96; *2H6* II.i.62, 88, 92), effectively ending most religious pilgrimages (*R&J* I.v.97–104; *1H4* I.ii.125–127; *R2* I.iii.49, 229, 263; *AYLI* III.ii.130; *RL* 791) within England. Some still went on pilgrimages outside of England, and though this was not a common practice, Shakespeare's audiences would have known that the "cockle hat and staff" (*Ham* IV.v.25–26) were the signs of a pilgrim to the shrine of St. James of Compostela in Spain (*AW* III.iv.4–8, III.v.29–35, 92–94); a cockle shell was (and still is) worn by those on their way to the shrine. The greatest pilgrimage of all was to Jerusalem (*R2* V.vi.49–50), and one who had returned from such a trip was called a palmer, from the palm branch he was entitled to carry (*2H6* V.i.97; *R&J* I.v.104).

Much controversy, even within the Protestant movement itself, sur-

Heaven and hell, from the *Roxburghe Ballads.* Reproduced from the Collections of the Library of Congress.

rounded questions of the afterlife. The Protestants retained a belief in heaven (*MAAN* II.i.41–47) and hell (*2H6* I.iv.40; *TNK* IV.iii.30–44), but they did away with the concept of purgatory (*R&J* III.iii.18), a state of temporary punishment before redemption that could be shortened by the prayers of those still living. The belief in purgatory prompted the rich, and even the middle-class, to leave bequests in their wills for prayers. A certain sum would be set aside for Masses to be said in the deceased's name, or to reimburse "beadsmen" (*R2* III.ii.116), hired paupers, to pray for his soul. In some cases, an entire building or portion of the local church would be endowed as a chantry (*TN* IV.iii.22–26; *H5* IV.i.298–303) in which priests would say prayers for the deceased. Often there was a special service one month after the burial, at which renewed prayers would be offered for release from purgatory. At the Reformation, these "month's mind" ceremonies were suppressed, and prayers for the deceased's soul were greatly restricted. However, the idea of purgatory, like that of limbo (a region adjacent to hell for the souls of unbaptized babies and virtuous pre–Chrisitan pagans—see *CE* IV.ii.32; *TA* III.i.149) remained a powerful part of the religious and poetic imagination. Strict Protestants, reacting against the seeming ease with which Catholicism's confession (or "shrift"—see *CE* II.ii.209; *3H6* III.ii.107; *AW* IV.iii.110–11; *MM* IV.ii.212; *R2* I.i.139–40; *R&J* III.v.234–35) and indulgences (*1H6* I.iii.35; *John* III.i.73–97) cleansed the soul (*3H6* II.iii.41; *R3* I.i.119), believed in a system of election, by which certain people were destined to be saved. This doctrine became complicated and controversial because people then wondered whether good works, which had been an essential part of Catholic practice, did any good at all in the maintenance of one's election to heaven. If one was predestined for heaven or hell, what was the point in being good? Was there free will?

Whatever one decided on that point, it was clear that the Protestant path was a rockier road to eternal bliss. The profoundly sinful nature of humanity was stressed again and again (*R&J* I.v.96, 109–12, III.iii.24;

2H6 III.iii.31; *3H6* IV.vi.44; *MAAN* V.i.273; *R3* II.i.121). Baptism and penance could restore the worshipper to the religious community, but they could not secure election. Good works alone, or the appearance of virtue, did not alter the fact that people were essentially bad and had to rely upon the miraculous favor of the divine to forgive them in spite of their perpetual sinning. The Puritans, who took this doctrine to extremes, were suspicious of almost any type of revelry or levity that implied a comfortable pleasure in the present or a confident hope of salvation. Dancing, gambling, drinking, May games, cockfighting, theatergoing, and a host of other forms of entertainment came under their critical eyes. The church fathers tended to be a little more lenient, and it was some time before English Puritans solidified into an organized separatist movement, but here and there a few genuine nonconformists, who refused to attend church or to have their children baptized, could be found. Because their numbers were small, they usually could be compelled to conform, at least outwardly. Those who refused baptism, for example, on the grounds that even the reformed rite was full of superstitious popery, were sometimes brought to the font by force and threatened with prison if they did not comply.

It took a brave person to resist the authorized church. Public opinion did not support those, like the Puritan Robert Browne (*TN* III.ii.31), who advocated separation of church and state or a severe revision of the Anglican Church. In cases of serious disagreement with church doctrine, especially where those disagreements threatened the sovereignty of the state, an outspoken critic might be accused of heresy, the punishment for which was death by burning at the stake (*MWW* IV.iv.9; *WT* II.iii.114; *John* III.i.118; *R&J* I.ii.93).

Liturgy and Practice

Religious texts were at the forefront of the battles for the nature of the new English church. From the beginning, the reformers had realized that it was essential for people to be able to read the Scripture that had so long been interpreted for them. Accordingly, the translation of Scripture and liturgy into English was of paramount importance. By late in Elizabeth's reign two competing texts vied for the souls of the English. The approved text was the Bishops' Bible. The text used by most people and by virtually all Puritans was the Geneva Bible, a smaller volume whose pages were crowded with anti–Catholic annotations. The establishment refused to accept the Geneva Bible, and the people had no affection for the Bishops' Bible, so another version was authorized by James I and issued in 1611. This "King James" version struck a chord and is probably still the best-known English translation of the Bible, though of course its late date means it was not the version that shaped Shakespeare's spirituality; which version had that honor is a matter of almost as much controversy as the original Bishops'-Geneva conflict.

Texts other than the Bible, including Richard Foxe's *Book of Martyrs*, the Psalter, and editions of John Calvin's sermons, could also be found in England's churches and homes. The *Paraphrases* of Erasmus was supposed to be owned by every church, though not every church complied. Every church, however, possessed the Book of Common Prayer, which contained the approved liturgy for services such as christenings, marriages, and burials. In order to encourage parishes to comply with new regulations and to root out old "superstitions," bishops or their delegates made periodic visits to the parishes and ran down a checklist covering everything from Sabbath observance to the location and form of the baptismal font. Questionnaires were also sent to the parishes from time to time, asking whether certain books or pieces of equipment were present. The influence of these visitations and questionnaires can be overestimated; parsons were free to lie on the latter, and the vigor and recommendations of the former depended entirely on the inspector. Many parishes succeeded in retaining "Catholic" trappings like rood lofts (*R3* III.ii.75, IV.iv.166) until after the Restoration, while others, with Puritan-inclined clergy, succeeded in evading commands to repair fonts.

Though the form of services was guided firmly by the Book of Common Prayer, there was some variation from place to place. The most important change from Catholic practice was the abolition of the Mass (*2H6* V.iii.16; *R&J* IV.i.38); although the sacrament of Communion, commemorating the Last Supper, was retained, much of the ritual surrounding it was abandoned. The altars were removed from the churches and a simple linen-covered table used instead, with a covered silver cup for the wine. Most churches offered Communion on the first or second Sunday of each month, and the goal was to have every person in the nation take Communion at least three times a year, with at least one of those times being on Easter.

Another change from Catholicism was the elimination, or at least the attempted elimination, of all objects deemed superstitious. These included rosaries (*3H6* II.i.162; *2H6* I.iii.58), reliquaries (containers for holy relics), supposed splinters of the True Cross, and the Agnus Dei, a wax disc with a lamb stamped on it that had been blessed by the pope. All of these were outlawed in 1571, and an act passed during James's reign gave justices of the peace the right to conduct searches for religious contraband. It was a strange new world, though some things remained constant, such as the importance of Sunday as the Sabbath. Laws regarding Sabbath conduct, hosts of tracts condemning any levity on that day, and even calendars that printed the "dominical" letter S in large red type (*LLL* V.ii.44) underscored Sunday's role as the anchor of the Christian week; it was one of the few aspects of the new religion that remained comfortingly the same.

Religious services began with morning prayer (*MWW* II.ii.95–96) at about seven or eight A.M., cathedral and college services usually began a bit earlier. Candles, which were closely associated with Catholic ritual, were used only for the Christmas morning service, which began before dawn. For the ordinary Sunday service, a text from the Old Testament was read, then a text from the Gospels. The "Litany and Suffrages," a series of petitions and prayers, were read, followed by Communion if it was being offered that day. A psalm was sung, then a sermon (*2H4* IV.ii.4–7; *AYLI* III.i.17; *Tim* II.ii.179) was preached, followed by another psalm and any scheduled baptisms. The readings were arranged so that the Psalter was read completely once every thirty days, the New Testament four times per year, and the Old Testament once per year. Sermons were preached from a pulpit, described by William Harrison as "a little tabernacle of wainscot," and ad libbed from minimal notes; though some parsons were accomplished preachers, others bored their captive flocks to tears (*AYLI* III.ii.155–57; *LLL* V.ii.917). The evening prayer service (*MWW* II.ii.95–96) began at two or three P.M. and followed a similar pattern, with another reading from the Old Testament and another from the New, this one taken from the Epistles. Catechism of the young, conducted in English, replaced the baptism of the morning service. Prayers for the intercession of individual saints were omitted, and the entire service was read in English. Sometimes special psalms were sung as a sign of thanksgiving; Psalm 115, which begins "Non nobis, Domine, non nobis" (Not unto us, Lord, not unto us), and the psalmlike hymn Te Deum (which begins "Te Deum laudamus"—we praise you, God) were offered on special occasions, such as military victories (*H5* IV.viii.122) or the birth of a royal heir.

All of this represented a substantial change from Catholic practice, yet it was insufficient for the Puritans (*TN* II.iii.140–51; *Per* IV.vi.9; *AW* I.iii.52–56). They objected to any music in the service; in this they opposed the personal practice of Elizabeth, whose chapel services included, according to a 1598 account, not only an organ but also cornets, flutes, other instruments, and a boy singer. The Puritans objected to the organ, to the reading of prayers in the choir (S 73) rather than in the main portion of the church, to kneeling when passing the Communion table, to the use of a font rather than a basin for baptisms, to the burial of anyone in consecrated ground, and to the making of the cross on infants' heads during baptism. One of their most visible rebelllions was in the matter of the surplice (*AW* I.iii.94–96), a wide-sleeved white linen robe that was mandated in 1566 for clergy during services. Clergymen with Purtian leanings found this too much like the vestments of a Catholic priest and wore a black gown only in protest. Yet it is too easy to see the church in this period as neatly divided between mainstream Anglicans and Puritans; the full separation did not come for a few more decades. An example of the conflicts is Samuel Harsnett, Archbishop of York, who endured the disapproval of the authorities because of his objection to the surplice. He would seem to have been a Puritan on these grounds, yet he disagreed with the Calvinists on the matter of free will and predestination, and with both Catholics and Puritans on the matter of demonic possession. Nothing about Renaissance religion was easy or straightforward.

Partly because it was so complicated, and partly because its importance was unquestioned, religion was nearly always on the mind of the English. Attendance at church was mandatory, so this cannot be taken as evidence of the fervor of the people, but there are plenty of other signs of the primacy of religion in people's lives. Religious books were the most common and best-selling publications. Documents, even those not intended for publication, such as diaries and letters, attributed almost every major event to the hand of God. Prayers (*MAAN* II.i.99; *MWW* I.iv.12–14; *TS* IV.i.71–72) were uttered every day, often several times a day—upon waking, upon retiring, and before meals (*1H4* I.ii.20–21; *MV* II.ii.188–89; *MM* I.ii.14–16; *Tim* I.ii.61–70, III.vi.66–70; *Cor* IV.vii.3–4; *MWW* I.i.252–53). Yet it is an oversimplification to say that the English were praying all the time. The clergy certainly complained that the people did not pray enough and too often skipped Sunday services to gamble, drink, dance, and conduct business.

Non-Christian Religions

Most of Shakespeare's religious references are to Christian doctrine and practice. However, since many of his plays are set in pre–Christian times, he includes a few references to other faiths. Greek and Roman religions centered on the temples (*Cor* III.iii.36; *Cym* V.v.398, 481–83) devoted to the worship of various gods. Each of these temples, in turn, became the focus of attention on the festival of its particular god or goddess, and in the meantime, people who had special petitions came to make offerings. Usually, they brought an animal as a sacrifice (*JC* II.i.166, 175–76, II.ii.5–6, 37–40; *T&C* V.iii.17–18; *Cym* V.v.398) and allowed it to be killed on the altar (*T&C* IV.iii.8) and, often, burned or cooked so that the smoke would rise to the heavens and delight the gods. The offering remained with the priests or priestesses of the temple or "fane" (*Cym* IV.ii.241–42), who promised to intercede for the petitioner with the deity. At some temples, a priest or a priestess gave answers to questions asked by the petitioners; these temples were called oracles (*Tim* IV.iii.121). Of the various types of Roman priests and priestesses, Shakespeare alludes to the Vestal Virgins (*MND* II.i.158), who kept the temple of Vesta (goddess of the hearth), and to the flamens (*Cor* II.i.216; *Tim* IV.iii.156–58), the sacrificers to the various gods. There were, in Republican Rome, fifteen *flamines*, three "major" and twelve "minor." The major flamens were those of Mars, Quirinus, and Jupiter, the last of whom was known as the *flamen Dialis*; he was forbidden to eat certain foods, to say the names of certain foods, to pass under a vine arbor, to sleep away from his bed for more than two nights in a row, to allow anyone else to sleep in his bed, or to permit a slave to cut his hair. *See also* Jews; Mythology.

Rope

Rope (*AW* IV.ii.38) was made of twisted hemp fibers and used for a variety of purposes, including harness traces, halters (*CE* IV.i.97–99), and gallows nooses, hence the phrase "crack-hemp" (*TS* V.i.45), meaning one destined to be hanged. It was also used, in much greater widths, on sailing ships (*Per* IV.i.54; *Temp* I.i.23–24, 31–33); it was blackened and waterproofed with pitch.

Ruff

Originating as the frill at the neck and sleeve edges of the smock or shirt, the ruff eventually developed into a separate collar. It reached its greatest width in the late 1580s, when on upper-class women it could be nine inches deep, with the wearer's head resting atop it like a bizarre confection on a white plate. Later the size diminished, with men in particular wearing small ruffs that barely extended beyond their chins. Ruffs were typically tilted up in back, and larger versions might have multiple layers or wire underpropping. Most people wore closed ruffs, which

Woman's open ruff with alternate teardrop edge, 1602.

Man's narrow open ruff with alternate teardrop pattern and bandstring ends showing, 1579.

Wide, closed "cartwheel" ruff, 1586

were tied together with thin, tasseled "bandstrings" to make a complete wheel-shaped enclosure of the neck, but some, especially unmarried ladies and bearded men, wore theirs open. Men allowed the band-strings to dangle decoratively; women pinned the front edges of the ruff to their partlets or bodices, so that the ruff followed the neckline of the garment.

The ruff (*2H4* II.iv.137; *AW* III.ii.7; *Per* IV.ii.104–5) was ideally made of cambric, holland, lawn, or lace. Among the middle class, it was made of whatever fine, white fabric was affordable. In some cases, it was made of "cut-work," fabric with patterns cut into it that resembled lace. Whatever the fabric, it was starched to a pefect and no doubt uncomfortable stiffness. The radiating curves of the ruff might be arranged so that, at their outer edge, they formed a series of circles or ovals, though ordinarily they made an undulating line sometimes described as a figure eight. This so-called figure eight actually more closely resembled a set of teardrops, arranged alternately point-up and point-down. The creases and curves were set into the wet, starched cloth by a hot iron called a poking stick (*WT* IV.iv.227). Ruffs ranged in height from one inch to several.

Not everyone wore a ruff. Some substituted a rebato (*MAAN* III.iv.6), an unfolded standing collar that ran from one side of the neckline, around the back of the head, and back to the other side of the neckline. Laboring people seldom wore ruffs, not because they preferred the rebato but because starched white collars showed dirt and inhibited movement, and thus were impractical on the farm or in the shop, kitchen, or forge. (Not that ruffs were particularly practical for the rich, either; Phillip Stubbes laughed up his sleeve at the fancy people in the streets on windy and rainy days, with their great cartwheel ruffs flapping madly or lying limp and dripping on their shoulders like dirty dishrags.) Working people were more likely to make do with an old-fashioned frilled or unfrilled

Queen Elizabeth wearing a rebato, c. 1585–90.

smock. Late in the sixteenth century, men began to make the transition from the ruff toward an integrated shirt collar that fell to each side of the neck in a soft, large, squared-off flap. This "falling band," as a nod to the ruff it replaced, often had an edging of lace and ties that evoked bandstrings. Some people wore multiple falling bands, with each layer slightly smaller than the one below it, to produce a terraced effect. *See also* Clothing.

Salamander

The salamander was a legendary lizard that thrived in and fed on the hottest fires, hence the comment "I have maintained that salamander of yours [a hot, red face] with / fire [strong drink] any time this two and thirty years" (*1H4* III.iii.49–50). The legend of the salamander may have arisen because people saw lizards or newts, carried in accidentally on their firewood, racing from their fireplaces. In a society that considered fire one of the four basic elements, the idea of a creature that sustained itself on pure heat was attractive to the imagination.

Sea Monster

Accounts of travel in the Renaissance were freely sprinkled with accounts of strange creatures (elephants, camels), wholly fictional creatures (griffins, basiliks), and actual creatures given the names of mythological beasts (a rhinoceros identified as a unicorn, a python identified as a dragon). The oceans were not exempt from attempts to catalog their fauna, and here, too, legend and observation were casually mingled. There were tales of whales that masqueraded as islands to drown hapless picnickers, biblical

A sea monster attacking a ship, from Konrad Gesner's *Icones Animalium Aquatilum in Mari*. Reproduced from the Collections of the Library of Congress.

leviathans, mermaids grotesque or seductive, winged Sirens, and even stranger beasts. The monster killed by Perseus in a myth recounted by Ovid is described as dragonlike, with a back hardened by barnacles, a softer belly and neck, and a fishlike tail. Pliny the Elder speaks of various creatures, including Nereids, being washed ashore, and claims that the skeleton of Perseus's beast was displayed in Rome; from the description of the bones—forty feet long with a thick spine—it sounds like the skeleton of a beached whale. Perhaps it is a whale, or one of the more exotic imaginary beasts, that is meant by the "sea-monster" of *King Lear* (I.iv.263). *See also* Mermaid.

Sequin

The sequin was an Italian coin that took its name from *zecca*, the word for mint. A *zecchino* was thus a little minted coin, and this in turn became sequin. In *Pericles* it is further altered as the "chequins" a pander hopes to amass for his retirement (IV.ii.26). The sequin was simply a gold ducat, but it developed this distinct name in the late fifteenth century when the rising price of gold necessitated a differentiation between the ducat of account (equal to 124 Venetian soldi, whatever the price of gold) and the ducat at its actual market rate. "Sequin" referred to this latter understanding of the coin, in which it was seen purely as a piece of metal of a given value rather than as the nominal equivalent of so many soldi.

Servants

In a time when everything had to be done by hand, servants were necessary to the smooth running of a household. Accordingly, everyone who could afford them—in other words, everyone with any pretensions at all to the middle class—had servants. Even the family of the servant Launce has a servant, a maid named Nan (*2GV* II.iii.21). Great households might have hundreds, some of whom did little other than attend the lord wherever he went, to emphasize his wealth and dignity. Other servants had specific and often arduous duties.

Types of Servants

The most skilled and responsible servants in a large household were the chamberlain, steward, bailiff, cook, housekeeper, butler, pantler, falconer, clerks (*2H6* III.i.179, IV.ii.85–109; *MAAN* II.i.105, 106), armorer, auditor, chaplain, gentleman of the horse, ladies' maids, and perhaps a few others. Some of these had the right to dine at the family's table in the great hall, while others were consigned to the lower tables to supervise their underlings' decorum. Shakespeare mentions few of these by name; his servants are mostly of the lower order or have no specified place in the household. The chamberlain, in very large households, was the master's chief personal servant, responsible for all the household servants and for, as his title implies, the master's bedchamber (*Per* I.i.153–54; *Cym* I.i.42–45). The best-known of all chamberlains was the Lord Chamberlain, who served the monarch and sat on the Privy Council.

Another type of personal servant was the page (*TS* Ind.i.105; *MWW* II.ii.110; *Cym* IV.ii.355; *AYLI* V.iii.5; *2H4* II.iv.380; *R&J* III.i.95), a boy or young man—in medieval times often the son of a relative or friend (*1H4* IV.iii.72)—who accompanied the master and ran his errands. He might be gloriously dressed, but he had no household department to run and thus only as much power as he derived from his influence over his master. Shakespeare's best portrait of a page is the character Moth in *Love's Labor's Lost*. He is brighter and better educated than the average servant—brighter, indeed, than his master—but for all his wit, he is still in a subordinate position. Cranmer, in *Henry VIII* (V.ii.25), lumps pages together with footboys (*1H6* III.iii.69; *TS* III.ii.69–70; *TA* V.ii.54–55), who had much the same functions as pages but without their quasi-gentlemanly status.

Male servants who served in the master's bedchamber were often quite powerful, with extensive authority throughout the household. The corresponding position for a woman—chambermaid, waiting-woman, or lady's maid (*TN* I.iii.49; *Lear* IV.i.63; *TNK* III.v.125–26; *AYLI* II.ii.5–7; *Temp* I.ii.46–48)—implied far less responsibility, but since she served the mistress of the household, she was in a position of great visibility. Maids' duties included everything from hairdressing to playing music, and they were indirectly responsible for their mistresses' chastity. For the latter reason, they also assisted or hindered their mistresses' sexual intrigues. The terms "lady's maid" and "waiting-woman" (*Cym* II.ii.ch.; *Mac* V.i.ch.) implied a more direct attendance on the mistress, while the term "chambermaid" (*R&J* V.iii.109) might mean a personal attendant or merely one who cleaned, made beds, and lit fires.

The chief servant in a household might well be a steward or a bailiff. The difference between them was explained by Conrad Heresbach in *The Whole Art and Trade of Husbandry*, pointed out that his bailiff "overseeth both my worke and my workemen," while the steward "looketh to the receaving of my revenues and commodities." The bailiff was thus a kind of foreman on the farm; according to Heresbach, he ought to be industrious, between thirty and sixty years old, capable of basic carpentry and veterinary medicine, trustworthy, and married to a woman who could supervise the maids in the same way that he supervised the men.

> [S]upplying his Masters place, he may be first up in the morning, and last that goeth to bed, & that he see the doores fast locked, and every man in bed, that the cattell have meat [food] enough, & be well littured [given straw], that he set forward, according to the time of the yeere, such as do loyter in their labor . . . and that he use sundry devices to cheere them up in their labor, sometime to helpe him that fainteth.

The bailiff was to ensure that sick workers were tended and that lax ones were disciplined. He had to maintain a delicate balance in his behavior; he was an upper servant and highly responsible, but he had to be well liked by the men and humble to his master. The best bailiff was often a man who had had a farm of his own but had lost it for some reason.

The steward was the head of the indoor servants, just as the bailiff was the head of the farm staff. He had a key to the storeroom and had to make sure that none of the servants stole, idled, or made habitual mistakes. It was also his duty to supply the household with all its wants, such as food, coal, and cloth, and to account for all the household expenses. He dealt with the local miller and directly supervised the butler, pantler, baker, cook, and other heads of household departments. In *Booke of Husbandrie*, John Fitzherbert thought

> hee ought to be a man that knoweth and feareth God, of a good conscience, constant, faithfull, wise, politique, circumspect, diligent, painful, laborious, sad [somber], and grave, in conversation: sober and gentle in speech: discreete and preudent in reformation: bearing like favour to all persons, . . . a mirrour of good manners, neyther to familier, nor yet to strange [standoffish], . . . glad to please his Maister and Mistris, and loath to offend: and finally, such a one as must thinke earnestly his Maisters profit his profit, and his Mistris losse his losse, his Maisters honour or worship his honesty.

Shakespeare does not show us the bailiff except in the sense of a public official somewhat like a police officer, but he includes a few stewards among his characters (*Lear* I.iii.ch.). One of these is Olivia's steward Malvolio in *Twelfth Night*, who appears to be competent at his job but has managed to alienate almost the entire household. Certainly he is "glad to please," but he is also definitely "to familier" with his mistress. A more ideal steward is presented in *Timon of Athens*. Flavius is "faithfull, wise, politique," and all else recommended by Fitzherbert, down to his complete identification of his own welfare with his master's.

In a smaller household, the functions of both bailiff and steward might be performed by one man. This is the case in Justice Shallow's house in *2 Henry IV* (V.i). Here, Davy acts as head of both the indoor and outdoor departments, for he brings an assortment of business to his master's attention, ranging from supervision of the cook and the discipline of lesser servants to the sowing of wheat and the repair of farm equipment. Later (V.iii), he also waits at table, which was usually the duty of a much less important servant, prompting a comment from Falstaff on his extraordinary versatility.

The other important servants in a large household were the butler (*WT* IV.iv.56), whose name was a corruption of "bottler." As this more accurate name implies, he was in charge of the household liquor. In some households he did the brewing; in others he merely took charge of the tuns of wine and hogsheads of beer and ale. The baker baked the bread and often the pastries such as pies and cakes. The cook (*WT* IV.iv.56; *2H4* V.i.12; *R&J* IV.iv.15; *H5* V.ii.152; *Tim* III.iv.117), who handled most other food preparation, also had a staff of assistants, and was, in large households, almost always a man. Food already prepared, ingredients, table utensils, and linen were the responsibility of the pantler (*Cym* II.iii.125; *WT* IV.iv.56; *2H4* II.iv.241–43), who kept the pantry and larder (*H8* V.iv.4) locked and accounted for its inventory at the end of each week. Some households gave the napkins, basins, and ewers, along with candles, snuffers, candlesticks, and torches, into the care of a separate officer of the ewery. The dining hall itself was the domain of the usher of the hall, or gentleman usher, who had assistants to help him seat and serve the guests.

In addition to the department heads, noble households had scores of lesser servants—yeomen (*TN* II.v.37–38), grooms, and children—to tend to the stables, fields, and house. Gamekeepers, woodmen, and huntsmen tended the game parks, saw to the welfare of deer and rabbits, and assisted in the hunt (*3H6* III.i.chs., IV.v.ch., IV.vi.84; *MWW* IV.iv.27–42; *MND* IV.i.139; *MM* IV.iii.164). Gardeners (*2H6* IV.ii.133) sowed, weeded, and gathered produce from the kitchen garden, tended the orchards, and cared for ornamental plants and hedges. Kitchen maids (*CE* IV.iv.74; *Cor* II.i.211–12; *Cym* V.v.177; *R&J* II.iv.41) turned the spits and scrubbed the pots and pans. Nurses fed and cared for infants, often being retained as servants to their young charges for the rest of their lives (*R&J* IV.i.92; *MAAN* III.iii.64–69). Porters (*CE* III.i.36; *1H6* II.iii. ch.; *MWW* II.ii.170; *Lear* III.vii.66; *Cor* IV.v.12–14; *Mac* II.iii.ch.; *H8* V.iv.ch.) kept the gates, determining whom to admit and whom to turn away. Though they sometimes fetched and carried for the families they served, they were distinct from the porters (*T&C* I.ii.255–56; *LLL* I.ii.71–72) who carried burdens in towns and on docks.

Various other servants cared for the family's wardrobe (*TN* II.v.37–38), did the laundry, brewed the beer and ale, slaughtered the livestock, gathered eggs, milked cows and made butter and cheese, stabled the horses, cleaned the house, carried messages (*1H6* II.v.19, 20; *2H6* IV.vii.ch.; *3H6* V.iv.ch.; *Lear* II.i.125–26; *TNK* V.iv.ch.), ran errands (*MAAN* II.iii.2–3; *H5* IV.i.150–52), and rode alongside, or even behind on the same horse, when members of the family traveled. Servants in husbandry did the farm chores, plowing, pitching hay into carts, threshing, sowing, reaping, and thatching roofs.

Lesser servants—called grooms (*2H6* IV.i.50–62; *TS* III.ii.212; *Mac* II.ii.5–6; *Per* IV.vi.194; *Cym* II.iii.127–28; *H8* V.ii.16–18; *R2* V.v.ch.), lackeys (*H5* III.vii.114; *AYLI* III.ii.296; *TS* III.ii.64, 70), and varlets (*T&C* I.i.1) by Shakespeare—did whatever tasks were most distasteful or required the least skill. They ran errands, scrubbed pots, shoveled dung out of the stables, held things so that the master's hands could be free, and waited in case they were needed. At mealtimes (*R&J* I.iii.100–104, I.v.1–17), they set the tables with saltcellars, trenchers, spoons, tablecloths, and napkins (*MV* III.v.59–60); filled cups with beer or wine (*A&C*

IV.ii.21; *WT* I.ii.346); offered water and a towel so that the master could wash his hands at the beginning of the meal; and ran back and forth to the kitchen to bring in new platters filled with food. At the end of the meal, they removed the dishes in the order that they had been served, swept the crumbs from the table, removed the bread and salt, bowed, and let the master wash and dry his hands again.

The fewer the servants in a household, the more of these duties they performed, though in smaller establishments, tasks like looking after the deer were omitted because there were no deer to look after. Davy, Shallow's versatile steward, does so many jobs that one wonders about the total size of Shallow's establishment, and whether there is a cook at all or whether Davy does the cooking, too. Caliban, of necessity, is Prospero's only human servant, and thus is tasked with a number of different chores. He carries wood, builds fires, catches fish, scrapes the trenchers, and scrubs the dishes (*Temp* I.ii.313–15, II.ii.182–85).

Working Conditions

Servants were often hired at statute fairs held in the fall, but they might also be recommended by a friend or relative of the employer. They were usually paid on a quarterly basis, and they were not paid very much, at least in cash wages (*LLL* I.ii.147–48, III.i.131–32). William Cavendish paid his butler 10s per quarter, or £2 per year, and his best-paid servants received only twice that amount. No wonder there was a proverbial saying, repeated by William Harrison, that ran, "Young serving men, old beggars." Fortunately, servants did not always have to rely solely on their wages. Most received room and board in addition to their pay, and many got some sort of perquisite as well. Farm servants might get the right to pasture a few of their own animals on their masters' land, a certain number of bushels of grain, special low prices for produce, or even such apparently useless commodities as the docked tails of sheep or the trimmings of horses' manes. Household servants, especially if they ran errands or carried messages, might be tipped by their masters or by the recipients of the messages (*2GV* IV.iv.176–77; *Per* II.i.157; *TN* I.v.281; *LLL* III.i.167–68; *H8* V.i.171–73). They might also receive perquisites such as leftover food and secondhand clothes; new clothes were also purchased or made for them. In the case of male servants, the clothing came in the form of livery (*2GV* II.iv.45)—a uniform, usually blue, with the employer's badge embroidered on the left sleeve.

Both servants and employers sometimes complained about each other. The servants no doubt found the work hard, the hours long, and the discipline irritating. Excessive beatings of servants were not condoned by society, but the definition of "excessive" varied from place to place, and it was considered perfectly all right to slap, whip, or punch a servant from time to time by way of rebuke (*TS* I.ii.17 s.d., 35, IV.i.71; *2GV* II.i.84,

III.i.376, IV.iv.28). Servants also had limited privacy, and masters tried to arrange the household so that nighttime wandering (in search of stolen food or a sexual partner) was difficult or impossible. Deference to the master, no matter how ridiculous his whims or how meager his intellect, was required at all times. The anxiety of Petruchio's servants as they await his review and approval (*TS* IV.i) is natural enough, for no servant wished to appear negligent or disrespectful.

Lodging and food were almost always less lavish than those allotted to the family; whether this bothered most servants is unknown, since they left very few records in their own words. In large households, there might be separate servants' quarters; in some homes, servants slept in garret rooms, on beds or pallets in an employer's chamber, in the stables, or on the threshing floor. However, the life could be comfortable enough compared to that of a smallholding farmer, especially in the home of a great lord, and then one shared to some extent in the employer's reflected glory. The status of a servant was always derived from the status of his employer.

The employers, for their part, felt a nearly familial responsibility for their servants, though they also tried to pay them as little and work them as hard as possible. From their perspective, a servant who stole (*Tim* IV.i.10–13) or gossiped about the family broke a sacred trust, and masters were advised to choose their servants very carefully to avoid betrayal or exposure of the rest of the household to bad habits (*2H4* V.i.68–79). Nonetheless, employers were fighting a losing battle, for a labor shortage in the late sixteenth century, which increased further from 1600 to 1620, made it hard to demand too much. A servant who was dissatisfied could always leave and find work elsewhere. The result was a certain amount of grumbling, better recorded than that among the servants, about the behavior of the opposing side. James Bankes, for example, complained that servants took no pride in work done well, so long as "they have meat, drink and wages. Small fear of God is in servants." *See also* Occupations.

Sheep

Sheep were the most valuable livestock in England, despite the fact that they could not pull a plow or a cart. They were eaten, when young as lamb and when old as mutton. Their fleece was usually a farm's biggest cash crop. They gave milk, about one-fifth as much as a cow. Their fat became candle tallow, their skin parchment (*2H6* IV.ii.79–80) and leather, their horns patches for the shepherd's shoes. Even their intestines (*MAAN* II.iii.58) and bones had purposes. But perhaps most crucially to the entire farm operation, they made manure that was the best and often the only type of fertilizer available for the fields. The wool industry was one of England's most important, and sheep were in such great demand that some substantial farmers circumvented the legal limit of 2,000 sheep per person

A ram, from Edward Topsell's *Historie of Foure-Footed Beastes.* Reproduced from the Collections of the Library of Congress.

by assigning sheep to themselves, their wives, their children, and their other relatives.

Shakespeare includes two calculations of the value of sheep in his plays:

SHALLOW: . . . How a score of ewes now?

SILENCE: Thereafter as they be. A score of good ewes may be worth ten pounds. (*2H4* III.ii.51–53)

. . . every 'leven wether tods, every tod yields pound and odd shilling; fifteen hundred shorn, what comes the wool to? (*WT* IV.iii.32–34)

In other words, ewes are worth a varying amount, according to their quality, but the good ones will bring in 10s each, and eleven wethers (rams, especially castrated rams) yielded a tod (28 lbs., or 12.7 kg) of wool, of about 2.5 pounds (1.1 kg) of wool per wether. Shakespeare's calculations were actually a bit on the low side. Renaissance sheep looked very little like their modern counterparts; selective breeding had only been recently introduced, and the animals were still leggy, horned, and bony, looking goatlike compared to modern-day sheep. Yet their stock was gradually improving, and a good wether in about 1600 might weigh 50 pounds (22.7 kg), be worth as much as 20s, and yield a 5-pound fleece each year.

There were three or four categories of sheep, depending on how one defines the word "wether." There were rams, uncastrated males, who could be kept only in small numbers because of their tendency to fight (*AYLI* V.ii.30–31). Wethers (*MV* IV.i.114), as noted above, might be rams, but were usually castrated males who were kept for their fleece. One of them, who led the flock, was given a bell and served as the "bellwether" (*MWW* III.v.105–6). Ewes (*MAAN* III.iii.69–71) were adult female sheep, and lambs were young sheep of either sex.

Lambs (*3H6* I.i.242, I.iv.5, II.v.75, IV.viii.49–50; *2GV* IV.iv.92; *LLL* II.i.219–22; *WT* I.ii.67) were born in early spring, usually in a special shed set aside for the purpose. They were weaned in early May and the ewes milked until August. Adults were shorn in June; year-old lambs in July, after being washed in a stream and allowed to dry for two days (*AYLI* II.iv.76–77). During the late spring and summer, sheep were led out to the pasture to graze in the morning and brought back to a fold (*V&A* 532), a temporary pen, at night. The fold was moved from place to place, to enable the farmer to manure whichever field he liked, and might be an actual enclosure, a virtual enclosure created by tying dogs at critical locations, or simply a few stakes set up on the theory that the sheep would stay close to the stakes in order to scratch themselves. In the winter, fresh grass was unavailable, so the sheep were fed hay, barley straw, pea stems, mistletoe, ivy, dried leaves, and clover.

A shepherd from the *Roxburghe Ballads*. Reproduced from the Collections of the Library of Congress.

Some of the sheep might be killed for food before winter arrived, to save the fodder (*2H6* IV.iii.3; *TA* II.iii.223).

At all times of the year, sheep required a good deal of care. The life of the shepherd (*1H6* I.ii.72, V.iv.ch.; *2H6* III.i.191; *AYLI* II.iv.42, III.ii.11–21, III.iv.46–48; *WT* III.iii.ch., IV.iv.326–27; *Cor* I.vi.25) was celebrated in pastoral poetry. Shakespeare has the beleaguered Henry VI compare it favorably to a king's existence, for it is composed of nothing but counting the hours, eating simple food, napping in the shade of a tree, and calculating

So many days my ewes have been with young,
So many weeks ere the poor fools will ean [bear young],
So many years ere I shall shear the fleece. (*3H6* II.v.35–37)

Nonetheless, it was not an easy life. It was full of alternating boredom and drudgery. Sheep were not bright animals (*LLL* V.i.49), and they were subject to disease (*Tim* V.iv.42–44), injury, and predation by stray dogs or, in times past, by wolves (*WT* III.iii.64–67). The shepherd had to be vigilant (*Lear* III.vi.41–42), and he had to take certain equipment with him—a knife, shears, a box of tar (mixed with butter or grease to make an ointment, or with pitch to make a marking compound), a dog, a board on which to lay sheep while treating them, and a crook (*WT* IV.iv.423) with a wide blade at one end, possibly to cut down leaves for the sheep to eat. The shepherd had to rise early (*MM* IV.ii.207–8), sleep lightly, and endure the cold, "blowing of his nails" to warm his hands (*3H6* II.v.3).

Shakespeare usually refers to sheep in the literal sense, as animals breeding (*MV* I.iii.75–90) or grazing on hillsides (*Temp* IV.i.62; *TA* IV.iv.91). The life of the shepherd figures prominently in *All's Well That Ends Well* and *The Winter's Tale*, though one of the most comprehensive passages about sheep actually occurs in *The Two Gentlemen of Verona*, where a series of puns turns on sheep's horns, silliness, tendency to wander off and be enclosed in the pound or "pinfold" for stray animals, tendency to follow the shepherd for fodder, and slaughter for mutton or to prevent the pasture from being "overcharged," that is, overgrazed (*2GV* I.i.74–101). Sometimes, however, he refers to them and Aesop's fable of the wolf in sheep's clothing (*1H6* I.iii.5; *2H6* III.i.55, 71, 77), a story that testifies less to the cleverness of the wolf than to the stupidity of the sheep. Sometimes "lamb" is used as an endearment, or as a metaphor for a gentle person (*LLL* IV.iii.7; *R2* II.i.174; *TS* III.ii.156). *See also* Animals; Farming.

Shield

Shakespeare's works range widely in setting; thus, the armaments and armor he mentions may be Renaissance, medieval, Roman, or even ancient Greek. How much he knew about ancient and medieval weapons and armor is unanswerable. Even if he knew, for example, how an Athenian hoplite (infantryman) was equipped, this is no guarantee that he envisioned his characters in this costume, and it is certainly not how his actors dressed onstage. Yet he does mention archaic as well as contemporary objects of war, so we will begin at the beginning—at least as far as Shakespearean settings are concerned—with ancient Greece.

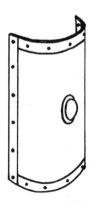 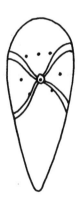 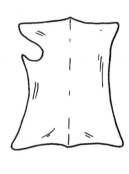

The evolution of the shield: (a) the convex rectangular Roman *scutum*; (b) the teardrop-shaped shield depicted in the eleventh-century Bayeux Tapestry; (c) horseman's targe, with angles to deflect lance blows and arrows, and with a hole near the armpit for a couched lance.

Round Shield. Italy. 16th century. Etched and gilded steel with brass rivets, w. 57.8 cm. © The Cleveland Museum of Art, 2001, Gift of Mr. and Mrs. John L. Severance, 1916.1504.

The hoplite's shield was shaped like a large, shallow bowl about half as high as the soldier who carried it. It was covered with oxhides; Ajax's, according to legend, had seven such layers (*A&C* IV.xiv.38). Inside, it had a wide strap into which the forearm slid, and smaller straps near the perimeter that could be grasped by the hand. Outside it had a painted device that served, like the later shield devices of medieval knights, to identify the bearer in the commotion of battle.

Roman shields (*A&C* V.ii.135; *TA* IV.i.127; *Cor* I.iv.23–24), on the other hand, were seldom round. They were initially oval and very tall, made of wood, and called *scuta*. By the third century C.E., the *scutum* was shorter, rectangular, and convex. It made a formidable defense when used by masses of soldiers, who overlapped their shields to make a sturdy angled wall or roof against enemy projectiles.

The shields of the early Middle Ages were usually round. Like ancient shields, they often featured a round "boss" or projection near the center that served as a cup for the fingers of the shield hand and helped to prevent knuckle abrasions. This simple round shield dominated until the eleventh century and survived afterward as the target (*A&C* I.iii.82, IV.viii.31; *1H4* II.iv.201–3; *3H6* II.i.39–40) or buckler (*2H6* III.ii.216; *3H6* III.iii.99; *1H4* II.iv.178–79; *2H4* III.ii.23). In *MAAN* V.ii.16–22, it is evident that the central boss has been retained and adapted to accommodate a spike ("pikes" attached "with a vice"). The buckler creates quite a bit of linguistic confusion, for it was variously known as the target, the rondache, or, erroneously, the targe. It could be made of iron, steel, or wood covered with embossed leather. Made obsolete by firearms, it was retained for a while in formal fencing, but was abolished in the late sixteenth century even for this purpose.

In about the eleventh century, shields became elongated. Made of leather-covered and iron-banded wood, they were strapped to the arm and neck. They can be seen in great numbers in the embroidery known as the Bayeux Tapestry. These shields are often described in texts as "kite-shaped" but in fact resemble upside-down teardrops more than the classic diamond-shaped kite. There was need for a shield of this shape to replace or augment the round buckler. The high oval top of the shield protected the soldier's face, since helmets did not yet have plate to cover the chin. The pointed bottom suited the shield for a man on horseback, who would find a wide-bottomed shield cumbersome but needed to be able to guard at least one of his legs.

Of course, this leaves the question of what he was to do about his other leg. Chain mail was one answer, but as stronger armor increasingly protected the rider's outer thighs and shins, the shield was no longer needed to perform this function. At about the same time, helmets that covered most of the face eliminated the need for an arched top to the shield. It therefore became shorter and flatter, more triangular, and more in keeping with the shield shape that we associate with coats of arms (*1H4* V.i.140; *LLL* V.ii.549; *R3* IV.iii.56). It also retained and expanded its function as a means of identification on the battlefield. Along with his crested helm, lance pennon, and horse's caparison, it heralded a knight's presence to friend and foe. The central boss vanished to allow more room for colorful designs, and the shield's size shrank to about three feet high by the beginning of the thirteenth century. Its bottom point served a function for foot soldiers as well. They preferred a larger shield called the pavise, using a pointed bottom or a sharp spike to keep it anchored in the ground as cover against arrows.

One of the later incarnations of the shield developed to protect the knight as he charged with a couched lance (horizontally balanced and braced against the right armpit), either in battle or in the formal mock combat of the joust. Called a "targe," this shield was roughly rectangular but usually had waves, flutings, folds, and curves, along with an overall concave shape, to deflect an enemy's blow. It also had an irregular, rounded gap in the top right side to allow the wielder's lance to protrude (*LLL* V.ii.549; *A&C* II.vi.38–39). Practical versions for battle were made of painted wood; only tournament and display targes were made of steel. *See also* Armor; Army; Helmet; Weapons.

Shilling

The idea of the solidus—a coin or weight of silver worth 1/20th of a pound and equal to 12 pence / denarii—was at least as old as Charlemagne, but the shilling of 12 English pence was a much later invention, dating from the reign of Henry VII. In the late fifteenth century, he introduced a testoon or shilling that forever altered the style of portraiture on English coins. Previously, monarchs had been portrayed as facing the coin's holder. This new coin, however, offered a profile of the king, and this style became standard.

Edward VI shilling, 1550. Actual size is 31 mm in diameter. © 2002 The American Numismatic Society. All rights reserved.

In the last twenty years of Elizabeth I's reign, the shilling followed a common type for silver coins. The obverse bore a portrait bust, in profile, of the queen, with the legend ELIZAB D G ANG FR ET HIB REGINA (an abbreviated form of "Elizabeth, Dei Gratia Anglie Francie et Hibernie Regina," or "Elizabeth, by the grace of God queen of England, France, and Ireland). The reverse showed a common device, the royal arms on a shield, quartered by a "long cross" that extended beyond the shield, and beyond the center of the coin, into the margin; it bore the legend POSVI DEVM ADIVTOREM MEVM (Behold, I have made God mine helper).

James I altered the coin slightly in the first year of his reign to include SCO (Scotie, Scotland) to the list of countries ruled. He also altered the royal arms, which previously had displayed the lions of England in two quarters and the fleur-de-lis of France, to which English monarchs still laid futile claim, in the other two. Now James moved this quartered design, in a miniature version, to the first and fourth quarters of his new shield, while the second and third quarters were occupied by the symbols of Scotland and Ireland, respectively. The new coat of arms was still divided and extended by the long cross, and had a new motto around the edge: EXVRGAT DEVS DISSIPENTVR INIMICI (Let God arise and let his enemies be scattered). Beginning with this coinage, the shilling bore a Roman numeral XII on the obverse, behind the king's head, to show its value. From 1604 to 1618 the design was essentially the same, but the reverse legend was altered again to QVAE DEVS CONIVNXIT NEMO SEPARET (What God has joined together, let no man put asunder).

In Shakespeare's works, the shilling is often mentioned, usually in the context of small to middling bills and debts. Falstaff borrows 30s (or a pound and a half) from Mistress Quickly (*2H4* II.i.101), and there are small wagers of 5 or 8 shillings in other plays (*MAAN* III.iii.77; *H5* II.i.95–96). Holland (fine linen) costs "40 shillings an ell" (*1H4* III.iii.72–75), shoes could be mended for a shilling (*H5* IV.viii.63–64), and 40 shillings seems to be a standard amount for imaginary financial transactions, much as one today might say, "If I had a dollar for every time (something common occurred), I'd be (rich to some particular extent)":

> I had rather than forty shillings I had such a leg, and so sweet a breath to sing, as the fool has. (*TN* II.iii.20–21)

> I had rather than forty shillings I had my Book of Songs and Sonnets here. (*MWW* I.i.188–89)

The shilling factors into a shepherd's calculation of the value of his flock's wool (*WT* IV.iii.32–34) and a bumpkin's assessment of the value of a gratuity (*LLL* III.i.167 s.d.–169). It even appears as a kind of collectible. Slender complains that Pistol has stolen two Edward VI shillings used as pieces in a game called shovel-board, each of which he purchased for "two shilling and two pence" (*MWW* I.i.148–50). *See also* Money.

Ships
See Transportation.

Sixpence
Introduced by Edward VI in 1549, the sixpence (*CE* I.i.55; *MAAN* II.i.37–38) was precisely what its name implies, a coin worth 6d or half a shilling. It was also sometimes called a "tester" (*2H4* III.ii.281; *TN*

II.iii.31–33), since it was originally issued as a shilling (or testoon) at the much-devalued rates of the end of Henry VIII's reign. Edward VI attempted to restore the currency to its actual value, and thus cut the face value of the testoon in half.

The sixpences of Elizabeth I from 1583 to 1603 bore her portrait in profile and an abbreviated list of the countries to which she laid claim of rulership. The reverse bore the long cross on the royal arms and the legend POSVI DEVM ADIVTOREM MEVM.

James I sixpence, 1624. Actual size is 25 mm in diameter. © 2002 The American Numismatic Society. All rights reserved.

James I's sixpences reflected the changes he made to most of his coinage. He was the reigning king of Scotland before he inherited the English throne, so he added Scotland to the list of his domains and the Scottish (and Irish) symbols to his royal arms. Thus his sixpences of 1603–4 bear, on the obverse, his portrait bust with the legend IACOBVUS ANG SCO FRAN ET HIB REX (James, King of England, Scotland, France, and Ireland) and, on the reverse, the revised arms with a long cross, the date in Arabic numerals, and the legend EXVRGAT DEVS DISSIPENTVR INIMICI (Let God arise and let his enemies be scattered). The sixpences of 1604–18 are almost exactly the same; only the reverse legend has been changed, to QVAE DEVS CONIVNXIT NEMO SEPARET (What God has joined together, let no man put asunder), a quotation reflecting his wishes for a peaceful union of Scotland and England.

Shakespearean sixpences serve as token sums and small fees for services: a page's tip (*2H4* II.ii.93), a barber's fee for a shave (*2H4* I.ii.25–26), a reward for a performance (*TN* II.iii.31–33; *MND* IV.ii.20–24), or the price of a shoddy pair of breeches (*Oth* II.iii.91–93). *See also* Groat; Money; Shilling.

Slave

It seems odd, at first, that Shakespeare should use the word "slave" so often. His was not a society torn apart, as was nineteenth-century America, by questions of slavery and freedom. On the contrary, the English accepted the ordering of society by class as not only inevitable but also natural and proper. There had to be a king (or queen); what alternative was there? No one seriously suggested a Roman-style republic or a Greek-style democracy as a viable option, though such suggestions would eventually be made and would result, in the seventeenth century, in the execution of a king. For the moment, however, there was a right and just order to things: king at the top, then nobles arranged neatly by rank and by the seniority of their titles, then knights banneret and bachelor, then esquires and other gentry, then yeomen, then mere husbandmen and "mechanicals" or manual laborers, then peasants (or "hinds"), with vagrants, whores, rogues, thieves, and other riffraff (including actors) at the stinking bottom of the heap. Slavery was not controversial; someone had to be at the bottom, and if slaves were there, it must be for a divinely ordained reason. Slavery was mentioned, even sanctioned, in the Bible, which made it blasphemous as well as anarchic to question it.

Neither was slavery particularly visible in England, where slaves' numbers were negligible. There were people poor enough and dependent enough on their local lords that they were no better off than serfs, but serfdom as a thriving institution was dead in England, as it was in most of Europe. African slaves existed in Europe, but their numbers were concentrated in Spain and Portugal, with fewer in Italy and hardly any in England. But there were slaves elsewhere: in parts of eastern Europe where serfdom still held sway, or where Tartars captured Christians to sell into bondage; in Islamic countries, which purchased both white and black slaves; and, of course, in the New World, where the Spanish and Portuguese, and to a lesser extent the Dutch, French, and English, sold slaves purchased from dealers in Africa.

There were slaves removed by time as well as by distance. Slavery had been common in the republican and imperial Rome so familiar to educated people of the Renaissance; at the end of the republic perhaps one-third of the population of Italy was composed of slaves. Roman slaves could be whipped, branded, sold, jailed, raped, and, in some cases, killed (*A&C* III.xiii.149–51). Their ranks were filled by prisoners of war, children born or sold into slavery, criminals, debtors, and babies who had been exposed by their biological parents and raised by their "saviors" as slaves. They had few legal rights; for example, they could testify in trials only if absolutely necessary, and then only after they had been tortured to ensure that their testimony was truthful. They could be freed and given Roman citizenship, and some owners allowed them to earn money or to graze cattle of their own on the master's land, but it was a miserable existence, and Shakespeare's attitudes toward slavery were most likely shaped by the twin influences of Roman literature, which accepted slavery as fundamental to society, and the Bible, which legislated the treatment of slaves but similarly tolerated the institution itself. His opinions certainly had little to do with personal experience or even national policy, for England would not begin a serious traffic in slaves until after 1650. Before that time, its efforts were haphazard and amateurish compared to the efficient Portuguese shipments of human chattel.

His attitude toward slavery seems mixed. On the one hand, we have Shylock's use of slavery as evidence of Venetian hypocrisy:

> You have among you many a purchased slave,
> Which like your asses and your dogs and mules
> You use in abject and in slavish parts,
> Because you bought them. Shall I say to you,
> "Let them be free! Marry them to your heirs!
> Why sweat they under burdens? Let their beds
> Be made as soft as yours, and let their palates
> Be seasoned with such viands"? You will answer,
> "The slaves are ours." (*MV* IV.i.90–98)

This passage would seem to imply a sympathy with the slave and a sense of the injustice of the institution of slavery. On the other hand, one of Shakespeare's most common uses of the word "slave" is as an insult, with the implication that the condition is a fully merited mark of baseness (*2GV* III.i.157, 377; *TS* IV.i.155; *R&J* I.v.57). Nor can Shylock's arguments be taken entirely at face value. He is the villain, after all, and his reasoning, in Shakespeare's eyes, has led him to several wrong conclusions that will ultimately cause his downfall. Shylock's argument is convincing from a twenty-first century perspective, but dangerously anarchic from a sixteenth-century one. In Shakespeare's world Christians were simply better than Jews and freemen better than slaves, and everyone knew it.

Shakespeare, then, mentions the slave so often not because he wishes to register a complaint. He uses slaves in the same way he uses kings—as symbols of the extremes of the human condition. The king is powerful, burdened by decisions, isolated yet never quite alone, the very pinnacle of humankind; the slave is powerless, deprived of any decisions, isolated yet never quite alone, the toe jam of humankind. The slave thus serves as a symbol of imprisonment, lowness of all kinds, or loss of control to love, external force, ignorance, or cowardice (*JC* III.ii.23; *TS* I.i.219–20; *2GV* III.i.41).

Sophy

In about 1500, Ismail Safi became the ruler of Persia and gave his name to a dynasty that lasted until 1736. His name also became synonymous in

English, as "sophy" or "grand sophy," with the title of the Persian shah or king (*TN* II.v.177, III.iv.284; *MV* II.i.25). The Sophy should not be confused with the Turkish sultan, who was quite a different ruler. Abraham Ortelius's *Theatrum Orbis Terrarum* calls Persia "The Empire of the SO-PHIES" and notes that it is separate from the Turkish empire and practices a different version of Islam. Similarly, in Thomas Heywood's play *The Four Prentices of London*, dating probably from the early 1590s, the Sophy and Sultan both appear as characters. Heywood, like Shakespeare, is not averse to a good anachronism—his play is set in the eleventh century, long before Safi came to the Persian throne.

Spectacles

Spectacles (*Lear* I.ii.34–35, IV.vi.170; *MAAN* I.i.185; *AYLI* II.vii.158) were made of glass lenses mounted in bone, horn, leather, or lead frames. The concave lens for nearsightedness was an invention of the early six-teenth century and was in fairly general use by Shakespeare's time by those who needed such devices. Spectacles were purchased, according to an Italian illustration of 1600, from vendors with stalls open to the street, who displayed their wares on tables and hanging from the awning above. The vendor might have a box with eight or ten pairs in it, and the customer tried on different lenses until he found a pair that worked reasonably well.

Glasses typically came in three types. The first was a pair of lenses, usually round, but also could be oval, for presbyopia (farsightedness), so that the wearer could look through the lenses to read and over them to see far away. These lenses were edged with a frame and joined by a bridge over the nose, but there were no earpieces. To keep the glasses from sliding, they were typically pinched into place low down on the nose—the pince-nez of a later era is the descendant of these eyeglasses.

The second type was similar to the first, except that something kept the spectacles in place. This might be a leather strap that fastened around the head or cords that passed in a loop behind the ears. The eyeglasses were usually modified in some way, for example, by having small holes at either side, to accommodate the strap or cord.

The third type was a single lens, used as a reading or magnifying glass for the farsighted and as a "perspective glass" by the nearsighted. The perspective glass had a small handle and hung around the neck; as is indicated in *All's Well That Ends Well* (V.iii.48–49), and as is true today of eyeglasses, the lens that worked for one produced only distorted images for another. The perspective glass was an upper-class accessory; poorer folk in need of vision correction would have worn simple two-lens spectacles in leather frames. Incidentally, Shakespeare's usage of the term "spectacles" is sometimes ambiguous and can be taken to mean the eyes, eyeglasses, or perhaps either (*2H6* III.ii.112, V.i.165).

Suicide

There is a curious duality in Shakespeare's works regarding suicide (*Mac* II.iii.4–5; *A&C* IV.xv.25–26), representing the very different beliefs about the practice in Renaissance Europe and in the ancient Rome from which so many of Shakespeare's plots are drawn. In Europe, Christianity forbade the taking of one's own life for any reason. It was one of the strongest taboos in the culture (*Cym* III.iv.76–78; *Oth* I.iii.352–53), and Shakespeare occasionally transports it beyond Christendom to places such as ancient Greece (*TNK* IV.iii.30–44) and even Rome; Lucrece, for example, treats suicide as a sin, even though this was a Christian, not a Roman, concept (*RL* 1154–76). The act was considered despicable. It smacked of the fate of Judas Iscariot (*LLL* V.ii.601–4); it implied a lack of faith in God's plan; it was even treasonous, for it deprived the king or queen of a subject. Lord Dyer, in 1554, declared it "an offence against nature, against God, and against the king." Suicides in Shakespeare's England were denied Christian burial. They were buried in or near a highway, preferably at a crossroads so that the evil associated with them would be drawn in different directions and thus weakened, usually with a wooden stake driven through the heart to keep them from rising as ghosts (*AW* I.i.141–43). Exceptions were made, as in Ophelia's case (*Ham* V.i.1–25), but if a suicide was buried in the churchyard, he or she was usually interred on the north side of the church, which was reserved for such ambiguous cases. The popular feeling against suicide was so strong that, though many people considered it, most rejected it as an option (*Lear* III.iv.53–54; *Mac* V.viii.1–2; *John* III.iii.54–56).

In ancient Rome, however, suicide was considered a dignified and even honorable way to exit life. It was a means of acknowledging defeat while still retaining control over one important act. Many prominent Romans, including the historical Brutus, Antony, Portia, and Cassius, ended their lives in this manner (*JC* IV.iii.153, V.iii.45–46, 95–96; *Ham* V.ii.343; *TA* II.iv.9–10, III.ii.16–22), usually by stabbing, sometimes by lying in a bathtub and slitting their wrists.

Sulfur

This nonmetallic element, yellow and crystalline in its pure form, appears a few times in Shakespeare's works, once in the context of its rotten-egg smell (*Cym* V.iv.85), but usually, since it is highly flammable, as a symbol of things hot or fiery (*Oth* III.iii.326). Its continual burning is one of the torments of hell (*Oth* V.ii.279–80; *Ham* I.v.2–4; *Lear* IV.vi.128–29), and lightning is often likened to a sulfurous flame, bolt, or stone (*Temp* I.ii.203–4; *Cym* V.v.240; *Cor* V.iii.152–53; *MM* II.ii.115–17; *Lear* III.ii.4–5; *Per* III.i.6). Occasionally it is referred to as "brimstone" (*TN*

II.v.48, II.ii.20–21; *Oth* IV.i.232); in the first and third of these examples, it is part of an angry exclamation: "Fire and brimstone!," a sort of Renaissance "Oh, hell!"

Sword

The sword is the weapon most frequently mentioned in Shakespeare's works. As with so many items of armor and weaponry, however, it can be difficult to envision just which sword he means. When he writes of "Brutus' sword" (*JC* V.i.58), for example, does he mean a Roman sword, or a Renaissance rapier anachronistically placed in Brutus's hand? Almost certainly, he means the latter, for the Renaissance theater was hardly noted for historical authenticity in its costumes or props. Nevertheless, it is worth mentioning, briefly, that the Greek "sword / Hung by a curious baldric" (*TNK* IV.ii.85–86) would have been, if accurately represented, a short, wide-bladed weapon. And there were two types of Roman swords, the long *spatha* for slashing and the short *gladius* for stabbing. The *spatha* was out of fashion by the days of the early empire, so it is perhaps the *gladius* that the conspirators wielded (*JC* III.i.107) and that Antony named "Philippan" (*A&C* II.v.23). Perhaps it is the *gladius* that occurs so often in the bloody *Titus Andronicus* (I.i.4, 68, 85, 128, 175, 204, 249, 288, 311, II.i.35, 59, III.i.72, IV.ii.86, 87).

Medieval Swords

The sword appears repeatedly in the history plays and tragedies, serving as a weapon, a metaphor, or a sign of rank. Here (*1H6* III.iv.9, 19; *2H6* IV.iii.IV.x.55, 68–72, 80; *3H6* I.ii.53; *R2* I.iii.128) it might be useful to imagine the classic medieval sword, even if Shakespeare did not. The medieval sword was a simple, cruciform (cross-shaped) weapon with a grip, a perpendicular guard on either side called a quillon, and a round or polyhedral pommel at the very end that helped to balance the weapon. The grip, quillons, and pommel together formed the hilt (*H5* II.Cho.9, II.i.66; *R3* I.iv.156–57).

The cruciform sword had a double-edged blade, though it was not primarily a cutting weapon. It was meant for thrusting or for bashing the other fellow's armor to pieces. That it was expected to hit objects—shields, helmets, swords—is reflected in the use of the phrases "unhacked swords" and "unhacked edges" when a battle is averted (*John* II.i.254; *A&C* II.vi.38). Conversely, a sign of energetic military action is the damage done to one's sword; a sword well used is "bended" (*H5* V.Cho.18) or, better yet, "hacked like a handsaw" (*1H4* II.iv.165).

There was a larger version of the cruciform sword, a gigantic weapon known as the two-handed (*2H6* II.i.46) sword, sometimes as long as six feet, which was often used more for ceremonial purposes than for actual

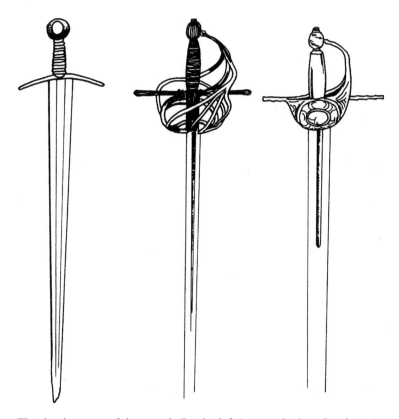

The development of the sword. On the left is a standard medieval cruciform sword, c. 1400, showing (from top): pommel, grip, quillons, and
blade. By the late sixteenth to early seventeenth centuries, the sword has
evolved into the longer, thinner rapier. The example in the center, with
its basket guard, retains the pommel, grip, and quillons, and includes a
set of gracefully curving pieces for the protection of the hand in dueling;
this sketch is based on a sword from c. 1580–1610 with an Italian hilt
and Spanish blade. The rapier on the right, based on an Italian sword of
c. 1610–30, uses a cup guard instead of a basket.

battle. There was also an intermediate version, the bastard or hand-and-a-
half sword, which could be wielded with either one or two hands, but the
two-handed and bastard swords were merely larger versions of the same
cruciform pattern.

Exceptions existed, but usually outside Europe. The scimitar (*MV*
II.i.24; *T&C* V.i.2; *TA* IV.ii.91) was a curved blade associated with exotic,
faraway places; Shakespeare usually assigns such a weapon to a Moor or a
legendary, ancient warrior. Another curved sword, the cutlass, appears
twice as the "curtle-ax" (*AYLI* I.iii.116; *H5* IV.ii.22). One type of European sword with a slight curve was the falchion (*3H6* I.iv.12; *Lear*
V.iii.278; *R3* I.ii.94), introduced in about 1200. It had a short, wide blade
that tapered toward the hilt and was especially popular in Italy, which may

be why Shakespeare assigns it anachronistically to Tarquin and to Caesar (*RL* 176, 509; *LLL* V.ii.613).

Renaissance Swords

In Shakespeare's day, there were a number of sword types, most of them much lighter and thinner than the medieval sword. The standard weapon was the rapier (*3H6* I.iii.37, I.iv.80; *LLL* I.ii.74, 173, 177; *TA* II.i.54, IV.ii.85), a thin, long, double-edged blade with a shallow channel down the middle. Its hilt had quillons like the medieval sword, designed to parry an opponent's blade. The rapier hilt, however, was usually much more complex, with guards in the shape of a cup or a series of curving wires. The first type of guard was called a cup hilt, the second a basket hilt (*2H4* II.iv.132). Cup hilts were particularly popular in Spain and Italy.

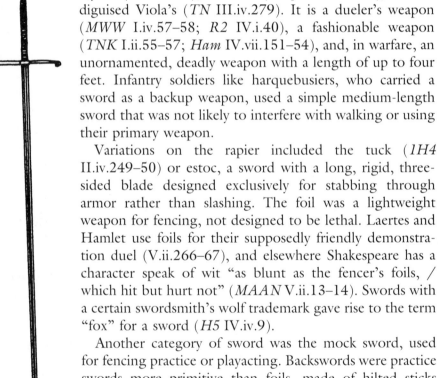

When a kind of sword is specified in Shakespeare, it is likely to be a rapier. The rapier is Falstaff's weapon (*2H4* II.iv.204), Nym's (*H5* II.i.59), Romeo's (*R&J* IV.iii.56–57), and the disguised Viola's (*TN* III.iv.279). It is a dueler's weapon (*MWW* I.iv.57–58; *R2* IV.i.40), a fashionable weapon (*TNK* I.ii.55–57; *Ham* IV.vii.151–54), and, in warfare, an unornamented, deadly weapon with a length of up to four feet. Infantry soldiers like harquebusiers, who carried a sword as a backup weapon, used a simple medium-length sword that was not likely to interfere with walking or using their primary weapon.

Variations on the rapier included the tuck (*1H4* II.iv.249–50) or estoc, a sword with a long, rigid, three-sided blade designed exclusively for stabbing through armor rather than slashing. The foil was a lightweight weapon for fencing, not designed to be lethal. Laertes and Hamlet use foils for their supposedly friendly demonstration duel (V.ii.266–67), and elsewhere Shakespeare has a character speak of wit "as blunt as the fencer's foils, / which hit but hurt not" (*MAAN* V.ii.13–14). Swords with a certain swordsmith's wolf trademark gave rise to the term "fox" for a sword (*H5* IV.iv.9).

Another category of sword was the mock sword, used for fencing practice or playacting. Backswords were practice swords more primitive than foils, made of hilted sticks (*2H4* III.ii.66). Actors and clowns used "lath" (wooden) swords and daggers in their performances (*2H6* IV.ii.1–2; *1H4* II.iv.138; *H5* IV.iv.73; *TA* II.i.41). Some men wore dancing swords, rapiers so light that they were good only

The tuck or estoc.

for show (*AW* II.i.34–35; *TA* II.i.39). (Horace Craig says that these purely decorative weapons did not exist in Shakespeare's time, but the preceding references seem unambiguous. Perhaps the dancing swords mentioned by Shakespeare were the light and useless weapons of a later age; perhaps they were simply serviceable rapiers that bore more elaborately ornamented hilts than usual.)

Those who could afford swords of the best quality preferred those forged in Spain (*R&J* I.iv.84; *AW* IV.i.48). Innsbruck or "Isebrook" steel was also highly valued, and the term became a generic one for any well-tempered blade; thus Othello praises "a sword of Spain, the ice-brook's temper" (*Oth* V.ii.253). Of the Spanish blades, those of Bilbao (called "Bilboa" in England) were especially well regarded for their elasticity; the "bilbo" or sword of Bilbao, it seems, could be bent double, for Falstaff is "compassed like a good / bilbo in the circumference of a peck, hilt to point" (*MWW* III.v.106–7).

Daggers

All dueling swords were intended to be paired with a dagger (*MND* V.i.149; *MAAN* IV.i.108; *H5* IV.i.56–57; *JC* III.ii.46; *Ham* V.ii.147; *R&J* V.iii.170–71; *R3* III.i.110–11), the smaller weapon being used to parry. Some were quite small; that in *The Tempest* (II.i.287) has only a three-inch-long steel blade. In most cases, "dagger," "knife" (*2H6* III.ii.195–97; *3H6* II.vi.48; *2H4* II.iv.130–32; *MAAN* II.iii.249; *TA* III.ii.16), "bodkin" (*WT* III.iii.84; *Ham* III.i.76), and "poniard" (*3H6* II.i.98; *MAAN* II.i.239–40; *AW* IV.i.78; *Ham* IV.vii.150–54, *TA* II.iii.120) appear to be used interchangeably.

A knife of some kind was a useful object to have on one's person, serving as a weapon, an eating utensil, and an all-purpose tool. Even a servant might carry one (*TS* IV.i.124). It was also, when the budget allowed, an ornament. Rich men had theirs made to match their rapiers. Even a child of noble birth might carry a dagger "muzzled, / Lest it should bite its master" (*WT* I.ii.156–57).

Using a Sword

The sword or dagger was kept in a scabbard (*1H6* II.iv.60; *MAAN* V.i.126; *TN* III.iv.279) or sheath (*2H6* IV.x.59; *1H4* I.i.17–18; *R&J* V.iii.171). The sheath was usually made of leather-covered wood with a metal plate called a chape (*AW* IV.iii.147) at the tip to keep the point of the weapon from piercing the leather. The scabbard was suspended from the belt or girdle by a loop called a hanger (*Ham* IV.vii.150–54) or carriage, which might be covered in velvet or otherwise ornamented. Philip Stubbes, in his *Anatomie of Abuses* (1583), complained that the entire sheath was now being made of velvet, and that respect for old-fashioned but practical leather had faded.

Swords and daggers required some care. They had to be sharpened periodically by using a whetstone (*2H4* IV.v.106–7; *MV* IV.i.121), for example, but compared to bows or guns they were low-maintenance weapons. They could be simple and practical enough to serve as forks to "toast cheese" (*H5* II.i.9), yet they were also glamorous weapons, more elegant than a simple quarterstaff (*LLL* V.ii.692–93), decorative, convenient to wear constantly, ancient in lineage, and redolent of the rich history and mythology of knighthood. After all, it was the sword that made a knight, for it was the sword that was used to dub him (*3H6* II.ii.59, 62; *R2* I.i.46, 78–79, 200). *See also* Duel; Weapons.

Tavern

There were far fewer taverns (*1H6* III.i.149; *1H4* II.iv.set) than alehouses in England. A 1577 survey of twenty-seven counties put the number at 300, compared to 14,000 alehouses. In part, this was because taverns' numbers were limited by law; a statute of Edward VI set London's maximum at forty. The lower number was also the result of the sorts of beverages served in the two kinds of establishments. Alehouses specialized in beer and ale, the national drinks, whose ingredients, barley and hops, were widely grown. Taverns, on the other hand, evolved from vintners' shops and sold primarly wine and brandy. These were almost exclusively imported beverages, since wine grapes grew poorly in England, and were drunk by middle- and upper-class men rather than by laborers.

The fare was not the only difference between alehouses and taverns. Alehouses were marked by a bush-topped pole; taverns, because of their connection to grape vines, by a growth of ivy (*AYLI* Epi.3–4). At alehouses, the emphasis was on drink; at taverns, there was some attention paid to "ordinaries" (*1H4* III.iii.178; *AW* II.iii.203; *A&C* II.ii.227) or simple meals. (In the first citation listed, the meal in question is a breakfast.) Because the tavern clientele was richer, taverns were more likely than alehouses to have separate rooms, each with its own character and name, such as "the Wild of Kent" (*1H4* II.i.57), the "Half-moon" (*1H4* II.iv.28), the "Pomgarnet" (pomegranate—*1H4* II.iv.39), the "Dolphin chamber" (*2H4* II.i.86), or the "Bunch of Grapes" (*MM* II.i.124–29). Bishop Earle, writing in 1628, declared taverns the socially superior type of drinking place, but Shakespeare's taverns seem sad and seedy places, staffed admittedly by "sweet" hostesses (*1H4* I.ii.40–41 and 47–50, II.iv.ch.; III.iii.ch.; *2H4* II.i.ch.) like Mistress Quickly, but otherwise characterized mostly by crime (*MWW* I.i.12–21), drunkenness, prostitution (*Lear* I.iv.242–47; *H5* II.i.33–36), and squabbles between staff and customers over payment of bills (*1H4* III.iii.77–89, 166; *Cym* V.iv.127–35). In *Richard II*, taverns are compared unfavorably to inns (V.i.13–15), though Pistol, upon marrying Nell Quickly, becomes outraged at being called a "host," which implies that he keeps an inn (*H5* II.i.28–32).

The vintner (*1H4* II.iv.ch.) or hostess of the tavern often had assistants called tapsters or drawers (*1H4* II.iv.4–28, 42–49). They darted to and fro, poured wine for those who summoned them (*V&A* 849), and reckoned up the bill at the end of the night. Customers often complained that the tapster had overcharged them, and a tapster's arithmetic was, to the outraged, as proverbially faulty then as a baseball umpire's vision is today (*AYLI* III.iv.29–31; *T&C* I.ii.117). *See also* Alehouse; Drink; Inn.

Tawdry Lace

This was a corruption of the phrase "St. Audrey's lace," and meant a necklace made of "thin and fine silk" popular in the sixteenth and early seventeenth centuries. The name came from St. Audrey (630?–679), originally known as Etheldreda, whose story is told by Bede. According to him, she foretold her death by plague, and in the meantime suffered a tumor on her jaw that caused great pain in her face and throat. (Other authorities state that she died of the tumor itself.) She told her doctor that she welcomed the agony, for she had worn "the needless burden of jewelry" around her neck in her youth, and to her the pain was a sign that God was purging her of her vanity. The tawdry lace may have taken its name from the connection with neckwear or from the fact that items of its kind may have been sold at a fair on or about St. Audrey's Day (June 23) and thus called St. Audrey's Fair. Certainly by the late seventeenth century, the trinkets sold at this fair had become so well known that the word "tawdry" became separated from the specific kind of necklace mentioned by Shakespeare (*WT* IV.iv.249–50) and came into general use as an adjective meaning cheap and showy.

Taxes

The English, by sixteenth-century European standards, were not overburdened by taxation (*2H6* III.i.60–63, 116; IV.vii.70–71), yet there has probably never been a tax in human history that was met with joyous welcome by its payers. No doubt Shakespeare drew on current resentments as well as his original historical sources when he wrote of the "burdenous taxation" (*R2* II.i.260) of earlier reigns (*R2* I.iv.47–50, II.i.246; *1H6* I.iii.64; *2H6* I.iii.130–33). Taxes came in many forms in his day, most of them royal prerogatives centuries old, though not all of them benefited the queen or king directly. One example of an indirect benefit was the right of a ruler to grant a monopoly (*Lear* I.iv.155) on the sale of some commodity, which did nothing to augment the royal purse but allowed the crown to reward a favorite without spending anything out of pocket. The people paid in the form of higher prices for the monopolized commodity. The crown itself need not fear to suffer from price increases, for another of its rights was that of purveyance.

Purveyance allowed crown officials called purveyors to purchase goods at a special below-market rate for use at the court. Sometimes they went directly to markets, manors, and villages, seizing the goods they wanted and paying the "king's price." Sometimes they "compounded" with the counties, which did the hard work of amassing the supplies and shipping them to court, gaining in exchange some control over what was sent. The purveyors were paid, but most of their income was acquired from their perquisite: a percentage of all the goods they acquired. Purveyance was much resented by the common people.

Much of the royal revenue came from customs duties. Exporters paid duties on wool, fells (hides with the wool still attached), sheepskins, and cloth, while importers paid duties on wine and cloth. Wool was such an important commodity for export that the wool duty was known as the "great custom." In addition, there were special taxes, called impositions, that served to regulate trade. For example, Mary I imposed a fine on anyone who imported sweet wine through any port other than the one to which she had granted the trade. Many import and export duties were classed together under the terms "tonnage and poundage"; tonnage, or tunnage, was an import duty imposed on wine imported in tuns or casks; poundage was levied on all other imports and exports, except bullion, by weight. Tonnage and poundage were the crown's most productive sources of customs revenue.

Customs duties were collected in one of two ways: by direct payment to the crown or by "farming." Ideally, all goods were landed at or shipped from one of England's principal ports, of which there were fewer than twenty. Merchants came to a collector and gave him a description of the applicable goods; he charged them the appropriate fee and gave them documents stating the type and quantity of cargo they were allowed to import or export. The collectors were responsible for turning the money over to the crown or its agent, and they in turn were inspected by controllers. Another type of customs official, the searcher, checked the merchants' documents against the cargo to make sure that the goods had been properly taxed.

In practice, the system seldom worked so smoothly. The custom houses were small, too small to handle the volume of goods being shipped to and from England, and officials could not adequately control goods that were unloaded elsewhere. In theory, the officials were responsible not only for their port but also for the shoreline halfway to ports in either direction along the coast, and the handful of agents assigned to each port could not protect against smuggling in such a large area. Merchants also attempted to evade customs by hiding packets in their clothes, disguising the contents of chests, forging documents, or switching chests before the searcher could inspect them. Furthermore, the custom officials were not above taking a bribe now and then.

In an attempt to remedy the evils of the system, or at least to make them someone else's problem, monarchs experimented with "farming" the customs (*R2* I.iv.45). In the same way that the crown leased royal lands to tenants who paid rents in goods, services, or money, the crown gave a contract for the customs to a tax "farmer" who paid a stipulated sum of money and was permitted to keep any duties in excess of that amount as his profit. After 1585, to increase accuracy in setting the farmer's payment, the crown won access to the books of its customs collectors. Elizabeth I returned briefly to direct collection of the duties in the 1590s, then gradually returned to national farming of the customs, a transition that was complete by 1604. In that year, the Great Farm of the customs cost £112,400 per year and permitted the holder of the contract to collect almost all duties, except the tonnage on wine, the impositions, and another kind of wine tax called prisage.

Prisage was one of the many miscellaneous sources of crown income. It began as the right of the monarch to appropriate wine directly from vintners (*AYLI* Epi.3–4) for his table. Well before Elizabeth's time, it had been converted into a cash payment. It supplemented her other sources of money, which included the rents on her lands, the sale of crown lands, forced loans wrested from wealthy merchants, fees paid by saltmakers for the right to operate their boiling cauldrons, and "first fruits," a fee paid by newly employed clergy that amounted to one year's salary. None of these sources of income required Parliament's approval or oversight.

Two types of taxes did. One of them, the fifteenth and tenth (*2H6* IV.vii.23–24), was a quota tax, with each county or borough given an amount it must raise. Collectors in each part of the country gave their bond to procure the specified sum, then tried to wring the taxes out of whomever they thought could pay. If they could not raise the tax through their efforts, they had to pay it out of their own purses. Perhaps this is the kind of tax that Shakespeare has in mind when he has Richard II say,

> Our substitutes at home shall have blank charters,
> Whereto, when they shall know what men are rich,
> They shall subscribe them for large sums of gold. (*R2* I.iv.48–50)

The other kind of tax was the subsidy, an assessed tax for which prominent citizens in each area became assessors. It was their job to estimate the wealth of each household, which was then charged a percentage of its valuation—usually 4s on the pound on land and 2s 8d on the pound on possessions. This was a harder tax to impose successfully, because it required the assessors to penalize their own neighbors, and many of them undervalued goods or simply failed to raise the expected amounts, afraid of living a hellish life afterward in a community filled with resentment. The subsidy and the fifteenth and tenth were imposed only in extraordinary circumstances, such as war or the fear of imminent war, because, unlike the duty on wine or a tithe of mined lead, they affected nearly everybody. Shakespeare's audiences would have been as indignant as the characters in his plays at the use of such measures for apparently frivolous causes, like a royal wedding or the transportation of a royal bride (*1H6* V.v.92–93; *2H6* I.i.131–32).

Theater

It seems superfluous to introduce an entry on theater, even though it is clearly the most essential of subjects when discussing a playwright. However, precisely because it is so essential, it is the one subject almost certain to be covered in every edition of every Shakespeare play. Every editor feels justifiably compelled to offer an explanation of the staging of plays in Shakespeare's time, and almost every preface includes some sort of diagram or description of the Globe or similar theaters. The exact shape of the original Globe and its immediate successor have been debated for centuries, and the recent reconstruction of the Globe has settled few of the controversies. Because this subject is covered so exhaustively elsewhere, then, only a few essential details will be discussed here.

Venues

Plays, in Shakespeare's day, were staged either in purpose-built theaters or in spaces originally designed for other uses, such as the great halls of schools and mansions or the open quadrangles inside large inns. Most London theaters at the time were actually constructed outside London, in Southwark, to escape the restrictions on theaters in the city itself. Some patrons walked or rode across London Bridge to get to the playhouses, but most took boats operated by watermen. Because the theaters attracted crowds, they were often criticized for encouraging disorder, corrupting morals, and spreading plague. In times of epidemic, they were closed to prevent the last, but no one did much about the first two. As a nod to religious observance, however, playhouses were closed on Sundays and during Lent.

The theaters of Southwark included a bearbaiting and bullbaiting arena; the Rose, just east of this; the Globe, south of the Rose across Maiden Lane; and the Swan, to the west just inland of Paris Garden stairs. The Rose,

The Globe Theater, or more likely a mislabeled Rose Theater, from a 1616 engraving by Cornelius Visscher. Reproduced from *Shakespeare's England*.

The "De Witt sketch" of the interior of the Swan Theater. Reproduced from *Shakespeare's England*.

not the first theater in the London area but the first in Southwark, was built in 1587 and demolished about 1606. The Globe was added in 1599 and rebuilt in 1613 after it burned during a performance of *Henry VIII.* The Swan was probably built in 1595, and in 1614, the bearbaiting arena was replaced by the Hope theater. Other London theaters included the Theater (whose materials were used in the building of the first Globe), the Curtain, the Fortune, and the Red Bull. Blackfriars and Whitefriars were enclosed theaters that, unlike the round open-air theaters of Southwark, could be used in comfort year-round. A venue called the Cockpit or Phoenix, constructed for cockfights in 1609, was converted into a theater after the close of Shakespeare's career. Almost all the open-air theaters were round—hence Shakespeare's description of the Globe as a "wooden O" (*H5* I.Pro.13)—but whether they were really round or merely polygonal has been much debated. The excavation of most of the foundation of the Rose in 1989 demonstrated that the Rose, at least, was polygonal.

Little is known of the interior of the theaters. The only surviving contemporary sketch of a stage (*H5* I.Pro.3) is a copy of one made by Johannes De Witt, a foreign visitor. It depicts the stage of the Swan, which, even if the drawing and its copy were accurate, does not necessarily tell us what the stage of the Globe looked like. We do not know for certain how wide or deep the stage was, or even what the stages or huts atop the main stage looked like; maps of London, including that by Cornelius Visscher, often relied upon sketches and maps by others, depicted structures that were out of date, and conflicted with each other. The number, size, and placement of huts and cupolas are still unknown. Deductions made on the basis of stage directions, contemporary descriptions, and other evidence pointing to the existence of two doors (*TN* II.ii.1 s.d.) leading to the backstage "tiring [dressing] rooms," an upper stage, a main stage, a thatched roof, three tiers of seats, an enclosed upper area called the "heavens" through which gods could descend (*Cym* V.iv.62 s.d.), and a compartment under the stage, or "hell," from which characters such as ghosts could emerge. Seats cost 2d or 3d; if one was willing to stand, he could get in for only a penny and join the other "groundlings" in the uncovered area around the stage (*Ham* III.ii.9–10). Silence was not a requirement for audience members. They often talked to the actors, shouted out jokes of their own, or hissed the villains in addition to laughing and applauding (*JC* I.ii.256–59; *H8* V.iv.59–60; *TNK* Pro.16).

Actors

There were no actresses. All women's parts were played by men, with the ingenues being played by boys whose voices had not changed (*AYLI* Epi.16–19; *A&C* V.ii.216–21). Some praised this technique for keeping women's virtue safe; there was a general belief that flirting, or adopting some compromising pose, onstage was nearly as dangerous and vile as doing it in real life. For some, particularly Puritans, there was no difference at all, and actors were thoroughly condemned by some as the devil's helpers. The law agreed, at least in part. A 1572 anti-vagrancy statute made actors (*JC* II.i.225–27; *AYLI* III.iv.57) without noble patrons subject to the same penalties as common vagabonds.

A ranting style of acting apparently was common in companies other than Shakespeare's, for he makes fun of actors who speak in a roaring, unnatural style (*1H4* II.iv.390, 400–401, 458–59; *Ham* III.ii.2–22), gesture frantically (*Ham* III.ii.4–5), and pace aggressively across the stage (*T&C* I.iii.153–61; *Ham* III.ii.28–35). He also criticizes comedians who attempt to upstage the rest of the players by laughing at their own jokes (*Ham* III.ii.36–45). Players tended to become known as either comedians (*TN* I.v.180) or tragedians (*AW* IV.iii.272), and some were famous for having played particular parts. Richard Tarleton, for example, was noted for his portrayals of a clown, or country bumpkin.

Plays and Genres

Plays were already beginning to diverge from more stylized, older forms. The Greek-style drama, with its unity of place, time, and action, had given way to plays that divided the action between multiple places, might include events that were years apart, and had not only a main plot but one or more subplots as well. Medieval morality plays, with one-dimensional heroes and villains named for the vices (*2H4* III.ii.324; *H5* IV.iv.73) or virtues they personified, had developed into dramas with multifaceted protagonists and antagonists. The commedia dell'arte, a form of Italian theater with stock characters such as the lecherous old man Pantalone (pantaloon—see *TS* I.i.47s.d.; *AYLI* II.vii.157–60), served only as a point of reference, not an inspiration. And the private revels, such as masques, pageants, and the Robin Hood plays of May Day celebrations (*TNK* Pro.20–21)—all of them lacking dramatic complexity—found a home in the theater only as a counterpoint or interlude, not as the main action. Pantomime, too, was seldom used, and then only in moderation, as in the play-within-a-play in *Hamlet*. Some of the characteristics of Roman theater, however had been retained: the division into five acts, for example, and the use of "high," "middle," and "low" styles for different classes of characters. Tragedies focused on noble-born characters speaking in high style, while comedies were supposed to focus on middle- or lower-class manners and mores.

Plays were performed on a rotating schedule, with a different work being presented each day except in the case of very new (*TNK* Pro.1–9) and popular works. These, which typically brought in much more money than older plays, might be performed for a few days in a row. It is unknown how much money Shakespeare's plays made. His rival Philip Henslowe's accounts show small figures in most cases—a few dozen shillings per performance—but a foreign visitor estimated that the amount was as much as £10 or £12, and there is no way of knowing how well informed he was.

Threepence

Introduced by Edward VI, the threepence is one of those little coins whose denominations seem so odd until one realizes that, as a quarter-shilling, it must have been somewhat convenient. Apparently, however, it was not convenient enough. Mary I overlooked it entirely. Elizabeth I brought it back in her second coinage of 1561–82, but abandoned it in her third coinage of 1583–1603, and James I did not revive it.

Elizabeth I threepence, 1582. Actual size is 18 mm in diameter. © 2002 The American Numismatic Society. All rights reserved.

Still, it appears on occasion in Shakespeare's plays, most notably in *Measure for Measure* II.i., where it occurs three times (90–92, 101, 240). However, in this scene and in *Coriolanus* II.i.75, the cost of something is described simply as "threepence," which could mean a 3d coin or a combination of smaller coins adding up to three pennies. The only undoubted reference to the coin itself is dismissive of both the coin and its condition: "a threepence bowed would hire me" (*H8* II.iii.36).

Assuming that the bent coin in question is the most recent issue, Elizabeth's coin of 1561–82, it looked almost exactly like other small silver coins of its time, differing from the 6d only in size and bearing, like the sixpence, a rose behind the queen's head to distinguish it from the similarly sized groat. *See also* Money.

Throne

When Shakespeare speaks of thrones (*3H6* V.vii.1; *R3* II.ii.100), it is possible that he has one of two specific chairs in mind. The first is the chair of state in the Houses of Parliament (*3H6* I.i.22–26, 51, 168), in which the monarch sat when he or she addressed the members. The chair of state was, for example, where the king or queen sat when opening and closing sessions of Parliament. The second is the coronation chair in Westminster Abbey, which was an important part of the coronation ritual. Built about 1300, the chair still exists. It rests on four carved lions and has a pointed back with two pillar-shaped finials on each side, open quatrefoils on the sides under the seat, and a large stone resting on a shelf and visible through the front and the openings on the sides. The stone is the Stone of Scone, captured from Scotland long before Shakespeare's time and associated in his day with the biblical patriarch Jacob. Jacob is supposed to have been standing on it when he had his vision of a ladder reaching to heaven.

Time

Time was measured differently in the Renaissance. It was less precise, more local, and thought of in larger units. It was less precise because the instruments by which it was read—sundials, hourglasses, and early clocks and watches—were vague, inaccurate, or both. Sundials (*H5* I.ii.210; *1H4* V.ii.83–84; *S* 77) operated only when the sun was shining; they also varied according to one's position on the earth, though scientists from Ptolemy on knew how to account for these differences. Hourglasses (*H5* I.Pro.31; *3H6* I.iv.25; *WT* I.ii.304–6; *Temp* V.i.223; *TNK* V.i.18; *Per* V.ii.1; *Cym* III.ii.71–73) could become temporarily clogged, and any unit less than an hour (*1H4* II.iii.35–36; *LLL* II.i.121–22; *R3* IV.i.28) had to be guessed at depending on the level of the sand, and of course the glass needed to be turned promptly when the sand ran out. And clocks and watches ran on gears that were far from perfect; even the best examples could be off by fifteen minutes a day.

Because the instruments for measuring time were imprecise, people often judged the time by the sky. They thought more in terms of dawn (*2GV* V.i.1–5), noon (*MM* II.ii.161; *A&C* I.iv.2), sunset, and the rise and fall of stars and the moon, than in minutes (*2H4* IV.i.83; *AYLI* IV.i.42–43) and seconds. Time was therefore local; there was no standardized sequence of time zones, for no one could travel fast enough to outpace the movements of the sun. Noon was noon wherever one happened to be, and clocks and watches were set or corrected according to the time when the sun reached its zenith. For the same reasons, and because of the unpredictability of travel, no one made appointments for 3:15 or 5:40, or even thought in terms of those times. When they had occasion to set a particular time for an occurrence, they thought in terms of its relation to sun, moon, or stars (*JC* II.i.2–3), or to a particular, roughly gauged hour (*1H4* II.i.1–2, 34–35; *2H4* III.i.32–34; *MAAN* III.iii.87–89, IV.i.82–83; *H5* I.i.93, IV.Cho.15–16; *JC* II.i.212, II.iv.23; *AYLI* IV.i.178–79; *Tim*

III.iv.7–8; *R3* III.iv.101, V.iii.31; *Oth* II.ii.8–10). One example, from *The Tempest*, mingles observations of the sun and the use of an hourglass:

PROSPERO: What is the time o' th' day?

ARIEL: Past the mid season [noon].

PROSPERO: At least two glasses [2:00 P.M.]. (I.ii.239–40)

Clocks, at this time, were not even made with minute hands, though, in a telling sign of how people conceived of time, they sometimes showed the monthly phases of the moon (*Oth* I.iii.84).

The day began, for many people, before dawn. Servants and farmers were among the earliest risers, and the rich tended to do everything later than those of lesser means. They also tended to eat more meals; most people contented themselves with a large dinner at noon and a lighter supper around five or six o'clock (*MV* II.ii.113–14; *LLL* I.i.234–36). Bedtime varied according to social class and according to the type of day; everyone tended to stay up late at celebrations (*MND* V.i.32–34; *TN* II.iii.1–3). During the day, people in towns and villages measured time either by natural signals or by the tolling of the local church bell. It rang on the hour (*H8* V.i.1; *R3* III.ii.4–5, IV.ii.108–11), and it was officially night either at the setting of the sun or at the tolling of the evening, or curfew, bell (*Lear* III.iv.114; *MM* IV.ii.76), usually at eight or nine P.M.; the night was then measured out in the periodic crowing of roosters (*Lear* III.iv.114; *Mac* II.ii.23–24) until dawn. Of all the nighttime hours, the most fearful was "first cock" (*1H4* Ii.i.19), or midnight (*2H4* III.ii.218; *H5* III.Cho.19, III.vii.91; *MM* IV.ii.65–66, V.i.280–81), at which time it was believed that evil spirits, witches, and ghosts were strongest (*MND* V.i.378–81; *Lear* III.iv.113–17). Another way of dividing the night was by "watches," four equal intervals between sunset and dawn.

Units of time longer than days included weeks (or "seven-nights"—see *MAAN* II.i.347), fortnights (periods of two weeks—*1H4* II.iii.38; *MWW* I.i.194), months, seasons, and years, often with the help of an almanac that contained a calendar (*JC* II.i.42; *Per* II.i.57–58; *Mac* IV.i.134). January 1 was New Year's, but the legal year actually began in March, so a legal document drawn up in February 1600 would bear a date in February 1599; this system was not altered until the mid-eighteenth century.

There are several excellent references to time in Shakespeare's works, many of which are cited above. Others that bear mentioning are the appearance of Time, with his hourglass, as the only character in *Winter's Tale* IV.i, the fictional date of "the fourscore / of April" (April 80th) later in the same play (*IV.iv.276–77*), and a dialogue between Falstaff and Hal that is practically a catalog of contemporary methods of telling time, mentioning noon, the time of day, hours, minutes, clocks, sundials, the sun, the moon, and the stars (*1H4* I.ii.2–16). *See also* Bell; Clocks and Watches.

Titles

In a society that valued and insisted upon class distinctions, the proper use of titles was extremely important. People were grouped loosely into several categories: the aristocracy, the gentry, the yeomanry, and the peasantry, with artisans and tradesmen generally falling into the hierarchy as the approximate equivalent of yeomen. The French casualties after Agincourt are divided according to rank; first the "princes, / . . . And nobles" are counted, then the "knights, esquires, and gallant gentlemen," then the common soldiers (*H5* IV.viii.80–99).

The nobles, composed in descending order of dukes (*1H6* III.i.170–74; *2H6* I.i.62–63), marquesses, earls (*1H6* III.iv.26; *2H6* I.i.8; *Mac* V.viii.63–64), viscounts, and barons (*2H6* I.i.8), and their respective wives (duchesses, marchionesses, countesses, viscountesses, and baronesses) were addressed in terms of extreme respect. Dukes and duchesses were referred to as His (or Her) Grace, and all the others as Lord or Lady, followed by the title name (for instance, Lord Cobham). The eldest son of a duke was an earl; the eldest son of an earl, a baron or viscount. All the other sons of nobles were technically esquires, although, as William Harrison pointed out, "in common speech all dukes' and marquises' sons and earls' eldest sons be called lords."

"Your Majesty" was appropriate only when addressing royalty (*2H6* I.ii.71); "my liege" (*H5* I.ii.3) could be used to any liege lord, but was most useful for reminding the sovereign of one's personal loyalty. "Your Grace" could be used either for royals, archbishops, or those of ducal rank; it is used for these purposes, and for cardinals as well, throughout Shakespeare's works (*LLL* II.i.32; *3H6* I.i.262; *2H6* I.ii.71, II.i.17, 137, III.i.44; *Lear* II.i.118; *2GV* III.i.52, 67; *R2* I.i.141). "Your Grace" could not, however, be used below the rank of duke, where only "your Honor" or "your Lordship / Ladyship" was called for; some, nonetheless, extended this courtesy to marquises and their wives. A character who uses the wrong form of address is, in fact, corrected in *Troilus and Cressida*: "Grace? Not so, friend. Honor and lord / ship are my titles" (III.i.16–17). "Your worship" was appropriate as a general, respectful address to a person of much higher station or greater authority than oneself. Costard, for example, uses it when talking to Berowne (*LLL* III.i.149).

The gentry—knights, esquires (*2H4* III.ii.59), and other professional or landed and idle gentlemen (*Cym* V.v.17)—were also addressed in respectful terms. A knight was called "Sir," followed by his first name, so Sir John Falstaff would have been known as "Sir John." The same courtesy was paid to priests, who were considered gentlemen (*R3* III.ii.108). A knight's wife was called "Lady" along with her husband's surname, so if Falstaff had ever married, his wife would have been Lady Falstaff; this method of addressing knights' wives is referred to by the newly knighted Bastard in

King John, who remarks with amusement, "now I can make any Joan a lady" (I.i.184). Gentlemen below the rank of knight were addressed as "Master" (*TN* IV.ii.1–3, 5–8; *MWW* I.i.75). If they were scholars who had taken a university doctorate, they were referred to as "Doctor" (*Ham* V.i.).Their wives might be addressed as "Dame," followed by the surname, though this title was often appended to the names of other ranks as well. It was sometimes used instead of "Lady" for a knight's wife and sometimes applied to any middle-aged or elderly housewife. Despite this vagueness, it is clear that the title "Dame" is a step down for the Duchess of Glouces-ter, who, after her attainder, is called not Her Grace the Duchess of Gloucester but simply "Dame Eleanor Cobham" (*2H6* II.iii.1). A title with a similarly broad application was "Dan," applied as a general title of respect to anyone prosperous and authoritative, from knight to substantial yeo-man. Shakespeare applies the term, which derives from the Latin *dominus* (lord), to "Dan Cupid" (*LLL* III.i.149).

There were forms of address, too, for the humbler members of society, though they were usually less formally applied. Yeomen expected to be addressed as "Goodman" (*R&J* I.v.79). Their wives might be called "Goodwife" or "Mistress" (*MWW* III.iii.35). Older people whose names were not known to the speaker were given familial titles, even when there was no known relationship between them. Such titles included "Father" (*MV* II.ii.68, 72), "Mother" (*2H6* I.iv.11–12), "Grandam" (grand-mother—see *R3* II.ii.1, 12, 20, 31, III.i.145, IV.iv.299), "Grandsire" (grandfather—*TS* IV.v.49), and "Nuncle" (mine uncle—*Lear* I.iv.106). These familial forms of address were a courtesy, used when the speaker was of lesser or equal stauts to the person addressed, and it was a sign of especially good manners for a speaker of higher station to use these terms, since he was not really required to do so.

Speakers of higher social station than their auditors were free to call them "sirrah" (*CE* III.i.83; *2H6* II.iii.82; *TS* Ind.i.74; *R&J* V.iii.281), a term that implied far less courtesy. It was an abrupt title used only for inferiors; to use it with an equal was a sign of casual friendship (*2GV* II.v.9); to use it to a superior was unthinkable. That Poins uses it when addressing Prince Hal is a symbol of the inappropriateness of the prince's friendships with tavern crawlers (*1H4* I.ii.177). Conrade takes offense when the term is applied to him and is quick to correct the speaker:

DOGBERRY: . . . Yours [your name], sirrah?

CONRADE: I am a gentleman, sir, and my name is Conrade.

DOGBERRY: Write down Master Gentleman Conrade. (*MAAN* IV.ii.12–16)

Within the family, husbands and wives had nicknames for each other; Hotspur and Petruchio both call their Katherines "Kate," and Hotspur's Kate calls him "Harry." Parents had nicknames for their children as well, and anyone who had an intimate or familial relationship with someone could use affectionate terms such as "bawcock" and "chuck" (*H5* III.ii.24–25). "You" was formal, and "thou" and "thee" more intimate; the latter terms fell out of use by the end of the seventeenth century, except among religious nonconformists. This may have been because it was too easy to give offense by presuming that one had the right to use the less formal mode of address. *See also* Etiquette.

Tools

Renaissance farmers and artisans used a variety of tools in their work that, in many cases, had remained unchanged in form and use since the Middle Ages, or even since the pre–Christian era. Farm tools included forks and rakes. In *Booke of Husbandrie*, John Fitzherbert gave instructions for the proper construction of a rake. One should make the teeth of dry wood, then "bore the holes with his wimble (auger—see *Mac* II.iii.123) both above and under, and drive the teeth upward fast and hard, and then wedge them above with dry wood of Oake, for that is hard, and will drive and never come out." The rake (*Cor* I.i.23) should be made of seasoned wood, for green wood would dry and warp, "and the teeth will fall out when hee hath most neede of them: wherby he shal hinder his worke and loose much hay." Other farm tools included a wide, shallow sieve for winnowing corn from chaff; ladders (*2H4* III.i.70; *T&C* I.iii.102; *JC* II.i.22–25); buckets and baskets; and scythes and sickles. Both the scythe (*TNK* I.i.77–79; *A&C* III.xiii.193–94) and sickle (*Temp* IV.i.134) had curved

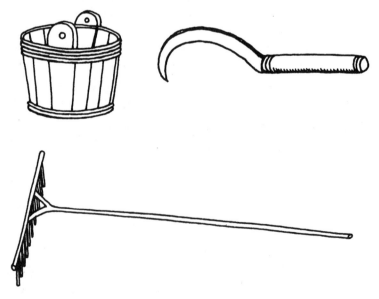

Wooden bucket (mid-sixteenth century); sickle and rake (1577).

cutting blades; the sickle was a short-handled implement wielded with one hand, and the scythe had a long handle, often with two perpendicular projections to serve as handholds for both hands.

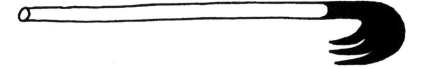

A skrapple, after Lawson.

If the farmer had an orchard, he also needed spades (*R&J* V.iii.186), weeding knives, a ladder with a platform on top for working near the tops of trees, a rake (*H5* II.iv.98) with iron teeth, "a skrapple of Iron thus formed for Netles and ground Ivy after a showr," and a hook for pulling branches down during the harvest, among other tools. For tending the fields, he needed plows, plowshares, coulters, harrows, rollers, harnesses, and either horse collars or yokes (*R&J* V.iii.111; *Cym* III.i.51) and ox-bows, depending on which type of animal did his plowing.

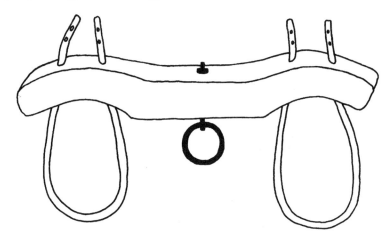

Yoke with ox-bows.

Experts on husbandry often divided their lists of recommended tools according to the outbuildings in which they were stored. As essentials for the stable, Thomas Tusser listed a rack and manger for feeding the animals—a contemporary illustration showed a rack made of widely spaced vertical bars through which the horses could nibble hay, a broom, pail (*Temp* II.ii.24), currycomb, whip, packsaddle, apron, and "crotchets and pins, to hang trinkets thereon." In *The Whole Art and Trade of Husbandry*, Conrad Heresbach offered a list that ran into dozens of items, including many of the tools already named, plus bills, "peasehookes," wedges, "draghookes," saws of various sizes (*1H4* II.iv.165), dung forks and pitchforks (the "pikes" of *Cor* I.i.23), shears (*MM* I.ii.29), tongs, scissors, mat-tocks (long-handled tools for breaking up earth, often with an axelike blade and a pick at the back end of the blade—see *R&J* V.ii.22, V.iii.186), files, lancets, gelding tools, presses, rulers, hammers, chip axes, winches and pulleys, fans (which, like sieves, were used for winnowing), flails (used for threshing), sacks, spindles, fire shovels and gridirons, wheelbarrows, and ropes. In the brewhouse, vessels such as tuns and barrels were re-quired, and in the bakehouse the cook needed coal rakes, sieves, and bolt-ing (sifting) tubs. The hay and corn barns needed wains, carts, wagons, coaches, sleds, and all of the plowing equipment mentioned above. Far-mers as well as woodmen needed axes (*3H6* II.i.54, II.ii.165–68, III.ii.181, V.ii.11; *TA* III.i.184–85; *Tim* V.i.211; *Per* I.ii.58) for felling trees.

Artisans used many of the same tools as farmers. Carpenters used axes, augers, hammers (*A&C* V.ii.210), and saws. To split boards into lumber, if they were doing this work instead of sawyers, they used axlike tools called adzes or wedges (*T&C* I.iii.316) that could be driven into a crack and then pounded with a hammer or mallet. They fixed planks together pri-marily with nails (*TNK* II.i.272; *2GV* II.iv.193). Doors often were strapped together with iron bands, and the boards were studded with wide-headed doornails (*2H6* IV.x.41). When building houses, they used a "line and level" (*Temp* IV.i.239), or plumb line, to ensure that vertical timbers stood straight. For any kind of construction, they needed rulers (or "squares") to measure accurately (*A&C* II.iii.6–7, V.ii.210; *WT* IV.iv.340–42; *LLL* V.ii.475). They, and many other workers with wood, had occasion to use metal hinges (*2H4* I.i.141).

Like carpenters, shoemakers had occasion to use short, wide-headed nails. Called hobnails, these were used as cleats on the soles of rustic shoes (*1H4* II.iv.366; *2H6* IV.x.60). The cobbler also used lasts (*R&J* I.ii.39–40), foot-shaped forms, on which to construct shoes. Anyone who worked with thread, including the cobblers, the knitters, the spinsters, and the tailors, needed "bones" (*TN* II.iv.43–45), or bone bobbins, on which to keep it wound. Before the thread was spun, its basic material, such as flax, was hung on a prong with a wide base and a handle below, called a distaff (*Cym* V.iii.33–34; *WT* I.ii.37; *TN* I.iii.98–100; *Lear* IV.ii.18); because most spinning was done by women, the distaff was a symbol of woman-hood, and in genealogy, the "distaff side" for centuries meant the line of maternal ancestry.

Stonecutters and carvers needed chisels (*WT* V.iii.78) and mallets (*2H4* II.iv.247). Many trades used wheelbarrows, though the example Shake-speare uses is a butcher hauling "offal" to the Thames for dumping (*MWW* III.v.4–6). The bellows was also a common item, in use wherever there was a need for an especially hot fire, such as in armorers' shops, smiths' forges, and iron smelters' furnaces. The bellows (*A&C* I.i.9–10; *Per*

I.ii.40–42) was a tube attached to an accordion-fanned, pear-shaped compartment of wood and leather, with two handles at the wide end so that it could be expanded and contracted, pushing air toward the forge or furnace. The folded or fluted sides of the bellows give the bellows mender of *Midsummer Night's Dream* his name. Almost anyone who worked with hot metal needed a bellows, as well as tongs, files (*TNK* III.ii.8), an anvil, and sundry hammers (*2H6* II.iii.76). Miners, who found the metal in the first place, worked chiefly with pickaxes (*Cym* IV.ii.389).

Shakespeare mentions a few other tools as well. The barber's scissors were not much different from scissors today, though his razor was obviously an old-fashioned straight razor (*TA* I.i.315; *Per* V.iii.74), with one sharp, deadly edge. The razor, like all sharp-edged tools, needed a whetstone (*AYLI* I.ii.52, 53; *T&C* V.ii.73; *Mac* IV.iii.228) to renew the edge; the blade could be drawn across the stone at an angle a few times, though professional knife grinders and sharpeners used a large round whetstone mounted vertically and turned by a foot pedal. Bricklayers and masons used trowels (*AYLI* I.ii.104) to spread mortar. Assorted knives were used in almost every trade, though the most specific type mentioned by Shakespeare must have had a very peculiar blade, for he describes "a great round beard like / a glover's paring knife" (*MWW* I.iv.19–20). A tool whose identity is easy to mistake is the crowbar, which is referred to as a "crow" (*CE* III.i.80), "an iron crow" (*R&J* V.ii.21), and a "wrenching iron" (*R&J* V.ii.22), but never as a crowbar. Paving stones were hammered into place with an enormous mallet, called a beetle, that required three men to lift it (*2H4* I.ii.231). *See also* Farming; Garden; Occupations.

Torture

Torture (*2H6* III.ii.11, 247; *Oth* V.ii.304; *R2* III.ii.198) was illegal in most cases in England. In *The Description of England*, William Harrison pointed out that the jailer himself was guilty of a felony if he tortured a prisoner to force the revelation of accomplices. However, in cases of treason or sedition, it was perfectly acceptable—hence the presence on the government payroll of torturer Richard Topcliffe—and it was used in other parts of Europe, including James VI's (England's James I's) Scotland. In most countries, the information elicited could be used as evidence in a criminal trial, though in England it was generally used only to lead investigators to admissible evidence, rather than serving as evidence itself. Torture could also be used to force a plea. Sometimes prisoners, seeking to preserve their fortunes for their heirs, attempted to use a loophole in the law that prohibited royal confiscation (*MM* V.i.424–27) unless a plea of guilty or not guilty was entered.

One torture tool, called the thumbscrews, was used on both fingers and toes. The device consisted of two metal plates that were slowly twisted together by means of screws, gradually crushing the bones of the digits between the plates. Another instrument of torture, called "the boots," was a set of metal boots, open at the front, into which wedges were driven to break the prisoner's leg bones. To add to the pain, boiling water or oil might be poured over the broken limbs. Sometimes fingernails were pulled off with pincers; a Scotsman, Dr. Fian, who was accused of witchcraft, not only had all his fingernails pulled off but needles driven into the wounds as far as they could go. His supposed colleague, Geillis Duncane, was tortured with "pilliwinkles [similar to thumbscrews] upon her fingers, which is a grievous torture, and binding or wrinching her head with a cord or roape." Female prisoners were sometimes sexually abused as part of their torture; prisoners of either gender could be starved or beaten.

Nevertheless, Shakespeare mentions none of these tortures, but he does include others in his works. One of these is the strappado (*1H4* II.iv.238), which involved tying weights to the prisoner's legs, binding his wrists with a rope, and hoisting him in the air by his bound wrists. He was then abruptly dropped most, but not quite all, the way to the ground, with the result that his arm, shoulder, leg, and hip joints were horribly wrenched and often dislocated. The same effect could be achieved far more slowly by use of the rack (*1H6* II.v.3; *2H6* III.i.376; *T&C* I.ii.143; *MM* V.i.312–13; *Lear* V.iii.315–17), which was a table with bindings for the ankles and wrists and a crank by which the two joints could be stretched farther and farther apart. On the theory that pushing could be just as painful as pulling, torturers also used heavy stones, added one at a time, to press the prisoner's chest until the bones began to crack. Pressing could be combined with the rack, sometimes with a stone beneath the spine to snap it when the collective pressure grew too great, and the torture was not uncommon; forty-four people were pressed to death in Middlesex alone between 1603 and 1625. Another version of "pressing to / death" (*MM* V.i.524–25) was "Skeffington's daughter," a series of bands that pinned the knees to the chest and the ankles to the buttocks. The twice-folded prisoner was then gradually squeezed with the bands until the chest buckled and blood burst from the fingers, toes, nose, and mouth. The "wheel" was another excruciating torture, in which the prisoner was tied to a large wheel and his bones smashed and broken until his arms and legs matched the curve of the wheel rim (*Cor* III.ii.2). *See also* Law.

Touchstone

In a time when all the coinage was real gold (*JC* IV.i.21, 25–27; *T&C* I.ii.108–9) or silver (*T&C* I.iii.65), counterfeiting was extremely profitable, and knowledge of the true value of a metal was important to miners and merchants alike. One way of testing the quality of a metal was to see how hard or soft it was. Gold and silver are both relatively soft metals, so some people used a touchstone (*Per* II.ii.37), a rock harder than gold or silver but presumably softer than baser metals or alloys. The suspect metal was rubbed against the stone to see if it left a colored streak; if it did, it was supposed to be genuine. If it did not, the reverse was true, hence the declaration in *Timon of Athens*, "They have all been touched, and found base metal" (III.iii.6). It is also an appropriate name for the fool in *As You Like It*, since the fool's role in the plays is often to point out the true nature of the characters around him.

Toys

Children had few purposely designed toys. An interest in childhood as a special time of innocence and delight had not yet developed in Western culture; children were still considered small, imperfect adults, and were dressed and treated as such. Accordingly, they, like their parents, had few playthings. They might have pets, such as a dog, a parrot, a goldfinch, or a monkey. Some children had balls to bounce or throw. Others had toys that helped them practice for adult duties, such as a miniature bow or gun for a boy. The "elder-gun" of *Henry V* (IV.i.197) is such a toy. Girls had dolls, which Shakespeare called "mammets" (*1H4* II.iii.91) or "a babe of clouts" (*John* III.iii.58)*—in other words, a rag or cloth doll. Shakespeare also mentions a "manikin" or puppet, but whether such a puppet would have been a child's plaything or part of the inventory of a professional performer is unclear (*TN* III.ii.52). Similarly, he writes of "rattles" (*MWW* IV.iv.51), and rattles were undoubtedly used by children, who blew up pigs' bladders (*1H4* II.iv.335–36) and filled them with dried peas, but rattles made of paper or parchment were also tools used by village goose-herds to gather their flocks.

One toy that is definitely not an adult tool is the gig (*LLL* V.i.63–65) or top (*TNK* V.ii.48–49; *WT* II.i.103; *MWW* V.i.24–26; *TN* I.iii.40–41), and it is the toy that Shakespeare mentions most. The top was usually a whipping-top, made of horn (*LLL* V.i.66–67) or wood, with a horizontal groove high up around its widest part. The top was set spinning, then kept going by striking the groove with a whip. Spinning a top in this manner was considered good exercise for adults and children alike in cold weather, but it was particularly associated with boys and springtime.

Transportation

Land Transportation

It is easy to read, and to understand intellectually, that for most of human history, transportation has been much slower and more difficult

---

The Complete Signet Classic Shakespeare combines two scenes in *King John*, so that the reference to the doll appears in many other editions of the play in III.iv.

than in the past 200, and especially the past 100, years. It is much harder, given the freedom with which we move, to enter emotionally into a world in which a journey of a few dozen miles could be a weeklong affair, fraught with dust, mud (*2H4* V.v.25), physical exhaustion (*LLL* IV.iii.304–5), and the very real danger of being robbed. To enter into this emotional understanding, we must try to forget about airplanes, cars, trains, even good and consistently passable roads. We must begin by realizing, as the poorest peasants must, that everywhere we go, we must get to by walking (*MAAN* II.iii.15–16) or by riding in a heavy cart or carrier's wagon (*AW* IV.iv.34) moving at the walking pace of the the horses or oxen pulling it. How far would you be willing to walk each day? How far would you have to walk to visit a relative, to conduct business in a city, to shop, or to sightsee? How many days could you spare from work, school, or family obligations to make such a journey? The answers to these questions explain why

A mounted rider from Jost Amman's *Adeliche Weydwercke*. Reproduced from the Collections of the Library of Congress.

many people rarely or never left the towns or villages in which they were born.

Those with slightly greater means had more options. They could ride horses or mules (*2H6* IV.i.54; *H8* IV.ii.6–7) of their own, buy a horse and sell it at journey's end, or rent a horse at an inn and later return it or pay a postboy to lead it back. Even so, riding could be slow and tedious. One could not simply gallop a horse all day, and trotting was jarring, so often the pace was a walk, and the only improvement over foot travel was that the horse was doing the walking. An itinerary provided by William Harrison from Dover to London is divided into six stages of 5 to 12 miles (8 to 19.3 km) each, at the end of each of which one presumes the rider was to stop at an inn for the night. Even if two of the six stages were ridden each day, that still means that a journey of 53 miles (85.3 km) took three days. Shakespeare himself offers a few clues about land speeds, stating that 20 miles (32.2 km) per day was a good rate of travel by horseback (*Cym* III.ii.67–68) and that a mile an hour, particularly for a rider with a message, was inexcusably slow (*Cor* I.v.16–18). Balthasar rides from Verona to Mantua and back, a distance of about 25 miles (40.2 km) each way, in two days (*R&J* V.iii.177), confirming the rate of 20 miles per day in *Cymbeline* as an approximation of a reasonable pace.

Those for whom speed or comfort was of the essence, and price no object, had additional choices. Rich women liked to travel in caroches or coaches (*MWW* II.ii.61–63; *R&J* I.iv.69), the latter an innovation of the 1560s. These were four-wheeled, horse-drawn vehicles, open at the sides and highly ornamented, sometimes topped with plumes of feathers, and differing from one another only in size. The caroche held only one person comfortably and was chiefly used in towns. The coach could hold a lady, her children, and her maids, with a coachman in the box up front and a couple of grooms riding alongside. A few women traveled in litters carried by men or horses.

Men and some women preferred to ride, and those in a hurry could hire post horses. These were animals kept at stations, usually in inns, and available for use by those carrying government correspondence. Private citizens could also rent them at a higher rate, exchanging them at each station for a fresh mount. Because the same horse need not be ridden all day, each one could be ridden harder, with heavy use of "Swit[che]s and spurs, swits and spurs" (*R&J* II.iv.72), and posting was therefore the fastest means of land travel (*R&J* V.i.21, 26; *R2* II.i.296). Traveling at this rate—70 to 150 miles (112.6 to 241.4 km) a day—must have been exhilarating but profoundly uncomfortable, for English saddles, as the secretary to the Duke of Württemberg noted in 1592, were "small and covered only with bare hide or leather, and therefore painful and hard to ride upon." Perhaps it was easier for the English, who (one hopes) had become used to such saddles, or perhaps the English innkeepers, who were required by special royal order to provide horses free of charge to the duke's suite, had deliberately provided their worst saddles as a means of revenge.

The roads (*2H6* II.iv.34) that all these travelers took were in generally poor repair. A 1555 act put them under the control of parish road surveyors, who could compel the local populace to work on road maintenance for a few days each year, but the system was inadequate, and there was no method of paving except for beds of cobblestones (*2H6* II.iv.8; *TNK* V.iv.58), which were horrifically bumpy for riders in any wheeled vehicle and in any case confined to the towns. Rural roads were dirt tracks, pitted with ruts, rarely identified with any signs, and often barely distinguishable from the fallows and meadows that adjoined them. In the winter, rain and snow turned them into impassable seas of mud. On these roads, carters (*Per* II.ii.50; *WT* IV.iv.326; *R3* II.i.123) or draymen (*T&C* I.ii.255–56; *R2* I.iv.32) hauling goods on packhorses or in wagons, "muleters" doing the same with teams of mules (*1H6* III.ii.68; *A&C* III.vii.35), drovers herding sheep or cattle, farmers bound for market with a cart and a string of single-file horses pulling it (the hind horse harnessed between the "fills" or cart shafts—see *T&C* III.ii.43), gentlemen and ladies bound for London or their country estates, and highwaymen willing to risk the noose for a few pounds made their slow way from point A to point B. Some roads, particularly the highways near London, were crowded with all this traffic (*2H4* II.ii.166–67; *R2* III.iii.153–56).

In most respects, this remained the state of land transportation for 200 years after Shakespeare's death. The exceptions were the condition of the roads, which were much improved during the eighteenth century, and the advent of the hackney coaches, London's horse-drawn taxis, in the 1620s. City streets, too, remained fairly constant throughout this period. They were dirty, often quite narrow, overshadowed by shop signs and the penthouses and jettied upper stories of timber-framed buildings. Garbage, human and animal waste, and rainwater swept along in gutters, or "channels" (*3H6* II.ii.141; *2H4* II.i.46; "kennel" in *2H6* IV.i.71), and more trash, ordure, and rain fell from the windows overhead and the sky. In these "foul ways" (*TS* IV.i.2), it was sometimes necessary to tiptoe (*TNK* I.ii.57–58) or to wear high-heeled overshoes to stay out of the filth. It helped somewhat to huddle near the walls, under the overhanging stories and away from the gutters, hence the granting of the place nearest the wall to a social superior (*R&J* I.i.13–14).

The one conveyance frequently mentioned by Shakespeare yet unknown in his time is the chariot. The Roman or Greek chariot was a small, two-wheeled vehicle, accommodating one or two standing passengers who held the reins of one to four horses. Given the vehicle's origins, it is not surprising to find it in plays set in the ancient world (*A&C* IV.xii.35; *Per* II.iv.7–9; *TA* I.i.249, II.ii.18, V.ii.47–55). It is, however, a bit odd to find the "car," often glossed as a chariot, in the histories set in medieval England (*1H6* I.i.21; *2H6* II.iv.13, III.i.129). Shakespeare is never fully historically accurate, so perhaps this is merely one of his many anachronisms. On the other hand, the word "car," from the Latin *carrus*, can also mean wagon, so perhaps this is the vehicle Shakespeare meant.

Water Transportation

It was usually faster to travel by water than by land. Shakespeare seldom offers any estimates of speed, though in a rare exception an embassy from Sicily to Delphi makes the round trip in an astonishingly short twenty-three days (*WT* II.iii.196–98). Likewise, he makes little mention of river travel, even the renewed freight and passenger services along the Thames, with which he must have been familiar. His one detailed description of a river boat concerns Cleopatra's barge, which cannot be presumed to resemble the ordinary Thames barges in any respect except their both having hulls, oars, and occupants (*A&C* II.ii.193–215). State barges were certainly ornate in Shakespeare's day, but perfume and purple sails were prob-

English ship, 1585. Left to right, the sails are a spritsail mounted on the bowsprit; a main foresail and top foresail on the foremast, with the "top" just visible between them; a mainsail and topsail on the mainmast, with the top visible again; and a lateen sail, mostly obscured by the large flag, hung from the mizzenmast. The raised deck near the foremast is the forecastle. Covering part of the forecastle and the forward part of the after castle are the shrouds, the ladderlike side ropes attached to each mast. Below the bottoms of the shrouds is a row of gun ports.

ably not in evidence. Another reference to a barge seems to indicate not a riverboat but an elaborate rowboat for use in a sea harbor (*Per* V.Cho.19).

Thus, most of Shakespeare's references to travel by ship (*R2* II.i.286) or boat (*1H6* IV.vi.33) are to ocean or sea voyages. He mentions several types of vessels, though by far the most common term he uses is "bark" (*CE* IV.i.86–100; *T&C* Pro.12, I.i.106–7; *Lear* IV.vi.18–20; *Temp* I.ii.144–48; *R3* III.vii.161; *TA* I.i.71–73; *S* 80). This he uses, accurately, as a general term for a small vessel, particularly a small merchant vessel. More specifically, a bark meant a three-masted ship with square-rigged (*Temp* V.i.224) sails on the front or foremast, square-rigged sails on the middle or mainmast, and fore-and-aft sails on the rear or mizzen mast. Additional sails called spritsails could be hung below a low, angled mast, called a bowsprit, at the ship's front, or bow.

Rigging, Masts, and Sails

Each of the three principal masts (*Lear* IV.vi.53–54) rose verically, or nearly vertically. At junctures, horizontal poles called yards crossed the foremast and mainmast, each about two-fifths the length of the one below it. At about the same point there was a platform supported by crosstrees and trestletrees on which sailors attending to the rigging could stand. The lowest platform was called the top (*TNK* IV.i.148), and from it rose the next section of the mast, called the topmast. A second platform was built at the top of the topmast where it joined the topgallant mast, and was called the topgallant.

Ropes called braces, at the juncture between yard and mast, controlled the yard's angle to the fore-and-aft (front to back) line of the ship. Square-rigged sails were suspended from these yards and anchored at the two lower corners to the ship or to the yard just below. A square-rigged sail could catch a good deal of wind, but it could not rotate well, and it was most useful if the wind was blowing in the exact direction that the ship needed to travel. If the ship was close-hauled, with its square-rigged sails turned nearly along the fore-and-aft line, the whole ship turned as close to the oncoming wind as possible, the sails full and the yards stable rather than shivering, it could sail no better than six points off the wind. This meant that if the wind was from the north, and the ship wanted to travel north, it would have to sail east-northeast for a while, then tack (turn— see *TNK* III.iv.10, IV.i.149) and sail west-northwest. Pointing the ship closer to the direction of the oncoming wind was called "luffing" her (*A&C* III.x.17).

Fore-and-aft sails had yards that adjoined, rather than crossed, the mast. They could be swung back and forth to make the most of the wind, even if the wind did not follow the ship's course. The addition of fore-and-aft sails made ships more maneuverable. Another version of the same concept was the lateen rig, also often used on the mizzenmast; this employed a top yard not fixed across the mast but suspended from it at an angle by a rope (*Per* IV.i.53–54; *Temp* I.i.23–24) called a halyard. Other ropes around the ship served a variety of purposes. Bowlines (*Per* III.i.43; *TNK* IV.i.146) ran from the weather (windward) side of the ship to the bow, helping to steady the sails when the ship was close-hauled (sailing as close as possible to the oncoming wind, as above). Stays stabilized the masts to the front and rear; shrouds (*H8* IV.i.71–72), from side to side. Lifts ran from points near the end of each yard to a point above the yard on the mast, supporting the yard; the portion of the yard outside the anchor points for the lifts was called the "yardarm," and it was from this part of the yard that sailors sentenced to be hanged were suspended.

If the wind called for all sails (*TN* I.v.200; *R&J* I.iv.112–13) to be set, then typically two or three sails were affixed to each of the bark's masts. The foremast and mainmast each had, from bottom to top and from largest to smallest, a course (*TNK* III.iv.10), a topsail, and, increasingly, a topgallant sail. The "maintop" of *Cymbeline* is thus the second-lowest sail on the mainmast, suspended from the maintop yard (IV.ii.319–20), and the "topgallant" of *Romeo and Juliet* is perhaps the topgallant yard, from which the uppermost sail hung, or the platform below it, or the topgallant mast itself (II.iv.194). Larger ships might have an additional mizzenmast called the bonaventure mizzen. By the early seventeenth century, still more sails were coming into use, including a square mizzen topsail and a spritsail topsail, added, as their names imply, to the upper parts of the mizzen and bowsprit. It was unusual for all these sails to be set at once; in stormy weather, the force of the wind might be too great, creating so much pressure on the sails that the masts or yards could break. Whenever a gale grew too fierce, therefore, or when a decrease in speed was desired, the order might be given to strike some or all of the sails (*3H6* III.iii.5).

This is in fact what is ordered in *The Tempest* (I.i.6–8, 34–35, 49–50). Fighting a storm, the ship's crew is first ordered to "Take in the topsail," presumably the main topsail, then to take down the topmast itself and make do with the "main course"—the mainsail (*TNK* IV.i.147). Later, when this strategy has proven insufficient to bring the ship away from shore, the boatswain orders "her two / courses"—that is, mainsail and foresail—set.

Other Parts of the Ship

Ships have literally hundreds of ropes, fasteners, openings, and other parts, each with its own particular name, but Shakespeare mentions few of them. He makes no reference, for example, to national flags, though he does interpret the flying of white flags as a peaceful overture (*Per* I.iv.71–72). One of his most common nautical terms is "helm" (*Cor* I.i.78; *A&C* II.ii.210), which he often uses to mean helmet but also uses in the sense of the wheel or tiller that controls a vessel's rudder (*A&C* III.x.2–3) and thus helps to turn it in a particular direction. Another term that he uses frequently is "anchor" (*Per* V.Cho.16; *MM* II.iv.4; *WT* I.ii.213–14; *R3* I.iv.26; *TA* IV.iv.38), a piece of equipment that, since it held a ship fast to something solid in an unpredictable and often turbulent environment, was often used in the Renaissance as a symbol of religious faith. There is a reference to the tar and pitch used to seal ropes and the ship's sides against water (*Temp* II.ii.52), and occasional mentions of specific parts of the ship, such as the bow, waist (the midsection of the ship, between the castles), poop (the highest rear deck, above and aft of the quarterdeck— see *1H4* III.iii.26–27), stern (*Per* IV.i.62), stem (the front timber, running from the keel upward—see *Per* IV.i.62), keel (*A&C* I.iv.50), and so on, the most extensive being the description of Ariel's appearance to the sailors in *The Tempest*:

> I boarded the king's ship. Now on the beak,
> Now in the waist, the deck, in every cabin,
> I flamed amazement. Sometime I'd divide
> And burn in many places; on the topmast,
> The yards, and boresprit would I flame distinctly. (I.ii.196–200)

This flaming apparition may be a creation of Shakespeare's imagination, or he may have read of or heard sailors ashore talking of St. Elmo's fire, an electrical discharge that can appear at the tops of masts and at the yardarms (but not in the cabins).

Types of Vessels

Though the bark was not the only type of ship in the Shakespearean period, most ships were rigged more or less alike, differing less in their number of sails or masts than in their size. The pinnace (*2H6* IV.i.9, 107) was smaller than a bark and usually square-rigged, relying mostly on its sails for power but also, from time to time, on oars (*Temp* II.i.123–24). It held as little as 20 tons (2,000 cubic feet, or 56 m³) and was three and a half to four times as long as it was wide, expressed in the latter example as a 4-to-1 "keel to beam" ratio. The reference to a pinnace in *2 Henry VI* is an anachronism, for the vessel was not introduced until the sixteenth century.

Another small ship was the hoy (*CE* IV.iii.39). It had a varying rig from place to place but generally had only one mast, often with a fore-and-aft sail and a square topsail. Too small, at about 60 tons (168 m³), to carry much cargo, it was chiefly used for ferrying pasengers from point to point along the coast.

Oars, manipulated by one to three banks of rowers, were the principal source of locomotion in a much larger type of vessel, the galley (*Oth* I.ii.39, iii.45, 107–200; *A&C* II.vi.80, IV.xi.3; *TS* II.i.372), which was found principally in the Mediterranean. On this type of ship, it was the one sail—usually square but sometimes lateen rigged—that was auxiliary. The galley looked markedly different from most other ships of the period, which had high sides, relatively wide beams, and high aft castles and fore-castles. It was long and narrow, with comparatively low sides and very little cargo room. The English found it an impractical vessel, for the huge numbers of rowers cost too much money to hire, and the galley was not seaworthy in rough Atlantic waters. Even in the Mediterranean, it was used more as a ship of war or as a passenger ship than as a merchantman.

Ships used for carrying goods differed somewhat from each other, though Shakespeare mentions only a few of the types. The caravel, a popular small ship in Portugal and Spain, never appears in his works. It was usually 75 to 80 feet (22.9 to 24.4 m) long, with three masts, two of which were square-rigged and one of which, the mizzen, was lateen-rigged. Neither does he include the two-masted Dutch bilander or the brigantine, a smaller version of the galley that took its name from its use by pirates, or "brigands." He does, however, make use of the hulk (*2H4* II.iv.65), a wide, large, not especially maneuverable cargo ship of about 400 tons (1,120 m³) with a rounded bow and stern; the argosy (*3H6* II.vi.35; *TS* II.i.369, 371), a large ship with medieval origins in the port of Ragusa (Dubrovnik); and the carrack, which was very similar, if not identical, to the hulk and the argosy.

The carrack (*Oth* I.ii.49–50; *TNK* III.iv.14) was a wide ship, with about a 2:1 keel-to-beam ratio and with a capacity of up to 1,500 tons (4,200 m³) according to one source, and 1,200 tons (3,360 m³) according to another. In either case, it was a massive ship, larger than a warship, and capable of hauling an enormous, and therefore immensely valuable, cargo. It was rigged much like other ships, square on the fore and main and lateen on the mizzen, and its distinguishing features were its very high forecastle and after castle.

The disadvantage of the high forecastle was that it was not streamlined enough for sailing close to the wind. A real innovation occurred in 1570, when Sir John Hawkins lowered the forecastle and created the galleon. This became the dominant ship of trade and war throughout Europe, including England, though the name "galleon" was in England chiefly associated with the Spanish examples of this design. The galleon's chief differences from the carrack, in addition to its lower forecastle, were its overall size, which was smaller than the carrack's, and its proportions, which were narrower. The galleon's keel-to-beam ratio was approximately 3:1.

An attempt was made in the late sixteenth century to capitalize on the strengths of both galleys and galleons. Galleons had far superior sailing capabilities, and galleys were more maneuverable in unfavorable winds or no wind at all. Accordingly, an intermediate type of ship, the galliass (*TS*

II.i.371), was developed. This was wider than a galley to accommodate masts and lateen sails, but it retained its rowers. It was never very successful as a warship, but it was a popular trading vessel, usually built about 25 feet (7.6 m) wide and up to 150 feet (45.7 m) long. Occasionally, it carried Chinese and Indian cargoes from Genoa or Venice to parts of northern Europe, but its lateen rig was not really suitable for Atlantic waters, and it was most often found in the Mediterranean.

The ships had decks (*Cym* I.iii.11), hatches (*Per* III.i.71–72; *Temp* V.i.98–99) or openings in the deck through which the lower levels could be reached, cabins (*Temp* I.i.14) for sleeping and dining, and cargo holds. Open vessels, with none of these amenities, were called boats. They were used for fishing or as tenders for ships. The largest, at about 50 feet (15.2 m) long, was called a longboat, and the smallest was a cock or cockboat (*Lear* IV.vi.20).

Navigation

Navigation was accomplished chiefly with charts, the astrolabe, and the compass. Charts, at this point, were still mostly drawings of shorelines, without much detail about depth, though measuring depth (*1H4* I.iii.201–2; *Lear* III.iv.37; *AYLI* IV.i.204–6) in fathoms was a practice already known and used. In very shallow water, a long rod could be used to measure depth, but in deeper water a long line, marked at intervals and tied to a lead weight, was employed. The weight was tossed ahead of the ship so that it would reach bottom just as the sailor holding the line passed over it. The astrolabe was a device that measured the height of the sun or a star and thus helped the crew, not very accurately, to determine the ship's latitude. Stars in general, and the North Star specifically (*MAAN* III.iv.56), were used by some sailors as guides, but far more useful in determining direction was the magnetic compass.

The compass was divided into thirty-two points, each representing a slightly different direction. The points from north to east, for example, ran as follows: north, north by east, north-northeast, northeast by north-northeast, northeast by east, east-northeast, east by north, and east. Shakespeare is fond of the compass, both in its literal sense as a navigational instrument and as a metaphor for a full circuit of any kind (*TNK* IV.i.141–44; *Cor* II.iii.24; *JC* V.iii.25; *Mac* I.iii.16–17).

Wind (*Cym* IV.ii.56; *H5* II.ii.12; *TNK* IV.i.146) and tide (*H5* I.ii.149) played a small role, under some circumstances, in assessing position, but they were far more important in the setting of a course. The ebb (low tide) and flood (high tide) were of particular significance in departures from port, for the best time to leave was when the flood tide was already in and any shoals were as deeply covered as possible (*2GV* II.iii.33–36; *2H4* V.ii.129–33). The most famous example of the tides as a metaphor for the human condition occurs in *Julius Caesar*:

There is a tide in the affairs of men
Which, taken at the flood, leads on to fortune;
Omitted, all the voyage of their life
Is bound in shallows and in miseries.
On such a full sea are we now afloat,
And we must take the current when it serves,
Or lose our ventures. (IV.iii.215–21)

Shakespeare occasionally refers to tides in other contexts. He makes one allusion to the midpoint between tides, when the water level remains apparently constant (*TN* I.v.158), and another to the sentence imposed on captured pirates, who were executed and then suspended in chains at the water's edge until three tides had submerged them and then receded (*Temp* I.i.57).

Personnel

The people aboard a ship included paying passengers (*CE* IV.i.86–100) and a crew whose size depended on the size and type of ship. The ship was steered by a pilot (*R&J* V.iii.117–18; *Oth* III.ii.1; *Mac* I.iii.28) and cleaned by swabbers (*TN* I.v.201; *Temp* II.ii.46). A quartermaster supervised the hold, and a purser the ship's accounts. A coxswain, the lowest-ranking officer with the right to use a whistle (*Per* III.i.8–10; *TNK* IV.i.147), was in charge of the rowers, and the boatswain (*Per* IV.i.62; *Temp* I.i.ch., II.ii.46), also endowed with a whistle, was responsible for ropes, rigging, anchors, cables, sails, flags, and the longboat or cockboat. The master (*Temp* I.i.ch., II.ii.46; *TNK* IV.i.147, 149) was the navigator aboard a man-of-war, and the captain aboard a merchantman. Seamen were divided into several classes: sailors (*2H6* IV.i.ch.; *Per* III.i.chs.), who were often older men; mariners (*Temp* V.i.98–99), the able-bodied seamen; younkers, or ordinary seamen; grommets, who were less experienced; and boys (*2H4* III.i.18–25; *TNK* IV.i.148).

Shipboard Conditions and Dangers

Life aboard ship was not much fun for any of these men. The food was terrible, consisting of beer, biscuits (*T&C* II.i.38–39), and a supplementary ration of beef or pork and peas four days a week, and fish, butter, and cheese the other three. The quantities were generous—2 pounds (.96 kg) of beef, 1 pound (.45 kg) of biscuit, and 1 gallon (3.8 l) of beer per day on meat days—but the quality was often atrocious, and the quantity could be reduced in time of need. Often the sailors were put at rations of "six upon four," that is, four rations divided among six sailors. Clothing was inadequate, seasickness was always a problem (*H5* II.Cho.37–40; *LLL* V.ii.394), and the pay was rarely high enough to satisfy the men. The 1578 English translation of a Spanish account described life aboard a galley in words that could have applied to many a ship of any nation. The water was "troubled, grosse, warm, and unsavourie"; the meat, "hard, burned, salty," and "indigestible as a stone"; the clothes, stiff from the salt water in which they were laundered and breeding "ytch and scurffe"; and the vermin, omnipresent. If a sailor would "but make a secrete inquirie," wrote the author, "in his necke and bosome, and a privie searche in his breeches, he shall find more lice then money in his pursse."

Yet these were actually the least of a sailor's troubles. There was a significant chance of drowning if the ship sank or he was swept overboard; few men at this time could swim (*Temp* I.ii.399–401). The opposite danger, dying of thirst, could happen if the ship was becalmed (*2H6* IV.ix.33) for a long period without rain. Privateers, who had a warrant from one government to interfere with the shipping of another, and pirates (*2H6* I.i.220, IV.i., IV.ix.33; *MM* I.ii.7–10, IV.iii.70–72; *A&C* I.iv.48; *Per* IV.i.chs.; *Ham* IV.vi.15–20), who stole without such a warrant, might capture the vessel, steal the cargo, and kill some of the men aboard.

The worst danger of all was shipwreck (*CE* I.i.60–94; *1H6* V.v.8; *3H6* II.ii.5; *H5* IV.i.97–98, 147–48; *Per* II.i.), which could be caused by lightning strikes, battle damage, innate defects in the ship, running aground due to navigational errors, and, most of all, storms (*Per* III.Cho.44–52; *TNK* III.iv.5–10; *TS* I.ii.200–201; *2H6* III.ii.82–113; *T&C* I.iii.34–45; *WT* III.iii.88–97). Small wonder that sailors, seeking any advantage at all over the fearsome element on which they worked, became superstitious. They had many traditions regarding omens such as the appearance of dolphins (good), the appearance of St. Elmo's fire (good), the shining of St. Elmo's fire on a particular seaman's face (bad—he would surely die within 24 hours), the presence on board of a man condemned to be executed (good, since fate had destined him for a death other than by drowning—see *2GV* I.i.149–51), and the keeping of a corpse on board overnight (bad—see *Per* III.i.47–52). Small wonder that sea travel was a perfect metaphor for the vagaries of fortune and the dangers that threatened every living soul (*2H6* V.iv.2–36). *See also* Horse; Navy; Travel.

Travel

Travel abroad was considered an indispensable part of a young man's education, if his family could afford to send him. Proteus's uncle makes the case in favor of such travel in *The Two Gentlemen of Verona* (I.iii.4–24). His voice is, however, decidedly in the minority in Shakespeare's works, just as voices in favor of travel always seemed to be in the minority among writers. People, it seemed, enjoyed travel for themselves, relishing the opportunity to observe foreign wonders and oddities (*2GV* I.i.12–13; *TN* III.iii.21–24). But they felt that foreign things ought to stay in foreign places, and resented any alien manners, clothes (*H8* I.iii.30–31), or practices that came back to England as a result of the travels of others. The resentment was probably greatest among those who had no funds to travel and felt unable to join in genteel conversation about "the Alps and Apennines, the Pyrenean and the river Po" (*John* I.i.202–3). No doubt sentiments such as those in *As You Like It* played well to London's xenophobic audiences:

> Farewell, Monsieur Traveler. Look you lisp and wear strange suits, disable all the benefits of your own country, be out of love with your nativity, and almost chide God for making you that countenance you are; or I will scarce think you have swam in a gundello [gondola]. (IV.i.31–36)

In *The Description of England*, William Harrison agreed in tone but differed in his complaints, charging that young men who went to Italy came back Catholic and waited on by overdressed, overly pretty pages. Of those who went there, he thought, "very few, without special grace, do return good men," a phenomenon he blamed on "the licentious and corrupt behavior of the people." However, for all the disapproval expressed, the only serious legal obstacles placed in the way of travel were caused by open or barely disguised hostilities with specific nations. For this reason, travel to Spain was always much rarer than travel to Italy. The government placed some restrictions on travel; every English citizen leaving the country had to have a passport (*H5* IV.iii.36–37), and there were limitations on the export of horses and currency, but these were not very intimidating hindrances to young men of good fortune. *See also* Places; Transportation.

Trees

Shakespeare's England was still substantially wooded (*2H6* IV.x.3), though far less so than it had been in the Middle Ages. The decrease in forest acreage was a cause for some concern, especially since the value of timber meant that even royal forests, preserved for deer hunting, were being gradually denuded of trees. The chief reason for this deforestation was the demand for charcoal, which was burned as fuel in several industries, including metal smelting.

Wood was also the favorite material for house construction. House frames were constructed of huge timbers, preferably of oak, which was the strongest of the available construction woods (*WT* II.iii.89–90; *Temp* V.i.45; *Cor* I.i.183); it was quartered rather than used in whole logs, to prevent splitting as it dried. It was often used unseasoned, causing it to warp in later years. Smaller pieces of oak were used as horizontal laths— thin strips to support the "daub" infilling between timbers—or vertical supports through which laths could be woven. Those who could not afford to build their houses of oak had to settle for less durable woods such as chestnut, hornbeam, elm, or poplar. Willow was typically used only for the cheapest cottages. Laths and vertical supports for laths could be made of chestnut or beech (*TNK* III.iii.41). Wattle, a lighter type of woven supprt for daub, could be made of twigs of hazel, ash, or willow. Inside the house, elm might be used for flooring, and softwoods such as pine (*2H6* II.iii.45; *WT* II.i.34; *Temp* V.i.48), imported from Scandinavia or North America, were used for various kinds of interior woodwork.

Oak, however, was still the king of the building woods and the best of all trees. It was strong while living; durable when cut; sacred to the god Jupiter (*3H6* V.ii.14); revered in ancient Rome as a symbol of heroism in battle (*Cor* I.iii.15); valued for its acorns, which fed swine (*Tim* IV.iii.420), and its bark, which was used in tanning; and preferred for the building of ships and heavy farm carts or wains. Other woods had secondary uses as well. Chestnut bark, like that of the oak, was used in tanning. Elm (*CE* II.ii.175; *2H4* II.iv.337; *MND* V.i.44–45) could be made into longbow shafts, carts, and plows. Ash, a lightweight wood, was useful for ladders, carts, plows, crossbows, battle lances, and spear poles (*Cor* IV.v.112). Hornbeam, like ash, was used for battle lances, and deal was used for the fragile type used in tournaments. Alder bark made a black dye. Hazel could be used for pitchforks; holly, for flails and ladders; thorn or hawthorn (*Lear* III.iv.45–46; *MWW* III.iii.69; *TNK* III.i.82; *MND* III.i.4), for carts, plows, and flails; crabapple, for walking staves (*H8* V.i.7); and poplar, for bowls, troughs, and dishes. Yew (*TN* II.iv.55; *R2* III.ii.117; *TA* II.iii.707) was considered the best wood for longbows and crossbows; it was a symbol of death for this reason and because its berries were poisonous. Accordingly, it was often grown in cemeteries (*R&J* V.iii.3; *2H6* III.ii.323) and associated with other symbols of darkness and evil (*Mac* IV.i.22–23). Willow or osier, which typically grew near streams and rivers (*AYLI* IV.iii.78), yielded a light, flexible wood that was unsuited for heavy construction, but rakes could be made of it, and the green branches were commonly used to beat refractory children (*MAAN* II.i.209–23). The willow was also a symbol of unrequited love (*MAAN* II.i.181–85; *TN* I.v.266; *3H6* III.iii.228).

Some trees yielded food, such as nuts or fruit (*R3* III.vii.166), and they were grown in orchards by those who could afford to spare the land. Apples, pears, plums (*2H6* II.i.95–103), walnuts, apricots (*TNK* II.i.295), and others were cultivated. Timber trees, too, required tending. When cut (*3H6* II.ii.165–68), they were "coppiced"—left to sprout again from the residual roots—and enclosed to prevent deer from grazing on the new shoots. Trees used as hedges, such as box (*TN* II.v.13), needed to have their branches split and woven or "pleached" to close gaps. Ornamental trees were bent or shaped as saplings (*Per* IV.ii.87–89). Orchard trees needed occasional pruning (*AYLI* II.iii.63–65; *TNK* III.vi.243–45) or grafting (*Cor* II.i.192–93). The tending of trees required a great deal of labor.

Trees, like so many other objects in Renaissance art, literature, and religion, often served as symbols of characteristics or ideas. This symbolism drew from classical mythology, the Bible, Druidic or magical beliefs, and physical characteristics of the species. A cedar was not, therefore, merely a kind of tree but also a symbol for something taller or loftier than its neighbors (*H8* V.v.53–54; *TNK* II.v.4–6; *RL* 664–65; *TA* IV.iii.46). The aspen was trembly (*2H4* II.iv.110), and thus cowardly. The cypress was an emblem of death (*TN* II.iv.52). Bay had classical associations from the laurel garlands awarded to Olympic victors and other honorees (*H8* IV.ii.92 s.d.; *R2* II.iv.8; *3H6* IV.vi.34); Andrea Alciato, author of *Emblemata*, said that a sprig of laurel placed under the pillow would bring true dreams. Palm (*H8* IV.ii.82 s.d.; *Tim* V.i.11), elder (*Cym* IV.ii.59–60; *LLL* V.ii.604; *TA* II.iii.272, 277), and olive (*2H4* IV.iv.87; *TN* I.v.208–9; *Tim* V.iv.82) had biblical connections: the palm was linked to Palm Sunday and thereby to Christ's entry into Jerusalem, and also to Psalm 92; the elder was supposedly the type of tree from which Judas Iscariot hanged himself; and the olive, like the dove, was associated with the reprieve from the great flood and was thus a symbol of peace (*3H6* IV.vi.34) and hope.

Long-standing folk beliefs about trees were also widespread. Cutting a tree could be frightening if, as many did, one believed in fairies or tree spirits. Some trees were believed to take revenge on their destroyers or to die out of mourning for their felled neighbors, and the superstitious steered clear of coppices at night. Hawthorn, elder, ash, willow, elm, and oak were all held to have such properties; hawthorn and elder were particularly associated with the fairies, and elder was believed by some to be the tree form of a witch, bleeding if cut. Hazel was associated with fertility and apple with divination. *See also* Architecture; Fairy; Food; Plants.

Triumph

The triumph (*A&C* V.i.66) was an ancient Roman celebration voted occasionally by the Senate to honor a victorious general. The general in question was crowned with laurel and given the chance to distribute spoils and rewards to his troops; then he climbed into a tower-shaped chariot with his children, the older boys, if any, being permitted to ride on the chariot's horses. A slave also rode in the chariot, holding a jeweled golden crown above the general's head but also reminding him from time to time that he was a mere mortal, not a god. The great attraction for the Roman people, the one so feared by Cleopatra and her court, was the exhibition at the head of the procession of the symbolic spoils of war, including strange beasts, effigies representing the geographical features of the conquered lands, heaps of treasure and armor, and high-born prisoners. At the end of the procession, the general arrived at the Forum, disposed of his prisoners by sending them to jail or to the executioner, and performed religious rites.

Unicorn

The unicorn, a mythical beast (*Temp* III.iii.21–22) described as early as 400 BCE, was supposed to have a deer's legs, a lion's tail, a horse's head and body, and one horn in the middle of its forehead. Pliny gave it an even more bizarre assortment of parts: a horse's body, a deer's head, an elephant's feet, a boar's tail, and a black horn two cubits long. Some legends held that the horn could be moved and wielded like a sword; others, that the horn could protect the animal from great falls if the horn touched the ground first. The unicorn was wild, but could be rendered mild by the presence of a pure young woman, hence its use as a symbol of chastity (*RL* 956). In the absence of virgins, however, it could be defeated by inducing it to charge until it ran its own horn into a tree (*JC* II.i.204; *Tim* IV.iii.335–37). In *The Historie of Foure-Footed Beasles*, the naturalist Edward Topsell gives a vivid though entirely fictional account of such a "capture":

> He [the unicorn] is an enemy to the Lyons, wherefore as soone as even a Lyon seeth a Unicorne, he runneth to a tree for succor, that so when the Unicorne maketh force at him, hee may not onely avoid his horne, but also destroy him; for the Unicorne in the swiftnesse of his course runneth against the tree wherein his sharpe horne sticketh fast, then when the Lyon seeth the Unicorne fastned by the horne without all danger, he fauleth upon him and killeth him.

The twelfth-century mystic Hildegard of Bingen identified the unicorn with Christ. She ascribed various magical properties, including proof against poison, to it and especially to its horn. She agreed with the notion that it was fascinated by virgins, who for her represented the Virgin Mary, but she felt that it was a class-conscious animal which would not be fascinated by low-born women, no matter how pure. Marco Polo actually saw a unicorn, but in his case it was a rhinoceros, and he found it to be nothing at all like the legends had promised. Nevertheless, belief in

A unicorn, from Konrad Gesner's *Icones Animalium Quadrupedam*. Reproduced from the Collections of the Library of Congress.

unicorns was widespread, and Elizabeth I had an object reputed to be a unicorn's horn, displayed for visitors, at Windsor Castle.

Wax

Beeswax was certainly used for candles (*2H6* II.iv.17 s.d.; *MWW* IV.iv.49–51); however, it was not only used in candle-making. It was soft and malleable, especially when warm (*V&A* 565–66; *R&J* III.iii.126–27; *MND* I.i.49–51), and so could be used to fix things in place (*JC* I.iii.45–46) or to make molds (*Tim* V.iii.5–6). Melted, it was dripped onto the loose edge of a folded letter to make a seal, then usually stamped with the impression of the sender's signet ring before it cooled completely (*2H6* IV.ii.81–83).

The wax was harvested from beehives, usually about 32 to 40 quarts (30.3 to 37.8 l) in volume, made of rye straw and brambles or wicker and clay. The bees were kept by farmers in a warm, dry spot and shielded as much as possible from the mice and moths that might damage the hives. After four or five years, when the hive had been fully inhabited and filled with honey and wax, the bees were moved to another hive and the old one emptied and burned. The melted wax was collected and sold. *See also* Bees.

Weapons

Shakespeare's characters tend to be heavily armed. In many cases, this seems natural; they are soldiers, kings, brigands, pirates, rebellious nobles, duelists, and jealous lovers. Yet even the women, merchants, and servants frequently turn up with weapons in their hands. Practically the only characters not equipped with bow or steel are the supernatural creatures. Puck, Ariel, and their like are apparently too powerful to require mortal armament.

The average person today, asked to think of a weapon used in Shakespeare's time, will probably think first of the sword, and perhaps second of the dagger or the bow. These weapons were certainly of great importance. However, there were plenty of other weapons in use in the Renaissance for personal defense, hunting, and warfare.

Short-Handled Weapons

There were several kinds of hand-to-hand weapons. The ax (*2H6* II.iv.49; *TNK* IV.ii.115; *R2* I.ii.21; *TA* III.i.168), for example, was more than a butcher's (*2H6* III.ii.189), woodman's, or executioner's (*MV* IV.i.125) tool. From the twelfth to the fourteenth centuries, it was a common weapon for both the cavalry and the infantry. Both versions bore a wide cutting blade with a sharp beak at the back; the chief difference between them was the length of the handle, which was approximately 5 to 6 feet (1.52 to 1.83 m) for the infantry version (*LLL* V.ii.573) and 2 feet to 2 feet 8 inches (.61 to .81 m) for the cavalry.

Sixteenth-century maces and fifteenth-century battle axes. Relative sizes not to scale.

The mace (*CE* IV.iii.28; *JC* IV.iii.265), on the other hand, was strictly a cavalry weapon. A medium-sized staff topped by a spiked or flanged metal weight, it was developed during the Middle Ages and increased in popularity during the Renaissance as a means of smashing enemy plate mail. It was used both in tournaments and in combat, and its knightly associations caused it to be adopted by civilian authorities as a symbol of rank.

Those of humbler status had to settle for the poor man's mace, known by many names—club (*1H6* I.iii.84; *LLL* I.ii.172; *TA* II.i.37), cudgel (*H8* V.iv.18; *MWW* II.ii.273–75; *MAAN* V.iv.113; *H5* V.i.52, 67, 68); bat (*Cor* I.i.56), billet (*MM* IV.iii.55), or truncheon (*2H4* II.iv.144; *H8* V.iv.51). A readily accessible piece of stout wood, the cudgel could be used to intimidate or incapacitate rioters or unruly tavern patrons. The common whip could also be pressed into service, though it was generally reserved for punishing wrongdoers (*2H6* II.i.136).

The Lance

The lance (*Cor* I.ix.40 s.d.; *1H6* III.ii.50; *2H4* IV.i.51; *MAAN* III.i.64; *Lear* IV.vi.166; *LLL* V.ii.642; *R3* V.iii.144; *TS* V.ii.175; *John* V.ii.157), like the mace, was a knight's weapon. It was used in the field in mass cavalry charges, with knights from opposing sides attempting to kill or unhorse each other before proceeding to combat with mace or sword. Essentially a glorified spear, the lance was a 12- to 14-foot (3.66 to 4.27 m) pointed staff of ash or hornbeam, flaring near the butt end to form a guard for the hand. Like a knight's surcoat, helm, shield, and caparison, it provided a means of ornament and identification, and was thus painted in bright colors. A pennon, or flag, was often attached.

A knight on the march typically carried his lance over his shoulder, horizontally, or across his saddle, perpendicular to the path. The pennon was furled around the staff. When the enemy, or a noble observer, was in sight, the lance was held vertically, with the butt end resting on the thigh or stirrup, and the pennon flying free. During a charge, it was held horizontally, the butt resting or "couched" against the right armpit, cradled by a special metal brace (the roundel or lance rest) incorporated into the armor. Right arm pulled up in a tight angle, legs almost straight in the stirrups, the knight galloped his horse toward the enemy. There is a reference to this posture in *Romeo and Juliet*; when Paris has made up his mind to have Juliet, he is said to have "set up his rest," with the sexual implications of a lance in readiness (IV.v.6).

The coordination of several difficult tasks in the cavalry charge—holding a heavy lance, aiming the lance accurately, standing in stirrups while armored, and controlling a powerful horse—made practice essential. To this end, and for the pure love of display and glory, knights engaged in the mounted joust (*R2* I.i.200, I.iii.74, 101, 103) at tournaments. The joust was very much like the cavalry charge; however, the lances in the joust were blunt-tipped and made of hollowed deal so as to shatter on impact (*T&C* I.iii.282–83).

For numerous reasons, including its knightly associations, the skill required to master its use, and, no doubt, its phallic shape, the lance was a quintessentially manly object. Shakespeare contrasts it with the traditionally feminine tool, the distaff, in *Cymbeline* (V.iii.33–34).

Pole Arms

Unlike the sword, mace, and lance, staff weapons or pole arms were usually wielded only by the infantry. (The lance was, of course, simply a glorified spear with a hand guard, but just try telling this to a knight for whom it was one of the chief symbols of his exalted rank. An attempt in the Middle Ages to develop an infantry lance failed in the long term.) Staff weapons, usually consisting of a pole with some sort of metal blade or point at one end, attached by sockets, rivets, or nails, were often derived from the farm tools brought to war by mustered medieval peasants—scythes, pruners, pitchforks, and so on.

The simplest staff weapon was the staff itself with no blade at all. It was a traveler's weapon, serving double duty as a walking stick (*2GV* II.iii.19,

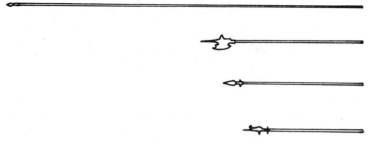

Approximate relative sizes of (bottom to top) the bill, parade spear, halberd, and pike. The spear is 7 feet long; the pike, 18 feet. Actual lengths of weapons varied somewhat, depending on the century and the country of origin.

II.v.24, 27–28) and a means of defense; in Shakespeare's day, it was not associated with serious warfare but with sport (*2H6* II.iii.58 s.d.), old men, hermits (*2H4* V.i.66), and petty thieves who struck from behind (the "long-staff sixpenny strikers" of *1H4* II.i.76). Crabapple wood appears to have been a common choice of material (*H8* V.iv.7). The staff also seems to have been perceived as a northern or a provincial weapon, judging from Costard's boast that "I will not fight with a pole, like a northern/man. I'll slash; I'll do it by the sword" (*LLL* V.ii.692–93). In some cases, like a mace or a scepter, it served as a "badge of office" (*2H6* I.i.25, II.iii.23).

One of the oldest of all weapons, the spear, either thrown as a javelin (*TNK* II.i.105–6) or held and thrust, was a principal piece of equipment in ancient Greece (*2H6* V.i.100; the "beam" of *T&C* V.v.9; the "charging staff" of *TNK* IV.ii.140). In Roman times, it was called a pilium and usually thrown; it was designed to be damaged on impact so that the enemy could not hurl it back at the Roman thrower. The spear's chief uses by Shakespeare's time were hunting (*AYLI* I.iii.117; *R3* III.ii.72) and ceremonial display. Sometimes it was a simple leaf-shaped point attached to a pole; sometimes it bore stops, called lugs, where the point joined the staff to prevent deep penetration. Ash wood is mentioned as a material for the pole (*Cor* IV.v.112).

Instead of the spear, which tended to be a little taller than the soldier wielding it, Renaissance armies used the pike (*Cor* V.vi.149; *2H4* II.iv.50–51; *1H6* I.i.116; *3H6* I.i.244; *H5* IV.i.40; *Cym* IV.ii.399), a small-tipped spear that grew over the centuries from 12 to 22 feet in length. The morris pike (*CE* IV.iii.28), a shorter version of the pike, was so named because it was believed to be Moorish in design.

A body of pikemen, massed in a square, their weapons towering above their heads like a weird, leafless forest, could be a fearsome sight. As soon as the enemy's cavalry charge began, each pikeman planted his weapon, bracing the butt end against the ground or his foot. Holding the pike with his left hand, he held his right on his sword hilt, ready to switch weapons as soon as the wall of sharp points had done its work against the oncoming riders and horses. After the development of firearms, pikemen were enlisted to defend the ranks of the musketeers. The English infantry of the first half of the seventeenth century was composed of approximately two-thirds musketeers and one-third pikemen.

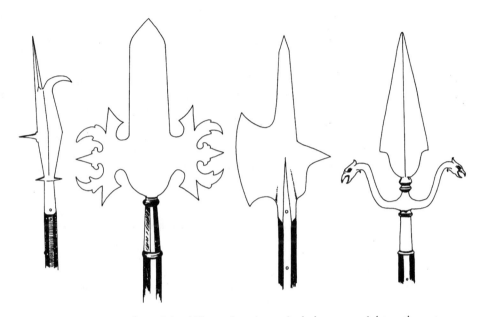

Pole arm blades. Left to right: bill, partisan (a particularly ornate eighteenth-century German example), halberd, linstock. Actual blade lengths, left to right: 13.8 inches (35 cm), 19.2 inches (48.7 cm), 15.5 inches (39.3 cm), 14.8 inches (37.7 cm).

There were several weapons with larger blades. The bill (*R&J* I.i.75) or gisarme, for example, had a large hooked blade, about 20 inches long in the fifteenth century, with two hooked lugs and a spike on the back. Its various surfaces made it a versatile weapon, capable of cracking plate mail, hooking and unhorsing a rider, or hamstringing a horse. Derived from a pruning tool in the thirteenth century, the bill was often replaced in the second half of the sixteenth century by the halberd or partisan, but it remained the weapon most closely associated with constables (*2H6* IV.x.13, II.iv.16 s.d.; *MAAN* III.iii.41; *Tim* III.iv.90), especially when varnished brown to inhibit rust (*Lear* IV.vi.91).

The partisan (*R&J* I.i.75, 97; *A&C* II.vii.14; *Cym* IV.ii.399) had a long, double-edged blade with a central ridge. It looked very much like an overgrown spear point with two large lugs curving from the base toward the point. From the mid-sixteenth century on, it was much used by infantry officers and by household guards of the royalty and nobility. In the seventeenth century it developed an octagonal shaft; making the staff of a weapon polygonal rather than round was a common improvement, for it made the weapon easier to grip.

Like the partisan, the fauchard was often used by bodyguards and palace guards. It was shaped like its ancestor the scythe, but had a sturdier blade and shaft, and the sharp edge was on the outside rather than the inside of the curved blade. The linstock (*1H6* I.iv.56 s.d.) looked very much like a spear, except that each of its lugs had a small opening to hold the match for lighting cannons. It thus served as a short-range weapon as well as a means of putting a safe distance between the artilleryman and the cannon.

Widely used in combat instead of or in addition to the pike, the halberd (*CE* V.i.185, *2H6* II.iv.16 s.d.; *3H6* IV.iii.20; *H8* II.i.53 s.d.; *R3* I.ii.1 s.d., III.iii.1 s.d., V.i.1 s.d.) originated in Sicily and Germany in the Middle Ages. Its shaft was about 6 feet long and its blade usually about 12 to 16 inches long, though some sixteenth-century examples had blades of up to 3 feet in length. Its blade had three principal features: an axlike blade for hacking at armor and lances, a beak or bill for unhorsing riders or parrying sword blows, and a spike for thrusting. It was long used by noncommissioned infantry officers. *See also* Army; Artillery; Bow; Firearms; Hunting; Jousting; Sword.

Wedding

Though Shakespeare usually greatly compresses the timetable, a Renaissance wedding actually began days or even years before the ceremony in a church. Thanks to a confusion of canon and civil law, dowry negotiations, traditional customs, and vague promises made between men and women, the exact moment at which a wedding began was often hard to pinpoint. It began at some point during courtship, when a man and woman exchanged certain types of promises, combined perhaps with a handclasp, a kiss, and a ring. How public this ceremony was, and what words were exchanged, determined whether or not the process of marriage had begun.

Betrothal

The ceremony of betrothal, or "handfasting," could take two forms. In both, the couple's hands were joined (*H5* V.ii.132; *MM* V.i.209–10), and they exchanged a kiss (*R2* V.i.71–75) and a ring, which was placed on the woman's right hand. Under ideal circumstances, the betrothal was performed in public, with the prior consent of the parents or guardian (*MAAN* V.iv.27–31), and in front of witnesses (*WT* IV.iv.393). The parties formed a contract *de futuro* or *de praesenti*, that is, in the future or in the present tense. A betrothal *de futuro* was expressed as "I will marry you" at some time to come, and might be conditional upon some other event, such as the death of an existing spouse (*AW* IV.ii.70–72). Angelo, in *Measure for Measure*, exploits the vagueness of the *de futuro* contract as a means of extracting himself from his promises to Mariana (III.i.213–17); though there were several ways of being released from such a commitment, his excuse, that she has lost her dowry, was not among them. Valid reasons for terminating the contract were mutual consent, physical disfigurement, proof of a prior contract *de praesenti* (*R3* III.vii.5–6, 176–90), long separation, grossly improper behavior by one of the parties, or a crime such as heresy or apostasy. Angelo, knowing these rules as well as anyone, attempts to shift his reason from the loss of her dowry to her fictitious misbehavior (*MM* V.i.217–222). However, a *de futuro* contract could not be canceled if the parties willingly cohabited with one another, as Mariana manages to arrange by deceiving Angelo (*MM* IV.i.72–75). Mariana's willingness to forgive Angelo's betrayal, and even to plead for his life, was not out of character for the times. Any marriage was sometimes better than no marriage at all, particularly if some sort of scandal had attended the repudiation. Rose Arnoldin, an Englishwoman, insisted in 1608 on the validity of her marriage contract with Francis Lane, even though he had seduced her with false promises, impregnated her, and pushed her into a well with intent of either abortion or murder. Angelo seems merely peevish by comparison.

Between "the contract of [a] . . . marriage and the day it / is solemnized" (*AYLI* III.ii.316–317), the arrangement was a marriage and yet not a marriage. Thus Paris greets Juliet as his wife and lays a legal claim to her (*R&J* IV.i.18–19, 35), and Kate is called Petruchio's wife once he has publicly claimed her but before the ceremony (*TS* III.ii.19–20), but Florizel, who has contracted a marriage with Perdita, confesses that they are not married, "nor are like to be" (*WT* V.i.205). In a way, the betrothal was the first step of the marriage ceremony, which would be repeated during the church service in the words, "I will" (the *de futuro* betrothal) and "I take thee" (the *de praesenti* betrothal), but it contained neither the solemnization by the priest nor the formal consummation. Canon and civil law differed on the status of the couple at this point and whether they could dispose of property independently or legitimately engage in sexual intercourse. It was a state of affairs that created many complications and would seem to have been an inconvenient way of making a match. Yet it served the purpose of creating a delay, during which the banns (*1H4* IV.ii.16–17), an announcement of the forthcoming marriage, could be read in the parish church of each party. The banns had to be read on three successive Sundays or holidays and might be anywhere from a day to a week apart. The delay and the public announcement allowed anyone who knew of an impediment to the marriage to make it known. There were at least thirty types of possible impediments to marriage, including the accidental castration of the groom or one party having served as godparent to the other or to the other's child. Cousins could marry, but aunts and uncles, nephews and nieces, the spouses of these relatives, and the spouses of one's previous wife or husband were all forbidden as marriage partners. If discovered after the marriage, impediments might be grounds for annulment (*1H6* V.iii.81–86; *AYLI* III.iii.88–92) and severe embarrassment, so they were best discovered beforehand.

Shakespeare includes several variations on the process of betrothal in his plays. Olivia's courtship of Sebastian proceeds with urgent haste from gift-giving to *de futuro* betrothal to *de praesenti* betrothal under a chaplain's supervision to public revelation of the clandestine arrangement (*TN* IV.iii, V.i.149–62). The betrothal of Julia and Proteus in *The Two Gentlemen of Verona*, however, takes place in private (II.ii), leaving Julia vulnerable to repudiation. Kate and Petruchio's betrothal takes place in such a flurry of nonsense from Petruchio that no one notices that Kate has not given her consent (II.i); nevertheless, she must have given consent in her heart, for even before the wedding ceremony she refers to herself as his wife. The betrothal in *The Winter's Tale* takes place according to the established form, though its unhappy conclusion arises from Florizel's refusal to obtain his father's consent to his choice (IV.iv); that in *The Tempest* has a similar fault, but this time it is quickly resolved because Ferdinand has failed to secure consent only because he believes his father to be dead (V.i).

Royal marriages (*John* II.i.423–539) often required an adaptation of the betrothal ceremony. Because the parties were often in two different countries, and because political necessity could mandate a change of mind on one side or the other if there was a delay (*1H6* V.v.25–35; *3H6* II.vi.88–97, III.i.29–31, III.iii.49–64), a betrothal by proxy was arranged (*1H6* V.iii.160–64; *2H6* I.i.1–13). One of the parties contracted the marriage with a deputy, often an ambassador, standing in for the other. On occasion, the ceremony was performed between two proxies, with neither the prospective bride nor groom actually present.

Weddings

Much preparation needed to take place before the actual wedding. Some of these preparations had been going on since the bride's infancy, when her mother began slowly amassing linens for the trousseau. In any family that could afford it, there were purchases of new clothes and household goods; the bride might have a new dress for the day, though she was more likely to select one that she already owned. A wedding day also needed to be set. Catholic prohibitions against marrying at certain times of year had been preserved, so that weddings were typically not scheduled near or during Lent, in the late spring before Ascension Day, and in the weeks of Advent prior to Christmas. In all, 144 days each year were off limits for weddings, though a license could be purchased to gain an exemption from the rules. If the bridal couple or their families were literate, invitations were written and sent to the guests; if the parties involved could not write, then notice of the event spread by word of mouth. The day of the week does not seem to have been particularly important; Shakespeare gives examples of weddings on Thursday (*R&J* III.iv., III.v.113–16), Sunday (*TS* II.i.386, 388), and Monday (*MAAN* II.i.346). Likewise, any time of day was acceptable, though the preference was for between eight A.M. and noon; in some cases the wedding was held at night or even at dawn. In *Much Ado About Nothing*, Hero is awake at five A.M. on what she supposes to be her wedding day, and the implication is that the time of the ceremony is not far off (III.iv.1, 50–51).

On the morning of the wedding, the bride (*R&J* III.v.116, 118) was awakened by music. With the help of her friends, she dressed (*Per* I.i.7; *TNK* V.i.136 s.d., 150) and trimmed her costume with ribbons and love knots. She tied her hose with blue, white, or red garters, combed her hair so that it fell loosely about her shoulders (*TNK* I.i.1 s.d.), and put on some sort of headdress or biliment—but not the frothy white veil of later centuries. Alternatively, she might carry a crown of flowers to be placed on her head after the ceremony. Flowers, worn as nosegays or elsewhere on the costume, were an integral part of the bride's attire. At this time, she might give presents, such as gloves, to her friends and guests; these gifts were usually paid for by the bridegroom (*R&J* IV.i.107) but sometimes the cost was split along gender lines, with the groom providing the men's gifts and the bride the women's. Refreshment of some kind might be served, with the whole wedding party getting a little tipsy before proceeding to church. Certainly by the time they reached the church doors, walking in procession accompanied by musicians and morris dancers, they were all feeling festive and even rowdy.

At the doors of the church (*MAAN* II.i.342–43; *MWW* IV.vi.31–32; *TS* IV.iv.88–89, V.i.5, 41), the groom might be presented with the dowry or a token of it, though sometimes this ceremony was saved until the feast later in the day. In Catholic times, the wedding was held here, just outside the church, but since the Reformation it had been performed inside. Often the bridesmaids proceeded to the altar first, followed by the bride, who was led by pages. The bride's father announced, when questioned by the parson, that it was he who gave his daughter to be married (*MAAN* IV.i.22–31; *AYLI* III.iii.64–71), in a gesture that signified both his consent to the marriage and the transfer of authority over the woman from father to husband. Richard Hooker defended this as an excellent custom that "putteth women in mind of a duty whereunto the very imbecility of their nature and sex doth bind them, namely, to be always directed, guided and ordered by others."

The bride stood on the groom's left, and the parson asked whether there were any objections or impediments (*MAAN* IV.i.11–17); if there were none, the ceremony proceeded with the exchange of vows (*AYLI* IV.i.120–35), the holding of hands, and the passing of a ring to the minister (along with the payment for his and his clerk's services, a fee that varied according to the means of the bridal couple but was usually between several pence and several shillings—see *1H6* V.iv.23–24). The minister passed the ring back to the groom, who placed it on the fourth finger of his wife's left hand. Often this was her betrothal ring, which was now moved from one hand to the other as a symbol of the completion of the ritual that had begun with her initial consent to the betrothal. (In the Catholic service, the priest anointed the ring with holy water before returning it—see *TA* I.i.324–26.) The minister, after some prayers and perhaps a sermon, announced that they were formally united in the eyes of God. The wedding party and guests partook of wine with floating bits of bread or cake called "sops" (*TS* III.ii.172), and then the couple emerged from the church as husband and wife. Grains of wheat were thrown at them, alms were distributed to the poor, and music and dancing followed them home.

A raucous feast followed, with much drinking, eating, singing, and bawdy joking about the wedding night to come (*Oth* II.ii.3–6; *MND* V.i; *R&J* IV.iv; *TS* III.ii.183–224; *John* III.i.228). A pile of cakes was stacked in front of the couple, and one might be broken over the bride's head. Its pieces were used to tell her fortune, its grain content being a symbol of fertility, and its breaking being a symbol of her soon-to-be broken maidenhead. Games, such as running at the quintain, might be organized by the groomsmen. The bride danced with all comers and gifts were presented. The wedding feasts of working-class couples might be held in taverns or alehouses, while those of the rich could involve elaborate masques, jousts, and hundreds of gallons of wine. At many wedding feasts, there was a potluck arrangement, with each guest, according to William Harrison (in *The Description of England*), "bringing such a dish or so many with him as his wife and he do consult upon."

At night, the bridal couple was followed, or even chased, to their bedchamber (*TS* III.i.82–83). There their friends undressed them (*Oth* II.iii.178–79), confiscating their ribbons, laces, and points and adorning themselves with the trophies. The greatest prizes of all were the bride's garters. Then the couple's stockings were removed, and the groomsmen threw the stockings—according to one account, backward over their shoulders without looking—at the bride. Whoever hit her head or nose would soon be married, according to superstition. Some accounts have the bridesmaids doing likewise with the groom's stockings. Any pins worn by the bride were thrown away, for keeping them was said to be bad luck. Ribaldry continued until the friends were scolded or chased from the chamber. Sometimes, before they left, they sewed the bride and groom together into the sheets. On rare occasions, such as the marriage of two noble heirs, a witness might stay in the room to ensure that consummation occurred. Otherwise, the bride and groom were left alone to consummate the marriage (*R&J* II.vi.36–37, III.v.202; *Per* II.v.90–91, III.Cho.9–11; *TNK* IV.i.109–13). In the morning they were awakened by music at their window, and the revelry continued, lasting sometimes for several days. *See also* Courtship; Marriage.

Weights and Measures

Units of measurement were poorly standardized. Within Europe, they differed widely. England, for example, used a system of inches and feet to measure short lengths. Much of the rest of Europe used the foot but not the inch, making up its foot with sixteen fingerbreadths or four handbreadths, and the length of this foot varied with place and time. Even within England, measures often differed from place to place, and they were arrived at haphazardly. The acre began as the amount of ground that oxen could plow in a day; the inch was the width of a man's thumb; the fathom was the distance between his middle fingertips when his arms were outstretched. There was plenty of room for error, despite government attempts at uniformity. Then there were separate types of measurements for different types of substances. Just as today, in the English system of measurement (which is retained only in the United States), an ounce of volume and an ounce of weight are not always the same, so in the Renaissance a hundred was fivescore—that is, 100—when counting people or most objects, but 112 when it applied to the number of pounds of something, and 120 when counting certain specific items like cattle or herrings. This could cause some confusion when measuring items like herrings, which were packed five hundreds to the cade (*2H6* IV.ii.35); a cade might contain five fivescore (500) or five great hundreds (600).

Units of weight were complex and confusing, for there were both troy and avoirdupois (*2H4* II.iv.260) pounds, the former equal to 12 ounces and the latter to 16 ounces.

Units of Weight

Unit	Equal To	Notes
Ounce	640 grains 31.1 g 28.35 g	*Lear* IV.vi.130. This weight is according to William Harrison, who defines 32 grains as 1/20th of an ounce, though the *Oxford English Dictionary* defines a grain as 1/5360 of a troy pound and 1/7000 of an avoirdupois pound. Harrison's arithmetic would yield 7,680 grains to the troy pound and 10,240 to the avoirdupois pound.

Unit	Equal To	Notes
Pound	12 ounces (troy) 16 ounces (avoirdupois) .373 kg .453 kg	*Cor* III.i.313; *WT* IV.iii.46–50. Troy weight was used for measuring precious metals and for calculating the supposed weight of units of volume. Avoirdupois was used for everything else. Thread, among other commodities, was bought in pounds or quarter-pounds.
Clove	7 pounds 3.17 kg	
Stone	14 pounds 6.34 kg	This weight was also called a half-quartern; it was a stone when wool was being weighed. A stone for beef was 8 lbs.
Quartern	28 pounds 12.68 kg	The same weight of wool was called a tod (*WT* IV.iii.32–33).
Half-hundred	56 pounds 25.36 kg	
Hundred	112 pounds 50.72 kg	Hundredweight was abbreviated as cwt. and was considered a "hundred" only for weighing, not for counting.
Weigh	224 pounds 101.44 kg	A measurement used in the weighing and sale of cheese, it was also sometimes defined as 256 lbs. (115.97 kg).
Sack	364 pounds 164.89 kg	The sack was a weight of wool equal to 26 stone.

Note: When two metric equivalents are given, the first is for troy-weight equivalent and the second for avoirdupois weight. When only one metric equivalent is given, it is for avoirdupois. Since Renaissance units differed from their modern counterparts (and even from each other), metric equivalents are merely approximations.

Jewels were weighed in carats (*2H4* IV.v.161; *CE* IV.i.28), each of which equaled 4 carat grains.

Units of length and area were numerous, more irregular than the English system today, and much more irregular than the metric system.

Units of Length

Unit	Equal To	Notes
Inch	3 barleycorns 2.54 cm	*1H4* II.iii.113; *Lear* III.iv.56; *A&C* I.iii.40; *Cym* V.v.52; *WT* I.ii.186; *LLL* V.ii.189
Foot	12 inches 30.48 cm	*LLL* V.ii.666; *Lear* IV.vi.25; *H8* V.iv.18; *John* I.i.183. Glass, timber, construction lengths and heights, and the depth and width of ditches were measured in feet.

Unit	Equal To	Notes
Yard	3 feet .91 m	*1H4* II.ii.24–25; *LLL* V.ii.667; *Ham* III.iv.209. The yard was used to measure cloth, laces, tapestries, silk, and similar materials, but not linen.
Ell	1 yard, 9 inches 1.14 m	*CE* III.ii.110; *1H4* III.iii.77. Linen was measured by the ell. Tapestries also were sometimes measured and sold by the ell.
Pace	5 feet 1.52 m	*H5* III.vii.128–30. This quotation illustrates one of the difficulties of measurements based on the dimensions of the human body.
Fathom	6 feet 1.83 m	*R&J* I.iv.85; *AYLI* IV.i.204–6; *Lear* III.iv.37, IV.vi.50; *WT* IV.iv.277. William Harrison defines it as 7 feet. It was used for measuring the depth of pits, wells, mines, and seafloor or shoals, and for measuring lengths of rope.
Pole	5½ yards 16½ feet 5 m	An acre (*Lear* IV.iv.7; *WT* I.ii.96; *Temp* I.i.64–65) was 40 poles in length and 4 poles in breadth, or an equivalent area of land. A perch of land (*Per* III.Cho.15) was one pole long, or square, measuring one pole on each side. The perch was used for measuring land, pales, and walls.
Rod	4 poles 22 yards 66 feet 20.1 m	The rod was also called a rodde, rood, farthingdeal (which meant a quarter of something), or yardland.
Furlong	variable	*WT* I.ii.95; *Temp* I.i.63–64. Literally, the unit meant a furrow long, which was as far as the plow went in one row, and could therefore be short or long, depending on the shape of the field. William Harrison defines it as 125 paces (208⅓ yards, 625 feet); another common measurement was 40 poles long, the typical longer measure of an acre-sized field (220 yards, 660 feet).

Unit	Equal To	Notes
Mile	8 furlongs	*1H4* II.ii.25–26; *2H4* V.v.65; *MM* III.ii.38; *Cym* IV.ii.293; *WT* IV.iii.99; *LLL* V.ii.185–98; *Cor* I.vi.16–17; *S* 44. William Harrison gives an alternate measurement: 278 turns of a cart wheel, which was usually 18 feet in circumference.
League	3 miles	*Temp* I.ii.145, II.i.251, III.ii.14–15; *MAAN* I.i.4; *MND* II.i.174; *H5* III.ii.43; *JC* III.i.286; *2GV* V.i.11. This was not a standard English measurement and was used chiefly as a poetic expression for any long distance. Shakespeare uses it for both land and nautical distances.

Note: Metric equivalents are given for the reader's convenience, but they correspond to modern, standard measurements for inches and feet. Renaissance measurements, as stated above, varied considerably from modern ones and from each other, so a Renaissance English inch should not be taken to be precisely equal to 2.54 centimeters.

Liquid measures were still more confusing, for the size of a pint, quart, or gallon varied over time and from place to place. William Harrison, in his *Description of England* (1587), defines units of volume in terms of troy ounces, dividing a pint into 12 ounces, not the 16 ounces of today. He lists the units of liquid measure as, in increasing size, spoonful or dram (*MV* IV.i.5; *AW* II.iii.223; *Oth* I.iii.105; today a dram is ⅛ oz.); assay, taste, or sippet, equal to 4 drams; farthingdeal, equal to ¼ pint; muytch, equal to 6 oz. or half a pint (*Cor* V.ii.56); pint (*2H6* II.iii.70) of 12 oz. or one troy pound; quart (*2H4* V.iii.64; *2H6* II.iii.72, IV.x.15; *MWW* III.v.3; *WT* IV.iii.8), equal to 2 pints; pottle, equal to 4 pints; and gallon, equal to 8 pints. Dry measures were the same up to this point and also included the apothecary's dram (*TN* III.iv.82–83; *Cym* III.iv.189), equal to 60 grains (*H5* II.iv.137–38), and the scruple (*TN* II.v.2, III.iv.82–83; *MAAN* V.i.92–93; *T&C* IV.i.70–71), which was one-third of a dram. Larger liquid and dry measures are given below.

Units of Liquid Measure

Unit	Equal To	Notes
Firkin	8 gallons 30.28 1	The firkin was 8 gallons for commodities that included ale, soap, and herrings, though herrings were also sold by the great hundred (120) or last (10,000). The firkin was 9 gallons for beer and 10.5 gallons for eels and salmon.

Unit	Equal To	Notes
Kilderkin	16 gallons	The kilderkin for beer was 18 gallons; for eels and salmon, 21. This measure was also known as a half-barrel.
Rundlet	18 gallons and 1 pottle	This measure was used for wine only.
Barrel	32 gallons	The barrel was 36 gallons for beer and 42 for eels and salmon. A barrel of wine (an uncommon size) was 31 gallons.
Hogshead	64 gallons	*LLL* IV.ii.87–88; *WT* III.iii.91–92; *Temp* IV.i.251. For beer, the hogshead was sometimes 72 gallons. William Harrison seems unsure of its exact size. For wine, the hogshead was 63 gallons.
Butt	84 gallons	*Temp* I.ii.146; *R3* I.iv.158, 273. This measure was for eels and salmon. A butt of wine was synonymous with a pipe of wine (see below), and 84 gallons of wine was known as a tierce.
Pipe	126 gallons	A measure of wine, also known as a butt.
Tun	252 gallons	*MWW* II.i.63. A measure of wine.

Note: See disclaimer on charts of length and weight units.

Units of Dry Measure

Unit	Equal To	Notes
Peck	2 gallons .009 cu m	*MWW* III.v.106–7. It was also called a farthingdeal (fourth part) of a bushel.
Bushel	8 gallons	*MV* I.i.116
Strike	2 bushels 16 gallons	*TNK* V.ii.64
Coomb	4 bushels	This was also sometimes called a raser or curnock.
Quarter	8 bushels 64 gallons	Grain was often measured in quarters, particularly when price was being discussed.
Weigh	6 quarters 384 gallons	The weigh could also be a quite different unit for weighing cheese.

Harrison wrote in *The Description of England* that these dry measures were used for seeds, roots, salt, and fruit. He noted that when measuring small things, such as grain or salt, the bushel or other measure was leveled, but that when measuring large objects such as apples or carrots, the bushel was heaped high.

Widow

When a woman married, she passed from the legal control of her father to that of her husband. Married women were considered in law to be under "coverture"—that is, their legal identity was covered or subsumed in the husband's. Accordingly, a wife could not own property, control her own wages, make contracts or wills, bring lawsuits, make purchases without her husband's consent, or collect rents on lands that had come with her as a marriage portion. The doctrine of coverture explains why men, for centuries of English history, were so eager to marry heiresses, for they thereby gained immediate and total control of any dowry, and a new bride's objections, if any, were meaningless to the courts.

When a husband died, all these legal controls disappeared, as did a host of protections and comforts. Many a marriage was loving and happy, and wives missed and grieved for their deceased husbands just as they do today (S 9). The widow (*1H6* III.i.84; *3H6* II.vi.18, III.ii.ch., III.iii.227, IV.i.99; *H5* I.ii.158; *AW* III.v.ch.; *TS* V.ii.ch.) also found herself an independent agent for very probably the first time in her life, and this could be exhilarating, terrifying (*John* II.ii.14), or both. Many women had no idea of how to handle business and were sometimes bilked by the unscrupulous (*2H6* V.i.188). They often found themselves raising children alone. They had to sort through papers to determine whether their husbands had died owing or owed any debts. Sometimes, upon finding records of a sum owed to a late hauband, the widow was denied the money and challenged on the grounds of her ignorance of financial transactions; such challenges were sometimes, but not always, successful. Sometimes a widow's inheritance was fought or withheld by other heirs, and she would have to defend herself in court. Such an inheritance, the "widow's portion," usually took one of three forms: dower, or one-third of the husband's lands for the remainder of her life (*TS* IV.ii.118, IV.iv.40–47); freebench, or one-third of the husband's tenancy, for life or until remarriage; or jointure, a settlement of land or an annuity written into the marriage contract (*AYLI* IV.i.52; *MWW* III.iv.48–49; *TS* II.i.363). The widows of tradesmen, moreover, who had probably been helping in the shop and supervising apprentices all through the marriage, often needed or wanted to continue running the family business. Several of London's printers and booksellers were women who had acquired their shops in precisely this way. A widow's life was therefore full of things to do, at least at first.

Some women thrived on the independence and the responsibility. Charmian, in *Antony and Cleopatra*, certainly feels that she would be such a woman: "Let me be married to three kings in forenoon," she tells the soothsayer, envisioning wealth and power, "and widow / them all" (I.ii.27–29). The Englishman William Page, writing for the benefit of his mother, wrote of widowhood as a woman's one chance to "be liker unto a man." Both he and Juan Luis Vives, who wrote on widowhood as part of a larger treatise on womanly behavior for Mary I, felt widows ought not to remarry, though Vives authorized remarriage if it was for avoiding fornication.

Remarriage was an option only for some women. Rich widows, granted a sudden ability to do exactly as they liked, were understandably reluctant to relinquish control to another man. Poor widows, often older, often saddled with children, and usually without any dowry to offer to a prospective husband, scraped by on the freebench if they had it, moved in with grown children in rare circumstances, and all too often sank into a miserable life of malnutrition, ill health, beggary, and eventual dementia or bitterness that could lead to being labeled a witch. This was a common stereotype of the widow—lonely, helpless, maltreated by all, and in special need of protection (*R2* I.ii.42–43; *John* III.i.33–34; *RL* 906). Middle-class widows, with shops or modest lands as a dowry, often felt the need for assistance in running their businesses or holdings and, unlike poor women, could offer a financial lure to prospective husbands. They were the most likely to remarry. When a printer died, for instance, there was an almost immediate contest for his widow between rivals eager to absorb inventory, presses, and shop space. On occasion, an ambitious apprentice might aspire successfully to his mistress's hand, becoming in one stroke the master of his own establishment. In Shakespeare's works, the queen of remarriage must surely be Mistress Overdone, in *Measure for Measure* (II.i.199–200), who has managed to secure nine husbands one after the other.

The community, meanwhile, paid close attention to the behavior of the new widow, waiting to see if she would comport herself with dignity. Vives recommended that, in all things, she behave as if her husband were still alive and responsible for her conduct. Page, noting the similarity between "widow" and the Latin *vidua* (empty), told her to maintain a perpetual hollowness that would be filled, in part, by patience, prayer, faith, and charitable works. He hoped she would remain single, not out of poverty or delight in her independence, but because there was a desolation in her heart, caused by her husband's death, that could never be assuaged by anything.

Neighbors hoped to see this virtuous behavior on the part of widows, but they at least half expected to see something quite different. The flip side of the popular image of the widow as a frail and helpless creature was an image of the widow as a ravenous sexual predator. She was believed by most to be incapable of living without the physical comforts of sex, and thus people expected her either to remarry or to engage in illicit affairs. Such is the state of Tranio's "lusty widow" who "shall be wooed and wedded in a day" (*TS* IV.ii.50, 51). The widow was often portrayed as simultaneously weeping for her old husband and looking for a new one;

Charmian, in her desire to be thrice wedded and thrice widowed in a single morning, is an example of the stereotype. Meanwhile, the widow, as a woman experienced in marriage but no longer under male control, was believed to wreak havoc in the homes of young brides by tutoring them in the ways of subversion and disobedience.

The marriage of a widow and a poor man, no matter what their actual emotional involvement, was virtually always perceived as a marriage of lust on her part and greed on his. There were fears, moreover, that a rich wife would dominate her husband. The popular feeling against such matches was intensified if the widow were older as well as richer than her groom. Whether she was poor or rich, young or old, happy or miserable, the widow was a figure who caused a sense of discomfort in those around her. *See also* Marriage; Women.

Windmill

Windmills (*1H4* III.i.157–60), like the water wheels that ran bellows and grain mills, used natural power for industrial purposes. The windmill was generally a very basic structure, consisting of a timber-framed and weatherboarded tower, not enormously tall, that had two main appendages. The larger and more obvious was the fan of blades or sails to catch the wind; the other was a hand-cranked tiller that adjusted the angle of the blades to enable them to make the most of the shifting winds. The average windmill generated about 20 to 30 horsepower, about twice the output of a water wheel, but, like the water wheel, it was worthwhile only in areas where geography favored its use.

Witch

It can be difficult, coming as we do from a world endowed with scientific method, to enter mentally into Renaissance. It was a time without a clear understanding of the origin and transmission of disease or the causes and significance of temporary astronomical phenomena. It was a time when many people could be ruined by the death of a handful of animals or the failure of a crop, a time in which people were born, grew old, and died in the same villages inhabited by their great-grandparents, surrounded for their entire lives by the same slowly changing cast of characters. If they wanted to escape from an ill-tempered neighbor or an overbearing parent, there were few options. It was a time in which a few misfortunes, combined with the wish to be rid of a quarrelsome or needy acquaintance, could formulate themselves into a belief that the acquaintance was the servant of the devil and had been the cause of the misfortunes. What is astonishing, in a world where coincidence, analogy, and tall tales were routinely accepted as ironclad evidence, is not that people believed in witches but that anyone resisted the myth.

Though belief in the existence of witches (*CE* III.ii.157, III.iii.11, IV.iii.65, IV.iv.146; *1H6* I.v.6–7, 21; *2H6* I.ii.91, II.i.170; *Temp* I.ii.258; *R3* III.iii.69; *A&C* IV.ii.37, IV.xii.47; *MAAN* II.i.173) was widespread, there were a few who disavowed them entirely or who believed in them only with substantial reservations about their powers. Samuel Harsnett, Archbishop of York, and his friend Richard Bancroft, Archbishop of Canterbury, disbelieved in witches. Harsnett wrote that only a man without "wit, understanding or sence" could seriously credit the idea that witches could transform themselves into animals.

> They that have their braines baited and their fancies distempered with the imaginations and apprehensions of Witches, Conjurers, and Fayries, . . . I finde to be marshalled in one of these five rankes: children, fooles, women, cowards, sick or blacke, melancholicke, discomposed wits.

He was not entirely alone in dismissing such "apprehensions." Reginald Scot, in his *Discoverie of Witchcraft*, would not go so far as to refute the Bible by denying all possibility of the existence of witches, but he redefined the concept. According to Scot, witches were merely frauds or "poor doting women" who had no magical powers. As proof, he offered the observation that "Such mischiefs as are imputed to witches, happen where no witches are; yea and continue when witches are hanged and burnt." He noted what most historians of witch trials have confirmed: that there were plenty of alternative explanations for supposedly supernatural phenomena, that there was no "credible witness" to any of the supposed acts of witchcraft, and that the accused witches were often the community's poorest, most helpless, most friendless, and least able to mount a logical defense. They were the contentious, the aged, the self-deluded, and the senile or insane. George Carleton, in a *The Madnesse of Astrologers* (1624), agreed. He rejected witchcraft, like astrology, as a matter of coincidence and the public's selective amnesia when predictions or threats were not borne out by later events.

The work of skeptics convinced some, particularly the better educated, but learning was not necessarily a guarantee of wisdom. George Gifford, in *A Discourse of the Subtill Practises of Devilles by Witches* (1586) and *A Dialogue Concerning Witches* (1593), was willing to concede that many so-called witches had been wrongfully accused and that illness arose from natural causes, but he maintained that witches did exist, that they did make pacts with Satan, and that "white" witches or cunning women were just as culpable as those who attempted harm. The general public was not so discriminating and believed all the worst tales about witches for a host of reasons: because the Bible said so, because so-and-so's child had fallen ill for no reason, because an old woman had looked grim or made a threat and then something bad happened, because an animal had behaved oddly, because the butter that had churned perfectly the last hundred times now inexplicably would not solidify, because the tales had appeared in print, because a witch had been found guilty in a neighboring town, and so on. The result was that people like the lay preacher John Darrell of Nottinghamshire, who claimed to be able to identify witches, periodically rose to prominence, and that at least fifty executions of "witches" took place in England between 1563 and 1603, two thirds of them from 1583 to 1603.

After James I came to the throne in 1603, belief in witchcraft (*H5* V.ii.279; *R3* III.iii.60, 71; *H8* III.ii.18–19; *TN* V.i.75) took on a new intensity, for the new king himself was an avowed believer in witches and had written a tract to that effect, published when he was still king of Scotland alone, and reprinted in London in the year of his accession. He had special reason to believe. In 1590–91, as James VI of Scotland, a supposed satanic plot against him, based in North Berwick, was "discovered" upon the torture of several suspected witches. James supervised some of the torture sessions personally and held that his deliverance from the plot was God's way of authenticating his right to rule. As many as a hundred people were tried in connection with the crime, which chiefly involved trying to wreck a ship carrying James and his Danish bride by casting a spell with human body parts and a christened cat. The methods of torture and the details of the plot were published, and the entire episode casts an interesting light on *Macbeth*. Shakespeare's only play set in Scotland, written while a Scottish king wore the English crown, *Macbeth* was a piece of egregious flattery lauding James's legendary descent from Banquo. The connection to the king was strengthened by the presence of the witches, who are clearly in league with Banquo's enemy, just as the North Berwick witches had been in league against James.

The Powers and Characteristics of Witches

Even though most people believed in witches, they differed to some extent in their beliefs about witches' powers. Gifford, conveniently for us, describes the most common popular beliefs before debunking them as products of weak logic and strong imagination. According to the characters in his *Dialogue*, witches "lame men and kil their cattel, yea they destroy both men and children." They are both numerous and ubiquitous; "there is scarce any towne or village in all this shire, but there is one or two witches at the least in it." They can change into hares, weasels, or cats. They kill swine and poultry and cause epidemics, storms, and crop failure; the storms were attested to by the Duke of Württemberg's secretary, who wrote in 1592 of England that "Many witches are found there, who frequently do much mischief by means of hail and tempests." They are attended by demonic animal familiars (*1H6* III.ii.122, V.iii; *2H6* IV.vii.109; *Mac* I.i.8–9), or "impes," "whom they nourish with milke or with a chicken, or by letting them sucke now and then a drop of bloud: whom they call when they be offended with any, and send them to hurt them in their bodies, yea to kill them, and to kill their cattell." Hares, toads, and cats were closely associated with witchcraft, and the discovery of such a creature in or near a suspected witch's house was often accepted as proof of her guilt.

All of these powers, in one form or another, were detailed in books, pamphlets, and the records of witch trials. Jean Bodin, who wrote a treatise on witches that was widely read in England, maintained that witches could change form, fly, make men impotent, and control the weather. Others thought they had, in addition to these skills, the ability to pass through walls or locked doors, to control minds, to kill with a look, to make livestock barren, to ruin the brewing or baking, to summon plagues of vermin, to cast hurtful spells by using the victim's possessions or a wax effigy, and to conjure demons. In exchange for these powers, they had to do all sorts of vile things, such as sacrificing babies, exhuming bodies, and eating blood or human flesh. In Continental and Scottish witch lore, witches were supposed to hold sabbats, in which they gathered together to desecrate holy objects, to cavort with demons, and to kiss the devil on his backside. The sabbat belief, which Gifford considered a delusion placed in the minds of foreign witches, entered England with James's reign, and was being offered into evidence in witch trials from 1612. Witches were routinely blamed for events that they could not possibly have caused, such as the destruction of the steeple of St. Paul's by lightning in 1561 and a shipwreck in 1583, the latter supposedly effected by a witch named Mother Gabley boiling eggs in cold water.

The typical person accused of witchcraft, according to Harsnett, was "an olde weather-beaten Croane, having her chinne and her knees meeting for age, . . . hollow eyed, untoothed, furrowed on her face, having her lips trembling with the palsie, going mumbling in the streetes, one that hath forgotten her *pater noster*, and hath yet a shrewd tongue in her head to call a drab a drab." Women were three times as likely as men to be indicted for witchcraft, a tendency explained at the time by the supposedly greater weakness, obstinacy, and evil of women, which made them perfect targets for the devil. An accused witch might be suspected because she had made threats against a neighbor, had been present at or near the time of a misfortune, looked ugly or old (*H5* IV.Cho.21), avoided making eye contact, or seemed unrepentant when challenged. Danger also attended the profession of the cunning man or cunning woman, who compounded cures and love potions, cast spells to find lost property, foretold the future, established the causes of animals' deaths, and, sometimes, claimed to be able to identify the work of harmful witches. It took only a grudge or a cross word to make people suspect the "white witch" of darker and more sinister magic.

Once accused, the suspect was subjected to additional tests to determine whether or not she was a witch. The means of verification included interrogation, torture, observing whether the accused could say the Lord's Prayer without stammering, and a search for the "devil's mark." This mark was some blemish or mole, or even a completely unmarked part of the skin that was supposed to be numb all the way to the bone. Female suspects were examined by groups of women for such marks and might be stuck with needles to determine whether a particular mark was the crucial proof of satanic influence. By the mid-seventeenth century, professional witch finders were equipped with retractable probes that could appear to pierce to the bone without actually causing any pain, thus proving that a devil's mark had been found.

Strategies for Control

When witchcraft was suspected, there were two principal means of addressing the threat: legal punishment and countercharms. Legal punishment began with the search for the witch marks and continued, in cases where a plot against the throne was suspected, with torture. Some of the Berwick witches were subjected to the thumbscrews, which smashed the finger or toe bones, or the "boots," metal boots in which wooden wedges were driven, crushing the bones of the legs and feet. Dr. Fian, one of the Berwick witches, not only wore the boots, but also had boiling water or oil poured on the broken limbs, after which his fingernails were pulled off with pincers "and under every nail there was thrust in two needles . . . up to the heads." Such extreme tortures were not always required to elicit a confession. Witches confessed as a result of sleep deprivation or under the influence of hallucinogens. They sometimes confessed because they were senile or insane. It is all too easy to imagine that some of them confessed because they were society's marginal, invisible people, alternately ignored and despised, and so desperate to be the center of attention that they were literally willing to die to be noticed and feared.

During Elizabeth's reign witchcraft, which had previously been a religious offense, was transformed into a criminal rather than a canon-law offense. A 1563 act made it a felony punishable by death (*2H6* II.iii.7) to murder by means of sorcery. Magic that led to injury was punishable by a year's imprisonment and four stints in the pillory (*MWW* IV.v.117) for the first offense, and death for the second. Seeking to locate treasure or lost property through witchcraft left one subject to a year's imprisonment and four times in the pillory. A revision of the act under James made it easier to sentence witches to death for a first offense. Nevertheless, not all witches who were accused were found guilty. Alice Freeman of Nottingham was acquitted after one of her accusers confessed that he and a noted exorcist had conspired to frame her. A 1605 case involving a Windsor girl named Anne Gunter ended without a conviction because it was proven to be a fraud devised by her father to rid himself of a local woman he disliked. Other cases were dismissed because the local magistrates simply did not believe in witches and had no wish to jail or execute innocent people.

Gifford, the Essex parson who believed in witches but not their powers, was torn between the ideas of merciless punishment and merciful skepticism. If witches can be absolutely and certainly proven to be present, says Daniel, the character in the *Dialogue* who speaks for the author, "they ought to be put to death." But it was of the utmost importance to be sure. Even in cases where two parties had quarreled, one had threatened, and the other had fallen ill or died, he maintained that it was difficult if not impossible to prove causation:

> There be naturall causes of tortures and griefe, of lamenesse, and of death in the bodies of men and beastes, which lie so hid and secret, that the learnedest physitians cannot espie them, but the divell seeth them, and can conjecture very neare the time when they will take effect. Then doeth he plie it, to bring the matter about that it may seeme he did it. If he have anie witch to deale by, he stirreth up some occasion to set her in rage with that party: and then he wil be sent, and telleth her he doth it. If he have no witch to deale by, yet he will set debate betweene the partie and some other, whom he may bring into suspition, as his greatest desire is to have innocent bloud shed.

In other words, it was impossible to tell whether the devil was acting through a real witch or through a complete innocent, even if all the ordinary "proofs" of witchcraft were evident, and by executing an innocent, the good people of the town or village would be committing a terrible sin. The entire concept of magic, he argued, was a fiction created by the devil to make himself seem more powerful and to stir up disbelief in God, and the best way to combat the devil's plan was to put no stock in magic of any kind, for good or for evil. Daniel dismisses virtually all of the traditional proofs of witchcraft, including the accounts of the supposed victims. Asked what he has to say to the case of a man who felt he had been compelled by witchcraft to kiss his cow under the tail, he replies, "I say he was farre in love with his cow." He insists that the courts are "to condemne none but upon sure ground, and infallible proofe," and his standards for "infallible proofe" were much higher than most of his contemporaries'.

The general public, disinclined to accept Gifford's claim that there was no good magic, used countercharms and spells to drive witches away, control them, or reduce their influence. Some went about whipping cats in the hope that these were transformed witches who would retain the wounds in their human form. Others used special phrases or words believed to avert evil influences; Shakespeare's "Aroint thee, witch" (*Lear* III.iv.122; *Mac* I.iii.6) appears to have been a formula of this kind. Gifford mentioned the conviction that the sacrifice of an animal, such as a hog or a hen, would balk the witch and drive away demons.

Other remedies involved heat; burning something that belonged to the witch or the person suspected of being bewitched (*3H6* III.iii.112; *R3* III.iii.67) was said to force the witch to come to the house of her victim. Gifford also lists a belief, current in Essex at least, that cattle can be unwitched, and the witch's face scratched, by having a pan of nails seething when the witch walks in the door. Bewitched cream could be made to yield butter if a red-hot poker or spit was thrust into the churn, wounding or driving away the witch who was believed to be present there, especially if the action was joined to words of banishment such as "If thou beest here have at thine eie." Gifford thought little of such remedies, perceiving them as Satan's devices to trick men into making burnt offerings to him, and he held that such "cures," when they appeared to work, did so because of the power of suggestion: "Imagination is a strong thing to hurt, all men doe finde, and why should it not then be strong also to help, when the parties mind is cheared, by beleeving fully that he receiveth ease?"

Shakespeare's Witches

Though Shakespeare often mentions witches, a few of these characters are worth special notice. He offers us a brief portrait of a "white witch" or cunning woman, the "Fat Woman of Brainford," who is accused of "the profession of / fortunetelling. She works by charms, by spells, by th' / [wax] figure" (*MWW* IV.ii.169–71). Although her charms seem to be unambitious by the standards of the *Macbeth* witches, she receives no more respect from the male characters than the weird sisters do. She is said to be not only fat but bearded as well, and is called "witch" and "hag" (IV.ii.81–83, 172–73, 188–89).

Other witches, like the Countess of Auvergne (*1H6* II.iii.36–38) and the Duchess of Gloucester, are noblewomen who seek to use magic for the acquisition of power. Eleanor, Duchess of Gloucester, was in fact a real person who was said to have employed "medicines and drynkis" to force Humphrey, Duke of Gloucester "to love her and to wedde her." The love potions were supposedly prepared by one Margery Jordemayne, the Witch of Eye, who was burned to death in 1441. Afterward, Eleanor was accused of hiring a soothsayer to cast her horoscope with the aim of determining whether she would ever be queen. The episode, much altered, appears in *2 Henry VI* (I.ii.74–82, I.iv.1–55, II.iii.1–12), complete with the conjuring of a demon; the arrest of the conjuror, witch, and duchess; and the eventual banishment of Eleanor and the execution of her assistants. Another historical figure, Joan of Arc, is portrayed by Shakespeare as the "damnèd sorceress" (*1H6* III.ii.38, V.iii.34, V.iv.1) that the English during the Hundred Years' War considered her.

However, the most detailed descriptions of witches and sorcery occur in *Macbeth*, a play that would have had special significance to James I. Here Shakespeare includes almost every one of the classic attributes of witches; the weird sisters are ugly, bearded (I.iii.39–46), accompanied by familiars, capable of conjuring spirits, able to foretell the future and to control the weather (I.iii.4–25), and inclined to kill livestock (I.iii.2) and to concoct noxious potions (IV.i.4–43). Furthermore, like virtually every other Shakespearean witch, they are female, just as most witches in the real world were thought to be. *See also* Demon; Magic.

Women

Emanuel van Meteren, a Dutch resident of England from 1558 to 1612, noted that women in England were treated differently from women in some other European countries. They were not shut up indoors but were permitted to move freely through the streets with uncovered heads and to socialize with friends or shop in the markets. William Rye states:

> They are well-dressed, fond of taking it easy, and commonly leave the care of household matters and drudgery to their servants. They sit before their doors, decked out in fine clothes, in order to see and be seen by the passers-by. In all banquets and feasts they are shown the greatest honour; they are placed at the upper end of the table, where they are the first served; at the lower end they help the men. All the rest of their time they employ in walking and riding, in playing at cards or otherwise, in visiting their friends and keeping company, conversing with their equals (whom they term *gosseps*), and their neighbours, and making merry with them at child-births, christenings, churchings . . . and funerals; and all this with the permission and knowledge of their husbands, as such is the custom.

During the same period, England was famously described as a "paradise for women, a prison for servants, and hell for horses," but women today might disagree with that assessment. Women were held to be full of faults, praised for only those virtues that made them docile wives, barred from full participation in public life, and denied equal rights. In literature, they met with worse treatment at times than in real life, and they were, in most respects, treated badly by Shakespeare, despite the age-old claim that he wrote strong female characters.

Men attributed to women a staggering catalog of faults and considered them the scourge of and a pernicious infuence on decent men everywhere, Women were supposedly stubborn, fickle (*A&C* V.ii.238–41), lustful, contrary, stingy, greedy, proud, vain (*Lear* III.ii.35–36), cowardly, physically and morally weak (*A&C* V.ii.122–24), imprudent, unthrifty, rash (*WT* III.ii.218–19), devious, deceitful (*1H6* II.i.50), hateful, garrulous, indiscreet (*WT* IV.iv.242–46; *JC* II.iv.9), jealous, and disobedient. Some women, of course, were many of these things, just as some were exactly the opposite. Shakespeare, however, chooses to repeat most of the calumnies against the sex as a whole. His company of actors, of course, would not be likely to object, since they were all male, even those playing the female characters. There was no doubt a delicious irony for Shakespeare's audiences in hearing a boy disguised as a girl disguised as a boy uttering pretending to be a girl criticisms of women (*AYLI* III.ii.346–55). The actor playing Rosalind in *As You Like It* was known by the audience to be a boy and thought falsely by the character courting him to be a boy, yet the fact that he was costumed as a woman gave him special license to revile "her" own sex and lent "her" criticisms a spurious authenticity, even though all the levels of deception were fully known to the audience.

Shakespeare did, undoubtedly, write strong and memorable female characters, but his strongest women, like Joan of Arc and Margaret of Anjou (whom he could not alter completely, since they were historical figures), are portrayed as villains. One of the chief vices with which he charges women is ill temper in one form or another. Margaret of Anjou is called a "wrangling woman" (*3H6* II.ii.176), and women are elsewhere characterized as "misbehaved and sullen" (*R&J* III.iii.143), self-absorbed (*1H4* I.iii.234–36), or scolding and shrewish (*AYLI* IV.i.169–73; *2H4* V.iii.34). They are inconstant (*1H4* II.iii.107–8; *T&C* V.ii.106–9), tearful (*3H6* II.iii.25–26; *RL* 1235–39), and weak-minded (*RL* 1240). The most common vices of which Shakespeare accuses women are cowardice and physical weakness. Sometimes, the terms are applied directly to the female characters (*JC* II.i.292–97, II.iv.8, 39–40; *MM* II.iv.128–29), as in *King John*:

I am sick and capable of fears,
Oppressed with wrongs, and therefore full of fears,
A widow, husbandless, subject to fears,
A woman naturally born to fears. (II.ii.12–15)

More often, the male characters are chided with behaving like women when they fail to meet some standard of courage or strength. It is "womanish" to be absent from battle, to cry, or to fear death (*T&C* I.i.110; *R&J* III.iii.109–10; *H8* II.i.37–38). Women, presented with bad news or a minor setback, fall to fainting and tears (*John* V.vi.21–22; *AW* IV.iii.109–10; *Tim* V.i.157–58), but men, proper men at least, should be ashamed to do so. Even the diguised Rosalind feels a responsibility to overcome her natural weakness:

I could find in my heart to disgrace my
man's apparel and to cry like a woman; but I must
comfort the weaker vessel, as doublet and hose ought
to show itself courageous to petticoat. (*AYLI* II.iv.4–7)

It is a sign of Rosalind's depth as a character that she is able to overcome the fact that she, too, is a "weaker vessel" (*LLL* I.i.266). Shakespeare may have been aware of the irony here—that circumstances, custom, and force of will can shape behavior as much as or more than gender. Looking back at his plays from a twenty-first-century perspective, we can see that the reason men have to be chided and goaded into battle or action with the accusation that they are womanish is because men, just like women, can be fearful and hesitant. Shakespeare was too good a dramatist not to be aware that everyone is capable of fear; he was too much a product of his time to rise above the idea that for men, fear was a common but unnatural response, while for women it was the natural, and therefore only slightly contemptible, state of affairs.

Women do have virtues in the plays, and we may divide their virtues into two categories: their Shakespearean virtues, which is to say the characteristics that made them interesting to watch onstage; and their societal virtues, the virtues for which women were praised by Renaissance culture at large. The former category is what endears Shakespeare's women to readers and audiences. The heroines are clever. They dress in men's clothing and go on daring adventures. They are, on occasion, quite brave. However, the Shakespearean virtues, some of which were definitely present in the real women of his time, were exactly the sorts of characteristics for which women were punished.

Women in the plays are given credit for a great deal of wit, and Shakespeare's heroines are generously endowed with this virtue, but in real life the woman who constantly got the better of men in verbal disputes was subjected to various forms of public humiliation. Chief among these were the ducking or cucking stool and the scold's brank or bridle (*H5* III.vii.52). The cucking stool was a chair, sometimes paraded through town on a wheeled platform or cart, into which the offending woman was tied. A jeering crowd watched as the chair was hoisted on a seesaw beam and the "scold" ducked once or several times in the nearest body of water. The scold's bridle was a leather or metal head cage with a bit or plate that held the tongue down and prevented the woman from talking. It was placed on her head, and she was exhibited publicly somewhere, usually for a

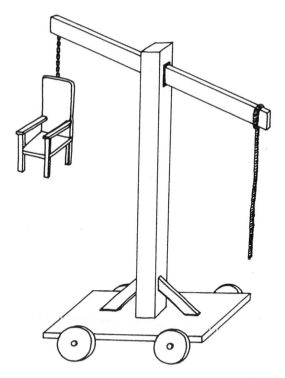

Cucking stool. The length of the cross beam depended on the distance from shore to a sufficiently deep point in the nearest pond or river. Sometimes the entire assembly was mounted on a tumbrel; in other places the beams remained standing at all times as a continual warning to women.

few hours, and similarly taunted regarding her newfound inability to speak. The reality in Renaissance England was that people liked a clever woman on the stage, but not in their homes or villages. Shakespeare also sometimes provides an excuse for a woman's wit, some extenuating circumstance that explains how she could be so clever. The most famous example of a woman in the plays outsmarting the men around her is that of Portia in *Merchant of Venice*, who secures an acquittal for Antonio, yet she does not arrive at her defense tactics on her own but merely repeats, eloquently, the defense told to her by a male lawyer.

Similarly, the sort of antics for which Shakespeare's heroines are so well known, such as dressing in drag or impersonating public officials, would have earned them not praise but condemnation, and perhaps a public whipping, in real life. They might even, for violating the code of maidenly modesty, have been accused of being whores (*MM* V.i.177–80).

Shakespeare's women are often brave, and on rare occasions this is presented as an unalloyed and appropriate virtue. Eleanor of Aquitaine is both tough matriarch and gallant knight, without being portrayed as a harridan. Indeed, her tone is at once jaunty and authoritative as she invites a gentleman to join her army:

> I like thee well: wilt thou forsake thy fortune,
> Bequeath thy land to him, and follow me?
> I am a soldier and now bound to France. (*John* I.i.148–50)

Elinor is a notable exception, for in most cases, bravery in a woman is mingled with some other quality, either in the woman herself or in the characters around her, that diminishes her courage in some way. Often, as with imputations of cowardice, the goal is to motivate or shame men:

> Had I been there, which am a silly woman,
> The soldiers should have tossed me on their pikes
> Before I would have granted to that act. (*3H6* I.i.243–45)

When women are in arms or endowed with unusual physical courage, it usually serves as an exhortation to the men around them (*3H6* V.iv.50–51; *R2* III.ii.118–19; *1H6* I.vi.16; *John* V.ii.154–58; *WT* II.iii.59–61; *Mac* IV.iii.186–88). There are a number of instances of women going to war in the plays. Elinor, Fulvia (*A&C* I.ii.89–95), Cleopatra, and Margaret of Anjou serve as commanders (*3H6* I.ii.68); Elinor, in the scene quoted above, brings along Blanche of Castile as well, and in *1 Henry IV* a loyal wife vows to accompany her husband on campaign (III.i.190–91). Most notable of all, perhaps, is Joan of Arc, who led the French to several victories against the English in the Hundred Years' War. Yet Margaret is a villain because she unnaturally dominates her husband (*2H6* I.iii.148; *3H6* II.ii.74, 90, II.vi.74), and the chief cause for celebration in her bravery is that she will probably bear brave sons as a result (*1H6* V.v.70–75). Margaret, like Fulvia and Cleopatra, is ultimately defeated, reinforcing the correct order of things, and Joan of Arc is not only defeated but burned as a witch. In any case, her victories can be attributed by the English to witchcraft; they are the result of "fear, not force" (*1H6* I.v.21). Most telling is her challenge to single combat of young Talbot, who declines to fight her because she is a lesser opponent (*1H6* IV.vii.37–43). In the language of the duel, the acceptance of a challenge was also the acceptance of the challenger's social equality, and this Joan never achieves.

The societal virtues of women also appear in Shakespeare's plays. These were the virtues that husbands, poets, and the authors of conduct manuals told women they ought to have, and every one was designed to create wives who were useful and trouble-free. The ideal woman was supposed to be chaste, so that the husband could be sure of his children's paternity; obedient (*MM* V.i.206), so that he never had to argue; quiet (*Lear* V.iii.274–75; *TS* I.i.70–71), so that he need not be bothered by her; thrifty, so that she might spend less of his money; modest, so that he need never feel threatened; skillful, so that he could save money by using her talents rather than those of expensive specialists; passive (*Per* II.iii.68–71), so that he could take the lead in all things; and pretty, so that he could display her with pride to his friends. Women's virtues, as listed by Shakespeare, fall into these and similar categories. "Women are soft, mild, pitiful [literally full of pity], and flexible" (*3H6* I.iv.141). Their three ideal characteristics are beauty, virtue (by which most people meant sexual propriety), and "government," or self-control (*3H6* I.iv.128–32). They should be "wise, fair, and true" (*MV* II.vi.56) and, above all, deferential to men and modest about their own strengths (*1H6* V.iii.177–78; *2H6* III.i.34–41; *H8* III.i.176–78).

The actual behavior of Shakespeare's characters, like the actual behavior of the real women of his time, often had little to do with such lists of virtues. Glimpses of realistic interaction, unlike the conventions of amazons, shrews, girls in boys' clothes, or prim and silent maidens, are scattered throughout the plays. There is Helena's appeal to girlhood solidarity (*MND* III.ii.215–19) and the sacrifice of girlhood friendship to grown-up passion, the bantering threats between Hotspur and his wife (*1H4* II.iii.86–88), and Launce's comic list of the virtues of his beloved milkmaid (*2GV* III.i.268–364), which probably has more resemblance to the actual characteristics of a valued wife than the catalogs compiled by conduct-book authors. Launce's milkmaid can fetch, carry, milk, brew, sew, knit, and spin. Her faults, too, are the sorts of faults one might find in a flesh-and-blood woman: she has borne a child out of wedlock, and she has bad breath in the mornings, a taste for sweets, no teeth (perhaps as a result of the taste for sweets), pride, shrewishness, a tendency to talk in her sleep, not enough thrift, and too much enthusiasm for liquor. That she is "slow in words" is first listed as a fault but declared to be a virtue, for a woman should ideally be quiet, and the sum of her character is that "She hath more hair than wit, / and more faults than hairs, and more wealth than faults" (348–49). Her wealth is, ultimately, her highest recommendation, outweighing toothlessness and shrewishness combined.

The odd thing about Shakespeare's women is that they are at once more and less than their real counterparts. They do much that real women could not, but they also reflect only a fraction of real women's experience. Shakespeare makes only passing references, for example, to the fact that, as van Meteren put it, "the women there are entirely in the power of their husbands except for their lives." A man could beat his wife, rape her, lock her up, remove her children from her and never permit her to see them again, take her property (*MV* III.ii.167–70), seize her wages, and prevent her from making a will (*John* II.i.193), and never violate a single law. He could not murder her, but in all other respects she was entirely within his legal control. This said, many women did work (*2H6* IV.ii.44–48), and some were masters of trades in their own right. Some followed their husband's trade, others had their own and accepted apprentices, male and female. In *The Description of England*, William Harrison noted that graziers' wives were just as good at their husbands at feeling an ox or bullock and guessing how much it was worth in meat, skin, and tallow; no doubt wives of other tradesmen and artisans had comparable skills.

Women were essential to the work of the farm and to the family economy, and while some continued to view them as annoyances fit only for the breeding of heirs, there were many husbands who doted on their wives (*Lear* I.iv.38–39) and mourned them deeply after their death. Beaten wives sometimes gained the support of their communities and found ways of shaming their husbands into better behavior. Some women, especially widows, were parties to lawsuits, and even more women testified as witnesses. Though they could not engage in single combat, since they were deemed to have no personal honor and to be merely extensions of their husband's or father's honor (*MAAN* IV.i.305–6); though they could not directly engage in politics except in very rare circumstances (*2H6* I.iii.119); though they could not vote or hold office; and though they had to remain passive in courtship (*T&C* III.ii.125–28), they found ways to break or circumvent the rules. Some debated with their husbands and thus influenced opinion; some found strength through friendships with other women; some went to the alehouses, drank, and flirted; some had premarital or extramarital affairs; some took their neighbors to task with words or blows; some, through trade, midwifery, marriage, piety, or natural leadership, became prominent in their communities. Few women followed all of the rules all of the time, and it was when they broke out of the restrictive ideal that they were characterized as shrews, scolds, and harridans. *See also* Housework; Marriage; Pregnancy and Childbirth; Witch.

Writing

The purposes of writing—expressing love, conducting business or diplomacy (*1H6* IV.i), recording government proceedings (*1H6* III.i.1–13, 100), making notes to oneself (*Cym* II.ii.24), recording legal transactions (*2H6* IV.ii.79–83), and so on—have not changed much in the past 400 or 500 years. The mechanics of writing, however, have changed dramatically. For example, even though some of the items on a Renaissance writing desk, such as paper and a "table-book" or notebook (*JC* IV.iii.96–97; *WT* IV.iv.600–603; S 77; *LLL* V.i.15 s.d.), would be recognizable to us, the paper was hand-laid linen, not made of wood pulp. If the document being prepared was really important, the more expensive parchment (*2H6* IV.ii.79–83; *R2* II.i.64; *JC* III.ii.129; *John* V.vii.32–34; *Ham* V.i.114–15), made of scraped sheepskin, might be used. Occasionally, Shakespeare makes reference to document forms that would have seemed exotic or ancient even to his contemporary audiences: scrolls (*1H6* III.i.150), for instance, or Roman wax tablets (*JC* III.i.216). Furthermore, the rest of the tools present would be unfamiliar, or known to us only as curiosities.

Pen and Ink

The pens (from the Latin *penna*, feather) were made of goose quills (S 83; *RL* 1297). Because of the wing curvature, right-handed writers found left-wing quills more comfortable to hold, while left-handed writers preferred feathers from the bird's right wing. Each pen (*MAAN* I.i.245; *H5* Epi.1; *T&C* Pro.24; *AW* II.i.80; *TN* III.ii.49; Sonnets 78, 79, and 81) was constructed by the user. The lower barbs were pared off with a penknife (*2H4* III.ii.272) and the pith of the feather removed. Then the end was sharpened to a point, a slit cut in the longer end, and an angle cut made in the shorter end. There was an art to the cutting and maintenance of pens: different cuts produced different types of script, the pens needed to be recut every time they became blunt or began to spatter or blot (*R2* II.i.64), and after each use the pens had to be washed and kept moist.

The quill pen was not the only writing utensil available in the Renaissance. Graphite pencils (*LLL* V.ii.43) came into use after the discovery of a large source in Cumberland in 1564; initially the messy substance, mistakenly known as "lead" for its resemblance to the metal, was wrapped in string to keep it from the soiling the user's hand, but wooden holders were soon devised. There were a few metal pens in existence, but they were not as flexible, and the supply of metal was always more uncertain than the supply of goose feathers, so the quill pen remained the dominant tool.

Next to the pen and penknife on the writing desk stood an inkhorn (*MAAN* III.v.59; *1H6* III.i.100; *2H6* IV.ii.108–9) into which the pen was dipped. One popular style of inkpot was a "countinghouse stan-

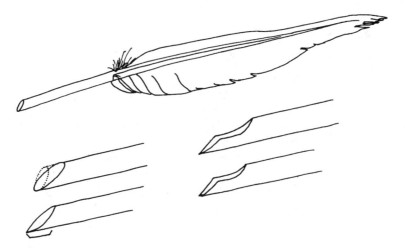

The manufacture of a quill pen. Top: The quill with its pith removed. Middle left: The tip is cut on an angle (original contour shown by dotted line). Bottom left: a slit is made in the longer side of the tip, between the brackets. Middle right: A pointed tip, finished by making a second cut halfway through the tip and upward. Bottom right: a chisel tip for making Gothic-style lettering.

dish," so named because it would have accommodated the numerous clerks of a counting house. It was a short cylinder, often with a wide, flat base. In the center of the cylinder was a dish for the ink, sometimes removable so that it could be easily cleaned. Arranged around this dish were several small holes so that multiple pens could be stood next to the ink, ready for use.

The ink (*MAAN* IV.i.139; *A&C* I.v.65; *LLL* V.ii.41; *TN* III.ii.43) was homemade from three principal ingredients. It began with gallnuts or "oak apples," nutlike growths created by the eggs of gall wasps, which were steeped to yield tannic and gallic acids. Copperas (hydrated ferrous sulfate, whose greenish color resembled oxided copper, hence its common name) was added to react with these acids and turn the ink black (*2GV* III.i.286; *Cym* III.ii.19–20; *S* 65). Gum arabic from the acacia tree bound the mixture and gave it its viscous consistency. This type of ink actually burned itself into the paper and tended to turn brown as it aged. There was another type of ink, made of carbon, gum, and water, that stayed blacker but did not adhere as well to the page when dry.

The last necessary item for a well-equipped writing desk was another cylindrical container, looking very much like a large saltshaker or a large metal thread spool, in either case concave and dotted with small holes on top. This shaker contained not salt but fine sand, which was sprinkled on the wet, inky sheets of paper to help them dry more quickly. The sand did not actually absorb the ink, as did the less common blotting paper. Instead, it drew the ink away from the paper and increased its surface area, helping it to dry by spreading it more thinly. Once the ink was dry, the page was tipped over the concave top of the shaker, and the sand spilled back into its box for reuse.

Handwriting

There were many styles of "character," or handwriting (*MM* IV.ii.198; *Lear* I.ii.64–65; *LLL* IV.ii.154; *Per* III.iv.3), in Shakespeare's day, but most people used only one or two styles, and no one used them all. Government offices and law courts used the "court hand," and several of these agencies, including the Court of Chancery, the Court of Common Pleas, the Pipe Office, and the Exchequer, had their own individual variations unique to their own clerks. The court hand was a cursive style intended for taking hurried notes of proceedings and keeping records in volume; as such, it could be written fast, but it was not particularly elegant. It was not used for personal correspondence.

The Italian cursive style, "the sweet Roman hand" of *TN* III.iv.28–29, was quite similar to the handwriting in use today. In the seventeeth century it became dominant, but in Shakespeare's time it was still a minority script, confined to those who found it interesting or fashionable and to women, who, according to Martin Billingsley in 1618, "(hauing not the patience to take any great paines, besides phantasticall and humorsome) must be taught that which they may instantly learne."

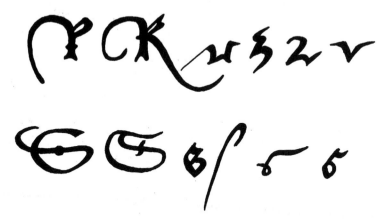

Examples of letters in the secretary hand. Top row: R, R, r, r, r, r. Bottom row: S, S, s, s, s, s.

Most business documents, letters, and literary works from the period are in a third writing style, the "secretary hand," which is practically undecipherable to the untrained modern eye. Part of the difficulty of reading it lies in its multiplicity of character forms. There were, for example, at least nine ways of making the letter *r*, some of which look like the number

2 or like mere squiggles; the two most common forms. A lowercase (minuscule) *c* could look like a modern *r*; an uppercase (majuscule) *e* could look more like a capital *C* with a *2* or an *E* inside it; the lowercase *e* often looked like an *o*, and so on. Some letters looked different when they came in the middle, at the beginning, or at the end of a word, or when they were preceded or followed by certain other letters. Hamlet found the entire process of penmanship tedious and "once did hold it . . . / A baseness to write fair, and labored much / How to forget that learning" (*Ham* V.ii.33–35).

Spelling also complicates matters for the modern reader of Renaissance documents. Printed books eventually led to standardized spelling, but in Shakespeare's day spelling, especially in personal correspondence, varied widely. Words we expect today to see written with double consonants, such as *well*, were often written with single ones: *wel*. The reverse was also true, with *horse* becoming *horsse*, and so on. Final *es* were added or dropped at whim. Even the spelling of Shakespeare's name is a consensus among scholars and does not reflect any consistency in the way he spelled his own name; even as late as the nineteenth century many knowledgeable people were still referring to him as "Shakspear" or "Shakespear." Aside from personal spelling variations, there were spelling conventions that have since fallen out of use. In the same way that *y* can be a vowel or a consonant, *u/v* and *i/j* were thought of as single letters in Tudor and early Stuart England. When one of these letters was being used as a vowel, it was spelled and pronounced *u* or *i*; when it was being used as a consonant, it was spelled and pronounced *v* or *j*.

There are further barriers to deciphering the secretary hand. The punctuation of the day was mostly the same as now, but with a few significant differences. There were fewer semicolons and many more colons used. Quotation marks were used seldom, and then for emphasis rather than quotation. The virgule, or slash, was frequently used as a comma or at the end of a section, and hyphens were doubled, so that they looked like an equals sign, when they were used in word breaks at the ends of lines. Most perplexingly, the exclamation point did not exist (and would not do so until 1650); instead, the question mark was used for both questions and exclamations.

There were also abbreviations and contractions that modern readers no longer use. The notable exceptions to this statement are the use of *&* for *and*, and the use of *ye* (the *y* being a version of the Old English letter *thorn*, which sounded like *th*) for *the*. These two usages have survived to the present day, the former in everyday text, and the latter in advertisements and shop names striving for a whiff of the antique. The other contractions have been abandoned: *dnus* for *dominus*; an *e* with a tail for *es*, *is*, plurals, and possessives; the tittle, a short line like a tilde to indicate a dropped *m* (as in *cõfort* for *comfort*), dropped *n*, or shortening of *-tion* to

-*con*; loops above the line for *er*, *or*, *ir*, or *ur* combinations; a *P* with a crossed or looped-back tail for the Latin words *per* and *pro*; a shape like an elongated number *9* for the Latin ending -*us*, the Latin word *con*, and the English ending -*ous*; the omissions of the middle letters in certain common words and titles (such as *Kt* for *Knight*, *yr* for *your*, and *Mr* for *Master*); and others. *See also* Books; Letters; Literacy.

Yeoman

A yeoman was technically a freeholder (one who owned his land outright) whose land brought in an income of 40 shillings (£2) per year. Lesser farmers and tenants, like leaseholders and copyholders, were mere "husbandmen." This was the theory. In practice, tenant farmers were often identified as "yeomen" in court documents if they were prosperous, and certain substantial yeomen were gentlemen in behavior, hobbies, and marital alliances, if not in name. In general, the term meant a middle-class farmer (*1H6* II.iv.81, 85, 95; *3H6* I.iv.123; *Lear* III.vi.10; *R3* V.iii.339; *H5* III.i.25; *1H4* IV.ii.15).

Z

"Thou whoreson zed, thou unnecessary letter!" (*Lear* II.ii.66).

Appendix: Chronology of Historical Events Referred to in Shakespeare's Plays

The introductions to editions of Shakespeare's plays often offer information about his historical accuracy or lack thereof. He tended to rely on one or two historical sources and on his own observations of human nature, and these tools served him well enough for dramatic purposes. However, his plays should not be taken as accurate representations of past events. He invents characters, crams events that were actually years apart into one act or even one scene, and swallows the prejudices of his time or his sources with little question. He makes no attempt, for example, to question the Tudor-era perception of Henry V as heroic or Richard III as monstrous. He had, furthermore, practical reasons to exaggerate the virtues and divine favor of certain characters at the expense of others. It was always advisable to flatter the current king or queen and his or her prominent ancestors. A complete list of the people Shakespeare portrays, the sources from which he derived his information, and the ways in which he alters or distorts the historical record would require a separate volume, but the list below offers dates and brief explanations of some of the more important events portrayed or alluded to in his works. (B.C.E. stands for "Before the Common Era" and C.E. stands for "Common Era"; these correspond to the B.C. and A.D. of the Christian calendar.) The abbreviations of the plays are the same as those used in the main text.

THE ANCIENT WORLD

c. 700 B.C.E. Numa Pompilius succeeds Romulus as Rome's second king (715–673 B.C.E.). He is followed by Tullus Hostilius, traditionally held to have ruled from 673 to 642 B.C.E., and Ancus Marcius (642–617 B.C.E.). All three are mentioned in *Coriolanus* (II.iii.241–42).

510 According to tradition, Lucretia, wife of Tarquinius Collatinus, is raped by Sextus, son of the Roman king Tarquinius Superbus,

leading to the ouster of Superbus and the founding of the Roman republic (*Cor* V.iv.44). The rape is the subject of the poem *The Rape of Lucrece*. The leadership of the rebellion by Lucius Junius Brutus, an ancestor of Marcus Junius Brutus, is alluded to elsewhere (*TA* IV.i.91; *JC* I.ii.159).

323   Alexander the Great (b. 356 B.C.E.; see *LLL* V.ii.; *WT* V.i.47–49) dies.

183   The Carthaginian general Hannibal (*LLL* V.ii.668) dies. He fought in the Punic Wars against Rome and, in a feat once considered impossible, invaded Italy by crossing the Alps.

57   Julius Caesar, after conquering the Helvetii and the Belgae, defeats the formidable Nervii, another Gallic tribe, at the battle of the River Sambre (*JC* III.ii.173).

53   Marcus Crassus, with Julius Caesar and Gnaeus Pompeius Magnus (Pompey the Great) a member of the first Roman triumvirate (meaning "rule by three men"—Rome was normally governed by two consuls), is slain by Parthians while attempting negotiations with them (*A&C* III.i.1–5).

48   Pompey the Great (b. 106 B.C.E.; see *LLL* V.ii., esp. 546–57) dies after being defeated at Pharsalus (*JC* V.i.74–75) in a civil war with Julius Caesar (*MM* II.i.245–48, III.ii.44–45; *JC* I.i.38–52). He fled to Egypt but was murdered (*2H6* IV.i.137–38) at the command of the Egyptian king Ptolemy XIII, brother and husband of Cleopatra. Caesar follows him to Egypt, intervenes in a fight for the throne between Cleopatra and Ptolemy, becomes Cleopatra's lover, and probably fathers her son Caesarion (*A&C* II.ii.229–30). He leaves Egypt and returns to Rome in 47.

46   After defeating Pompey's supporter Metellus Scipio in Africa, Caesar returns to Rome and celebrates a triumph.

44   On March 15, Julius Caesar is assassinated at a session of the Senate held in the portico of a stone theater built by his former co-triumvir and rival Pompey the Great (*JC* III.i). Some of the assassins are men with grievances against him; some, like Decius Brutus and Caius Trebonius, are his trusted lieutenants; still others, like Gaius Cassius and Marcus Brutus, had supported Pompey in the civil war but had been forgiven by Caesar. On March 17, the Senate, led by Marcus Antonius (Mark Antony), votes an amnesty for the conspirators and a public funeral for Caesar. Caesar's legacy to the Roman people, the sight of his bloodstained toga, and Antony's short funeral oration incite the citizenry of Rome to a frenzy, and they riot and drive the conspirators out of the city. Shortly thereafter, the grandnephew and adopted son of Caesar, Gaius Julius Caesar Octavianus, arrives in Rome and begins a protracted struggle with Antony for the support of Caesar's former

troops. In July, Cassius and Brutus, who have still not dared to return to Rome, demand better provinces to rule and are rebuffed; they conclude that the amnesty will not hold. In September, Cicero begins a series of speeches called philippics against Antony's rule.

43   Early in the year the Senate elects Aulus Hirtius and Gaius Vibius Pansa as consuls. Cicero's philippics continue, and Octavian is given a military command. Antony, in defiance of the Senate, marches against the conspirator Decius Brutus, who is stationed in the town of Mutina (Modena), and begins a siege. The Senate, in response, sends Hirtius, Pansa, and Octavian to fight Antony. A battle in April outside Mutina ends in a defeat and withdrawal for Antony; Hirtius is killed in battle and Pansa mortally wounded (*A&C* I.iv.56–58). Antony acquires reinforcements while the Senate, believing him completely powerless, brands him a public enemy. Antony, however, brings his reinforcements back to the now undefended Mutina and defeats Decius Brutus, who flees to the hills and is killed by bandits. Octavian, treated treacherously by the Senate, marches troops into Rome, seizes control of the government, rescinds the amnesty offered to Caesar's assassins, and pardons Antony. Octavian, Antony, and Marcus Aemilius Lepidus are named coconsuls, forming the Second Triumvirate. Three hundred senators and 2,000 *equites* (knights) are proscribed; many are executed, and most have their assets seized. One of those murdered is Cicero (*JC* IV.iii.175).

42   Brutus and Cassius are defeated and commit suicide in two battles at Philippi, in the province of Macedonia. Cassius is defeated and kills himself after the first battle, and Brutus is defeated in the second battle three weeks later (*JC* IV.ii–V.v).

41   Antony's brother, Lucius Antonius, and Antony's Fulvia stage a rebellion against Octavian (*A&C* I.ii.89–95). Unfortunately, they have not consulted Antony first, and he declines to aid them; they are defeated, and Octavian gains control of Gaul. Antony meets Cleopatra and becomes her lover (*A&C* II.ii.188–89).

40   Antony's wife Fulvia dies (*A&C* I.ii.119), and to cement a new accord with Octavian, he marries Octavian's sister Octavia (*A&C* II.ii). Quintus Labienus, a Roman defector to Parthia, invades Rome's Asian provinces with a Parthian army and takes Syria and Asia Minor (*A&C* I.ii.100–103), while Pacorus, son of the Parthian king, takes Palestine. In 39 and 38, however, one of Antony's lieutenants, Ventidius, will recapture these territories (*A&C* III.i.1–5).

35   Sextus Pompeius Magnus, also known as Pompey the Younger, is captured and executed by Mark Antony's troops (*A&C* III.vi.24–25). The younger son of Pompey the Great, he was proscribed by

the Second Triumvirate in 43 and became a successful pirate off the Italian coast (*A&C* I.ii.184–90, I.iv., II.vi.35, II.vii).

33 The Second Triumvirate, which has had the official recognition of the Senate, legally ends. Octavian abandons his title, but Antony continues to behave as if he is still invested with power.

32 The Roman people, already dismayed at Antony's liaison with Cleopatra, are further shocked to hear that he has divorced Octavia and that his will—or what purports to be his will—asks that he be buried next to Cleopatra. Antony, who has raised a navy with substantial help from Cleopatra, goes to Greece and sets up his headquarters at Actium. Octavian declares war not on Antony but on Cleopatra.

31 Harassed by the forces of Octavian and Octavian's general Agrippa, Antony and Cleopatra are finally pinned in at Actium. Antony decides to make a run for it, slipping his boats out and then hoisting sail at the last minute. He positions himself correctly, but while the well-trained crews of Cleopatra's sixty ships hoist sail expeditiously and escape, miscommunication or mutiny among Antony's men leads to a botched execution of the orders. Antony manages to elude capture with only a fraction of his fleet. The remainder of the fleet takes Antony's hasty departure as a betrayal and switches sides to Octavian (*A&C* III.vii–xi).

30 Octavian pursues Antony and Cleopatra to Alexandria, where they both commit suicide. Caesarion is put to death, but Cleopatra's two children by Antony are allowed to live.

27 Octavian, later known as Augustus Caesar, begins his reign as emperor, ruling until his death in 14 C.E. Shakespeare sets *Cymbeline* during his reign (III.i.1).

4 Herod the Great, ruler of Judaea, dies (*A&C* I.ii.29–30). His lands are divided by Augustus Caesar into three parts, each to be ruled by one of his sons. One of these, Herod Antipas, rules Galilee until 39 C.E.

A SLICE OF THE MIDDLE AGES: 700–1100 C.E.

751 Childeric III, last Merovingian king of the Franks, is deposed and replaced by Pepin the Short (*AW* II.i.79; *H5* I.ii.65), first of the Carolingian kings. See *Henry V*, I.ii.65–68, in which Pepin the Short is given as an example of kingship descending through the female line. Though there were a number of Frankish Pepins, this one (714?–768) is probably the one meant in *LLL* IV.i.122 and *H8* I.iii.10. The "Clotharius" of *H8* I.iii.10 could refer to any of four Merovigian kings named Chlotar, who ruled the Franks 558–61, 613–29, 657–73, and 717–19.

772–77   The Frankish emperor Charlemagne defeats and begins to forcibly Christianize the Saxons, a northern German nation of pagans. This conquest of the "Salic" lands (so called because they lay between the Sala and Elbe rivers) is referred to in *Henry V* (I.ii.44–47). At issue is the Salic law of inheritance, followed by the French heirs to Charlemagne's kingdom. The Salic law forbade the passage of the crown through the female line; a woman could therefore neither inherit the throne nor pass any kind of right to it to her sons.

England, however, did not follow Salic law, and the succession, in the twelfth century, had by Henry V's time already passed through the female line. The only living legitimate child of Henry I, Matilda, had been proclaimed queen in 1141, but a civil war had resulted in her ouster by her cousin Stephen, whose right to the throne came through his mother Adela, daughter of William the Conqueror. Further civil wars followed, ending only when Matilda's son, Henry, was named Stephen's heir.

In *Henry V* I.ii, the Archbishop of Canterbury is attempting to summarize the English right to the French crown on the basis of this discrepancy in inheritance law. If one accepts descent through the female line, then the English have a claim to the French throne; if the Salic law is valid, then only male-line descent is acceptable. Oddly, however, in a detail of his lecture that has little bearing on its main thesis, Canterbury's math seems flawed. He claims that Charlemagne conquered the "Salique" lands

> four hundred one and twenty years
> After defunction of King Pharamond,
> Idly supposed the founder of this law,
> Who died within the year of our redemption
> Four hundred twenty-six; and Charles the Great
> Subdued the Saxons, and did seat the French
> Beyond the river Sala, in the year
> Eight hundred five. (56–64)

In other words, according to Canterbury, Pharamond died in 426, and the French won the Salic land 421 years later, in 847. It is possible that Canterbury means not the initial conquest of the Saxons, but the supression of their rebellions, but these rebellions took place in 782 and 792–804, not 847. Even Canterbury himself, in the last two lines above, suggests that the latter rebellion is the one he means, for the settlement of the French in Saxony takes place "in the year / Eight hundred five." Charlemagne died in 814, and by 847 Saxony was in the hands of his grandson, Louis the German.

The answer appears to lie in the words "four hundred one and twenty." This is an awkward construction in any case, but seems to imply the number 421, "four hundred [plus] one [plus] twenty." If, however, we assume it means "four hundred [minus] one and twenty," Canterbury's math suddenly makes sense. This would mean that the French settlement took place *379* years after 426, in 805, as Canterbury later states.

814   Charlemagne dies, and his empire is inherited by his son Louis (*H5* I.ii.76).

840   Louis dies, leaving his lands to his three sons, Lothair, Louis the German, and Charles the Bold. Each son inherits a substantial territory, with Lothair having ultimate authority over the other two. This solution is unacceptable to the two younger sons, and after three years of war, Charles inherits much of modern-day France, Lothair becomes Holy Roman Emperor with lands stretching from northern Italy to the North Sea, and Louis takes control of much of modern-day Germany, including Saxony.

987   Hugh Capet secures the French throne, becoming the first Capetian king and triumphing over the more legitimate Carolingian claimant, Charles of Lower Lorraine. In *Henry V* (I.ii.69–77), his accession is used as a counterexample to Salic law. He claims descent from Lingard, daughter of Charles the Bold (whom Shakespeare calls "Charlemain").

1035   Sweyn, son of Danish and English king Canute the Great, is ousted as king of Norway. The "Sweno, . . . Norway's king" referred to in *Macbeth* (I.ii.59) is probably this man. Although there were more prominent and long-reigning kings named Sweyn, they were kings of Denmark. Sweyn Forkbeard (Canute the Great's father) ruled Denmark until 1014; Sweyn II (or Sweyn Estridsøn), Canute's nephew, will rule Denmark from 1047 to 1074. However, though Canute ruled England, Norway, Sweden, and Denmark, neither of these other two Sweyns ever ruled Norway.

1054   Earl Siward of Northumbria invades Scotland to support Malcolm Canmore's claim to the throne. Malcolm, son of the murdered King Duncan, ousts the usurper Macbeth, formerly earl of Moray, at Dunsinane, near the town of Perth.

1066   Edward the Confessor (who ruled England 1042–66) dies. King Harold, who succeeds, is conquered and killed at the battle of Hastings. William of Normandy becomes England's king.

KING JOHN: 1199–1216

1199   Richard I (the Lionheart) dies, leaving his nephew Arthur of Brittany, son of his brother Geoffrey, as his heir. However, Richard's brother John seizes power instead. France, under Philip II, supports Arthur, whose mother, Constance of Brittany, has placed him in Philip's care. Above all, Arthur's cause serves as an opportunity for France to attack England and perhaps retake some of its land. As a pretext, it is claimed that John has waged war in Normandy without his liege lord Philip's permission. Philip demands that John pay homage to him—the French held that England's French lands were fiefdoms that could be granted or withdrawn at the king's will—and that he surrender substantial possessions in France to Arthur and to Philip himself (*John* I.i.1–30).

Eleanor of Aquitaine, introduced as a character in *John* I.i, is John's mother, widow of Henry II, possessor of Aquitaine in her own right, and a formidable political intriguer who accompanied her first husband on a crusade to Jerusalem. The character of the Bastard, also introduced in this scene, is entirely fictional.

A convocation of lords from Anjou, Maine, and Touraine meets in the city of Angers and, on April 18, declares for Arthur. Le Mans refuses John entrance. He flees to England, where on May 27 he is crowned. He returns to France almost immediately, determined to take Angers and Tours, which control the main roads across the country. In a fortunate turn of events, the Angevin baron William des Roches, irritated by Philip's high-handed destruction of a castle in his dominions, joins John's side, and on September 22, Constance and Arthur agree to a peace with John. A truce with Philip follows in December.

1200   Philip and John meet cordially on January 15 and conclude a treaty on May 22. John gets to keep most of his French territories as long as he acknowledges that he holds them as a fief from Philip. Philip also extorts a customary payment, a kind of feudal inheritance tax, and John agrees to pay it, even though his father and elder brother were never required to do so. The marriage of Blanche of Castile, daughter of John's sister Eleanor, and the future Louis VIII of France, both still children, is arranged, and Blanche's dowry includes some territories still disputed. Finally, Arthur is made John's vassal, and John's relationships to certain rebellious lords are arbitrated by Philip. In short, the terms of the peace make John subservient to Philip in ways that the past two kings of England would not have found acceptable (*John* II.i–ii).

One of the characters in King John, Austria, is actually a fictional combination of two separate men, both of whom had a connection to Richard I. Guy, the viscount of Limoges, rebelled against Richard; it was his castle that Richard was besieging when he was killed by an arrow. The duke of Austria, on the other hand, captured Richard in 1192 and sold him to Emperor Henry VI of Germany, who then held him for a ransom that was never fully paid. Constance makes it clear that Shakespeare has combined the two (*John* III.i.40–55), making the new character doubly disloyal.

To further solidify his hold on France, John now holds two ecclesiastical trials, one in Normandy and one in Aquitaine, and has his childless marriage to his cousin Isabelle annulled. On August 24, he marries another Isabelle, the twelve-year-old daughter of the count of Angoulême. Unfortunately, she is already betrothed to Hugh of Lusignan; this match, had it gone through, might have eased long-standing rivalry between the two families (and also, in the process, made them able to resist England's power in the region). John returns to England with his new bride, and on October 8 they are crowned at Westminster.

John proves inventive, almost desperate, in his attempts to garner more revenue for the crown. He sells all sorts of rights and honors, and extorts new payments for the continuation of old privileges, such as those of England's Jews.

1201   Eleanor of Aquitaine fetches Blanche of Castile from Spain and delivers her to her French bridegroom. Eleanor then retires to the abbey of Fontrevault in Anjou, but, hearing of the unrest in Poitou following John's remarriage, she warns him of impending war and has others try to warn him as well. John, however, continues to antagonize French lords, including Hugh of Lusignan, and Hugh appeals to King Philip for redress.

In August, Constance of Brittany, reconciled to John at last (as she never is in Shakespeare's play), dies (*John* IV.ii.122–23).

1202   Philip summons John to a French court; John refuses to attend, and war begins between France and England. Philip declares John's French lands forfeit, knights Arthur of Brittany, and makes him lord of Aquitaine, Poitou, and Anjou. Philip, however, does not yet have clear legal authority to seize Normandy. While he seeks this, John attempts to generate outrage over his dispossession.

In July, John receives word from Eleanor of Aquitaine that she is being pursued by a rebel army led by Arthur. When John reaches her on July 31, after a desperate forced march, she is trapped in the keep of Mirebeau with Arthur's forces in control of the town. At dawn the next day, John's army storms one of the town gates, traps the rebel leaders, and rescues Eleanor—a job that Shakespeare gives not to John but to his fictional Bastard (*John* III.ii). Arthur and one of his partisans, Geoffrey de Lusignan, are imprisoned in Falaise.

John now stupidly alienates one of his most powerful supporters, William des Roches; to this error he will add, in 1203, the release of the Lusignan leaders, who will promise good behavior but renege. Most damaging is the disappearance of Arthur during this year. By 1203, he will be nowhere to be found, with rumors—impossible to sort out reliably now—circulating of his accidental death, his murder at John's hands, or his murder on John's orders (*John* III.ii). One story, adopted by Shakespeare, has Arthur's custodian, Hubert de Burgh, swayed from his orders to blind and castrate the boy. According to this rendition of the tale, de Burgh instead says that Arthur is dead, in the hopes of quelling the rebellion (*John* IV.i; IV.ii.67–102, 182–269). Outrage fans the

flames, and he recants, but no one now believes that Arthur is
alive. Many of the rumors claim that Arthur has drowned; one
story, almost too dramatic to be believed, but possibly informed
by a reliable source, has John killing Arthur himself in a fit of
drunken pique at Rouen, then tying his body to a stone and casting him into the Seine. Shakespeare has him die trying to escape
(*John* IV.iii). The French are incensed by Arthur's death, but the
English are unimpressed by it, and even the pope feels (later, in
1216) that he deserved an ignominious death for his rebellion
against a liege lord.

1203   Many of John's French vassals turn against him, and he loses most
            of his French lands.

1204   News of fresh losses in Normandy arrive shortly before the death
            of Eleanor of Aquitaine on April 1 (*John* IV.ii.120–21). Over the
            next few years, John will continue to lose ground in France, but
            he will also continue to strengthen the navy, which will begin
            taking French ships as prizes and will successfully defend England
            from invasion in 1213.

1205   Hubert Walter, Archbishop of Canterbury, dies. John attempts to
            push the election of John de Gray, Bishop of Norwich, as his
            successor; confirmation of a royal choice for a see is customary,
            though not automatic. The monks of the cathedral priory, in re-
            sponse, lobby for Rome to give the post to their prior, Reginald.
            In December John holds an election by the monks in his presence,
            at which they unanimously choose de Gray, his candidate.

1206   A delegation of monks arrives in Rome, announcing that they now
            support de Gray for archbishop. Pope Innocent III, confused and
            irritated by the claims of the various delegations now before him,
            at first tries to hold a new election, then offers a new candidate,
            Stephen Langton of Lincolnshire, whom the monks unanimously
            accept. John, furious that he has not been permitted to hand-select
            a new candidate, objects strenuously; Innocent replies that the
            election has been handled according to Church law and that John
            must accept Langton. The pope consecrates Langton (on June 17,
            1207), and John retaliates by expelling the monks of the Canter-
            bury priory and refusing to admit Langton to England.

1208   Pope Innocent III, whose nominee for Archbishop of Canterbury,
            Stephen Langton, has been rejected by King John, places England
            under a papal interdict, which means that the sacraments cannot
            be administered in England until the king relents (*John* III.i).
            Shakespeare, writing in an England that had rejected the pope's
            authority, emphasizes John's rebellion—which historically in-
            cluded arresting and ransoming priests' mistresses—rather than his
            subsequent submission to papal authority.

1209   Pope Innocent III orders John excommunicated. Shakespeare, as always, compresses events, putting the long-dead Constance in the same scene (*John* III.i) and making the excommunication, rather than Philip's ambition and John's troubles with his barons, the cause of the broken truce and the loss of the French possessions.

1213   John accepts Langton as Archbishop and hands his own crown to the papal legate, Pandulf. Pandulf holds the crown for a few days (a few seconds in Shakespeare's version—see *John* V.i.1–4) and then returns it to John, making John a papal vassal.

1215   John, under duress from his nobles, signs the Magna Carta, a document granting the people of England (mainly its nobility) certain legal rights. Immediately afterward, John tries to undo the charter, soliciting support from his liege lord, the pope. The pope supports England in the resulting conflict, though many of John's nobles support an attempt by the French dauphin Louis (later Louis VIII) to invade England and seize the throne. John's brilliant siege of Rochester, however, convinces many barons to abandon their cause.

1216   In May, Louis lands an invasion force. He gets as far as London, though John maintains control over the rest of the country (*John* IV.iii.114–15, V.i.30–32, V.ii). In October, while crossing the Wash, a large estuary in East Anglia that is dry at low tide, the king's baggage train is destroyed by a miscalculation of the tide's effects; the chroniclers differ in their accounts, but the version blaming quicksand and a mistimed departure across the tidal flats is more plausible than the version blaming whirlpools that suddenly arose and slaughtered the entire infantry contingent. Shakespeare gives the incident to the Bastard and has troops rather than mere mules and household goods lost as a result (*John* V.vi.39–41). On October 19, just days later, King John dies at the bishop of Lincoln's castle and is succeeded by his young son Henry III (*John* V.vii). The rebellious English nobles, having no quarrel with Henry, abandon Louis. Shakespeare presents Prince Henry as unusually mature; he is only nine years old at his father's death.

HENRY III: 1216–72

1270   France's King Louis IX dies. He is mistakenly referred to by Shakespeare as "King Lewis the Tenth" in *Henry V* (I.ii.77) as an example of kingly descent through the female line. It was Louis IX whose grandmother was Isabella (81), wife of Philip II Augustus.

EDWARD III: 1327–77

1328   Charles IV of France dies, leaving no sons, so the succession passes to Philip of Valois, a nephew of Philip IV (the Fair).

1337   On May 24, Philip VI of France confiscates Gascony, claiming that English kings have held it as a fief and that he can revoke their ownership of it if they misbehave. On October 7, Edward III, who is descended from French kings on his mother's side, claims France as well as Gascony, beginning the Hundred Years' War.

1339   In the fall, Edward III invades France.

1346   On August 26, the Battle of Crécy, twelve miles north of Abbeville, results in a defeat for the French. An exhausted French force of 8,000 cavalry and 4,000 crossbowmen and mercenaries, divided from their infantry, wades into English longbow range. Sun in the French army's eyes and rain on their bowstrings lead to a retreat by the crossbowmen and a slaughter of the cavalry by the English archers, who have kept their own bowstrings dry inside their helmets. Edward's son, the Black Prince (*AW* IV.v.42; *R2* II.iii.100), fights desperately for his life, and his father orders him to be left to succeed or fail without assistance, saying, "let the boy win his spurs, for if God has so ordained it I wish the day to be his." The Black Prince survives, but many of the French and their allies are killed, including the blind King John of Luxembourg, who insisted upon being led into the battle and was slain with all of his attendants (*H5* I.ii.105–14, II.iv.53–62). The infantry, arriving the next day, are similarly routed, and a number of high-ranking prelates with them are slain.

     Meanwhile, David II of Scotland invades England, but northern troops left behind by Edward attack near Durham and capture David; he will remain in captivity in England until 1357 (*H5* I.ii.159–65).

1371   John of Gaunt (or Ghent), so called because he was born in Ghent, marries Constance, daughter of Pedro the Cruel of Castile and León. John is the third son of Edward III and Queen Philippa. Constance is his second wife; the first, Blanche of Lancaster (d. 1368), brought him the title of Duke of Lancaster upon her father's death. Much loved and respected, she was the posthumous inspiration for Chaucer's *Book of the Duchess*.

1376   On June 8, Edward, the Black Prince, heir to Edward III, dies at Berkhamsted, England. On Christmas, Edward III recognizes the prince's son Richard as his heir and requires his court to swear loyalty to Richard.

1377   Edward III of England dies. He is invoked as inspiration for Henry V's invasion of France in *Henry V* I.ii.103–4. Another of Edward III's sons, John of Gaunt, has in many ways the strongest claim to the throne. He is England's wealthiest and most powerful man, with a palace in London, the Savoy, that dwarfs any belonging to the crown. Most important, he is an adult, and the Black Prince's son Richard is a mere child. However, John is unpopular, especially in London, and he quickly swears allegiance to Richard II.

RICHARD II: 1377–99

1381 A peasant rebellion erupts in many parts of the country as laborers reject the ties of serfdom and an excessive poll tax. Leaders emerge in various parts of the nation, among them Wat Tyler, a roof tiler from Kent whom Froissart calls "a wicked and nasty fellow." The Kentish rebels march to London, arriving June 12. Richard II moves into the Tower of London, the best fortified of his London residences. On June 13, the king and his ministers set out to negotiate with the rebels but, seeing the size of the rebel force, turn back midway across the Thames. This enrages the rebels, who assault St. Mary's, Southwark (now Southwark Cathedral), Marshalsea Prison, the Chancery records house, and London Bridge. Entering London itself, they release the prisoners in the Fleet and destroy the contents of the Savoy, John of Gaunt's immense palace. Tyler forbids looting but authorizes the burning of the palace. Other buildings are burned as well, and Richard speaks to the crowd from the Tower, inviting them to a parley at Mile End.

On June 14, Richard meets with the rebels, who swear loyalty but demand that his ministers be surrendered to the mob. He grants them the abolition of villeinage and other demands, and promises them any ministers found guilty of treason in a court of law. Meanwhile, rebels seize the Tower of London and kill several prominent men, spiking their heads on London Bridge and threatening the king's mother, Joan, the Fair Maid of Kent, with sexual assault.

The next day, a newly arrogant Wat Tyler meets with the king at Smithfield and makes more demands. Lord Mayor Walworth scuffles with Tyler and wounds him. Then, one of Richard's attendants, a man named Standish, kills Tyler with his sword; the king calms the mob and pardons Tyler's adherents. Later, Richard renounces all of his concessions to the peasants except for the repeal of the poll tax. This breach of a promise, even a promise made under duress, angers the English.

Another of Richard's actions this year that leads to public discontent is his disinheritance of a child. When Edmund Mortimer, third earl of March, drowns in December, Richard gives away his possessions to his own servants instead of allowing Edmund's heir, seven-year-old Roger Mortimer, to inherit them.

1382 Richard II marries Anne of Bohemia.

1384 The increasingly autocratic and greedy Richard II is told by a Carmelite friar named John Latimer that John of Gaunt is plotting an assassination. Confronted, Gaunt defends himself so eloquently that it is Latimer who is arrested. A group of knights then captures and executes Latimer before he can stand trial. Popular opinion stands with the unjustly accused Gaunt, who has been a more sympathetic figure in England since the destruction of the Savoy.

1384–85   France sends troops to Scotland with the apparent intention of invading England from the north. Accordingly, an army being raised to invade France is redirected toward Scotland. The expedition is a failure, and the army never engages the French, who sail back to France after sacking Cumberland. Richard deliberately rejects the advice of the wiser and more experienced John of Gaunt, who turns his attention to seizing the Spanish throne.

1386   "John of Gaunt, / Which did subdue the greatest part of Spain" (*3H6* III.iii.81–87) in an attempt to assert his claim by marriage to the Spanish throne, conquers Galicia but fails to capture Castile. He will eventually renounce his claims to the Castilian throne in exchange for a pension and the marriage of one of his daughters to Castile's King Henry III.

1387   Richard II engages in a protracted struggle with Parliament over his powers and responsibilities. Chief among his opponents is his uncle, Thomas Woodstock, Duke of Gloucester. Richard promises to bring five of his least popular ministers to trial, but purposely allows most of them to escape, and Gloucester engages in open rebellion. In his war against Richard he is joined by Henry Bolingbroke (whose surname came from his birthplace, Bolingbroke Castle in Lincolnshire), son of John of Gaunt. Richard finally agrees to reforms in order to keep his throne.

1388   On February 3, all five of Richard's accused ministers are tried in Parliament, four of them in absentia. The only one present, Sir Nicholas Brembre, protests his innocence and offers to prove it in a trial by combat, whereupon over 300 members of Parliament fling down their gloves to signify their willingness to prove his guilt. Several men, including Brembre, are hanged or beheaded for their supposed treason, which appears to have consisted mainly in being a bad moral influence on the king.

     In August, a Scottish army invades England and captures Henry Percy (the Harry Hotspur of *1H4*).

1392   Richard alienates the citizens of London by extracting a forced "gift" of £10,000 from them.

1394   In March, John of Gaunt's wife, Constance, for whom he has never felt much affection, dies. Richard II's beloved wife, Anne of Bohemia, dies in June and is deeply mourned by her husband. A third woman of note, Mary Bohun, wife of Henry Bolingbroke, also dies. She bore Henry six children, including the future Henry V.

1396   John of Gaunt marries his mistress Catherine Swynford; Richard II legitimizes her children (including an ancestor of Henry VII) under the surname Beaufort. Richard himself marries the seven-year-old daughter of King Charles VI of France, Princess Isabelle. The French marriage is unpopular in England, but John of Gaunt's support for the match helps to some extent.

1397   Richard's chief foes, Gloucester, Arundel, and Warwick, are arrested. Later, Arundel's brother Thomas, Archbishop of Canterbury, is also arrested and charged with treason. The archbishop and a penitent Warwick are banished. Arundel, at the insistence of the speaker of the House of Commons, Sir John Bushey, is beheaded. Gloucester never managed to appear at the trial and appears to have been murdered in Calais at Richard's command (*R2* I.ii). Loyal nobles are rewarded with titles; Henry Bolingbroke becomes Duke of Hereford, Thomas Mowbray becomes Duke of Norfolk, and Edward Plantagenet, Earl of Rutland, becomes Duke of Albemarle (Shakespeare's Aumerle). Richard's half brothers on his mother's side, John and Thomas Holland, become the Dukes of Exeter and Surrey, respectively.

1398   In January, Henry Bolingbroke denounces Thomas Mowbray, Duke of Norfolk, to the king (*R2* I.i), claiming that Mowbray told him of a plot to kill Bolingbroke, Mowbray, Aumerle, Exeter, John of Gaunt, and the Marquess of Dorset, and insisted that they either flee or oppose the plot. Attempts to reconcile Bolingbroke and Mowbray fail, and they meet to do combat on September 17. Richard, desiring neither to increase Bolingbroke's popularity nor to acknowledge any truth in Mowbray's charges of vengeful plotting, determines that neither shall win and stops the battle. Bolingbroke is banished from England for ten years, Mowbray for life (*R2* I.iii, I.iv).

1399   John of Gaunt dies; Richard II seizes his assets (*R2* II.i), which would ordinarily have passed to Gaunt's banished son Henry Bolingbroke, and expands Bolingbroke's banishment from ten years to life. Richard departs for Ireland to quell a rebellion, in Shakespeare's version leaving behind a queen much more mature than the ten-year-old Isabelle would have been (*R2* II.ii). In June, Bolingbroke invades England with only about 300 followers, landing at Ravenscar (*R2* II.ii) and proceeding in July to Doncaster, where Henry Percy, Earl of Northumberland, Ralph Neville, Earl of Westmorland, and Percy's son, Harry Hotspur, join his cause. Other supporters, too many to feed, join him as he moves on to Berkeley Castle in Gloucestershire (though he does not pass through the Cotswold Hills, as stated in *R2* II.iii.9). The Keeper of the Realm, Edmund, Duke of York, youngest of Edward III's sons, was about as indecisive as II.iii depicts him: unwilling to take sides, essentially loyal to Richard, but wishing no ill to Henry Bolingbroke.

On July 27 Richard leaves Ireland to defend himself against his cousin's invasion. On the same day, York surrenders Berkeley to Bolingbroke, the new Duke of Lancaster. Two days later, York and Lancaster arrive at Bristol, where they capture Richard II's loyalists the Earl of Wiltshire, Sir John Bushey, and Sir Henry Green (*R2* III.i). The men are executed, and their severed heads are sent to London, York, and Bristol to be displayed on the city gates. Another loyalist, Sir William Bagot, flees.

Aumerle, now in league with Lancaster, convinces Richard to split his army and to delay his arrival in Chester. By the time he meets Salisbury on August 11, Chester has fallen to Lancaster, and Salisbury's army, having heard rumors of Richard's death, has disintegrated (*R2* III.ii). Richard, assured by Northumberland and Archbishop Arundel that Henry has no intention of deposing him, agrees to enter into negotiations, and is ambushed and captured by Henry's forces. Taken first to Flint Castle (*R2* III.iii), he is later removed to the Tower, where, on September 29, he abdicates (*R2* III.iv, IV.i; *1H4* I.iii.145–55).

On the following day a Parliament-like assembly, but not a Parliament because there was no king to open the session, met at Westminster Hall. The group met in the hall that still stands today, with its magnificent hammer-beam roof, though the construction, ordered by Richard, was not yet finished. For dramatic purposes, Shakespeare squeezes both Richard's abdication, which had taken place the previous day, and the quasi-Parliamentary session into a single scene. Henry would have been a fool, however, to permit Richard to speak at the session, since Henry was a usurper, and everyone present knew it. He was not even the next in line to the throne after Richard; that honor fell to the young Roger Mortimer, Earl of March. It was bad enough that he had to seek the approval of the legislators, and still worse that Richard's remaining adherents, including the Bishop of Carlisle (*R2* IV.i.115–49), spoke eloquently on his behalf. Yet by the end of the session, Henry was named king, and he was crowned on October 13 (*R2* IV.i), the first of England's monarchs to be anointed with oil from the ampulla said to be have been given to Thomas à Becket by the Virgin Mary.

Henry IV immediately proves less vengeful than Richard, settling for the removal of Albemarle's (Aumerle's), Surrey's, and Exeter's dukedoms and Carlisle's bishopric. The dispute over Albemarle's complicity in the murder of the Duke of Gloucester, like the abdication, did not take place on September 30. However, unlike the abdication, it did take place in Westminster Hall, in a session of Parliament (on October 16 and 18). Shakespeare takes even more liberties with the formation of a plot against Henry (*R2* IV.i.325–33), for its participants did not meet until December 17. More plausible, but still unlikely, is the inclusion of the death of the banished Duke of Norfolk. Henry's old adversary had died in Venice on September 22 while returning from a crusade to Jerusalem.

On October 28, Richard is quietly removed from the Tower and later taken to Pontefract Castle ("Pomfret") in Yorkshire. The farewells of Richard and Isabelle (*R2* V.i) are completely invented; one should remember that Isabelle was at this time only eleven years old. Similarly, although Henry made a grand entrance into London and was greeted by huge and enthusiastic crowds (*R2* V.ii), Richard was not part of a procession. On the contrary, Henry wanted him out of sight and out of mind. About a month after his coronation, Henry sends a deputation to France asking if Charles VI would mind marrying the widowed or soon-to-be-widowed Queen Isabelle to his own son, the future Henry V. The offer is quickly rejected.

HENRY IV: 1399–1413

1400   A plot to kill Henry IV on January 6 fails after the Earl of Rutland (formerly the Duke of Albemarle) accidentally allows his father, Edmund, Duke of York, to discover the plot (*R2* V.ii). The incident of the letter comes straight from one of Shakespeare's sources, Raphael Holinshed's *Chronicles*. Henry vacates Windsor, but the people support him, and London, which has still not forgotten Richard's bad behavior, refuses to rise to his defense. On January 8, the Earl of Kent (the former Duke of Surrey) and the Earl of Salisbury are beheaded; the same fate eventually befalls the Earl of Huntingdon (the demoted Duke of Exeter), but not the accidental informer Rutland (*R2* V.iii). Henry returns to Westminster on January 15.

Sometime before January 29, Richard II dies at Pontefract. The cause of his death is not known; Shakespeare lifts the Piers Exton incident (*R2* V.iv, V.v; *2H4* I.i.204–5) from Holinshed, but Richard may have starved himself out of spite or have been smothered. He is buried in Hertfordshire. Henry's vow of a pilgrimage (*R2* V.vi) belongs to a much later part of his reign and probably had nothing to do with guilt over Richard's death.

In August, Henry IV leads an invading army into Scotland—the last English king to do so—with the idea of humiliating King Robert III for an incursion into England earlier in the year. The expedition is a failure.

1401   A Welsh rebellion is led by Owen Glendower. Three armies under Henry's command invade, but are never able to engage the Welsh and are forced to retreat and disband. Conway Castle, captured by the Welsh rebels, is retaken by the middle-aged Hotspur and the teenage Prince of Wales; the two were not, as Shakespeare implies, nearly the same age (*1H4* I.i.87). Shakespeare deemphasizes both the young prince's military victories and his riotous partying and odd antics, making him seem playful and inexperienced.

1402   On April 3, Henry marries Joan, daughter of Charles II of Navarre and widow of the Duke of Brittany, by proxy. On June 22, at a battle at Pilleth, Radnorshire, Edmund Mortimer is captured by Welsh forces under Owen Glendower (*1H4* I.i). Henry raises three armies to invade Wales, but he is never able to engage the Welsh, and is forced to retreat and to disband the armies. On September 14, English forces under Northumberland and Harry Hotspur battle Scots at Homildon Hill ("Holmedon"), winning a great victory but in the process highlighting Henry's failures and the shortcomings of his heir, the Prince of Wales.

Shakespeare includes the outcomes of both battles in *1 Henry IV* I.i. Henry demands, with no legal justification, that all the Homildon prisoners be sent to him to be ransomed; Hotspur yields all but the Earl of Douglas. On October 20, Hotspur, Northumberland, and Henry quarrel over the failure to surrender Douglas and over rumors that Edmund Mortimer, uncle of the Earl of March (who had a better claim to the throne than Henry did), had gone over to Glendower's camp (*1H4* I.iii). Henry, either believing the rumors or simply wanting a rival claimant to the throne out of the way, refuses to permit the Percys to ransom Mortimer, who is the brother of Hotspur's wife, Elizabeth. Henry calls Hotspur a traitor, causing an irreparable breach.

Shakespeare's version combines the Mortimer uncle and nephew into one character, confuses the Mortimer Earls of March with the unrelated Scottish Earls of March, gives Harry Percy the nickname "Hotspur," which was first applied to him centuries after his death, and makes the expansion of the rebellion take place on the same day as Hotspur's quarrel with Henry.

1403   On January 19, Joan and Henry meet at Exeter. On February 7, they hold a face-to-face wedding at Westminster, and Joan is crowned queen on February 26. Edmund Mortimer, uncle of the Earl of March, marries Owen Glendower's daughter. In May, the Prince of Wales invades Wales and destroys two of Glendower's strongholds. In July, the Percys rebel (*1H4* I.iii). Shakespeare shows us Hotspur's preparations and, for some reason, calls his wife Elizabeth "Kate" (*1H4* I.iii, III.i).

Henry IV quickly raises an army to meet the challenge (*1H4* IV.ii). Shakespeare indicates that the rebels are already at Shrewsbury and puts Hal in the room with his father when the news is delivered, though actually the rebels were at Chester, and Hal was on campaign in Wales when he heard of the rebellion (*1H4* III.ii). On July 21, the Percy forces meet the king's army near Shrewsbury (*1H4* IV.i, IV.iii; *2H4* Ind, I.i), after failed negotiations in the morning (*1H4* V.i.,V.ii). Both the king and the Prince of Wales fight bravely, the latter despite an arrow wound in his face. The king kills as many as thirty rebels in a desperate battle, and an effort by Hotspur, Douglas, and a small picked band to force their way to the king and kill him fails (*1H4* V.iii, V.iv). Hotspur is killed, Northumberland's brother Worcester and the freed Earl of Douglas are captured (*1H4* V.v), and the rebel army retreats.

On July 23, Worcester and two other rebels are executed. Hotspur's body is publicly exhibited; later its head and quarters are hung on the gates of York, London, Bristol, Chester, and Newcastle. Northumberland is arrested and deprived of his castles but not executed.

In depicting the battle, Shakespeare makes both Sir Walter Blunt (a standard-bearer) and Sir Richard Vernon considerably more important than they seem to have been in real life. He also introduces Henry's younger brother, John of Lancaster, who was only thirteen and was not present at the battle. In the play, Blunt negotiates for peace, whereas in real life this function was performed by the abbot of Shrewsbury. Hal's offer of single combat has no historical foundation. However, Blunt, along with others, was disguised as a decoy king, and it is possible, though not proven, that Hal killed Hotspur. There is only slight evidence that Hal saved his father's life during the battle. Shakespeare portrays the Earl of Northumberland as too sick to come to Shrewsbury (*1H4* IV.i; *2H4* I.i), though in fact he had recovered and was on his way, but did not arrive in time.

1404   Charles VI of France, who has conceived an implacable hatred for Henry IV, continues to authorize raids on the English coast, while Parliament remains hostile to Henry and refuses to give him sufficient funds to defend the nation. Another plot against the throne, this time led by a group that believes Richard II is still alive, fails. In August, a French fleet intended to bring supplies to Owen Glendower gathers at Harfleur. Support for the Lollards, the followers of reformer John Wycliffe, grows.

1405   The Earl of Northumberland concocts another plot against Henry IV (*2H4* I.i, I.iii, II.iii, III.i), this time with Thomas Mowbray, Earl of Nottingham, and Richard Scrope, Archbishop of York. On May 29, in the "Forest of Gaultree" (Galtres, north of York), Ralph Neville, Earl of Westmorland, negotiates the disbanding of the rebel forces in exchange for concessions up to, but not including, Henry's abdication (*2H4* IV.i, IV.ii). Once the armies are gone, the rebels are arrested, and Mowbray and Scrope are executed (*2H4* IV.iv.83–85). Shakespeare places most of the blame for the betrayal at John of Lancaster's door, though historically it seems to have been Westmorland who deserves both the credit and the blame for ending the rebellion.

The execution of Scrope in particular causes much dismay and murmurs of blasphemy, and Northumberland escapes entirely. The rebellion, moreover, prevents Henry from making a campaign into Wales to quell Glendower's continuing uprising. Henry grows increasingly ill with a skin complaint that resembled leprosy but was possibly some other disfiguring condition (*2H4* II.ii.46).

1406	Prince Hal fights a battle with the Welsh rebels on St. George's Day; one of Glendower's sons is killed.
1408	Northumberland stages yet another rebellion, and this time is killed at the battle of Bramham Moor. In *2 Henry IV*, the king learns of the outcomes of both this and the rebellion of three years earlier in the same scene (IV.iv.97–99).
1412	Henry IV's health, which has been poor for some time, takes a turn for the worse in the fall. He lapses into unconsciousness in December, recovering in time for Christmas.
1413	Henry IV slips in and out of a coma. At his request, he is conveyed to Westminster Abbey to pray and suffers a seizure, whereupon he is carried into a drawing room known as the Jerusalem Chamber. Believing the name of the room to relate to a prophecy that he would die in Jerusalem, he orders his deathbed set up here (*2H4* IV.v.234–40). In *2 Henry IV*, the seizure, the rebellion of 1405, and the death of Northumberland in 1408 are compressed into a single scene (IV.iv.102–32). On March 20, Henry dies at the age of forty-five (*2H4* IV.v, V.ii).

On March 29, the Lord Chief Justice is replaced by Sir William Hankford, despite the episode invented to illustrate the magnanimity of the new king, Henry V (*2H4* I.ii.55, V.ii.70–71). It is not likely either that the young Prince Hal ever assaulted the old Chief Justice or that the Chief Justice left his office in disgrace—he was old enough to retire, and he received a pension of venison as a sign of royal favor.

HENRY V: 1413–22

1413	Henry V removes Richard II's body from Hertfordshire to Westminster Abbey and has him buried beside his first wife, Anne of Bohemia. On April 9, Henry V is crowned. Almost from the moment of his coronation, he leaves behind the frivolity of his youth and becomes extraordinarily pious, even severe. Evidence of his change of heart is given when one of his old drinking companions, a knight named Sir John Oldcastle, is arrested for leading the Lollards of the West Country. The Lollards were proto–Protestants, followers of John Wycliffe, who rejected many of the sacraments and traditions of the Catholic Church. In September, Oldcastle is interrogated and found guilty of heresy; on October 19, however,

he escapes. Henry, as far as we know, offers no aid to his old friend but begins trying to hunt him down, a process that will take four years.

1414   John of Lancaster is made Duke of Bedford; Henry V's youngest brother, Humphrey, is made an Earl and the Duke of Gloucester. Both brothers appear as characters in *1 Henry VI*. In January, more than 100 Lollards are hanged in St. Giles's Fields.

1415   Henry sends his uncle Thomas Beaufort (Earl of Dorset, but referred to by Shakespeare by the title he will bear after 1416, Earl of Exeter) to demand that the disorganized and politically divided French recognize Henry as king (*H5* II.iv). Failing that, they are to deliver Normandy, Maine, Anjou, Touraine, half of Provence, 1.6 million gold crowns in overdue ransom, the hand of Princess Katherine, and a staggering dowry of 2 million gold crowns. The French counter with an offer of some land, Katherine, and a still astounding dowry of 800,000 crowns; the English reject this offer and use it as an excuse to go to war (*H5* II.Cho.28–32). The incident of the tennis balls, dramatized in *Henry V* I.ii, probably never happened. The French, who had a mad king and two factions, the Burgundians and the Armagnacs, warring for the succession, were in no state to offend their greatest enemy. Henry begins to raise a huge army and a fleet of 1,500 ships to carry them and their followers to France (*H5* II.Cho.).

In the summer, the Earl of March reveals a plot to assassinate Henry and place himself on the throne. Henry calls a meeting with the three conspirators: Richard of Carisbrough, Earl of Cambridge; Sir Thomas Gray, a cousin of Hotspur's; and Henry, Lord Scrope, nephew of the Archbishop who was executed for rebelling against Henry IV. He confronts them with their guilt—though he neither produces papers to support his accusations nor lures them into condemning another supposed traitor first, as in Shakespeare's play—and they confess and are executed (*H5* II.Cho.22–30, II.ii). On August 9, the Earl of March, whose chief fault was deliberating ten days before revealing the plot to Henry, is pardoned, and on August 11, the English army sets sail, leaving the king's brother John as regent.

Landing near the town of Harfleur, Henry begins a five-week siege (*H5* III.i, III.ii), during which his men are plagued by flies, fever, and dysentery. Thousands of them are killed by disease or so incapacitated that they are sent home, greatly diminishing the English force. At last the town, after being permitted to send a message requesting help, and being rebuffed by the Dauphin Louis (*H5* III.iii.45–47), capitulates on September 22 (*H5* III.iii.49–50). Shakespeare's version of the French reaction (*H5* III.v), like his version of the earlier negotiations, grossly exaggerates both the sanity of Charles VI and the stupidity and arrogance of the dauphin, and the scene between Katherine and her maid (*H5* III.iv) is of course entirely fabricated.

Henry, meanwhile, instead of retreating sensibly by water back to England, decides to march the 150 miles to Calais with his much-attenuated army. On October 8, he leaves Harfleur in the command of Thomas Beaufort (later, as stated above, Earl of Exeter—see *H5* III.iii.51–53). All goes well until he is required to cross the Somme, for the best fords are too heavily fortified against him. He is forced to march his army almost 60 miles out of the way before the crossing can be made (*H5* III.v.1). On October 24, the French army is in sight, with a numerically superior and much better rested force.

Disheartened, Henry does precisely what the Constable, in Shakespeare's play, predicts:

> Sorry am I his numbers are so few,
> His soldiers sick, and famished in their march;
> For I am sure, when he shall see our army,
> He'll drop his heart into the sink of fear
> And, for achievement, offer us his ransom. (*H5* III.v.56–60)

Henry sends a messenger to the French, offering to retreat, to give up Harfleur and his other conquests, and to pay restitution, but no reply arrives. Shakespeare not only makes no mention of Henry's offer of ransom, he has the French make the offer and has Henry refuse it (*H5* III.vi.119–67, IV.iii.79–91).

Almost all night, as for many of the preceding days, it rains. There is no evidence for or against Henry's nighttime rounds of the camp, as portrayed in IV.i, except that such an excursion (most likely undisguised) would have been in character for a popular general. The soldiers Bates and Williams are fictional, but Sir Thomas Erpingham, aged fifty-eight, was indeed present at the battle.

On the morning of October 25, the lines of battle are drawn up between the villages of Tramecourt and Agincourt (now Azincourt), on rain-soaked fields bordered by forest. Henry's reply to a wish (not from Westmorland, but probably from Sir Walter Hungerford) for more men (*H5* IV.iii.17–19) is embellished by Shakespeare but probably happened in some form. Less accurate is Shakespeare's placement of Exeter at Agincourt, when he had actually been left behind to guard Harfleur.

The opening in the woods is too small to let the superior French forces form wide battle lines that might conceivably surround the English; they are forced instead to march in narrower columns, arranged in three large groups that advance one after the other. In addition to the disadvantageous ground, they are hampered by two other considerations: their inferior range of fire (they have only crossbowmen, who take much longer to fire than the English longbowmen), and the mud of the fields, which captures the armor-clad horses and their heavy, armor-clad riders like a trap.

Wave after wave of Frenchmen wades into the mud, only to be slaughtered by English arrows, and the third section of the army, seeing the fate of the first two, flees (*H5* IV). About 7,000 of the 20,000 French are killed. The English casualties number no more than 1,600 and probably far fewer. Shakespeare, following his historical source Holinshed, exaggerates the numbers on both sides, putting the number of French dead at 10,000 and the number of English dead at 29 (*H5* IV.viii.79–105).

There are more dead and fewer prisoners than expected, for Henry could be fierce in vengeance and gave, for reasons still not entirely clear, an order to kill all but the highest-born and most ransomable prisoners (*H5* IV.vi.37). Contrary to Gower's supportive statements (*H5* IV.vii.5–10), many of Henry's soldiers openly rebelled at this command, which was against the rules of war.

On October 29, news of the victory reaches London, and Henry reaches Calais (*H5* V.Cho.6–7). On November 23, Henry arrives in London to a tumultuous welcome, which he receives without smiling and without permitting his battered armor to be displayed as proof of his personal bravery (*H5* V.Cho.14–25). On December 18, the dauphin dies and is replaced as heir to the French throne by his younger brother John, a member of the Burgundian faction.

1417   Henry raises another army, requisitioning six feathers from every goose in his kingdom to fletch the army's arrows. He sails to France, takes Caen and slaughters every man in the town except for the clergy, receives the surrenders of Argentan and Alençon, and besieges the town and then the castle of Falaise for a total of ten weeks before achieving victory there as well.

In April, the Dauphin John dies, and his title passes to another son of Charles VI, also named Charles (all of these sons, incidentally, are brothers of Isabelle, the young widow of Richard II). The new dauphin belongs to the Armagnac faction, and he is almost immediately opposed by his mother, the pro–Burgundian Queen Isabella.

Henry Beaufort, Bishop of Winchester, England's Lord Chancellor, is made a cardinal (*1H6* I.iii.19) and papal legate, but is forced to resign his offices by Henry V (*1H6* I.iii.24).

Sir John Oldcastle, finally captured, is hanged and then "burnt hanging" as a heretic. Oldcastle's name—and apparently only his name—was lifted by Shakespeare from an account of young Prince Hal's drinking companions (*1H4* I.ii). The fictional Oldcastle was made a drunkard, a coward, and a boor, and his descendants naturally objected, so Shakespeare changed his name to Falstaff. This name was lifted from an equally unoffending historical personage, Sir John Fastolf, who fought at Agincourt and Patay and remained a knight of the Garter until his death. The other drinking companions, too, were renamed: Harvey became Bardolph, and Russell became Peto. Shakespeare explicitly indicates that his creation is not meant to be the historical Oldcastle (*2H4* Epil.32), who was a courageous soldier and was eventually included in Richard Foxe's *Book of Martyrs*.

1418	In July, Paris is captured by Queen Isabella's Burgundian faction. On July 31; the English begin a six-month siege of Rouen.
1419	On January 19, Rouen surrenders to the English. In March, the Dauphin Charles fails to show up at an appointed parley between himself and Henry. On May 29, however, Henry meets with the Duke of Burgundy and with Isabella, acting on behalf of her insane husband. They engage in unsuccessful but promising peace negotiations, and Henry meets Katherine of Valois for the first time.
1420	The Treaty of Troyes makes peace between France and England, recognizes Henry V as Charles VI's heir, and disinherits the dauphin (*H5* V.ii). Henry and Katherine marry on June 2. They leave for England on December 27, stopping first in Rouen.
1421	On February 7, Henry and Katherine arrive at Dover. Katherine is crowned on February 23. In March, Henry's brother Thomas, the Duke of Clarence, is killed in battle against the disinherited dauphin's forces. On June 10, Henry, after raising an army of 4,000 men, departs again for France. A son, the future Henry VI, is born to Katherine on December 6 at Windsor, but Henry V will not live to see his child.
1422	In May, Katherine joins Henry V in France, leaving her infant son in England. On August 31, Henry, who has been gravely ill for several months, dies at the age of thirty-four (*1H6* I.i). His rival, Charles VI, dies on October 11, depriving Henry of the French crown by a matter of weeks. The dauphin is crowned Charles VII of France, though the infant Henry VI is nominally king of France as well as of England. On November 7, Henry is buried in Westminster Abbey. Shakespeare's account of his funeral (*1H6* I.i) includes news of the losses of Guyenne, Compiègne (mistakenly called Champaigne), Rheims, Rouen, Orléans, Paris, Gisors, and Poitiers, all of which were actually lost between 1427 and 1450.

HENRY VI: 1422–61

1422	Humphrey, Duke of Gloucester, uncle of the infant King Henry VI, becomes Protector, and another uncle, John, Duke of Bedford, becomes Regent of France (*1H6* I.i). The new king's council includes Thomas Beaufort, Duke of Exeter, Henry VI's great-uncle.
1423	Bedford, uneasy at the growing French support for Charles VII, tries with only limited success to impose an oath of loyalty to Henry VI.

1424   Henry Beaufort, Bishop of Winchester since 1404 and Henry VI's great-uncle, is made chancellor. He will largely control the English government from about 1435 to 1443.

1425   In January, Edmund Mortimer, Earl of March, dies in Ireland (not in the Tower, as Shakespeare would have us believe in *1H6* II.v). This scene, like the countess of Auvergne episode (*1H6* II.ii–iii) and the Temple garden incident (*1H6* II.iv), is an invention. The many historical inconsistencies and inaccuracies of *1 Henry VI* can be blamed on dramatic necessity, errors in Shakespeare's principal source (Edward Hall's *Chronicle of the Union of the Two Noble and Illustre Famelies of Lancastre and Yorke*), and Shakespeare's inexperience—the *Henry VI* plays were among his first efforts.

Henry V's widow, Katherine of Valois, marries Owen Tudor, grandfather of the future Henry VII. Henry VI, at the age of three and a half, opens Parliament.

Humphrey, Duke of Gloucester, whose feud with the Bishop of Winchester is worsening, convinces the Lord Mayor of London to prevent the bishop from crossing London Bridge. A riot ensues, with several injuries and some property damage (*1H6* III.i).

1426   Henry Beaufort, Bishop of Winchester, is made cardinal and papal legate again (*1H6* V.i.28). There is no truth to the implication, later in the scene (51–54), that he purchased his office. At a Parliament held on February 18 in Leicester (not London), he and Gloucester are ordered to patch up their differences.

The restoration of the teenage Richard, Duke of York, to his title and lands in this scene is entirely fictitious, as is the implication in the list of dramatis personae that he is not yet a duke at the beginning of the play. Henry VI does, however, confer one honor on the fourteen-year-old Richard in 1426; he knights him on May 19.

1428   The English begin besieging the French city of Orléans, which is defended by Jean (1403–68), the illegitimate son of Louis I, Duke of Orléans (1372–1407) and thus known as "the Bastard of Orléans." At this time, Jean is the brother of the current Duke of Orléans (*1H6* IV.iv.26), Charles, and an adviser of his cousin the Dauphin Charles. The English siege is at first led by Thomas Montagu, Earl of Salisbury, who is killed by a cannonball in the fall (*1H6* I.iv) and replaced by William de la Pole, Earl of Suffolk, and John Talbot, Earl of Shrewsbury. Since Salisbury has no son, his title passes to his daughter Alice's husband, Richard Neville (1400–60). Richard's son, also named Richard (1428–71), will marry the daughter of Richard de Beauchamp, thereby inheriting the title Earl of Warwick and becoming so influential in the Wars of the Roses that he will become known as "the Kingmaker." Shakespeare's account of Salisbury's wound is largely faithful to the historical record; it was supposedly a boy who fired the fatal shot. However, Salisbury was buried in England, not France (*1H6* II.ii.12–17).

The fight between John Talbot, first Earl of Shrewsbury, and Joan of Arc (*1H6* I.v) has no historical foundation. Joan did come to the relief of Orléans (*1H6* I.vi), but it was not retaken by the English (*1H6* II.i); Shakespeare's account of a surprise attack on the French is lifted from a description of the taking of Le Mans.

Richard de Beauchamp, Earl of Warwick (misidentified as a Neville in *2H4* II.i.66), is placed in charge of Henry VI's education, a post he will hold until 1436.

1429	On March 8, Joan of Arc meets the dauphin and eventually gains his permission to try to lift the siege of Orléans (*1H6* I.ii); her identification of the dauphin, despite his being disguised and despite the charade of one of his nobles posing as a prince, is really supposed to have happened. Her forces repulse the English, capturing John Talbot, first Earl of Shrewsbury, at Patay (*1H6* I.i.105–46) on June 18 (not August 10, as in the play). In *1 Henry VI*, this siege is presented as nearly simultaneous with Henry VI's accession (I.i). Because of this difficulty, Talbot will be shown later in the play fighting before his capture. Furthermore, this same 1429 battle supposedly features cowardly behavior by Sir John Falstaff, though the messenger carring the report of cowardice is placed by Shakespeare in the context of 1422, and Falstaff's death occurs in *Henry V* in 1415. The historical Sir John Fastolf, a talented and dedicated soldier, fled from Patay only after his own men, misunderstanding an order, made a retreat, and his own position became untenable.

On July 17, Charles VII is crowned again, this time at Rheims (*1H6* I.i.92), in accordance with French tradition. Shakespeare places news of this event in the same scene as Henry V's funeral in 1422. In September, Charles makes an unsuccessful attempt to seize Paris.

Henry VI is crowned King of England on November 6. Gloucester's Protectorate ends shortly thereafter, though Shakespeare anachronistically continues it to at least 1445 (*2H6* I.i.145).

1430	Joan of Arc is captured by the Burgundians (not by the Duke of York, as in *1H6* V.iii) on May 23 and sold to the English for 10,000 francs. Shakespeare's portrayal of her as a devil-worshiping witch (*1H6* V.iii) is in keeping with historical opinion in his day. The French, of course, believed that Joan's victories had been ordained by God; the English, conversely, believed that her capture and execution had been God's work.
1431	Henry VI is crowned King of France (*1H6* IV.i; *2H6* I.i.92). The incident in which Falstaff is deprived of his Garter is an invention, and Talbot misidentifies Patay as "Poictiers" (*1H6* IV.i.14–26). In *Richard III*, Shakespeare mistakenly indicates that Henry is

crowned in Paris at the age of nine months (II.iii.17), which was instead the age at which he inherited the throne.

Joan of Arc is burned as a heretic in Rouen on May 30.

1433   Lord Talbot is released by the French.

1434   René (the "Reignier" of *1H6*), son of Louis II of Naples, inherits the title of Duke of Anjou from his brother, Louis III. When Joanna II of Naples dies, he becomes titular King of Naples as well. His daughter Margaret of Anjou will become wife of England's Henry VI.

1435   John, Duke of Bedford, dies on September 14. On the same day, an English deputation influenced by the petulant Duke Humphrey of Gloucester withdraws from peace talks, and exactly one week later, the Burgundians make a separate peace with the French, leaving the English in an untenable situation in France. The notion that Joan's sorcery was to blame for the disaffected Philip of Burgundy's departure from an English alliance is absurd; for one thing, Joan and Philip probably never even met, and for another, she was already dead by the time the Burgundian-English alliance fell apart (*1H6* III.iii). Similarly, Charles of Orléans was not freed (*1H6* III.iii), nor did Rouen fall to the French (*1H6* III.ii), until many years after her death.

1436   Richard, Duke of York, becomes head of the war in France. He is accompanied by Richard Neville, Earl of Salisbury, son-in-law of that Salisbury killed at Orléans.

1437   The Earl of Warwick travels to France to replace the Duke of York, leaving the teenage Henry VI mostly to his own devices. Henry demonstrates that, while he is exceptionally pious, he is neither a person of strong will nor a very good judge of character. In November, Charles VII enters Paris (*1H6* V.ii) to popular acclaim.

1438   Albert II (*1H6* V.i.2) becomes Holy Roman Emperor.

1439   The Earl of Warwick dies in France and is replaced by Richard, Duke of York.

1440   Lord Talbot and John Beaufort, first Duke of Somerset (older brother of Henry Beaufort, and half brother of Henry IV), recapture Harfleur. Somerset's daughter Margaret will marry Edmund Tudor and will become mother of Henry VII, grandmother of Henry VIII, and great-grandmother of Elizabeth I.

Duke Humphrey of Gloucester, a much more self-serving and incompetent man than Shakespeare depicts, suffers two public-relations blows when a French prisoner is ransomed against his advice and when he brings ill-considered charges of treason against Cardinal Beaufort and John Kemp, Archbishop of York.

1441   Duke Humphrey of Gloucester's second wife, Eleanor Cobham (originally a lady-in-waiting to his first wife), is arrested (*2H6* I.iv) and found guilty of sorcery (*2H6* II.i, II.iii, II.iv). Supposedly, she had melted a wax figurine of the king in an attempt to kill him and replace him with her husband, next in line to the throne. Both her accomplices are executed, Roger Bolingbroke by being hanged, drawn, and quartered, and Margery Jourdain by being burned at the stake, but Cobham herself is allowed to live, no thanks to her husband, who immediately sacrifices her to ensure his own political survival. (Shakespeare removes the blame for his cowardice by making him unable to lighten her sentence.) Cobham is sentenced to walk three days through London carrying a lighted candle; carrying a taper while dressed only in a shift or smock was a common punishment for offenders against England's religious codes. Afterward, she is banished to the Isle of Man, where she dies in 1455. Hume (who appears as "Hum" in *2H6* I.ii, I.iv) and John Southwell (*2H6* I.iv) are also historical personages.

One of the investigators into the Duchess of Gloucester's conduct is William de la Pole, Earl of Suffolk. His father was the Earl of Suffolk killed at Harfleur, and his elder brother, who succeeded to the title, was one of the two English peers slain at Agincourt. Suffolk is a faithful servant of the crown and a competent administrator, though Shakespeare portrays him as ambitious and lecherous.

1442   Lord Talbot is created the first Earl of Shrewsbury by Henry VI (*1H6* III.iv.26)

1443   Somerset is made captain-general of Guyenne, over the protests of the Duke of York; he is not, as suggested in *1 Henry VI* (IV.i.164–65), made head of the cavalry. The specifics of IV.iii and IV.iv are thus fictitious, though the increasing rancor between the Yorkist and Lancastrian factions is not.

1444   The Earl of Suffolk meets at Tours with Count René of Anjou, a man of extensive political connections, to arrange a marriage between Henry VI and the count's daughter, Margaret of Anjou, a lovely and intelligent fifteen-year-old. In May, Margaret arrives in Tours, and on May 24th she is betrothed to the English king with Suffolk as proxy. There is nearly a year's delay in finalizing the marriage, however, because Charles VII and Count René are busy with military matters. The delay causes the English to suspect that the count is asking for gifts or concessions in exchange for his daughter's hand, a suspicion apparently confirmed by Henry's gift of Maine and Anjou to the count (*2H6* I.i). The rumors cause the public to turn on Suffolk, whom they incorrectly believe is to blame for this territorial loss. Suffolk never captured her in war as in *1H6* V.iii, nor did he convince the king to marry her (V.v); he was sent by the king expressly to make the match. Nor can it be said of Anjou and Maine that Warwick "did win them both" (*2H6* I.i.117); Shakespeare has confused Salisbury's son Richard Neville, born in 1428, with his father-in-law, Richard Beauchamp, from whom he inherited the earldom (and who, in any case, did not win those provinces singlehandedly).

Somerset dies in England, possibly by suicide. A truce, which lasts about five years, is concluded between France and England (*1H6* V.i).

1445	In March, Margaret of Anjou marries Henry VI of England (*2H6* I.i) by proxy. She arrives in England, at Portsmouth, on April 9, after a rough Channel crossing. Sick in bed until April 23, she then travels to the abbey of Titchfield to marry the twenty-three-year-old Henry in person. She is crowned Queen on May 30 in Westminster Abbey. Gloucester, the next in line to the throne if Henry VI remains childless, is unhappy about the match.
1447	On February 10, Parliament convenes at Bury St. Edmunds (*2H6* II.iv.70–71, III.i). Gloucester arrives on February 17 with a contingent of cavalry and is promptly arrested. He dies suddenly on the 23rd; murder is suspected by many, including Shakespeare, but Gloucester's death was very possibly a natural one (*2H6* III.ii). His longtime rival Henry Cardinal Beaufort dies in April (*2H6* III.ii), leaving the kingdom in the hands of Suffolk. Suffolk becomes Lord Chamberlain, constable of Dover, Lord Warden of the Cinque Ports, and Admiral of England in rapid succession. On September 29, Richard, Duke of York, is chosen as lieutenant in Ireland; Shakespeare makes this event contemporaneous with Gloucester's death (*2H6* III.i.309–83). Moreover, he attributes to the duke a plan for insurrection involving both the army in Ireland and the rebel Jack Cade; however, there is no evidence whatsoever of any plan to rebel at this early date, let alone any credible evidence of the duke's being remotely acquainted with Cade. Shakespeare also blames Suffolk for Gloucester's death (*2H6* III.ii), but there is likewise no evidence that Suffolk had anything to do with it. He has Cardinal Beaufort die almost immediately after Gloucester, presumably at Bury and in a state of confusion, rather than clearheadedly at Winchester, as actually occurred (*2H6* III.iii).
1448	In February, Maine is surrendered to Margaret of Anjou's father, and popular opinion blames William de la Pole, Earl of Suffolk. Suffolk continues to amass power, becoming Governor of Calais. On July 2 he is made Duke of Suffolk.
1449	Salisbury's son, Richard Neville, inherits the earldom of Warwick from his father-in-law, Richard Beauchamp. In July, Richard,

Duke of York, leaves to take office as lieutenant of Ireland, a post he has avoided taking up for eighteen months because it will isolate him from power. He has, as outlined in *2 Henry VI* II.ii, a very good claim to the throne himself, and rightly sees his mission to Ireland as a way of diluting his influence. York is succeeded in his French command by Edmund Beaufort, since the death of his brother, the Earl of Somerset in 1445.

In France, where Somerset will manage to botch everything he touches, a force leaving Maine raids a town in Brittany, ending the fragile truce between the French and the English. The English quickly lose Verneuil, Mantes, Lisieux, and Rouen.

1450   The English lose more French towns, including Vire, Caen, and Falaise, reducing their possessions to Calais and part of Guyenne. Despite Somerset's command of the army, the duke of Suffolk is blamed for the reversal of fortune. On January 28, he is arrested and sent to the Tower. Sentenced to five years' exile, he sets sail on May 1 (*2H6* III.ii.242–97) but is immediately captured by a royal ship, *Nicholas of the Tower*, sent by an unknown person or faction. Suffolk is given a day and a night to offer his confession, and then he is rowed away from the ship and beheaded with a sword. The idea that pirates were behind the attack (*2H6* IV.i) is implausible, and Queen Margaret and Suffolk were never anything but political allies, so the tender farewell between them is pure fiction (*2H6* III.ii.300–413).

On June 1, a group of rebels from Kent camp at Blackheath outside London (*2H6* IV.ii). They are led by a man named Jack Cade, who is neither as uneducated nor as low-born as Shakespeare indicates. He is followed by some working-class men, to be sure, but also by a number of landowners who are displeased by excessive taxation, the selling of political offices, and the control of parliamentary elections by a few powerful men. The King's Council refuses all the rebels' demands and sends in the army, but unwisely splits the army so that one part of it is defeated and the other part mutinies. The rebellion spreads and Jack Cade, claiming to be a Mortimer descendant of Edward III (*2H6* IV.ii.135–45), enters London on July 3 (*2H6* IV.iii–viii). (Incidentally, though the ranks and names of some of Cade's followers are known, Bevis and Holland, who appear in *2H6* IV.ii, are neither historical followers nor entirely fictional; these were the names of two actors in Shakespeare's company.) Henry VI flees London, after putting Lord Say (James Fiennes, Lord Treasurer) and his son-in-law William Crowmer, the Sheriff of Kent, in the Tower to appease Cade's men. On July 4, Cade has these two beheaded (*2H6* IV.vii), and rioting and looting spread. Lord Scales and Matthew Gough, positioned in the Tower, attempt to retake the city in a long battle that lasts all night and in which Gough is slain (*2H6* IV.v–vii).

The next day, Cade's forces retreat to Southwark, setting fire to London Bridge as they go. There they free the prisoners of the King's Bench and Marshalsea prisons.

Two emissaries meet with Cade and offer him a pardon for himself and his followers; Cade, however, believes the pardons worthless and stages an attack in Rochester, whereupon he is attainted (declared an outlaw and deprived of civil privilege), and many of his men desert him (*2H6* IV.viii). He flees (*2H6* IV.ix.10) and is tracked to a garden by an East Sussex sheriff, Alexander Iden, who kills him when he resists arrest (*2H6* IV.x). (The garden, by the way, is unidentified by the chroniclers, and was not necessarily Iden's own, as Shakespeare would have it.) Eight other rebels are later executed.

Meanwhile, conflict between the Lancastrians and the Yorkists intensifies. The Lancastrians hold that Henry IV's seizure of the throne was justified and that his heirs are the lawful possessors of the crown. The Yorkists have a better claim legally but are out of power; they maintain that the succession should have passed to the Earls of March and thence to the last earl's nephew, Richard, Duke of York. The conflict polarizes around the hated and incompetent Duke of Somerset, leader of the Lancastrian faction, and Richard, leader of the Yorkists. In August, Richard returns without permission from Ireland to urge the king to dismiss Somerset. Heading an army of 4,000 men, he makes his way to the king, who agrees to include York in a new Council (*2H6* IV.x.24–30).

1451	The siege of Bordeaux takes place; Shakespeare incorrectly locates it in the 1430s (*1H6* IV.ii). Parliament demands that the Duke of Somerset be banished, along with about thirty other unpopular courtiers. The king refuses.
1452	Richard, Duke of York, still protesting his loyalty, calls upon the people of Shrewsbury to rise up in an attempt to remove Somerset's pernicious influence. He marches on London for the second time in two years (Shakespeare combines both marches into one incident). Refused entrance to the city, Richard continues to Cade's former home, Kent, and camps at Dartford. On March 1, Henry VI goes to meet him at Blackheath. A delegation to York promises that Somerset will be arrested. York dismisses his army but at Blackheath sees Somerset still very much at liberty and still favored by the king. Furious at the betrayal, he does not lose his temper, as Shakespeare portrays (*2H6* V.i), but remains calm. The playwright also introduces, anachronistically, York's sons Edward and Richard, who were, respectively, nine years old and in utero.
1453	England is driven from all of France except Calais after a defeat at Castillon in which Lord Talbot is killed (*1H6* IV.v–vii). Talbot's son John, who becomes the second Earl of Shrewsbury, dies in 1460, fighting for Henry VI in the Wars of the Roses. (The second

earl's great-great-grandson, George, will one day be the jailer-host of Mary, Queen of Scots.)

In the summer, Henry VI falls ill with a dementia that is eerily similar to that of his maternal grandfather, Charles VI of France. He is still ill on October 13, when he hears—but does not understand—that Margaret has given birth to a son, apparently securing the Lancastrian succession. By November, Guyenne has been completely reconquered by the French; Somerset is blamed and arrested.

1454   In January, Queen Margaret demands to be made regent for her ill and incompetent husband; she is rejected, and on March 27 York is made protector during Henry VI's illness. He begins to pack the court with Yorkists but rules well. In late December, Henry VI recovers, and the Lancastrians begin to seize power again.

1455   Somerset is released from the Tower and ousts York himself as captain of Calais. In May, he and the queen hold a meeting to counter the Yorkist threat, and the Yorkists mobilize an army again, demanding that a set of traitors, headed by Somerset, be yielded to them. The king refuses, and a battle ensues in the streets of St. Albans on May 22. The Lancastrians Somerset, Northumberland, and Clifford are all killed near the Castle Inn; Shakespeare gives the honor of Somerset's slaying to York's son Richard, who was actually two years old at the time of the battle (*2H6* V.ii). Henry and Margaret spend the night in St. Albans and then withdraw to London with Warwick, Salisbury, and Gloucester as escorts (Shakespeare has them flee as soon as the battle is over) (*2H6* V.ii–iii; *3H6* I.i.1–3).

1457   Henry Tudor, the future Henry VII, is born to Margaret Beaufort after the death, during her pregnancy, of her husband Edmund Tudor.

1460   In September, York begins amassing an army for a fourth march on London. Arriving on October 10, he demands that the unenthusiastic House of Lords confirm his right to the throne. On October 24, an Act of Accord gives Henry VI the crown for the remainder of his life but makes York his heir (*3H6* I.i). Margaret of Anjou, furious at the disinheritance of her son, flees to Scotland (*3H6* I.i.258–62) and begins collecting lords and armies loyal to the Lancastrian cause.

In December, fighting takes place at Worksop and at York's castle of Sandal near Wakefield (*3H6* I.ii–iv). The Lancastrians prepare to besiege York there; he attacks them on December 30 and is killed. His severed head is displayed afterward wearing a paper crown (*3H6* I.iv.175–78, II.i.107–8). York's son, the Earl of Rutland, is killed by young Clifford (*3H6* I.iii). The Earl of Salisbury is captured and executed on the last day of the year; his son, Sir Thomas Neville, was killed in the battle the day before. Shakespeare fails to place Salisbury at the scene but inserts John Neville, Marquis of Montagu (who was actually in London at the time), into *3H6* I.ii. It should be remembered that York's son Richard is now only eight years old.

EDWARD IV: 1461–83

1461 Edward, Earl of March, York's oldest son and now Duke of York himself, defeats the earls of Pembroke and Wiltshire in February at Mortimer's Cross, Herefordshire. Pembroke (Jasper Tudor, son of Katherine of Valois and Owen Tudor, and uncle of the future Henry VII) and Wiltshire manage to escape, keeping Edward in the west, anticipating their next move. London is taken by the Yorkist Richard Neville, Earl of Warwick, who confines Henry VI to the Tower. However, Warwick, with Henry in tow, loses the second battle of St. Albans in mid–February. Henry is left alone in the chaos of the battle and retrieved by his wife and son (*3H6* II.i).

Margaret's army pauses at Barnet, thus losing the opportunity to take London, which seizes the moment and rises against her. It is Edward who enters London, on February 26. The Council names him the rightful King on March 3, and later that month he begins to campaign against Margaret. On March 28 and 29, the bloody battle of Towton (*3H6* II.iii–vi) is a victory for the Yorkists, though at the cost of thousands of men on each side. Of the Lancastrians, Northumberland, Clifford, Neville, and Sir Andrew Trollope are killed; on the Yorkist, side, Lord FitzWalter is the only aristocrat slain. The Lancastrian Earls of Devon and Wiltshire are executed afterward. Richard and George, Edward's brothers, were not at the battle at all, but were in Holland at the time. The heads of the Earl of Devon and three others replace that of Richard, the former Duke of York, on the gates of the city of York; Shakespeare supposes that Clifford's is one of the three unnamed heads (*3H6* II.vi.51–52).

On June 28, Edward is crowned at Westminster Abbey. His brothers George and Richard, brought over from Holland for the coronation, are made the Dukes of Clarence and Gloucester, respectively (*3H6* II.vi.102–8).

Warwick travels to France to negotiate a marriage between Edward IV and Louis XI's sister-in-law, Bona of Savoy (*3H6* III.iii).

1462 Margaret of Anjou, who has fled to France with her son, begins a series of negotiations with Louis XI (*3H6* III.iii). She offers him Calais in exchange for an invasion force, and he agrees, but their arrangement is blocked by the Duke of Burgundy.

1463   Margaret of Anjou again attempts an invasion of England, and again fails.

1464   The new Duke of Somerset, Sir Ralph Percy, and Sir Humphrey Neville rebel in Northumberland. They are defeated at Alnwick on April 25, and Percy is killed. On May 15 Somerset, too, is defeated, captured, and beheaded. Henry VI, who is present at the battle, escapes and wanders the countryside for almost a year before being apprehended while eating dinner in Ribbesdale (*3H6* III.i). He is arrested and taken to the Tower.

         On May 1, Edward IV secretly marries Elizabeth Woodville (*3H6* III.ii, III.iii.174, IV.i), widow of a Lancastrian knight, Sir John Grey, and member of a large and ambitious family. Warwick is furious when the marriage becomes public in September, both because he has been negotiating a more politically advantageous match (*3H6* III.iii) and because he fears the Woodvilles will eclipse his own family in influence.

1468   Jasper Tudor, Earl of Pembroke, is attainted. His title is awarded to Sir William Herbert, a supporter of Edward IV.

1469   Against Edward IV's direct order, Warwick marries his older daughter, Isabel Neville, to George, Duke of Clarence (*3H6* IV.i.118, IV.ii.12). (The Somerset who appears in *3 Henry VI* IV.ii is a combination of the third and fourth Dukes of Somerset; the third was first a Lancastrian, then a Yorkist, and finally a Lanscastrian again, and was executed in 1464; the fourth was a consistent Lancastrian.) The battle presented in *3 Henry VI* IV.iii included neither Edward nor Warwick, but shortly after the battle, the Archbishop of York, Warwick's brother, arrests Edward, a maneuver that fails and renders the country chaotic. The Nevilles return Edward to London, whereupon he pardons them and his brother George. Shakespeare omits this reprieve and skips directly to Edward's flight to Holland the next year (*3H6* IV.iv–v).

1470   Edward IV puts down an insurrection in Lincolnshire that is proven, by captured documents, to have been incited by Warwick and Clarence. After attempting to summon them, he pursues them. They flee to France in April, and on July 22, Warwick begs Margaret of Anjou, his old adversary, for forgiveness (*3H6* III.iii). They forge an uneasy alliance against Edward and betroth her son, the sometime Prince of Wales, to Warwick's younger daughter, Anne Neville (*3H6* III.iii.241–50). On September 9, Warwick invades England, with the understanding that Margaret will follow with reinforcements (*3H6* III.iii.202–65, IV.vi). The Marquis of Montagu, Warwick's brother and the former Earl of Northumberland before his title was granted to another by Edward, turns coat and joins Warwick, forcing Edward to flee to Holland on October 2 (*3H6* IV.iv–v). Elizabeth Woodville and her daughters claim sanctuary at Westminster Abbey. On October 21, the mentally unstable and entirely unkingly Henry VI is returned to nominal power (*3H6* IV.vi) and paraded before the people wearing his crown. In November, Elizabeth Woodville gives birth to a son (*3H6* V.v.90), who will reign pitifully briefly as Edward V (*3H6* V.vii.16–20).

Edward IV, always a notorious womanizer, takes a mistress, Jane Shore, who will remain influential for much of the rest of his life.

1471   Edward IV, sponsored by Charles the Bold of Burgundy (*3H6* IV.vi.90), lands at Ravenscar on March 14, claiming that he wants nothing but his dukedom (*3H6* IV.vii.28). Clarence, who has been supporting his father-in-law Warwick, switches sides again and joins Edward (*3H6* V.i.81–85), who marches on London on April 5. London's forces have left to meet Queen Margaret, a desperate Lancastrian public-relations effort involving a display of King Henry that backfires as people compare him against the tall, handsome warrior Edward IV. Edward takes the city bloodlessly on April 11. Henry returns to the Tower (*3H6* IV.vii.52–64).

Montagu and Warwick are defeated and killed at the battle of Barnet on April 14, Easter Sunday (*3H6* V.ii–iii). Margaret and her son, Prince Edward, land and find a receptive populace, but their army is dogged by Edward IV's and arrives exhausted at Tewkesbury, where they are attacked and defeated on May 4 (*3H6* V.iv–v). Prince Edward is slain, though the manner of his death remains a mystery.

Margaret, not present at the battle, is captured along with Anne Neville and imprisoned in the comfortable style accorded to royal prisoners. It is at this battle of Tewkesbury that French soldiers are first used by Warwick in the Wars of the Roses, despite the stage directions of *3H6* IV.ii. In the aftermath of Tewkesbury, the fourth Duke of Somerset, upon whom the "Somerset" of *3 Henry VI* is in part based, is executed by the Yorkists. Henry, Earl of Richmond, the future Henry VII (*3H6* IV.vi.67–76), flees to Brittany, for he is now the principal Lancastrian heir. On May 21, Henry VI dies, probably the victim of murder, in the Tower (*3H6* V.vi). *Richard III* I.ii is set at his funeral, though the scene contains dates or events that occurred months or years later and refers to Anne Neville as Prince Edward's wife, though the two were only betrothed, not married. This latter error may not, in fact, be an error at all, for the existence of a marriage contract was considered binding, and Shakespeare elsewhere refers to contracted couples as husband and wife.

The late Earl of Warwick's fortune now falls to his two daughters: Isabel, married to Clarence, and sixteen-year-old Anne. Clarence, attempting to prevent his brother from marrying Anne, tries to hide her, but Richard finds her and moves her to the church of St. Martin-le-Grand.

1472   Richard of Gloucester marries Anne Neville.

1475   Margaret of Anjou is ransomed by Louis XI (*3H6* V.vii.37–40). She will spend the rest of her days in France, though Shakespeare has her return in *Richard III* I.iii.

1476   Isabel Neville, wife of Clarence, dies. Edward, afraid of a rival and of diplomatic difficulties with France, forbids his brother to marry the daughter of the lately deceased Charles the Bold of Burgundy. Clarence turns against his brother again and accuses Elizabeth Woodville of witchcraft and poisoning.

1477   In June, Clarence, who has become increasingly unstable and reckless, is arrested and sent to the Tower (*R3* I.i).

1478   In January, Clarence is tried and found guilty of treason. On February 18, to spare him a public execution, he is drowned in the Tower in a butt of malmsey wine (*R3* I.iv, II.i.81–135, II.ii). Shakespeare's account falsely blames Richard, not Edward (or the disloyal and stupid Clarence himself), for Clarence's murder.

1482   Richard, Duke of Gloucester, becomes extremely popular after leading a successful raid into Scotland. He is not as deformed as Shakespeare would have us believe; he is shorter than his brothers, to be sure, with one shoulder a bit higher than the other, and with something wrong with his left arm, but his military career indicates that he could not have been too badly impaired, for he was a vigorous hand-to-hand fighter.

     Margaret of Anjou dies.

EDWARD V: 1483

1483   Edward IV dies on April 9, just shy of his forty-first birthday (*R3* II.ii). He does not die after an illness, as Shakespeare depicts, but quite suddenly and while in apparent good health except for his ever-increasing weight. His son, the twelve-year-old Edward V, becomes king. His governor is Elizabeth Woodville's brother Lord Rivers; his treasurer is his older half brother Lord Richard Grey, Marquess of Dorset. The Woodvilles are confident that their majority on the Council will overturn Edward IV's desire to have Richard of Gloucester as protector.

     Richard, in turn, allies himself with Henry Stafford, Duke of Buckingham, a nephew of the Lancastrian Dukes of Somerset and the victim of a forced marriage to one of Elizabeth Woodville's sisters. Richard and Buckingham launch an aggressive public-relations campaign on Richard's behalf, meanwhile plotting to block the coronation of the boy king on May 4. On April 29, Gloucester and Buckingham rendezvous with the royal party on the pretext of accompanying them to London. Because Northampton could not accommodate two large groups, the prince's party had moved on to Stony Stratford. The news is brought to Richard in Northampton by Rivers and Grey, who eat dinner with him and are arrested by him on the following day. Richard then moves to Northampton and seizes the young prince. Shakespeare shows the Woodvilles working to bring the boy to London, and Richard and Buckingham working to intercept him at the end of *Richard III* II.ii. Later, Shakespeare perhaps reveals some confusion about all the movements back and forth between Stony Stratford and Northampton when he has the Archbishop of York report on the prince's party's progress:

> Last night, I hear, they lay at Stony Stratford;
> And at Northampton they do rest tonight;
> Tomorrow or next day they will be here. (II.iv.1–3)

Rivers and Grey are sent to Sheriff Hutton, one of Richard's castles, and moved to "Pomfret" (Pontefract) only later (*R3* II.iv.42). They are executed (*R3* III.iii) at the later castle on June 25; therefore Hastings, as we shall see, could not have known of their deaths (*R3* III.ii.49–50).

Richard arrives with his nephew in London on May 4 (*R3* III.i) to find the terrified Elizabeth Woodville hiding in Westminster Abbey with her five daughters and her second son, the nine-year-old Duke of York (*R3* II.iv.65). Richard allays public fears of a coup by riding proudly with his nephew to St. Paul's and by rescheduling the coronation for June 22. In mid–May, however, he removes Edward to the Tower (*R3* III.i.62–68) and requests that the boy be joined by his brother. Elizabeth Woodville initially refuses, but after being cajoled and subtly threatened by the Archbishop of Canterbury, finally allows it. Shakespeare, for economy's sake, shows the two princes proceeding to the Tower together (*R3* III.i), though actually the young Duke of York arrived there a few days after his elder brother. He now has control of the boys, but not of Lord Hastings, the Lord Chancellor, who remains loyal to Edward IV's intentions for the succession.

On June 13, at a meeting at the Tower, Richard reveals a supposed plot against himself, taking the form of witchcraft organized by Elizabeth Woodville and Jane Shore (once Edward IV's mistress and now the mistress of Lord Hastings—see *R3* III.iv.67–71, III.v.31). He summons armed men, who arrest Hastings and three other men: Stanley, Rotherham, and Morton. Hastings is beheaded immediately, his death being accompanied by a proclamation that is too long to have been composed on the spot and provides further evidence of Richard's duplicity (*R3* III.vi). Shakespeare's account of the incident, except for its placement after the deaths of Rivers, Grey, and Vaughan, closely follows his historical sources, Sir Thomas More and Edward Hall (*R3* III.iv).

Richard now begins to assault Edward IV's legitimacy (*R3*

III.v.86–94) and the validity of his marriage to Elizabeth Woodville (*R3* III.v.75), with a view to making himself the only rightful
heir to the throne. The "Doctor Shaw" for whom he sends at the
end of *R3* III.v is Ralph Shaa (referred to by More and Holinshed
as John Shaa), a priest who preaches Richard's right to the crown
at St. Paul's Cross on June 22. The other clergyman mentioned
here, Friar Penker or Pynkie, is also a historical personage. However, the timeline is slightly compressed here; Buckingham's unenthusiastic reception at the Guildhall took place on June 24, and
the meeting with Richard at Baynard's Castle on June 25 (*R3*
III.vii). There, a deputation led by Buckingham asks Richard to
take the throne, in response to which he feigns surprise. He at last
pretends to yield to their request and has Rivers, Lord Richard
Grey, Sir Thomas Vaughan, and Sir Richard Haute executed that
day. Shakespeare has the citizens fooled by Richard's deception,
but the historical accounts indicate that none of the participants
were really confused about the act of theft taking place.

Sir Robert Brackenbury becomes lieutenant of the Tower;
Shakespeare anachronistically makes him Clarence's custodian six
years earlier (*R3* I.i).

RICHARD III: 1483–85

1483   Richard III is crowned July 6, and his wife, Anne, is crowned
Queen (*R3* IV.i). The elderly Archbishop of Canterbury, no doubt
still smarting from being used as a tool in the usurpation, refuses
to attend the banquet afterward. Nor would Elizabeth Woodville
or her son from her first marriage, the Marquess of Dorset, have
been on their way to the Tower to visit the confined princes. Elizabeth Woodville was still in sanctuary, and all access to the princes
had been denied for weeks; Dorset had escaped from sanctuary,
evaded packs of hounds, and was making his way to France.

From late June onward, the "princes in the Tower," Edward
IV's two sons, are seen more and more rarely, until finally they
disappear altogether. Certainly the victims of murder, they are
probably killed on Richard's orders sometime during August by
the agents of a Suffolk knight, Sir James Tyrell (*R3* IV.ii–iii).
These agents, a murderer named Miles Forest and a groom of
Tyrell's named John Dighton, smother the boys, and Tyrell has
them buried within a staircase in the Tower, where their bodies
will be discovered in 1674.

Richard makes his nine-year-old son Prince of Wales. Shortly
afterward, his friend and ally the Duke of Buckingham rebels
against him, perhaps to secure the crown for himself or perhaps
to distance himself from the increasingly unpopular king—in any
case not, as Shakespeare would have us believe, over the Hereford
title (*R3* IV.ii). He seems to have been advised by the Lancastrian

Bishop of Ely, John Morton (*R3* IV.iii.46–48). The coalition is strengthened by the now-ousted Woodvilles, including Elizabeth Woodville, who has been plotting with Margaret Beaufort to marry their two children: Elizabeth of York, as Edward IV's eldest daughter the legal York claimant to the throne, and Henry Tudor, the leading Lancastrian contender. A revolt scheduled for October 18, however, begins prematurely in the south, and Buckingham is arrested (*R3* IV.iv.531) and beheaded (*R3* V.i) on November 2. Henry Tudor, headed for England (*R3* IV.iv.433–39), turns back to Brittany to avoid capture (*R3* IV.iv.521–27), and receives the homage of some of the rebels on Christmas Day.

At about this time, Shakespeare reintroduces Margaret of Anjou, who is already dead and in any case never came back to England after being ransomed in 1475 (*R3* IV.iv).

1484	Richard's son and heir, Edward of Middleham, dies on April 9. Henry of Richmond, meanwhile, is being courted as an ally by both the Duchy of Brittany, ruled by Duke Francis, and the Kingdom of France, now ruled by Charles VIII and his older sister and regent, Anne of Beaujeu.
1485	On March 16, Queen Anne dies after a long, wasting illness caused, some say, by poison (*R3* IV.ii). It is feared that Richard murdered her so that he could marry his niece, Elizabeth of York (*R3* IV.iv.204–430). Only the insistence of his advisers that such a marriage would mean instant and nationwide insurrection dissuades him from his purpose. On March 30, he makes a public statement rejecting the idea and averring (despite evidence to the contrary) that he is deeply grieved at the death of Anne Neville.

On August 7, Henry of Richmond's army, composed of Welshmen and Normans, lands at Milford Haven in southern Wales; Shakespeare combines the insurrections of 1483 and 1485 and has him land not at Milford Haven but "At Pembroke or at Ha[ve]rford west in Wales" (*R3* IV.v.10). Despite some early setbacks, Shrewsbury opens its gates to him, and soon reinforcements arrive, led in many cases by disenchanted Yorkists. Many other lords contribute to Henry's victory not by joining him but by refusing to bring troops into the field to support Richard. Thomas, Lord Stanley, Henry's stepfather, and Sir William Stanley, Thomas' brother, are among these. On August 22, they bring 8,000 men to Bosworth Field, near Leicester (*R3* V.ii.12), where Richard's army of 12,000 is preparing to battle Henry's army of about 5,000. Ordinarily, they might have joined Henry immediately, but Lord Stanley's son, Lord Strange, is being held as a hostage by Richard. Lord Stanley, however, rejects the overtures of both sides, replying to Richard's threat to kill Lord Strange that he has other sons to spare. Shakespeare combines both Stanleys into one man and brings him, inaccurately, to Henry's camp on the eve of the battle (*R3* V.iii).

An initial charge by the Duke of Norfolk fails to shatter Henry's center, commanded by the Earl of Oxford. Norfolk and Oxford come to blows, after which Norfolk is killed by an arrow to the throat. Henry rides toward the Stanleys to enlist their aid and is fiercely beset by Richard himself (*R3* V.iv), while Lord Stanley continues to delay. Sir William Stanley, however, charges with 3,000 men and saves Henry from the onslaught. Richard's horse is killed (*R3* V.iv), and he continues to fight on foot until after his men have urged him to flee and then taken to their heels. His last words, as he dies with a small gold crown around his helmet, are "Treason! Treason!" Henry is informally crowned on the battlefield (*R3* V.v) and orders the arrest of the Duke of Northumberland, whose delay in choosing sides very nearly cost him the throne. Richard's body is dragged naked through the mud back to Leicester and buried in an unmarked grave, later given a monument by Henry VII.

HENRY VII: 1485–1509

1489   The Mediterranean island of Cyprus is purchased by Venice. Conflict over its possession is the historical background of *Othello*.

1501   Catherine of Aragon, daughter of Ferdinand and Isabella of Spain, marries Arthur, Prince of Wales, elder son of Henry VII. Henry has three other children as well: a younger son, also named Henry; and two daughters, Mary and Margaret. Mary will become Queen of France out of duty and then Countess of Suffolk out of love; Margaret will marry the King of Scotland, James IV.

1502   Arthur, Prince of Wales, dies of "a consumption," leaving Katherine of Aragon a widow. The subject of whether her brief marriage was ever consummated will later become a matter of great importance.

1503   On June 23, Katherine of Aragon is contracted (but not yet married) to the future Henry VIII. There is still debate about whether or not her first marriage was consummated; if it was not, she would need only a dispensation from her earlier betrothal. If it was consummated, as the current agreement implies, she needs further permission to marry a man deemed by the church to be her lawful relative (*H8* II.iv.49–51).

1504   Katherine of Aragon and Henry Tudor, Prince of Wales, receive a papal dispensation to marry.

HENRY VIII: 1509–47

1509   Henry VII dies on April 21. After the funeral in May, the new king, Henry VIII, marries Katherine of Aragon, and they are crowned together at Westminster.

1513	At the battle of Flodden between the English and the Scots, James IV of Scotland is killed. His widow Margaret, Henry VIII's sister, becomes regent for their son, the infant James V.

1514   Thomas Wolsey, a butcher's son from Ipswich and for some time the king's master almoner, becomes Bishop of Tournai, Bishop of Lincoln, and finally Archbishop of York.

     Nicholas Hopkins, a Carthusian prior at Henton, predicts that Henry VIII will have no heirs and that Edward Stafford, Duke of Buckingham, will one day be king (*H8* I.i.221); the reference to Hopkins as "A monk of the Chartreux" in the same line is another way of calling him a Carthusian, for the Carthusians took their name from one of their great foundations, the Chartreuse or Charterhouse. In the following scene, Shakespeare mistakenly calls the prior "Nicholas Henton" (*H8* I.ii.148–72).

1515   Thomas Wolsey becomes a cardinal and Lord Chancellor of England.

1520   Henry VIII and Francis I of France meet at Guisnes (Guînes), among a mass of pavilions and costumes so gorgeous that the meeting is known as the Field of Cloth of Gold (*H8* I.i.7–51). The two monarchs have much in common, but Henry at least, is irritated by Francis, who makes the critical error of defeating Henry in a wrestling match. In the same year, Thomas Howard, Earl of Surrey, becomes lieutenant of Ireland (*H8* II.i.41–43).

1521   In May, Edward Stafford, Duke of Buckingham, a leader of the faction that detests Cardinal Wolsey, is tried for treason. Arguably next in line for the crown (after Henry and Katherine's only surviving child, Mary) and the son of a man who died fighting to place Henry VII on the throne (*H8* II.i.107–18), he is sentenced to be "drawn on a hurdle to the place of execution, there to be hanged, cut down alive," dismembered, disemboweled, beheaded, and quartered (*H8* I.i.199–201, II.i.7–8). Few regret his death, for he is unpopular both at court and among his own tenants. Among those who testify to his having spoken treasonously is his surveyor (*H8* I.i.115), Charles Knyvet. It is not known whether Henry personally interrogated Knyvet (*H8* I.ii), but certainly Knyvet's testimony, whether true or false, was extremely damaging to the duke.

     George Neville, Lord Abergavenny, Buckingham's son-in-law, is also briefly confined to the Tower (*H8* I.i). Released, he will later show his displeasure for Henry's treatment of Katherine by withdrawing from court and, in 1535, by conspiring against Henry.

     Meanwhile, Anne Boleyn, sister of a former mistress of the king's, returns from some time in France.

1522   After the French invade the territory of Charles V, Holy Roman Emperor and King of Spain (*H8* II.ii.25), England declares war on France (*H8* I.i.95–96).

1526–27   Henry VIII is infatuated with Anne Boleyn, who, unlike his other mistresses, resists his advances. Shakespeare has them meet at York Place, Wolsey's Palace on the Thames, but the actual manner of their first meeting is unknown (*H8* I.iv). The masquers dressed as shepherds in this scene, however, are quite characteristic of the young Henry, who adores jousts, dances, and revelry of all kinds.

     Simultaneously, Henry begins working for a French alliance, to be sealed by a betrothal of his daughter Mary to a French prince, and for a divorce from Katherine so that he may marry Anne Boleyn. His pretense that a chance ambassadorial comment occasioned a crisis of conscience over his marriage is, however, just that: a pretense (*H8* II.iv.169–73).

1528   Cardinal Lorenzo Campeggio (often known by the Latin form of his name, "Campeius") arrives in London to adjuicate, with Wolsey, the matter of the legality of Katherine and Henry's marriage (*H8* II.ii). He has been in London once before, in 1518, to conclude a treaty between the powers of western Europe; that visit coincided with Katherine's last pregnancy. Shakespeare has him note the absence of Richard Pace, a learned man now committed to the Tower for his support of Katherine. In Pace's place is Stephen Gardiner, a man of Wolsey's, who becomes one of Henry's lawyers in the divorce case, the royal secretary, and eventually Bishop of Winchester (*H8* II.ii). Shakespeare implies that Pace is already dead at this juncture (*H8* II.ii.130), but in fact Pace will live six years longer than Wolsey.

1529   On June 18, Wolsey and the Papal Legate Lorenzo Campeggio (whose Latin name is Campeius) open a hearing at Blackfriars on the legitimacy of Henry VIII's marriage to Katherine of Aragon (*H8* II.iv). Henry has grown increasingly impatient with Katherine's inability to give him a living son, and he has decided to challenge the legality of their marriage on the grounds of consanguinity—in other words, their family relationship through her prior marriage to his brother. Henry appears at the hearing by proxy, but Katherine attends in person, arguing that the hearing is unlawful because the place and judges are biased against her and because the same matter is already pending in Rome. The first full session of the court takes place on June 21, with Katherine again in attendance and Henry now present in person. Katherine defends herself, pleading her helplessness as a foreigner and a woman, stressing her obedience and fidelity throughout their marriage, touching upon her many pregnancies and, sadly, on the many stillbirths and infant deaths that followed, and finishing with a direct statement that Henry could tell, on their first night together, that she had come to him as a virgin. He does not reply, and she continues with a discussion of the wisdom of their fathers in agreeing to their union and of the bias of her own defenders, who dare not displease their king. Then she departs, refusing a summons to remain.

After she leaves, Henry makes a tepid speech about his regret at having to obey his conscience and set aside his queen, and Wolsey makes a show of disclaiming responsibility for planting the idea of a divorce in the king's mind.

On June 25, Katherine is declared "contumacious"—in contempt of court—and evidence is heard on the question of the queen's virginity at her marriage to Henry. Henry himself, however, does not testify. A last attempt is made to convince the queen to submit to the divorce; Wolsey and Campeggio visit her in her apartments, interrupting her with a skein of white silk around her neck as she and her ladies sew. As in Shakespeare's version, she insists that they speak in English (*H8* III.i) and remains adamant that her marriage is true and lawful.

On July 22, Wolsey's failure is complete. He has not been able to bully or cajole Katherine into giving way, and now the divorce case has been advoked to Rome (removed to Rome's jurisdiction). There, with Katherine's great-nephew Charles V's influence over the pope, ultimate failure seems likely. Wolsey's foreign policy, too, comes to naught, as Charles V and Francis I sign a peace treaty that leaves England with little to show for its wars except debt.

On September 19, Campeggio comes to court to take his formal leave of the king, since the matter of the divorce has been moved to Rome; he does not steal away, as Suffolk says in the play (*H8* III.ii.56–58). With him comes the disgraced Wolsey, determined to have an audience with the king. Henry is cordial to him at first, but draws him aside and angrily shows him a letter, the contents of which are not known, in Wolsey's own handwriting (*H8* III.ii.77–228). On September 20, Anne Boleyn keeps Henry busy all day, and he has no time for Wolsey. On September 22, Wolsey is commanded to surrender the Great Seal (*H8* III.ii.229–31); he does, and it is brought to Henry by the Dukes of Norfolk and Suffolk. Wolsey, as ordered by Henry, retires to Esher (*H8* III.ii.232). His replacement as lord chancellor is Sir Thomas More.

Wolsey, meanwhile, is deprived of the bishopric of Winchester, the abbacy of St. Albans and, moreover, of York Place, the property of the Archbishops of York. Henry insists that Wolsey make the palace over to him and renames it Whitehall. However, he continues to claim that he values Wolsey, sends him a ring as a token, and sends physicians to him when he is ill at Christmas.

1530	Wolsey is given permission to move to Richmond, but later he is ordered to remove himself to York. Shakespeare makes him prophetically aware that he will never rise to power again (*H8* III.ii), although the historical Wolsey probably had hopes of eventually being restored to the king's favor.

In May, the Lord Chancellor, Sir Thomas More, resigns his post over his inability to approve of "The King's Great Matter," his divorce from Katherine of Aragon.

On November 4, Wolsey is arrested for treason. Traveling south for his trial, he dies at Leicester Abbey on November 29 (*H8* IV.ii).

1532	On September 1, Anne Boleyn is created Marchioness of Pembroke; Shakespeare erroneously places this event just after the arrival of Campeggio in 1528 (*H8* II.iii.62–65).

1533	In January, Henry VIII secretly marries Anne Boleyn, who is pregnant with their child. Some sort of public legitimation of this marriage is now urgently necessary so that the long-awaited (and presumably male) heir can legally inherit the throne. Shakespeare places a report of the secret marriage in *Henry VIII* III.ii.41–42, predating the fall of Wolsey. Katherine of Aragon is moved to Ampthill, a manor in Bedfordshire, where a group led by the Dukes of Norfolk and Suffolk tells her that she must stop calling herself queen and be content to be referred to as Princess Dowager of Wales (*H8* III.ii.69–71).

On May 8, Thomas Cranmer, recently made Archbishop of Canterbury, summons Katherine to a court at Dunstable, near the manor of Ampthill. She refuses to attend, and on May 23 he declares her marriage to Henry unlawful and annuls it. On June 1, received by large but unenthusiastic crowds, Anne Boleyn is borne to Westminster and crowned (*H8* III.ii.46, IV.i). On September 7, at Greenwich, she gives birth to a princess (*H8* V.i), the future Elizabeth I, who is christened on September 10. Thomas Cranmer serves as her godfather (*H8* V.iii.161–62, V.iv–v). Katherine and Henry's daughter Princess Mary, now legally illegitimate, is deprived of most of her servants and made an attendant on her baby half-sister.

1534	In April, Sir Thomas More is sent to the Tower of London for his opposition to Henry's marriage to Anne Boleyn. In May, Katherine is removed to Kimbolton with a small group of attendants. Shakespeare shows her receiving a visit there from Eustache Chapuys, the ambassador of the Holy Roman Emperor (*H8* IV.ii), whom he terms "Capucius." However, Chapuys is not of noble blood, as Shakespeare has Katherine state. He is refused admittance to her, though he is able to establish lines of communication with her by means of a diversion involving a jester.

1535	Katherine of Aragon's daughter Mary falls ill, and Henry VIII sends her his own physician, Dr. Butts, who appears as a character in *Henry VIII* V.ii. Katherine's pleas to see her daughter and to protect her from Anne Boleyn (whom she suspects of poisoning Mary) are rejected.
1536	On January 2, Chapuys is at last allowed to meet with Katherine of Aragon, now close to death, at Kimbolton (*H8* IV.ii). He remains with her for a few days, receiving her wishes for the disposal of her few remaining possessions. She dies on January 7.
1540	Thomas Cromwell, architect of the king's separation from Rome and marriage to Anne Boleyn, is arrested and executed.
1543	Thomas Cranmer, Archbishop of Canterbury, is accused of heresy. Henry agrees that he shall be arrested at the Council table, but warns Cranmer of the plot beforehand, gives him a ring as a sign of the royal favor, and scolds Cranmer's enemies when they attempt to spring their trap the next day. Shakespeare places the incident in 1533 (*H8* V.ii–iii) and puts Thomas Cromwell, arrested in just such a manner in 1540, at the scene.

EDWARD VI: 1547–53
MARY I: 1553–58

1555	A fifteen-month siege of Siena ends when the occupying French forces surrender to a Florentine army led by Cosimo de' Medici. This is perhaps what Shakespeare intends when he refers to "the Tuscan wars" in *All's Well That Ends Well* (II.iii.276).

ELIZABETH I: 1558–1603

1564	William Shakespeare is baptized in Stratford-on-Avon on April 26. His date of birth is not recorded, but is traditionally held to be April 23.
1571	After a year-long siege, the Turks drive the Venetians out of Cyprus and take control of the island; conflict over Cyprus serves as the historical backdrop of *Othello*.
1574	Amurath (Murad) III of Turkey accedes and has his brothers strangled; Henry V refers to the incident anachronistically in *2 Henry IV* V.ii.47–48.

JAMES I: 1603–25

1616	William Shakespeare dies on April 23.
1623	The First Folio of Shakespeare's works is published.

Bibliography and Topic Guides

For information in a given field, you may consult the following references. Works other than the one you are now reading are listed first, followed by a list of relevant entries within *All Things Shakespeare*.

GENERAL INFORMATION ABOUT THE RENAISSANCE AND SHAKESPEAREAN ENGLAND

Alciato, Andrea. *Emblemata*. London, 1550. Reprint. Translated by Betty I. Knott. Aldershot, UK: Scolar Press, 1996.

Cipolla, Carlo M. *Before the Industrial Revolution: European Society and Economy, 1000–1700*. 2nd edition. New York: W. W. Norton, 1980.

Collier, John Payne, ed. *A Book of the Roxburghe Ballads*. London: Longman, Brown, Green, and Longmans, 1847.

Harrison, William. *The Description of England*. London, 1587. Reprint. Edited by Georges Edelen. Ithaca, NY: Cornell University Press (for the Folger Shakespeare Library), 1968.

Hazlitt, W. C., ed. *Inedited Tracts: Illustrating the Manners, Opinions, and Occupations of Englishmen During the Sixteenth and Seventeenth Centuries*. London: Roxburghe Library, 1868.

Levi, Peter. *The Life and Times of William Shakespeare*. New York: Henry Holt, 1988.

McMurtry, Jo. *Understanding Shakespeare's England*. Hamden, CT: Archon Books, 1989.

Ortelius, Abraham. *Theatrum Orbis Terrarum*. Antwerp, 1570. Reprint and first English translation. London: I. Norton, 1606.

Paradin, Claude. *The Heroicall Devises of M. Claudius Paradin*. London, 1591. Reprint. Delmar, NY: Scholars' Facsimiles and Reprints, 1984.

Reed, Michael. *The Age of Exuberance: 1550–1700*. London: Routledge and Kegan Paul, 1986.

Rye, William Brenchley, ed. *England as Seen by Foreigners in the Days of Elizabeth and James the First*. London, 1865. Reprint. New York: Benjamin Blom, 1967.

Shakespeare's England: An Account of the Life & Manners of His Age. 2 vols. Oxford: Clarendon Press, 1916.

Stow, John. *A Survey of London*. London, 1598.

Stubbes, Phillip. *The Anatomie of Abuses*. London, 1583. Reprint. New York: Garland, 1973.

ANIMALS AND PLANTS

Astley, John. *The Art of Riding*. London, 1584. Reprint. Amsterdam, NY: Da Capo Press, 1968.

Blundeville, Thomas. *The Arte of Ryding and Breakinge Greate Horses*. London, 1560. Reprint. Amsterdam, NY: Da Capo Press, 1969.

Caius, Johannes. *Of Englishe Dogges*. Translated by Abraham Fleming. London, 1576. Reprint. Washington, DC: Milo G. Denlinger, 1945.

Cummins, John. *The Hound and the Hawk: The Art of Medieval Hunting*. New York: St. Martin's Press, 1988.

Fussell, G. E., and K. R. Fussell. *The English Countryman: His Life and Work from Tudor Times to the Victorian Age*. London: Andrew Melrose, 1955. Reprint. London: Orbis, 1981.

Gerard, John. *The Herball: Or General Historie of Plants . . . Very Much Enlarged and Amended by Thomas Johnson*. London: Adam Islip, Joice Norton, and Richard Whitakers, 1633.

Gesner, Konrad. *Icones Animalium Aquatilum in Mari*. Tiguri: C. Froschoverus, 1560.

———. *Icones Animalium Quadrupedam Viviparorum et Oviparorum*. Tiguri: C. Froschoverus, 1560.

———. *Icones Avium Omnium*. Tiguri: C. Froschoverus, 1560.

Kerridge, Eric. *Farmers of Old England*. Totowa, NJ: Rowman and Littlefield, 1973.

Langdon, John. *Horses, Oxen and Technological Innovation: The Use of Draught Animals in English Farming from 1066 to 1500*. Cambridge: Cambridge University Press, 1986.

Lawson, William. *The Country House-Wives Garden . . . Together with the Husbandry of Bees*. London: John Harison, 1648.

———. *A New Orchard and Garden*. 2nd edition. London: John Harison, 1648.

Nigg, Joseph. *The Book of Fabulous Beasts*. New York: Oxford University Press, 1999.

Riddle, Maxwell. *Dogs Through History*. Fairfax, VA: Denlinger, 1987.

Seebohm, M. E. *The Evolution of the English Farm*. 1927. Reprint. London: George Allen and Unwin, 1952.

Swainson, Charles. *The Folk Lore and Provincial Names of British Birds*. London: Elliot Stock, 1886.

Topsell, Edward. *The Historie of Foure-Footed Beastes*. London: W. Jaggard, 1607.
———. *The Historie of Serpents*. London: William Jaggard, 1608.
Tusser, Thomas. *Five Hundred Points of Good Husbandry*. London: Company of Stationers, 1630.
    Entries within this book: Animals; Basilisk; Bees; Birds; Cattle; Dog; Dragon; Falconry and Fowling; Farming; Flowers; Garden; Griffin; Horse; Hunting; Phoenix; Plants; Sheep; Trees; Unicorn.

BEHAVIOR

Anglo, Sydney, ed. *Chivalry in the Renaissance*. Woodbridge, UK: Boydell, 1990.
Bacon, Francis. *The Charge of Sir Francis Bacon Touching Duells*. London, 1614. Reprint. Amsterdam, NY: Da Capo Press, 1968.
Bryson, Anna. *From Courtesy to Civility: Changing Codes of Conduct in Early Modern England*. Oxford: Clarendon Press, 1998.
Craig, Horace S. "Dueling Scenes and Terms in Shakespeare's Plays." *University of California Publications in English* 9, no. 1 (1940): 1–28.
Montagu, Ashley. *The Anatomy of Swearing*. New York: Macmillan, 1967.
Wildeblood, Joan. *The Polite World: A Guide to the Deportment of the English in Former Times*. London, 1965. Reprint. London: Davis-Poynter, 1973.
    Entries within this book: Court; Courtship; Duel; Etiquette; Hygiene; Oaths; Titles.

CHURCH AND STATE

Attwater, Donald, ed. *Penguin Dictionary of Saints*. Harmondsworth, Middlesex, 1965. Reprint. London: Penguin, 1983.
Barber, Richard. *The Knight and Chivalry*. London: Longman, 1970.
Braddick, Michael J. *The Nerves of State: Taxation and the Financing of the English State, 1558–1714*. Manchester, UK: Manchester University Press, 1996.
Brownlow, F. W. *Shakespeare, Harsnett, and the Devils of Denham*. Newark: University of Delaware Press, 1993.
Bryson, Frederick Robertson. *The Point of Honor in Sixteenth-Century Italy: An Aspect of the Life of the Gentleman*. New York: Columbia University Press, 1935.
Bulfinch, Thomas. *Bulfinch's Mythology*. Reprint. New York: Avenel Books, 1978.
Burford, E. J., and Sandra Shulman. *Of Bridles and Burnings: The Punishment of Women*. New York: St. Martin's Press, 1992.
Cross, F. L., ed. *Oxford Dictionary of the Christian Church*. Oxford, 1957. Reprint. Oxford: Oxford University Press, 1993.
Davis, David Brion. *The Problem of Slavery in Western Culture*. Ithaca, NY: Cornell University Press, 1966.
Ferguson, Arthur B. *The Chivalric Tradition in Renaissance England*. Cranbury, NJ: Associated University Presses, 1986.
Glassman, Bernard. *Anti-Semitic Stereotypes Without Jews: Images of the Jews in England 1290–1700*. Detroit: Wayne State University Press, 1975.

Hamilton, Edith. *Mythology*. Boston, 1942. Reprint. New York: Penguin, 1979.

Harding, Christopher, Bill Hines, Richard Ireland, and Philip Rawlings. *Imprisonment in England and Wales: A Concise History*. London: Croom Helm, 1985.

Howson, Brian. *Houses of Noble Poverty: A History of the English Almshouse*. Sunbury-on-Thames, UK: Bellevue Books, 1993.

Norwich, John Julius. *Shakespeare's Kings: The Great Plays and the History of England in the Middle Ages, 1337–1485*. New York: Touchstone, 2001. Reprint of Penguin ed. 1999.

Peters, Edward. *Torture*. New York: Basil Blackwell, 1985.

Phillips, William D., Jr. *Slavery from Roman Times to the Early Transatlantic Trade*. Minneapolis: University of Minnesota Press, 1985.

Rudorff, Raymond. *The Knights and Their World*. London: Cassell, 1974.

Thomas, J. E. *House of Care: Prisons and Prisoners in England 1500–1800*. Nottingham, UK: University of Nottingham, 1988.

Woodcock, Thomas, and John Martin Robinson. *The Oxford Guide to Heraldry*. Oxford: Oxford University Press, 1988.

Entries within this book: Baptism; Bell; Coronation; Crime; Execution; Government; Heraldry; Inheritance; Inns of Court; Jews; Knight; Land; Law; Mythology; Prison; Rape; Religion; Slave; Taxes; Torture. *See also* Appendix: Chronology of Historical Events Referred to in Shakespeare's Plays.

THE ECONOMY

Cameron, David Kerr. *The English Fair*. Stroud, UK: Sutton, 1998.

Havinden, Michael, ed. *Husbandry and Marketing in the South-West 1500–1800*. Exeter, UK: University of Exeter Press, 1973.

Kent, J.P.C. *Roman Coins*. New York: Harry N. Abrams, 1978.

Porteous, John. *Coins in History*. New York: G. P. Putnam's Sons, 1969.

Sutherland, C.H.V. *English Coinage 600–1900*. London: B. T. Batsford, 1973.

Entries within this book: Angel; Business; Crown; Crusadoes; Doit; Dollar; Drachma; Ducat; Farthing; Groat; Halfpenny; Mark; Markets and Fairs; Noble; Penny; Pound; Quart d'Écu; Sequin; Shilling; Sixpence; Taxes; Threepence.

EDUCATION AND KNOWLEDGE

Bennett, H. S. *English Books and Readers 1558–1603*. Cambridge: Cambridge University Press, 1965.

Charlton, Kenneth. *Education in Renaissance England*. London: Routledge and Kegan Paul, 1965.

Dawson, Giles E., and Laetitia Kennedy-Skipton. *Elizabethan Handwriting 1500–1650: A Guide to the Reading of Documents and Manuscripts*. London, 1968. Reprint. Chichester, UK: Phillimore, 1981.

Jewell, Helen M. *Education in Early Modern England*. New York: St. Martin's Press, 1998.

Nickell, Joe. *Pen, Ink, & Evidence: A Study of Writing and Writing Materials for the Penman, Collector, and Document Detective.* Lexington: University Press of Kentucky, 1990.

Plomer, Henry R. *Abstracts from the Wills of English Printers and Stationers, from 1492 to 1630.* London: Blades, East & Blades (for the Bibliographical Society), 1903.

Reed, Talbot Baines. *A History of the Old English Letter Foundries.* Revised by A. F. Johnson. London: Faber and Faber, 1952.

Thomas, Keith. "The Meaning of Literacy in Early Modern England." In *The Written Word: Literacy in Transition.* Edited by Gerd Baumann. Oxford: Clarendon, 1986.

Tilley, Morris Palmer. *A Dictionary of the Proverbs in England in the Sixteenth and Seventeenth Centuries.* Ann Arbor: University of Michigan Press, 1950.

Updike, Daniel Berkeley. *Printing Types: Their History, Forms and Use.* Vol. II. Cambridge, MA: Belknap Press of Harvard University Press, 1962.

Whalley, Joyce Irene. *The Pen's Excellencie: Calligraphy of Western Europe and America.* New York: Taplinger, 1980.

Williams, George Walton. *The Craft of Printing: The Publication of Shakespeare's Works.* Washington, DC: Associated University Presses, 1985.

Entries within this book: Art; Books; Education; France; Letters; Literacy; Music; Poetry; Writing.

FAMILY LIFE

Buck, Anne. *Clothes and the Child: A Handbook of Children's Dress in England 1500–1900.* Carlton, UK: Ruth Bean, 1996.

Cavallo, Sandra, and Lyndon Warner, eds. *Widowhood in Medieval and Early Modern Europe.* Harlow, UK: Pearson Education, 1999.

Cressy, David. *Birth, Marriage, and Death: Ritual, Religion, and the Life-Cycle in Tudor and Stuart England.* Oxford: Oxford University Press, 1997.

Gittings, Clare. *Death, Burial and the Individual in Early Modern England.* London: Croom Helm, 1984.

Heywood, Thomas. *Three Marriage Plays:* The Wise-Woman of Hogsdon, The English Traveller, *and* The Captives. Edited by Paul Merchant. Manchester, UK: Manchester University Press, 1996.

Jones, Paul Van Brunt. *The Household of a Tudor Nobleman.* Cedar Rapids, IA: Torch Press, 1918.

O'Hara, Diana. *Courtship and Constraint: Rethinking the Making of Marriage in Tudor England.* Manchester, UK: Manchester University Press, 2000.

Pearson, Lu Emily. *Elizabethans at Home.* Stanford, CA: Stanford University Press, 1957.

Taylor, Lou. *Mourning Dress: A Costume and Social History.* London: George Allen and Unwin, 1983.

Entries within this book: Baptism; Children; Courtship; Death; Marriage; Nursing; Pregnancy and Childbirth; Rape; Toys; Widow.

HEAD TO TOE

Ashelford, Jane. *Dress in the Age of Elizabeth I.* New York: Holmes and Meier, 1988.

———. *A Visual History of Costume: The Sixteenth Century.* London, 1983. Reprint. New York: Drama Book Publishers, 1986.

Boorde, Andrew. *The First Boke of the Introduction of Knowledge, a Compendyous Regyment or a Dyetary of Helth,* and *Barnes in Defence of the Berde: A Treatyse Made, Answerynge the Treatyse of Doctor Borde upon Berdes.* Reprint. Edited by F. J. Furnivall. London: Early English Text Society, 1870.

Buck, Anne. *Clothes and the Child: A Handbook of Children's Dress in England 1500–1900.* Carlton, UK: Ruth Bean, 1996.

Corson, Richard. *Fashions in Eyeglasses.* London, 1967. Reprint. London: Peter Owen, 1980.

———. *Fashions in Hair: The First Five Thousand Years.* London: Peter Owen, 1984.

———. *Fashions in Makeup from Ancient to Modern Times.* New York: Universe Books, 1972.

Croutier, Alev Lytle. *Harem: The World Behind the Veil.* New York: Abbeville Press, 1989.

Cumming, Valerie. *Gloves.* London: B. T. Batsford, 1982.

Cunnington, C. Willett, and Phillis Cunnington. *The History of Underclothes.* 1951. Corrected reprint. Mineola, NY: Dover, 1992.

De Marly, Diana. *Fashion for Men: An Illustrated History.* New York, 1985. Reprint. London: B. T. Batsford, 1989.

Ffoulkes, Charles. *The Armourer and His Craft from the XIth to the XVIth Century.* London, 1912. Reprint. New York: Dover, 1988.

Fliegel, Stephen N. *Arms and Armor.* Cleveland, OH: Cleveland Museum of Art, 1998.

Foster, Vanda. *Bags and Purses.* London: B. T. Batsford, 1982.

Greene, Robert. *A Quip for an Upstart Courtier.* London, 1592. Reprint. Menston, UK: Scolar Press, 1972.

Harrison, Michael. *The History of the Hat.* London: Herbert Jenkins, 1960.

Lister, Margot. *Costume: An Illustrated Survey from Ancient Times to the 20th Century.* Boston, 1968. Reprint. Boston: Plays, Inc., 1987.

Martin, Paul. *Armour and Weapons.* London: Herbert Jenkins, 1967.

Roth, Hy, and Robert Cromie. *The Little People.* New York: Everest House, 1980.

Scarisbrick, Diana. *Jewellery in Britain 1066–1837.* Norwich, UK: Michael Russell, 1994.

———. *Tudor and Jacobean Jewellery.* London: Tate Publishing, 1995.

Singman, Jeffrey L. *Daily Life in Elizabethan England.* Westport, CT: Greenwood, 1995.

Stubbes, Phillip. *The Anatomie of Abuses.* London, 1583. Reprint. New York: Garland, 1973.

Taylor, Lou. *Mourning Dress: A Costume and Social History.* London: George Allen and Unwin, 1983.

Williams-Mitchell, Christobel. *Dressed for the Job: The Story of Occupational Costume*. Poole, UK: Blandford Press, 1982.

Wood, Edward J. *Giants and Dwarfs*. London, 1868. Reprint. Folcroft, PA: Folcroft Library Editions, 1976.

   Entries within this book: Armor; Beard; Clothing; Cosmetics; Doublet; Dwarf; Etiquette; Eunuch; Fabric; Giants; Gloves; Hair; Helmet; Hygiene; Inkle; Jewelry; Lead; Pomander; Pregnancy and Childbirth; Ruff; Spectacles; Tawdry Lace.

HEARTH AND HOME

Blakemore, Robbie G. *History of Interior Design and Furniture from Ancient Egypt to Nineteenth-Century Europe*. New York: Van Nostrand Reinhold, 1997.

Brackett, Oliver. *English Furniture Illustrated*. Revised and edited by H. Clifford Smith. London: Spring Books, 1958.

Brunskill, R. W. *Traditional Buildings of Britain: An Introduction to Vernacular Architecture*. London: Victor Gollancz, 1981.

Cescinsky, Herbert. *English Furniture from Gothic to Sheraton*. 2nd edition. Garden City, NY: Garden City Publishing, 1937.

Clifton-Taylor, Alec. *The Pattern of English Building*. 4th edition. London: Faber & Faber, 1987.

Dawson, Percy G., C. B. Drover, and D. W. Parkes. *Early English Clocks: A Discussion of Domestic Clocks up to the Beginning of the Eighteenth Century*. Woodbridge, UK: Antique Collectors' Club, 1982.

Fastnedge, Ralph. *English Furniture Styles from 1500 to 1800*. Harmondsworth, UK, 1955. Reprint. Harmondsworth, UK: Penguin, 1962.

Forde-Johnston, James. *Great Medieval Castles of Britain*. London: The Bodley Head, 1979.

Gloag, John. *The Englishman's Chair*. London: George Allen and Unwin, 1964.

Hackwood, Frederick W. *Inns, Ales, and Drinking Customs of Old England*. London, 1909. Reprint. London: Bracken Books, 1985.

Johnson, Paul. *The National Trust Book of British Castles*. London: The National Trust/Weidenfeld and Nicolson, 1978.

King, Donald, and Santina Levey. *The Victoria & Albert Museum's Textile Collection: Embroidery in Britain from 1200 to 1750*. New York: Canopy Books, 1993.

Lawson, William. *The Country House-Wives Garden . . . Together with the Husbandry of Bees*. London: John Harison, 1648.

———. *A New Orchard and Garden*. 2nd edition. London: John Harison, 1648.

Levey, Santina M. *Elizabethan Treasures: The Hardwick Hall Textiles*. New York: Harry N. Abrams, 1988.

Martin, A. Lynn. *Alcohol, Sex, and Gender in Late Medieval and Early Modern Europe*. New York: Palgrave, 2001.

Platt, Colin. *The Great Rebuildings of Tudor and Stuart England: Revolutions in Architectural Taste*. London: UCL Press, 1994.

Pounds, N.J.G. *The Medieval Castle in England and Wales: A Social and Political History.* Cambridge: Cambridge University Press, 1990.

Riccardi-Cubitt. *The Art of the Cabinet.* London: Thames and Hudson, 1992.

Roberts, George Edwin. *Cups and Their Customs.* London: John Van Voorst, 1863.

Schweig, Bruno. *Mirrors: A Guide to the Manufacturing of Mirrors and Reflecting Surfaces.* London: Pelham Books, 1973.

Summerson, John. *Architecture in Britain 1530–1830.* 9th edition. New Haven, CT: Yale University Press, 1993.

Thornton, Peter. *Seventeenth-Century Interior Decoration in England, France and Holland.* New Haven, CT: Yale University Press, 1979.

Wilson, C. Anne, ed. *"Banquetting Stuffe": The Fare and Social Background of the Tudor and Stuart Banquet.* Edinburgh: Edinburgh University Press, 1991.

Wolsey, S. W., and R.W.P. Luff. *Furniture in England: The Age of the Joiner.* New York: Frederick A. Praeger, 1969.

Entries within this book: Animals; Architecture; Clocks and Watches; Drink; Fabric; Fire; Food; Furniture; Household Objects; Housework; Key; Lighting; Mirror; Needlework; Toys; Trees.

LEISURE

Amman, Jost. *Adeliche Weydwercke.* Reprint. Frankfurt am Main: J. W. Ammon and W. Serlin Bucch., 1661.

Auden, W. H., Chester Kallman, and Noah Greenbrg, eds. *An Elizabethan Song Book: Lute Songs, Madrigals and Rounds.* London: Faber and Faber, 1957.

Barber, Richard. *The Knight and Chivalry.* London: Longman, 1970.

Bartlett, Vernon. *The Past of Pastimes.* N.p.: Archon Books, 1969.

Bell, R. C. *Board and Table Games from Many Civilizations.* London: Oxford University Press, 1960.

Chappell, William. *The Ballad Literature and Popular Music of the Olden Time.* London, 1859. Reprint. New York: Dover, 1965.

Clephan, R. Coltman. *The Tournament: Its Periods and Phases.* London, 1919. Reprint. New York: Frederick Ungar, 1967.

Cummins, John. *The Hound and the Hawk: The Art of Medieval Hunting.* New York: St. Martin's Press, 1988.

Dolmetsch, Mabel. *Dances of England and France from 1450 to 1600.* London: Routledge and Kegan Paul, 1949.

Evans, G. Blakemore, ed. *Elizabethan-Jacobean Drama.* London: A&C Black, 1987.

Foakes, R. A. *Illustrations of the English Stage 1580–1642.* London: Scolar Press, 1985.

Graves, Thornton Shirley. *The Court and the London Theaters During the Reign of Elizabeth.* Menasha, WI, 1913. Reprint. New York: Russell and Russell, 1967.

Kiernan, V. G. *The Duel in European History: Honour and the Reign of Aristocracy.* Oxford: Oxford University Press, 1988.

Opie, Iona, and Peter Opie. *Children's Games with Things.* Oxford: Oxford University Press, 1997.

Rudorff, Raymond. *The Knights and Their World.* London: Cassell, 1974.

Sachs, Curt. *World History of the Dance.* New York: Seven Arts, 1952.

Strutt, Joseph. *The Sports and Pastimes of the People of England.* London, 1801. Reprint (revised and enlarged 1903). New York: Augustus M. Kelley, 1970.

Turberville, George. *The Noble Art of Venerie or Hunting.* London, 1575. Reprint. London: Thomas Purfoot, 1611.

Entries within this book: Dance; Entertainment; Falconry and Fowling; Fishing; Games; Hunting; Jousting; Masque; Music; Theater; Toys.

MAGIC, SUPERSTITION, AND WITCHCRAFT

Allen, Don Cameron. *The Star-Crossed Renaissance: The Quarrel About Astrology and Its Influence in England.* New York: Octagon Books, 1966.

Briggs, K. M. *The Fairies in English Literature and Tradition.* Chicago: University of Chicago Press, 1967.

Brownlow, F. W. *Shakespeare, Harsnett, and the Devils of Denham.* Newark: University of Delaware Press, 1993.

Cirlot, J. E. *A Dictionary of Symbols.* New York: Philosophical Library, 1962.

Geneva, Ann. *Astrology and the Seventeenth Century Mind.* Manchester, UK: Manchester University Press, 1995.

Gifford, George. *A Dialogue Concerning Witches & Witchcraft.* London, 1593. Reprinted from the London 1603 edition. London: The Percy Society, 1842.

Grafton, Anthony. *Cardano's Cosmos: The Worlds and Works of a Renaissance Astrologer.* Cambridge, MA: Harvard University Press, 1999.

Hazlitt, W. C. *Fairy Tales, Legends and Romances Illustrating Shakespeare and Other Early English Writers.* With two preliminary dissertations, *On Pigmies* and *On Fairies*, by Joseph Ritson. London, 1875. Reprint. New York and Hildesheim: George Olms Verlag, 1977.

Kittredge, George Lyman. *Witchcraft in Old and New England.* Cambridge, MA, 1929. Reprint. New York: Russell & Russell, 1956.

Nigg, Joseph. *The Book of Fabulous Beasts.* New York: Oxford University Press, 1999.

Notestein, Wallace. *A History of Witchcraft in England from 1558 to 1718.* Washington, DC, 1911. Reprint. New York: Russell & Russell, 1965.

Phillpotts, Beatrice. *Mermaids.* New York: Ballantine Books, 1980.

Sidky, H. *Witchcraft, Lycanthropy, Drugs, and Disease: An Anthropological Study of the European Witch-Hunts.* New York: Peter Lang, 1997.

Entries within this book: Alchemy; Astrology; Basilisk; Demon; Dragon; Fairy; Griffin; Magic; Mermaid; Mythology; Phoenix; Salamander; Sea Monster; Unicorn; Witch.

SCIENCE, TECHNOLOGY, AND MEDICINE

Allen, Don Cameron. *The Star-Crossed Renaissance: The Quarrel About Astrology and Its Influence in England.* New York: Octagon Books, 1966.

Boorde, Andrew. *The First Boke of the Introduction of Knowledge, a Compendyous Regyment or a Dyetary of Helth*, and *Barnes in Defence of the Berde: A Treatyse Made, Answerynge the Treatyse of Doctor Borde upon Berdes*. Reprint. Edited by F. J. Furnivall. London: Early English Text Society, 1870.

Brain, Peter. *Galen on Bloodletting*. Cambridge: Cambridge University Press, 1986.

Carleton, George. *The Madnesse of Astrologers*. London, 1624. Reprint. Amsterdam, NY: Da Capo Press, 1968.

Croutier, Alev Lytle. *Harem: The World Behind the Veil*. New York: Abbeville Press, 1989.

Fludd, Robert. *Utriusque Cosmi Historia*. Frankfurt, 1624.

Galen. *On the Usefulness of the Parts of the Body*. Translated by Margaret Tallmadge May. Ithaca, NY: Cornell University Press, 1968.

Geneva, Ann. *Astrology and the Seventeenth Century Mind*. Manchester, UK: Manchester University Press, 1995.

Grafton, Anthony. *Cardano's Cosmos: The Worlds and Works of a Renaissance Astrologer*. Cambridge, MA: Harvard University Press, 1999.

Haggard, Howard W. *The Doctor in History*. New Haven, CT: Yale University Press, 1934.

Knobel, E. B. "Astronomy and Astrology," In *Shakespeare's England*, Vol. I. Oxford: Clarendon Press, 1916.

Lindemann, Mary. *Medicine and Society in Early Modern Europe*. Cambridge: Cambridge University Press, 1999.

Loudon, Irvine, ed. *Western Medicine: An Illustrated History*. Oxford: Oxford University Press, 1997.

Major, Ralph H. *A History of Medicine*. Vol. I. Springfield, IL: Charles C. Thomas, 1954.

North, John. *The Norton History of Astronomy and Cosmology*. New York: W.W. Norton, 1995.

Siraisi, Nancy G. *Medieval and Early Renaissance Medicine: An Introduction to Knowledge and Practice*. Chicago: University of Chicago Press, 1990.

Steele, Robert. "Alchemy," In *Shakespeare's England*, Vol. I. Oxford: Clarendon Press, 1916.

Stevens, Serita Deborah, with Anne Klarner. *Deadly Doses: A Writer's Guide to Poisons*. Cincinnati, OH: Writer's Digest Books, 1990.

Vesalius, Andreas. *Humani Corporis Fabrica Librorum Epitome*. Basel: J. Oporini, 1543.

Waite, Arthur Edward, ed. *The Hermetical and Alchemical Writings of . . . Paracelsus*. Vol. II. Boulder, CO: Shambala, 1976. Reprint of London: James Elliott, 1894, edition.

Webster, Charles, ed. *Health, Medicine and Mortality in the Sixteenth Century*. Cambridge: Cambridge University Press, 1979.

Westman, Robert S., and J. E. McGuire. *Hermeticism and the Scientific Revolution*. Los Angeles: William Andrews Clark Memorial Library, 1977.

Entries within this book: Alchemy; Anatomy and Physiology; Astrology; Astronomy; Bleeding; Disease and Injury; Eunuch; Humors; Insanity; Medical Practitioners; Plague; Pox; Pregnancy and Childbirth; Weights and Measures; Windmill.

TIME AND SPACE

Adair, John. *The Royal Palaces of Britain.* London: Thames and Hudson, 1981.

Astley, John. *The Art of Riding.* London, 1584. Reprint. Amsterdam, NY: Da Capo Press, 1968.

Barker, Felix, and Peter Jackson. *The History of London in Maps.* London, 1990. Reprint. New York: Cross River Press, 1992.

Blundeville, Thomas. *The Arte of Ryding and Breakinge Greate Horses.* London, 1560. Reprint. Amsterdam, NY: Da Capo Press, 1969.

Cattermole, Paul. *Church Bells and Bell-Ringing: A Norfolk Profile.* Woodbridge, UK: Boydell Press, 1990.

Cavalli-Sforza, Luigi Luca, ed. *African Pygmies.* Orlando, FL: Academic Press, 1986.

Clout, Hugh, ed. *The Times London History Atlas.* New York: HarperCollins, 1991.

Croutier, Alev Lytle. *Harem: The World Behind the Veil.* New York: Abbeville Press, 1989.

Dawson, Percy G., C. B. Drover, and D. W. Parkes. *Early English Clocks: A Discussion of Domestic Clocks up to the Beginning of the Eighteenth Century.* Woodbridge, UK: Antique Collectors' Club, 1982.

Fraser, Antonia. *The Wives of Henry VIII.* New York: Vintage Books, 1992.

Hackwood, Frederick W. *Inns, Ales, and Drinking Customs of Old England.* London, 1909. Reprint. London: Bracken Books, 1985.

Hibbert, Christopher. *The Virgin Queen: Elizabeth I. Genius of the Golden Age.* Reading, MA: Addison-Wesley, 1991.

Hutton, Ronald. *The Rise and Fall of Merry England: The Ritual Year 1400–1700.* Oxford: Oxford University Press, 1994.

Lewis, Naphtali, and Meyer Reinhold, eds. *Roman Civilization. Sourcebook I: The Republic.* New York: Harper & Row, 1966.

Mattingly, Garrett. *Catherine of Aragon.* Reprinted New York: Quality Paperback Books, 1990.

Norden, John. *Norden's Maps of London and Westminster.* London, 1593. Reprint. London: London Topographical Society, 1899.

Ortelius, Abraham. *Theatrum Orbis Terrarum.* Antwerp, 1570. Reprint and first English translation. London: I. Norton, 1606.

Price, Percival. *Bells and Man.* Oxford: Oxford University Press, 1983.

Saxton, Christopher. *An Atlas of England and Wales.* London, 1579.

Scarisbrick, J. J. *Henry VIII.* Berkeley: University of California Press, 1968.

Sherman, Stuart. *Telling Time: Clocks, Diaries, and English Diurnal Form, 1660–1785.* Chicago: University of Chicago Press, 1996.

Speed, John. *The Theatre of the Empire of Great Britaine.* London, 1611.

Tooley, R. V. *Maps and Map-Makers.* London, 1949. Reprint. New York: Dorset Press, 1990.

Turner, Ralph V. *King John.* London: Longman, 1994.

Warner, W. L. *King John.* 1961. Reprint. Berkeley: University of California Press, 1978.

Entries within this book: Bell; Clocks and Watches; Earthquake; Eunuch;

Gypsy; Holidays; Inn; Maps; Places; Pygmy; Sophy; Time; Transportation; Travel; Weights and Measures.

WAR AND PEACE

Barber, Richard. *The Knight and Chivalry*. London: Longman, 1970.

Bryson, Frederick Robertson. *The Point of Honor in Sixteenth-Century Italy: An Aspect of the Life of the Gentleman*. New York: Columbia University Press, 1935.

Cipolla, Carlo M. *Guns and Sails in the Early Phase of European Expansion 1400–1700*. London: Collins, 1965.

Clements, John. *Renaissance Swordsmanship: The Illustrated Use of Rapiers and Cut-and-Thrust Swords*. Boulder, CO: Paladin Press, 1997.

Clephan, R. Coltman. *The Tournament: Its Periods and Phases*. London, 1919. Reprint. New York: Frederick Ungar, 1967.

Ferguson, Arthur B. *The Chivalric Tradition in Renaissance England*. Cranbury, NJ: Associated University Presses, 1986.

Ffoulkes, Charles. *The Armourer and His Craft from the XIth to the XVIth Century*. London, 1912. Reprint. New York: Dover, 1988.

Fliegel, Stephen N. *Arms and Armor*. Cleveland, OH: Cleveland Museum of Art, 1998.

Fludd, Robert. *Utriusque Cosmi Historia*. Frankfurt, 1624.

Hale, J. R. *Renaissance War Studies*. London: Hambledon Press, 1983.

Hall, Bert S. *Weapons and Warfare in Renaissance Europe: Gunpowder, Technology, and Tactics*. Baltimore: Johns Hopkins University Press, 1997.

Kiernan, V. G. *The Duel in European History: Honour and the Reign of Aristocracy*. Oxford: Oxford University Press, 1988.

Martin, Paul. *Armour and Weapons*. London: Herbert Jenkins, 1967.

Reid, William. *Weapons Through the Ages*. New York: Crescent Books, 1976.

Rudorff, Raymond. *The Knights and Their World*. London: Cassell, 1974.

Turner, Craig, and Tony Soper. *Methods and Practice of Elizabethan Swordplay*. Carbondale: Southern Illinois University Press, 1990.

Webb, Henry J. *Elizabethan Military Science: The Books and the Practice*. Madison: University of Wisconsin Press, 1965.

Woodcock, Thomas, and John Martin Robinson. *The Oxford Guide to Heraldry*. Oxford: Oxford University Press, 1988.

Entries within this book: Alarum; Armor; Army; Artillery; Bow; Fencing; Firearms; Helmet; Heraldry; Jousting; Navy; Shield; Sword; Weapons. *See also* Appendix: Chronology of Historical Events Referred to in Shakespeare's Plays.

WORK

Fitzherbert, John. *Booke of Husbandrie*. 1598. Reprint. Norwood, NJ: Walter J. Johnson, 1979.

Fussell, G. E., and K. R. Fussell. *The English Countryman: His Life and Work from Tudor Times to the Victorian Age*. London: Andrew Melrose, 1955. Reprint. London: Orbis, 1981.

Greene, Robert. *A Quip for an Upstart Courtier*. London, 1592. Reprint. Menston, UK: Scolar Press, 1972.

Heresbach, Conrad. *The Whole Art and Trade of Husbandry, Contained in Foure Bookes*. Enlarged by Barnaby Googe. London: Richard More, 1614.

Heywood, Thomas. *The Four Prentices of London*. Edited by Mary Ann Gasior. New York: Garland, 1980.

Kent, J.P.C. *Roman Coins*. New York: Harry N. Abrams, 1978.

Kerridge, Eric. *Farmers of Old England*. Totowa, NJ: Rowman and Littlefield, 1973.

Langdon, John. *Horses, Oxen and Technological Innovation: The Use of Draught Animals in English Farming from 1066 to 1500*. Cambridge: Cambridge University Press, 1986.

Pearson, Lu Emily. *Elizabethans at Home*. Stanford, CA: Stanford University Press, 1957.

Porteous, John. *Coins in History*. New York: G. P. Putnam's Sons, 1969.

Roberts, Nickie. *Whores in History: Prostitution in Western Society*. London: HarperCollins, 1992.

Schopper, Hartmann. *Panoplia*. Frankfurt: S. Feyerabent, 1568.

Seebohm, M. E. *The Evolution of the English Farm*. 1927. Reprint. London: George Allen and Unwin, 1952.

Smith, Elmer Lewis. *Early Tools and Equipment*. Lebanon, PA: Applied Arts Publishers, 1973.

Sutherland, C.H.V. *English Coinage 600–1900*. London: B. T. Batsford, 1973.

Tusser, Thomas. *Five Hundred Points of Good Husbandry*. London: Company of Stationers, 1630.

Entries within this book: Art; Business; Fabric; Farming; Fire; Fishing; Gloves; Iron; Law; Leather; Medical Practitioners; Money; Occupations; Prostitution; Servants; Tools.

Index

Page numbers in **bold** indicate the location of the main entry.

Nightgown, 133
Nightingale, 89–90, 501
Nine Men's Morris, 312–13
Nine Worthies, **513–14**
Niobe, 501
Nits, 390
Noble, **514–15**
The Noble Art of Venerie or Hunting
(1575, 1611),172, 196, 378
Noddy, 402
Noncome, 398
Nonconformists, and baptism, 75
Norden, John, 457
Norfolk, 534–35
Norfolk, Duke of. *See* Howard, John,
Duke of Norfolk; Howard, Thomas,
Duke of Norfolk; Mowbray, Tho-
mas, Duke of Norfolk
Normandy, 532–33, 707, 708, 709,
720
Northampton, 735–36
Northamptonshire, 534–35
Northumberland, 3rd Earl of, 732.
See also Percy, Henry, 1st Earl of
Northumberland; Percy, Henry,
2nd Earl of Northumberland
Notes, 483
Novum, 310
Numa Pompilius, 701
Numbers, 550
Nun, 578
Nuncheon, 277
Nuncle, 629
Nurse, 543, 595
Nursery, 36
Nursing, **515–16**
Nuthook, 442
Nutmeg, 206, 207, 280, 293, 552
Nuts, 185, 292, 361
Nymph, 498

Oak, 257, 296, 630, 647, 648, 649;
and Jupiter, 493
Oaths, 260, 421, 439, **519–20**; and
Jupiter, 493
Oats, 250, 253, 255, 286–87, 367
Oboe. *See* Hautboy
Obolus, 335

Occupations, **520–23**
Oceanus, 498
Octavia, 703, 704
Octavian. *See* Caesar Octavianus, Ga-
ius
Octavo, 98, 100; cost of binding, 107
Ode, 549
Oedipus, 502
*Of English Dogs. See De Canibus An-
glicis*
Old age, 66, 137, 186
Oldcastle, Sir John, 719, 722–23
Olives, 291, 319
Olive tree, 495, 649
Olympus, 497, 499, 536–37
Omens, 456, 559; regarding bees, 80;
regarding birds, 85, 90–91, 92, 93,
559. *See also* Astrology
Omphale, 505
Onion, 285, 289, 290, 316
*On the Revolutions of the Celestial
Spheres. See De revolutionibus or-
bium coelestium*
Opal, 413
Opposition, 66
Ops, 497, 498
Oracle, 584
Oranges, 115, 291
Orb, 141, 142, 553
Orchard, 38, 317, 319, 320, 631,
648
Orchésographie (1588), 163
Ordinaries: heraldic term, 346–48, inn
meals, 617
Organ, 486, 583
Orléans, 532–33, 724, 725
Orphans, 7
Orpheus, 505
Ortelius, Abraham, 113, 123, 190–91,
202, 457, 533, 608
Osprey, 90
Ossa, 497
Ostler, 367, 395
Ostrich, 90
Otter, 22, 193, 387
Ouches, 409
Ounce, 22, 667, 670
Ousel, 90

About the Author

KIRSTIN OLSEN is an independent author. Her several books include *Understanding Lord of the Flies* (2000), *Daily Life in 18th-Century England* (1999), and *Chronology of Women's History* (1994), all from Greenwood Press.